\# 0009066535

DOWNTOWNS

DOWNTOWNS

REVITALIZING THE CENTERS OF SMALL URBAN COMMUNITIES

MICHAEL A. BURAYIDI, EDITOR

Published in 2001 by
Routledge
29 West 35th Street
New York, NY 10001

Published in Great Britain by
Routledge
11 New Fetter Lane
London EC4P 4EE

Routledge is an imprint of the Taylor & Francis Group.

Copyright © 2001 by Routledge

Printed in the United States of America on acid-free paper.

Library of Congress Cataloging-in-Publication Data

Downtowns : revitalizing the centers of small urban communities / Michael A. Burayidi,
editor.
p. cm. – (Contemporary urban affairs)
Includes bibliographical references and index.
ISBN 0-8153-3361-7
1. Urban renewal – United States – Case studies. I. Burayidi, Michael A. II. Routledge
reference library of social science. Contemporary urban affairs

HT175 .D69 2001
307.3'42162'0973--dc21   00-047673

CONTENTS

LIST OF TABLES

RICHARD BINGHAM

Most of the literature on revitalizating downtowns has been based on the experiences of large urban centers. In *Downtowns: Revitalizing the Centers of Small Urban Communities*, Michael A. Burayidi and his colleagues seek to remedy that fact. They seek to provide a starting point for understanding the unique development problems of downtowns in small urban communities.

This series of case studies of fifteen chapters seeks to examine some principles of downtown revitalization, urban design and infrastructure redevelopment, waterfront and brownfields redevelopment, and retail and commercial redevelopment. Burayidi concludes the book with a summary of the key experiences shown in the case studies:

a) Work within the political culture;
b) Place emphasis on local funding of downtown projects;
c) Create an image and sense of place for downtown;
d) Monitor programs and progress;
e) Make downtown revitalization a community effort;
f) Develop a long-term vision for downtown; and
g) Learn from others.

The book clearly shows that downtown revitalization works in small as well as in large cities, and that common principles apply.

ACKNOWLEDGMENTS

I wish to thank all the workers in small cities across the country who contributed to the success of this project by giving of their time and providing the necessary information that made possible the writing of the chapters in this book. Without their support, this book would not have been possible. I also wish to thank the University of Wisconsin, Oshkosh's Faculty Development Program for providing me the financial support for getting my research and this book completed. Chapter four benefited tremendously from previous research on small cities conducted by Ben Ofori-Amoah. I am indebted to him for the insight he provided on this matter.

I am deeply grateful to my children Dennis and Rodney for withstanding a period of great family turmoil even as this book was underway. I hope they will grow up to understand. Finally, I wish to thank Jelka Cucuz for her keen interest and support of my research and for accommodating my strenuous academic lifestyle.

CHAPTER 1

Introduction: Downtowns and Small City Development

MICHAEL A. BURAYIDI

Since the 1920s, there has been a steady decline in the economic health of downtowns in the United States. The middle class and businesses that once provided the thriving economic force of cities have moved to the surrounding suburban fringe, leaving in their wake, lower income households, vacant lots, and abandoned buildings.

A number of reasons have been given for this trend in economic activity decentralization. First, land in the built up parts of cities is often difficult and costly to assemble for developers since land in the central city is usually owned by several people. Added to this is the uncertainty of environmental pollution on already developed sites which could increase the cost of land development to exorbitant levels. By contrast, the fringe of cities provides virgin land that is easy to assemble and to develop. Thus, firms are drawn to the fringe because of the lower land costs.

Second, American downtowns were shaped by pedestrian activity and mass transit. Due to the high densities in downtowns in the pre war years, and easy access to downtown locations via mass transit, this provided for a thriving market place. However, in the post war period, the federal highway program and homeownership subsidies for the middle class aided the suburbanization of population and business. Housing became more affordable for the middle class because of federal mortgage insurance programs and lower downpayments. Much of the new housing was built in the suburbs. Firms sought locations near highways to increase their visibility to auto-oriented customers and to take advantage of the middle class population that now lived outside of city centers.

The Problem

The decentralization of economic activity away from the downtown area to the fringe has posed several problems for cities. First, business decentralization has created a mismatch between work places and places of residence, especially for low income residents of cities. For example, about 71 percent of the black population reside in central cities, a majority of whom are low income households, but since 1948 suburban areas have received over 80 percent of the new employment in manufacturing, retail and wholesale trade (Darden 1991). Thus, newer and better jobs are locating away from the central city. Lower income households are unable to obtain housing in the suburbs because of exclusionary zoning laws that prevent the development of low income housing in these neighborhoods. As a result, these households have had to reside in the downtown and commute to work in the suburbs.

The second effect of economic activity decentralization is that cities lose tax revenues from those businesses and middle class households that locate outside city boundaries. This increases the fiscal strain on cities whose residual population is increasingly poorer and more dependent on public services.

Another concern of economic decentralization for cities is the sprawl and the loss of agricultural land that this trend causes. For example, the Minneapolis-St. Paul metropolitan population grew by 9.7 percent between 1970 and 1984, but the amount of urbanized land grew by 25.1 percent. The result is that large tracts of farmland that had once been used for farming is now consumed by sprawl development (Fischer 1995). This trend is evident even in smaller metropolitan regions. For example, in the Fox Valley region of Wisconsin, all four counties reported a decrease in farm acreage and in number of farms between 1970 and 1996. Fond du Lac had a decrease in farm acreage by 8.3 percent, Green Lake by 2.6 percent and Winnebago by 18.2 percent.

The increased decentralization of business and population from the downtowns has also been costly to cities in the provision of infrastructure amenities. A study by the Washington, DC Farmland Trust compared the cost of servicing residential, commercial, industrial and agricultural land in three metropolitan farm communities in Minnesota—Farmington, Lake Elmo, and Independence—and came to the conclusion that the cost of servicing residential development in all three communities exceeded the property tax revenues generated. The cost of providing such public services as fire services, streets, education, and police protection costs the cities $1.02 for every $1.00 of revenue generated in property taxes. Alternatively, farmland consumed 77 cents of every tax dollar raised (Fischer 1995).

Economic activity decentralization also increases the cost of transportation for city and suburban residents. A 1991 study by the U.S. Department of Transportation and the Federal Highway Administration found that Americans spend an annual average of $3,500 to own and operate a car. Frequently, those who live in the suburbs commute to work in white collar jobs in central cities while central city residents must commute to their blue collar jobs in the suburbs. This spatial mismatch of jobs and places of residence increases travel time and pollution in cities.

The Response

Since the 1950s, these shifts in economic activity have provided a fodder of research for urban scholars (see for example, Bluestone *et. al.* 1981; Sternlieb 1963; Vernon 1959). The research has documented not only the problem, but also some of the policy responses that cities are using to stem the tide of economic decentralization and inner city decay. For example, a study by Skelcher

(1992) of downtown revitalization strategies in Galesburg, IL; Madison, IN; and Hot Springs, SD, shows that the use of historic preservation, enhancement of the visual qualities of Main Street, and business diversification, have helped to stimulate the economies of these cities' downtowns.

For cities located on bodies of water such as rivers and lakes, waterfront development has been the instrument for downtown revitalization. Thus, cities such as Louisville, KY; Milwaukee, WI; Portland, OR; and Rochester, NY; have all embarked on such a downtown redevelopment strategy (Robertson 1995). Yet, as Walzer and Kline observe in chapter Thirteen of this volume, some cities have continued to rely on the office sector as a critical component of their downtown revitalization strategy.

Despite the overwhelming literature on downtowns, however, the research findings and derivative policies have mostly been based on the experience of large urban areas such as Seattle (Daniels 1982), Los Angeles (Lloyd 1991), or New York City (Quante 1976). Yet, most U.S. cities, and a majority of the U.S. population live in small urban areas (defined as settlements of 100,000 or less). Where small urban areas have been studied, these have usually been suburbs of the large metropolitan areas or their dormitory communities. At this point in time, we know very little about the pattern of economic activity shifts in free standing small urban areas, beyond the anecdotal comments of journalists in local newspapers.

Evidence from the few studies that have been conducted on such free standing small urban communities indicate that there is a distinctive difference in the forces that shape these small cities versus those of the large urban centers or their suburbs. Thus, Mattingly (1991) identified more differences than similarities between small and large urban areas in his study of location dynamics of physician offices in Bloomington-Normal, IL. In particular, he found that contrary to studies that indicate a trend towards office concentration in the large cities and their suburbs, the central business districts of small urban areas experienced office decentralization.

Filling in the gap in our knowledge of the economic activity shifts that are taking place in free standing small cities will greatly enhance our understanding of the phenomenon of business decentralization and our ability to provide appropriate policy responses in addressing the decline of downtowns. Economic development practitioners and policy makers in free standing small cities will also benefit from such findings. In dealing with problems resulting from business disinvestment and economic activity decentralization from their downtowns, these practitioners have had to rely on policies and programs derived from the findings on large urban centers that may not be suited to small cities.

This book provides a starting point for understanding the peculiar developmental problems of downtowns in small urban communities, across the nation. In this volume, contributors discuss the experiences of downtown redevelopment in over fifty such communities and how these communities have wrestled with, and in several cases, succeeded in bringing their downtowns "back from the

edge." Along the way, the authors point to the challenges and obstacles to downtown revitalization, but most especially, the lessons from these revitalization
efforts are discussed so that cities in similar situations can avoid these costly lessons. This compendium of case studies is, thus, a guide to downtown revitalization in small urban communities.

The book is organized under four different themes. Principles of downtown
revitalization and four specific case studies are discussed in Part One. In chapter
two, Robertson first discusses the key differences between the downtowns of
large and small cities and then lists some criteria that cities must bear in mind as
they undertake the revitalization of their downtowns. Following from this, case
studies of downtown revitalization in three states and one province in Canada are
discussed. Readers are admonished to bear in mind the principles outlined by
Robertson and to critically assess the extent to which these principles are followed. It becomes apparent in reading the examples of downtown revitalization
in these cities, that the closer a community adheres to these principles the more
successful is its efforts at revitalization.

In chapter three, Hardt explains how theories of bifurcation and sprawl in
Billings, MT, have influenced the development of the city. Hardt tells of how
community participation is vital to efforts at downtown revitalization. In chapter
four, I discuss downtown revitalization in four urban communities in Wisconsin.
I identify four primary strategies used by these cities. The chapter also covers
some of the problems that arise in assessing revitalization efforts in these communities. Downes and others, provide a comparative discussion of similar efforts
in five Oregon communities in chapter five. The authors stress the importance of
a visionary and dynamic leadership to downtown revitalization of small urban
communities. Finally, Horne discusses how Brandon, a small community in
Manitoba, Canada, is galvanizing efforts to revitalize the city's downtown.
Horne's discussion in chapter six sheds more light to the assertion that there is
such a thing as, "the north American city." Brandon, Canada, shares similar
developmental patterns and problems as the other U.S. cities discussed in this
volume.

Part Two is devoted to a discussion of the role of urban design and infrastructure to the economic health of downtowns. Indeed, one of the factors of
mainstreet renewal, as suggested by the National Trust for Historic Preservation,
is design. McClure and Hurand in chapter seven discuss the use of co-design and
community workshops in identifying the physical threads that bind a downtown
together and contribute to its aesthetic appeal, while Sen and Bell in chapter eight
provide a discussion of their experiences with physical design improvements for
cities in several workshops they held with mayors in small communities in the
northeast. In the concluding chapter of Part Two, Garr shows in chapter nine how
the political culture in Santa Cruz influenced the city's policies and recovery
efforts after the Loma Prieta earthquake.

Most U.S. cities owe their origins to a location near a water body. Factories
and industry located close to water bodies to provide access to transportation for

their raw materials and finished products. However, as water transportation became less of a factor in firm location, new development occurred away from the original settlement sites. Thus, these communities now have to contend with the water related types of development such as harbors, manufacturing plants, and ship yards that once provided the life blood for the communities, but that now lie idle, abandoned or underutilized. In Part Three of this book, Kotval and Mullin in chapter ten as well as Simmons in chapter eleven discuss how small cities are coping with this problem. Using examples from their planning practice and research on waterfront revitalization in cities both in the United States and Europe, Kotval and Mullin provide examples of successful efforts while pointing out some pitfalls that other cities must avoid.

Simmons examines the devolution of state brownfield policy at the local level in Wisconsin, and how cities in the Fox Valley are taking advantage of such a policy to nurture their shorefronts back to health. In the end, Simmons cautions that local environmentalism and a broadly construed vision, based on sustainable developmental principles, holds the key to waterfront and brownfield renewal in these cities.

While infrastructure, waterfront, and brownfields redevelopment have been important aspects of downtown development, most cities still view commercial development as the most vital part of downtown's health. Consequently, a lot of effort is put into attracting and retaining retail and professional services in the downtown. To what extent should a city go, to promote commercial revitalization? McClure, in chapter twelve, suggests that cities need to monitor the supply of retail space against demand in order to avoid over building of commercial space. Such an approach, he argues, will also prevent blight from occuring in the already built up parts of the city, especially the downtown. McClure provides an economic tool for monitoring the demand and supply of retail businesses to ensure that they are in equilibrium, using Lawrence, KS, as an example to make his case.

In chapter thirteen, Walzer and Kline discuss perceptions of downtown conditions in rural and metropolitan communities, examine the strategies pursued by these communities to revitalize their downtowns, and highlight the success stories of downtown revitalization in five small urban communities—Carril, IA; Galesburg, IL; Lanesboro, MN; LaFayette, IN; and New Cordell, OR. Haque observes in chapter fourteen that the key to successful downtown revitalization is a partnership between local, private, and public institutions especially the utilization of manpower available at local universities. He discusses successful revitalization programs in Dothan and Auburn, MS.

Siphoning through the wealth of experiences and revitalization initiatives shared by the contributors, I identify the elements of "best practices" in chapter fifteen, the concluding chapter of the book.

References

Bluestone, B., P. Hanna, S. Kuhn, and L. Moore, 1981. *The Retail Revolution: Market Transformation, Investment, and Labor in the Modern Department Store.* Boston: Auburn House.

Cassidy, R. 1972. "Moving to the Suburbs: When Business Flees the City." *The New Republic*. 166: 20–23.

Daniels, P.W. 1982. "An Exploratory Study of Office Location Behavior in Greater Seattle" *Urban Geography* 3 (1): 58–78.

Darden, Joe T. 1991. "Residential segregation in Urban America: Present Trends and Future Implications." in Lang, Marvel. *Contemporary Urban America*. University Press of America, Lanham, MD: 195–219.

Fischer, Adelheid. 1995. "Where Goes the Neighborhood?" *Mpls-St Paul Magazine* (May 1995): 62–67, 94–99.

Frieden, Bernard J. 1990. "American Business Still Wants to Go Downtown." *Wall Street Journal* (January 16): A16

Lloyd, W. 1991. "Changing Suburban Retail Patterns in Metropolitan Los Angeles" *Professional Geographer* 43: 335–344.

Mattingly, Paul F. 1991. "The Changing Location of Physician Offices in Bloomington. Normal, Illinois: 1870–1988" *Professional Geographer* 43 (4), 465–474.

Quante, W. 1976. *The Exodus of Corporate Headquarters From New York City*. New York: Praeger.

Robertson, Kent A. 1995. "Downtown Redevelopment Strategies in the United States: An End of the Century Assessment." *Journal of the American Planning Association* 61 (4): pp. 429–437.

Skelcher, Bradley. 1992. "What Are the Lessons Learned from the Main Street Pilot Project, 1977–1980?" *Small Town* 22 (4): 15–19.

Sternlieb, G. 1963. "The Future of Retailing in the Downtown Core" *Journal of the American Institute of Planners* 29: 102–112.

Vernon R. 1959. *The Changing Economic Function of the Central City*. New York: Committee for Economic Development.

Part One

Some Principles of Downtown Revitalization and Four Case Studies

CHAPTER 2

Downtown Development Principles for Small Cities

KENT ROBERTSON

Cities across the United States, regardless of population size, geographic location, or economic base, have been actively engaged in downtown development activities for many years. Cities large and small see a healthy core as integral to their overall heritage, tax base, sense of community, identity, economic development appeal, and image. However, as Burayidi has indicated in chapter one, most of the attention in the media and scholarly publications has focused on downtown revitalization in large cities the likes of Denver, Baltimore, Cleveland, and Seattle. Downtowns in small cities with populations under 100,000 have received minimal attention despite the fact that for every Seattle there are scores of smaller cities that can boast equally impressive downtown success stories. While downtown development in large and small cities share some common elements, it is important to understand the most critical components of successful downtown development salient specifically to small cities.

The purpose of this chapter, therefore, is to elucidate eight key principles that underscore successful downtown development efforts in small cities. These principles are drawn from four sources. First, a national survey of downtown problems and strategies in 54 small cities (population 25,000–50,000) was conducted in 1995 by the author (Robertson 1999). Second, in-depth site visits to Auburn, NY; Bangor, ME; Carson City, NV; Texarkana, TX/AR; and Wausau, WI; were made in 1997 (Robertson 1998, 1999). Third, professional newsletters were consulted, such as the National Main Street Center's *Main Street News* and the Downtown Research and Development Center's *Downtown Idea Exchange,* along with other relevant literature. Finally, the author has had the opportunity to work with and learn from a number of small cities through the facilitation of downtown visioning sessions and the presentation of downtown revitalization seminars.

Downtown Development Literature

In light of the widespread efforts to revitalize downtowns nationwide, the volume of scholarly literature devoted to this subject has been surprisingly thin the past decade; moreover, the vast majority of this sparse literature has emphasized large cities. For example, Frieden and Sagalyn's *Downtown, Inc.* (1989) examines the development process involved with major downtown projects such as Boston's Fanueil Hall, Seattle's Pike Place Market, and San Diego's Horton Plaza, while

Urban Design Downtown (Loukaitou-Sideris and Banerjee 1998) primarily looks at corporate plazas in Los Angeles and San Francisco in their analysis of the design of downtown open space. The relevance of their findings to small cities, most of which will not have large development projects and buildings, is limited at best. Other studies have focused on large cities in their research of specific downtown development strategies, such as retail (Robertson 1997; Sawicki 1989), parking (Mildner *et. al.* 1997; Voith 1998), stadiums (Rosentraub *et. al.* 1994), open spaces (Loukaitou-Sideris 1993; Mozingo 1989), and pedestrianization (Byers 1998; Robertson 1993).

The literature on small city downtowns can best be described as descriptive, non-analytical, and usually limited to the author's experience in a single city. Examples include articles in professional magazines that feature Columbus, IN (Campbell 1998); Santa Monica, CA (Lockwood 1997); Puyallup, WA (Seachord 1997); Pullman, WA (Ryder and Gray 1988); Bonaparte, IA (Meek 1995); Harrisburg, PA (Means 1997); Grand Forks, ND (Suchman 1998); and Richmond, IN (Oldham 1999).

There are several exceptions to this rule, however, that merit discussion. Francaviglia's *Main Street Revisited* (1996) is a rare scholarly publication that examines the origins, evolution, and design of small city main streets throughout the country and how these relate to the modern day image of what "main street" should look like. The magazine *Small Town* has published two articles (Brooks and Searcy 1995; Kenyon 1989) that report on studies/surveys of a cross-section of small city downtowns in Georgia; both articles conclude that the primary function of many downtowns has shifted from economic purposes to social and community-related purposes. The National Main Street Center (1988) published a report that presented the findings of their national survey of main street programs, almost all of which were located in small cities. Tyler (1998) studied 16 small cities in Michigan and found that business mix is the key indicator of downtown health, while Ryan, Brantz, and Brault (1998) examined the downtown retail mix in Wisconsin cities with populations of 2,500–15,000. Finally, as mentioned in the introduction, I have conducted a national study of small city downtown issues and strategies; one significant conclusion was that a strong sense of place is a key component for successful downtowns to possess (Robertson 1999).

Differences Between Large and Small City Downtowns

Downtowns in large and small American cities are likely to share a number of common characteristics. Regardless of city size, downtowns are likely to be situated very close to the historic beginnings of the city, often next to a body of water. Many of the city's most historic and important buildings—in terms of both architecture and public use—are downtown, such as city halls, theatres, bank buildings, post offices, courthouses, hotels, and libraries. Downtown districts maintain a strong public identity amongst local residents—although not always positive—and these districts possess greater densities than elsewhere in the region. Finally, the downtowns in cities of all sizes began a downward spiral during the post World War II decades as a result of the rising popularity of the private automobile, massive public expenditures into highways, and rapid suburbanization.

Despite some common elements, small city downtowns contain numerous features that set them apart from their larger cousins. Bangor, ME, provides an excellent example of these differences. These characteristics present a different set of challenges and opportunities, and therefore are important to understand.

First, small city downtowns are more human scale. They generally do not contain large skyscraper-like structures that make people feel diminutive. They lack the huge throngs of people on the sidewalks during rush hour. Distances between destinations within the downtown are negotiable on foot.

Second, small city downtowns are not plagued with some of the problems that confront larger cities. Traffic congestion and fear of crime, for example, are often cited as major impediments to the use of large city downtowns, but these problems usually are relatively minor in smaller cities.

Third, larger city downtowns are dominated by a corporate presence both in terms of physical structures (e.g., hotels, office buildings) and economic influence. The corporate center approach has been identified as a primary downtown development strategy in large cities (Frieden and Sagalyn 1989). This situation is rarely the case in smaller cities, especially in cities with less than 25,000 population.

Fourth, most small city downtowns lack the large signature projects that are key components in larger city redevelopment efforts. Large city downtowns usually contain multiple large-scale development projects such as a sports stadium/arena, indoor shopping center, convention center, and/or a mixed-use center that act as development anchors.

Fifth, the retail structure differs in smaller cities. Regional and national chains are far less interested in locating in small cities due to the reduced market area, and only a small percentage of small city downtowns still possess a department store (in fact, how to reuse a vacant department store continues to be a challenge in many cities). Downtown retailing is dominated by local independents.

Sixth, the downtowns of most small cities are not divided up into districts. In large city downtowns, due to their sheer size, downtowns may contain a financial district, riverfront, historic quarter, entertainment district, civic center area, shopping corridor, amongst others, each with their own distinct function, character, and feel (Robertson 1999).

Seventh, many small city downtowns are closely linked to nearby residential neighborhoods. Often within easy walking distance, these neighborhoods contain older homes where downtown employees and consumers may reside. This is rarely the case in larger cities because of the greater distances and the prevalence of a transition zone between downtown and neighborhoods that contain industrial uses, automobile-oriented businesses, and surface parking lots.

Eighth, small city downtowns are more likely to still possess a higher percentage of historic buildings than large cities (Kenyon 1989). The demand for new development, which usually leads to the demolition of older structures, did not materialize in small cities over the past few decades as it has in larger market areas.

These notable differences between downtowns of large and small cities dictate that a targeted set of principles be developed for successful downtown development in small cities.

PRINCIPLE NO. 1: THE IMPORTANCE OF A STRONG PRIVATE/PUBLIC PARTNERSHIP

The majority of successful downtowns possess two interrelated ingredients. First, an active and well-organized downtown association can help downtown businesses and property owners work together towards their mutual benefit, somewhat similar to the organization of a shopping mall (Robertson 1997). With a broad base of volunteers and a full-time downtown manager (Stitt 1996), downtown associations are well-equipped to engage in activities related to marketing, recruitment, promotions, and event planning, and to serve as a unified voice representing downtown interests. Second, city government needs to be a supportive partner in downtown development activities. The city can demonstrate its commitment by granting downtown high priority in the comprehensive plan and budgeting process, by investing in public improvements such as sidewalks, streetlights, and infrastructure, and by providing incentives for building façade improvements and business expansions (e.g., a low interest revolving loan fund).

Three excellent examples of balanced partnerships can be found in Auburn, NY; Bangor, ME; and St. Cloud, MN. The Auburn Downtown Partnership (ADP) has worked closely with the city planning and economic development department on a host of successful downtown projects ranging from new streetlights to the construction of downtown housing. City staff sit on the ADP Board and serve as key resource people. The city devoted nearly one-half of its comprehensive plan to the downtown district. A similar close relationship exists in Bangor between the city's department of community development and the Bangor Center Corporation (BCC), an organization funded by special assessments on downtown properties. A city staff member administers the BCC. In St. Cloud, the Downtown Council worked with the city to implement major streetscape improvements and to renovate an historic theatre. The Mayor sits on the Downtown Council's Board of Directors. Revolving loan funds are available for downtown improvements in all three cities.

The results are often less than desirable where the public/private balance is lacking. Carson City, NV possesses an active community development department that has been a strong advocate of downtown. Unfortunately, private sector involvement is limited to a small subcommittee within the chamber of commerce. The opposite prevails in Texarkana (TX/AR), the downtown of which is situated within two cities and two states. An increasingly dynamic downtown organization has emerged within the past few years which has helped to bring downtown interests together from both sides of the border and to initiate numerous downtown projects. City involvement, particularly on the more populous Texas side, can best be described as apathetic. Efforts to revitalize the downtown of the small Minnesota town of Foley have a steep hill to climb despite the impressive efforts launched by a grassroots citizen-based group (e.g., a visioning session and a successful grant). The town does not possess a downtown organization, not even a chamber of commerce, and its city council has expressed minimal commitment towards the well being of downtown Foley.

No discussion of partnerships and organization would be complete without mention of the popular Main Street Approach, sponsored by the National Trust for Historic Preservation. Strong organization of downtown interests, which includes linkages with government agencies and other organizations, is one of the four tenants of the Main Street Approach; the other three tenants are design that enhances visual qualities and historic architecture, promotions and marketing, and economic restructuring and diversification (Dane 1997). In my national survey of small city downtowns (Robertson 1999), the Main Street Approach ranked as the most successful amongst 16 downtown development strategies. Many states have developed very productive statewide main street programs that help to provide technical assistance and a network among main street communities. Some of the successful state programs that have been featured in professional magazines include Mississippi (Kelly 1996), Oklahoma (Ehrenhalt 1996), Indiana (Kronemyer 1997), and Iowa (Buehler 1996). The vast majority of main street communities across the United States are small cities.

PRINCIPLE NO. 2: DEVELOP A VISION/PLAN FOR DOWNTOWN

Far too many cities, often responding to a development opportunity, economic hard times, and/or funding availability, forge ahead with downtown development activities with little sense of the value of these activities or how they will shape the downtown. Individual projects are implemented in a vacuum without the context of a long-term downtown vision and plan. Mayor Jim Marshall of Macon, GA, stated the following (Hudnit 1998, 72):

> Good projects are not enough; they have to fit into an overall plan, and they must be feasible as well as desirable. It makes no sense to propose projects without the benefit of context.

A vision of what the community would like the downtown to be—functionally, physically, socially, economically—is a critical step in the revitalization process (Palma 1998). The visioning process should include much more than just a handful of community or downtown power brokers. It should bring together a wide variety of downtown interests (e.g., business owners, property owners, customers, workers, residents, government officials, institutional representatives) for the purpose of discussing, debating, and reaching consensus of the most desirable direction for downtown to proceed. Extending the vision process to include interests outside of downtown is always advisable to help make this a community-wide vision for downtown.

Two cities that I have worked with help to illustrate this point. In Jonesboro, AR, a group of well-positioned individuals representing the local hospital, university, newspaper, largest bank, and so on, were concerned about the downward direction of their downtown and organized a series of public forums in 1999 to solicit people's ideas. The forums were lively, well attended, nicely covered by local media, and included a wide cross-section of community interests, including many residents of a nearby minority neighborhood. The next step will be to hire a consulting firm to conduct a more formal visioning session and to create a downtown plan based on the visioning results. The St. Cloud Downtown Council sponsored a two-day visioning session in 1998 to help determine the future course of action for the downtown. Participating in the sessions were representatives from various city departments, the arts council, the convention and visitors bureau, a labor organization, several banks, a downtown hotel, and numerous downtown business and property owners; the President of St. Cloud State University and a representative from the local newspaper, neither of which are located downtown, also participated. I facilitated a SWOT Analysis (Strengths, Weaknesses, Opportunities, and Threats) and an action planning session to help the group prioritize their future direction. Several of the group's recommendations have received attention.

Once the vision for downtown's future has been established, the next step is to create a formal plan that incorporates the values and ideas derived from the visioning participants. This plan should clearly articulate the goals, objectives, and priorities for downtown development, transportation dimensions, design elements, specific locations for various types of desired projects, and linkages between primary downtown locations. The downtown plan could either be a component of the city comprehensive plan (e.g., Auburn, NY) or a plan specifically created for downtown by a consulting firm (e.g., Jonesboro, AR). Once the vision and plan are in place, they help to guide future decisions regarding the need, priority, location, and appropriateness of future revitalization proposals by providing an overall context.

PRINCIPLE NO. 3: DOWNTOWN SHOULD BE MULTIFUNCTIONAL

The healthiest downtowns contain a wide range of activities that serve to bring different types of people downtown for different reasons at varied times of the day and week. Traditionally, the primary downtown functions were shopping/services and employment. Even though most small cities have seen the level of downtown retailing decline in recent decades, these two activities are still very important. Other functions compliment this traditional commercial orientation. Downtown has long been the location for government-related structures such as city halls, county courthouses, libraries, post offices, and police stations. Often the oldest churches in the city are in the downtown area, thereby attracting people during the weekend and evenings. Entertainment activities (e.g., taverns, nightclubs, movies, microbreweries) and cultural attractions (e.g., theatres, museums) also bring people downtown at times other than the traditional 9AM-5PM on weekdays. Many professionals, such as lawyers, accountants, financial advisors, and realtors, choose to locate their offices in the downtown. More recently, tourism has constituted an increasingly popular development strategy (Snepenger *et. al.* 1998). A few small cities have even erected convention and sports facilities downtown in the hopes of attracting large numbers of visitors.

The above activities primarily seek to bring people to the downtown from elsewhere. In recent years, however, many downtowns have recognized the advantages of having more people actually live downtown, thereby providing a human presence throughout the week and a market for downtown businesses. Over two-thirds of the cities in my national survey listed downtown housing as an ongoing strategy (Robertson 1999). Downtown housing comes in many forms. Market rate condominiums were created through the conversion of a hotel in Wausau, WI, and an industrial building in Bangor, ME. Bangor also rehabilitated an abandoned department store into senior housing, while senior projects have also been built in Anoka, MN; Auburn, NY; and St. Cloud, MN. In Auburn, a student apartment building was erected to serve a nearby community college. Upper floors of commercial buildings, long underutilized, have been successfully converted into affordable housing in numerous cities (Holcombe 1993). Finally, the majority of the cities I worked with have older neighborhoods within close walking distance of the downtown that provide a desirable location for certain people, including downtown workers.

Most small city downtowns possess an inherent advantage over other locations within their city and region: a multitude of activities within close walking distance (regional malls, for example, rarely have churches, housing, law offices, museums, and libraries that one can reach on foot). Downtowns seeking to improve their vitality have learned to build upon and enhance the functions that are already prevalent and then, as appropriate, add new complimentary functions.

PRINCIPLE NO. 4: TAKE ADVANTAGE OF DOWNTOWN'S HERITAGE

Arguably the greatest asset intrinsic to most small city downtowns is their close relationship to the city's heritage. Given that the city most likely originated where the present day downtown is situated, the streets, parks/squares, waterfront, and many of the older buildings are deeply ingrained into the city's collective history, evolution, and memory. The older buildings constitute the most visible manifestation of this heritage, and preserving and maintaining these

buildings have been cited as the most significant feature for successful downtown development in Georgia (Brooks and Searcy 1995). There are also strong
economic arguments supporting preservation over new construction. It is more
labor intensive, thus keeping more money within the community; it can attract
tourism dollars into the city; it is often less costly and disruptive; and it takes
advantage of already built infrastructure (Rypkema 1998).

The importance of heritage has been recognized throughout the country. The
most frequently cited asset in the national survey of small city downtowns was
preservation/architecture/heritage while historic preservation was the most commonly utilized development strategy (Robertson 1999). The preservation of a
landmark structure that many people identify with can prove to be a catalyst for
downtown vitality. For example, historic theatres have been successfully rehabilitated in Texarkana, St. Cloud, Bangor, and Wausau, while Auburn converted
a strategically located bank building, with its prominent clock tower, to offices
and a restaurant.

The heritage of any community, however, consists of much more than a collection of buildings. Downtown can be linked to many important events, experiences, and memories to a broad spectrum of people throughout the city and
surrounding region. It was where parades and festivals took place, where cele-
brations occurred following wars, where major civic decisions were made at city
hall and county courthouses, where many people worshipped, utilized the library,
attended school, and/or went to the theatre. Downtown has the unique ability to
tap into the collective memory of many individuals, an essential component for
a strong sense of community and sense of place. Even though people will still
shop at Wal-Mart or a distant suburban shopping mall, they will feel little sense
of ownership at these places, nor will they constitute any special sense of place
to its users.

Given this tremendous advantage over shopping malls, big box discounters,
and highway commercial strips, it is amazing how many downtowns have chosen to ignore their heritage and instead try to replicate suburban commercial
environments. Across the country downtowns have razed older buildings and in
their place erected surface parking lots and suburban-style structures with blank
walls and parking lots in front. Many building owners slipcovered their older
buildings with aluminum façades in a misguided attempt to modernize the look
of their businesses. Not only are these efforts usually unsuccessful in luring back
customers, they serve to damage the traditional fabric, density, and sense of place
that can make downtown an attractive alternative to newer shopping venues.

PRINCIPLE NO. 5: LINK DOWNTOWN TO THE WATERFRONT

A high percentage of small city downtowns are located on water, which undoubtedly played a critical role in the origins and overall heritage of that community.
People are naturally attracted to water, and the presence of a body of water serves
to heighten one's sense of place (Breen and Rigby 1994). It is an amenity rarely

found by newly constructed commercial structures (has anyone ever seen a big box discount store overlooking a body of water?). The survey of small cities found that waterfronts were considered the second most attractive asset possessed by downtowns and waterfront development was the third most successful strategy (Robertson 1999).

The main street is usually situated within one or two blocks from the waterfront. The keys to taking advantage of this natural amenity are to provide clear pedestrian links between the core of downtown and the water and to provide an attractive and interesting waterfront setting. Some downtowns are cut off from the waterfront by parking lots, railroad tracks, busy streets, or industrial buildings. The design of open spaces and buildings, both new construction and rehabilitation, needs to provide easy access to and viewing of the water. Bangor, ME, located at the confluence of the Kenduskeag and Penobscot Rivers, has made effective use of its proximity to water. The narrow Kenduskeag River, which splits the downtown in half, has been developed to include continuous public access via a nicely landscaped linear park, a pedestrian bridge, and an inviting open space on a little island. On the Penobscot River, a former industrial corridor has been cleaned up and redeveloped to include a community park, an office building, and a microbrewery. The fact that the Penobscot is located about seven blocks from the heart of downtown presents a special challenge to planners attempting to provide clear and user-friendly pedestrian linkage. In contrast, St. Cloud, MN, built a convention center and a hotel on the Mississippi River, thereby blocking public access from downtown.

Principle No. 6: Downtown Should Be Pedestrian-Friendly

One essential element of most successful downtowns is the prevalence of an environment that is very walkable. People will often choose to walk if the pathways/sidewalks are comfortable, safe, interesting, and enjoyable; if distances between destinations are deemed walkable; and if destinations are clearly linked by a network of sidewalks and pathways (e.g., the core of downtown with the riverfront or a nearby neighborhood). Downtowns have a tremendous built-in advantage over most other commercial areas in this regard. Traditional downtown districts evolved when walking and transit were the primary means of transportation, and consequently were compact with destinations relatively close to each other. Unless the fabric has been gutted over time with torn down buildings, surface parking lots, and buildings with blank walls or set back from the sidewalk, downtowns can continue to provide a setting where walking is an enjoyable, practical, and efficient mode of transport.

There are numerous benefits of having a pedestrian-friendly downtown. Our image of a vibrant downtown always contains a multitude of people walking on the sidewalks; no matter how aesthetically pleasing the downtown may be, it looks dead without the presence of pedestrians. Economically, the more a person is enticed to walk, the more storefronts he/she will encounter, thereby increasing the pool of potential customers for businesses to draw from. This principle has been well understood by managers of suburban shopping malls for decades. Finally, the attribute of a multifunctional downtown described in Principle No. 3 is diminished when people are discouraged from walking between functions. It does little good to have the library one block from a series of interesting little shops if people find the walk to be difficult or uninteresting.

Downtowns nationwide have implemented many strategies aimed at the pedestrian. Some of the most common include providing pedestrian amenities (e.g., flowers, landscaping, benches, interesting lighting, banners, brick pavers, street trees, widening sidewalks, reducing traffic speeds, and making streets easier to cross. Since parking facilities serve as a major pedestrian impediment, some cities have realized the benefits of locating parking lots/garages in less conspicuous places —such as behind main street buildings—that are clearly marked with directional signage. Linking these parking facilities directly to major downtown destinations is a key to this strategy. Encouraging building and business owners to have attractive building façades, awnings, and interesting store windows helps to make the journey more enticing to people on foot. A few cities have provided pedestrian-only corridors in their downtowns. Examples include a pedestrian bridge over the Kenduskeag River in Bangor, ME; a pedestrian alley in Carson City, NV; and successful pedestrian malls in Wausau, WI; and Auburn and Ithaca, NY.

PRINCIPLE NO. 7: ESTABLISH DESIGN GUIDELINES

Given the importance of heritage, sense of place, and a pedestrian-friendly environment to a healthy downtown, cities and downtown associations are strongly advised to pay special attention to downtown design. This will help to ensure that the redevelopment of older structures and the construction of new buildings integrate with the inherent character and fabric of the downtown. Not providing any guidance to building and business owners can often result in buildings that do more damage than good. For instance, the erection of a suburban-style store set back from the sidewalk with a parking lot in front will probably interrupt the continuity of the streetscape, rendering it less friendly to pedestrians and compromising the integrity of the other traditional buildings on the block. For buildings old and new, technical guidance is needed for matters concerning setbacks, windows, signage, awnings, rooflines, doorways, materials, color, and massing, and how these factors relate to surrounding structures.

Design can be influenced in several ways. The strictest method is for the city to pass a design ordinance for building façades. Bangor, ME enacted such an ordinance for its downtown in 1983 that regulates every building and structure located within a defined area of the downtown. A Code Enforcement Officer is vested with full authority to enforce and administer this ordinance, and must grant permission for all exterior alterations to existing buildings. Many cities have passed special ordinances regulating signage in the downtown (McMahon

1991). More palatable to many downtown businesses and to politically sensitive city councils is the use of design guidelines. These generally are not mandatory unless tied to some form of financial assistance. For example, both Auburn, NY, and Carson City, NV, have adopted design guidelines which are voluntary for most but required for building owners who have made use of low interest revolving loan funds for building improvements. Finally, a number of downtown organizations, particularly those associated with the National Main Street Center, have established design committees which offer an array of technical design assistance to interested building owners. The Main Street Program in Pullman, Washington (pop. 25,000), for example, has provided design assistance through a volunteer committee for many years (Ryder and Gray 1988).

PRINCIPLE NO. 8: DO NOT OVEREMPHASIZE THE IMPORTANCE OF PARKING

Parking has long been the scapegoat for a declining downtown. In city after city, many downtown businesses declare, "if we only had more parking, we could be more competitive". They steadfastly cling to this belief despite the opinions of experienced experts who have discounted the importance of parking to the revitalization of downtowns (Stitt 1996; Smith 1998; Rypkema 1999). In his study of 16 small city downtowns in Michigan, Tyler (1998) found that parking was the characteristic least correlated with a healthy downtown. In all but the most popular downtowns, spaces are available at any time of day within 1-2 blocks of any destination. Most of these spaces are not located directly in front of one's destination. Therefore, the key usually is not to build more spaces but to more effectively manage the existing spaces and to better inform the public as to the whereabouts of available parking (e.g., directional signs, brochures, maps, newspaper advertisements).

Surface parking lots are especially damaging to a downtown. They impede pedestrian circulation, constitute an unsightly use of land, add less to the tax base than most alternate uses, reduce downtown densities, and usually serve to detract from downtown's overall value and appeal. Where absolutely necessary (i.e., small cities with less than 15,000 population), lots should be generously landscaped and located on the edges of downtown or behind main street buildings. In small cities with larger populations, parking garages/ramps often utilize land more efficiently. As with lots, location and design are still key factors (Edwards 1995). They should not be located along downtown corridors where heavy pedestrian use is desired and, ideally, should be underground or above ground to allow more attractive uses to be on street level. It is important to remember that parking itself never attracts people downtown, and therefore should constitute a supporting role, not the centerpiece, of downtown development efforts.

Final Thoughts

One final observation underscores the successful implementation of all of the above principles: Be patient. The decline of small city downtowns took decades to occur, and revitalization efforts always take many years of small, steady, incremental steps before noticeable improvements are evident to all. A major conclusion of mayors involved in downtown development was that the process takes time, perseverance, and constant energy from multiple directions (Hudnit 1998). "Big fix" solutions rarely work, especially in smaller cities. Rather a continuous series of small-scale organizational, aesthetic/design, and economic improvements that makes downtown distinctive from other settings— a strong sense of place—is the foundation for successful downtown development in small cities.

References

Breen, Ann, and Dick Rigby. 1994. *Waterfronts: Cities Reclaim Their Edge.* New York: McGraw-Hill.

Brooks, Rusty, and Cindy Searcy. 1995. "Downtowns in Georgia". *Small Town* 26 (November): 14-29.

Buehler, Beth. 1996. "Main Street Iowa: Celebrating the Spirit". *Main Street News* (July): 1-7.

Byers, Jack. 1998. "The Privatization of Downtown Public Space: The Emerging Grade Separated City in North America". *Journal of Planning Education and Research* 17: 189-205.

Campbell, Robert. 1998. "Modernism on Main Street". *Preservation* 50 (September): 38-45.

Dane, Suzanne. 1997. *Main Street Success Stories.* Washington, D.C.: National Main Street Center.

Edwards, John. 1995. *The Parking Handbook for Small Communities.* Washington, D.C.: National Main Street Center.

Ehrenhalt, Alan. 1996. "Return to Main Street". *Governing* (May): 18-27.

Francaviglia, Richard. 1996. *Main Street Revisited.* Iowa City: University of Iowa Press.

Frieden, Bernard, and Lynne Sagalyn. 1989. *Downtown Inc.* Cambridge, Massachusetts: MIT Press.

Holcombe, Greg. 1993. "Upper Floor Housing: An Innovative Approach". *Main Street News* (April): 1-5.

Hudnit, William. 1998. "Downtown: Still the Heart and Soul of a Region". *Urban Land* 57 (February): 70-75.

Kelly, Steve. 1996. "The Main Street Program in Mississippi". *Economic Development Review* (Summer): 56-59.

Kenyon, James. 1989. "From Central Business District to Central Social District: The Revitalization of the Small Georgia City". *Small Town* 20 (March): 4-17.

Kronemyer, Bob. 1997. "Indiana Main Streets: Tips for Successful Downtown Revitalization". *Indiana Business Magazine* 41 (June): 17-24.

Lockwood, Charles. 1997. "Onward and Upward in Downtown Santa Monica". *Planning* 63 (September): 14-16.

Loukaitou-Sideris, Anastasia. 1993. "Privatization of Public Open Space: The Los Angeles Experience". *Town Planning Review* 64: 139-167.

Loukaitou-Sideris, and Tridib Banerjee. 1998. *Urban Design Downtown.* Berkeley: University of California Press.

McMahon, Edward. 1991. "Regulating Signs". *Main Street News* (January):1-9.

Means, Annette. 1997. "Downtown Revitalization in Small Cities." *Urban Land* 56 (January): 26-31, 56.

Meek, Mary. 1995. "Bonaparte, Iowa Organizes a Comprehensive Volunteer Effort to Save Its Downtown." *Small Town* 26 (May): 4-9.

Mildner, Gerard, James Strathman, and Martha Bianco. 1997. "Parking Policies and Behavior." *Transportation Quarterly* 51 (Winter): 111-125.

Mozingo, Louise. 1989. "Women and Downtown Open Space." *Places* 6: 38-47.

National Main Street Center. 1988. *Revitalizing Downtown 1976-1986*. Washington, D.C.

Oldham, Renee. 1999. "Richmond, Indiana: A Changing Vision." *Main Street News* (March): 1-6, 11.

Palma, Dolores. 1998. "Local Officials Can Learn Strategies for a Successful Downtown." *Nation's Cities Weekly* 21 (January 5): 7-8.

Robertson, Kent. 1993. "Pedestrianization Strategies for Downtown Planners: Skywalks v. Pedestrian Malls." *Journal of the American Planning Association* 59 (Summer): 361-370.

Robertson, Kent. 1997. "Downtown Retail Revitalization: A Review of American Development Strategies." *Planning Perspectives* 12 (October): 383-401.

Robertson, Kent. 1998. "Small-City Downtowns." *Urban Land* 57 (October): 48-51, 94-95.

Robertson, Kent. 1999. "Can Small-City Downtowns Remain Viable?: A National Study of Development Issues and Strategies." *Journal of the American Planning Association* 65 (Summer): Vol. 65, 3(Summer): 270-284.

Rosentraub, Mark, David Swindell, Michael Przybylski, and Daniel Mullins. 1994. "Sport and Downtown Development Strategy." *Journal of Urban Affairs* 16: 221-239.

Ryan, Bill, Jerry Braatz, and Aaron Brault. 1998. "Retail Mix in Wisconsin's Small Downtowns." *Let's Talk Business* (November): 1-2.

Ryder, Barbara, and Kelsey Gray. 1988. "Developing a Downtown Design Assistance Program in Pullman, Washington." *Small Town* 19 (March): 4-13.

Rypkema, Donovan. 1998. "Preserving for Profit." *Urban Land* 57 (December): 66-69.

Rypkema, Donovan. 1999. "15 Reasons Why Downtowns Don't Need More Parking." *Main Street News* (May): 16.

Sawicki, David. 1989. "The Festival Market Place as Public Policy." *Journal of the American Planning Association* 53 (Summer): 347-361.

Seachord, Dan. 1997. "Bringing Investment Back Downtown: A Case Study of Puyallop, Washington." *Small Town* 28 (March): 22-29.

Smith, Kennedy. 1998. "The P Word." *Main Street News* (August): 15.

Snepenger, David, Steven Reiman, Jerry Johnson, and Mary Snepenger. 1998. "Is Downtown Mainly for Tourists?" *Journal of Travel Research* 36 (Winter): 5-12.

Suchman, Diane. 1998. "Rebuilding Downtown Grand Forks." *Urban Land* 57 (February): 80-83, 94.

Stitt, Bert. 1996. "The Lies of Downtown." *Small Town* 27 (July): 18-25.

Tyler, Norman. 1998. "Evaluating the Health of Downtowns: A Study of Michigan Small Cities." *Let's Talk Business* (July): 1-4.

Voith, Richard. 1998. "The Downtown Parking Syndrome: Does Curing the Illness Cure the Patient?" *Business Review*. Federal Reserve Bank of Philadelphia (January): 3-11.

CHAPTER 3

The Emergence of a Competitive Core: Bifurcation Dynamics in Billings, Montana[1]

MARK D. HARDT

Billings Montana is a small metropolitan city, having approximately 90,000 residents and an additional 35,000 in surrounding communities. Despite its small size, Billings was the first of three Montana cities to achieve metropolitan status, and is the state's largest city. Originally settled as a railroad town, the city's business and industrial core was long oriented in the vicinity of the rail terminal and was surrounded by residential neighborhoods. Since 1980 the city has had substantial population growth, with rates of increase during the decade (21.5 percent) nearly equalling its growth in the previous two decades (25 percent). The rate of growth has remained consistent through the first half of the 1990s, and estimates indicate a continuance of growth.

The recent period of growth has not been uniformly distributed, and can be described as reflecting the kind of urban sprawl that has become a concern even in small Montana cities, and in cities throughout the U.S. Billings' growth and development has disrupted previous land use patterns, with the downtown core becoming increasingly constrained and characterized by high rates of business turnover and declining property values. As the downtown has stagnated, economic development has shifted to the western end of the city which runs roughly parallel to Interstate 90 and spreading in that direction from the Rimrock Mall— the largest mall in the region. To a lesser extent economic development has also occurred in an area known as "the heights." The north and east of the original city are framed by 400 to 500 foot sandstone cliffs known as the rimrocks. Directly accessible only by a single road that connects it with the downtown core, and indirectly by a road running parallel to the rims and leading to the airport, the heights developed as an isolated section of the city. Unlike the downtown core and the sprawl on the western side of the city, both of which are accessible from I-90, the main transportation artery in the heights is a state highway. This has encouraged economic development by businesses that cater directly to a relatively isolated population.

Development in the heights and the western edge of the city has led to a bifurcation of Billings' business district. Instead of a common core, the city can instead be characterized as having a hierarchy of economic zones, with a rapidly sprawling zone to the west, a more moderately sprawling zone in the heights, and a stagnating inner core.

This chapter examines the ecological constraints, and prior decisions, actions, and governmental policy that have resulted in the decline of Billings' downtown and the emergence of competing economic sectors. While some attention is given to understanding why the outer sectors have developed in the manners they have, the focus throughout is to determine why a downtown core—vibrant as recently as the early 1970s—has lost its luster.

Frameworks for Analysis

Two theoretical perspectives, both having roots in the natural sciences, help to provide divergent—yet overlapping—explanations of metropolitan growth and its impacts on downtown development. These are the human ecology model and the bifurcation model. Human ecology, on the one hand, tends to be macroscopic in nature, and assumes that a dynamic expansion occurs in a natural, rather uniform and predictive manner. The bifurcation model utilizes variables found in ecological studies, but introduces a microscopic element, assuming that the seemingly rational decisions of individual actors lead to unpredictable patterns that are only sporadically uniform and predictable. The core issue for human ecology is the "understanding of how a population organizes itself in adapting to a constantly changing yet restricting environment" (Berry and Kasarda 1977, 12). This is a central concern of the bifurcation model as well. It is the shared concern of the two models that serves as the guiding framework for analysis in this chapter.

Both models make reference to environmental conditions. In the ecological model, populations exist in an environment, and environmental features—both directly and indirectly—influence the size and structure of populations. The view leads to a postulation that there is a tendency of social systems to move toward stabilization within the web of life. The equilibrium position is a basic assumption of human ecology. Besides population and environment, contemporary ecological analyses include two remaining reference variables or rubrics—organization and technology. These four variables are functionally interdependent and mutually reciprocal (Duncan 1959). Thus both change and stability in a community are a result of the interactions between these rubrics. Equilibrium is attained when the various functions of an urban system are complementary and provide the conditions needed for each to survive; when the number of individuals is sufficient to maintain the complementary functions; and when units are spatially and temporally distributed so that accessibility of one to others bears a direct relation to the frequency of exchanges between them (Hawley 1968, 334).

To the extent that any of these conditions are not being met, a lack of equilibrium occurs. Therein lies the disruptive nature of urban growth. As people and economic entities move into a city, an outward expansion occurs and the previous state of equilibrium is disrupted. While the physical environment can inhibit the direction of the process, it is nevertheless assumed that centrifugal movement—which begins in the central locus of the city—will occur in a fairly uniform and orderly fashion. Such change, however, disrupts the necessary balance between the four reference variables and, during a period of disequilibrium, imposes a need for the urban system to make adjustments to new conditions in order for equilibrium to be re-established. The systems—rather than individual—level of analysis that is typical of human ecology necessitates a reliance on quantitative data to assess the manners in which groups and aggregates behave (Palen 1997). The Bifurcation model has its roots in catastrophe theory, first developed in physics and chemistry in the 1960s and 1970s. By 1980 the theory was being applied to the study of urban and regional systems, most extensively by Allen (1983, 1997), Allen and Sanglier (1981), Beaumont, *et. al.* (1983), and Dendrinos (1983).

The bifurcation model partly shares an interest with human ecology in a systems approach, and with an approach emphasizing the importance of environmental factors. The model is critical, though, of any model emphasizing stasis or equilibrium. To maintain equilibrium requires a stable state, in particular in terms of energy, material, and information. "Should these flows change, for any reason, the possibility of a change in structure must be admitted" (Crosby 1983, 9). While this echoes the ecological model, there are important distinctions. First, while the ecological model strives for the scientific goal of simplicity by referencing four basic variables (Palen 1995), the bifurcation model contends that there are too many variables affecting a system for equilibrium to be maintained (Crosby 1983). Second, an important feature that cannot be anticipated by a purely systems approach is the impact of human decision making. As Crosby put it:

> The fact is that we take actions because we make decisions, not because we are particles in a force field. It is this distinction that requires us to examine human decision making as the key to understanding process in social systems (Crosby 1983, 14).

The uncertainty of decision making, coupled with the time lag between the making of a decision and the completion of an action lead to unstable and unpredictable patterns. Instead of tending toward equilibrium, then, the bifurcation model sees cities as being beset by local instabilities (Allen 1997). It is at points of instability, or bifurcation points, that new, unexpected, and unpredicted opportunities arise. It is from such bifurcation points that any semblance of order is seen.

The bifurcation model has potential as an applied model for understanding urban growth. Its inclusion of systemic variables make it useful at a macro-sociological level, while its emphasis on human decision making and its effects on systemic patterns make it a useful tool for including a micro-sociological approach. In addition, its recognition of societal/environmental influences connect the model to the otherwise antithetical model of human ecology. Nevertheless it must be recognized that the bifurcation model remains largely a mathematical model, one relying heavily on computer simulations. Systemic variables tend to be added to the model, with "noise" being introduced as regular intervals to assess morphological changes in an urban system.

This chapter does not attempt to make a systematic comparison of these two models. They are used, instead, as a framework for understanding opportunities and constraints to development of the core of a small metropolis confronted with urban sprawl. The macro-sociological systemic analysis shared by both models is examined first, focusing on population characteristics that have held, and still hold, for the downtown core. Also analyzed in this segment of the chapter are physical and environmental features, as well as technological issues—transportation in particular—that have affected the core. Finally, instead of a simulation of decision making, information derived from key informants and other sources are used to develop an understanding of the uncertainties that have lead to the current patterns of urban development found in Billings.

Ecological Opportunities and Constraints

Billings was established by the Northern Pacific Railroad in 1882. As a railroad town the original settlement was laid out to be oriented, in a grid fashion, to the railroad depot. The city's downtown core lies to the north of the depot. This proximity to a major transportation route served the city well, as long as railroads were the major transportation mode.

The downtown core is rather small, encompassing an area of only about six city blocks in any direction. A land use survey conducted in the mid-1990s shows a mixed use core predominated by business and office space (28 percent), governmental facilities (16 percent), retail establishments (12 percent), and service centers (8 percent). The vacancy rate at the time stood at 12 percent. While housing is one key to sustaining a vibrant downtown, ensuring the constant presence of people for a variety of reasons, housing in downtown Billings represented only one percent of available space (Jacobs 1961). One informant, active in current downtown development activities, reported that vacancy levels have not changed substantially, though no follow-up land use survey has been conducted.

In 1997, the only major department store in Billings—located at the very intersection that is considered the heart of the downtown core—closed. The closure had adverse impacts on surrounding establishments that could cater to the customer base the department store drew. Since its closure the building has been partitioned into business and office space, usages that do not attract the same volume or constancy of customers. The closure did not only represent the loss of a business. The Hart-Albin building is a cultural landmark, and its vacancy symbolized the lost allure of the downtown core.

Even if vacancy rates have not deteriorated, observation suggests that turnover rates are high, though the absence of any more recent land use survey makes it impossible to state how high. This compact core confronts a number of ecological constraints on development and expansion, with each border presenting different conditions. Its southern border runs parallel to the railroad tracks and encompasses the original train depot, to the southeast of the core. The city's historical district is along Montana Avenue, immediately adjacent to the depot. More will be said about this district later.

The railroad tracks serve as a dividing line that is common among many cities: the "southside." It is one of the lowest income areas in the city, dominated by low and moderate income housing. Its major institutional features include the city's main post office, the Chamber of Commerce's Visitors Center, the state women's prison, two oil refineries and a sugar beat processing plant.

The downtown core is directly accessible to I-90 (located approximately one and a half miles to the south) and the city's international airport (located about a similar distance to the north) via 27th Street North. This main thoroughfare bisects the southside and serves as the eastern border of the core. The border is important for a number of reasons. First, its immediate vicinity contains most of the local, county, state, and federal office buildings—along with retail and financial institutions. Second, beyond the immediate perimeter of the core, the eastern zone is comprised by a wide expanse of mixed use zoning. This expanse stretches a mile and a half from the core to the state fairgrounds, a year around facility known as MetraPark. The street leading directly from downtown to MetraPark is the principal route into the heights.

The northern and western borders of the core are densely populated and comprise mostly of moderate to upper income housing, including both single and multiple dwellings. The high population density in these areas provides a socio-economic resource for business, but a resource that is not strongly attracted to the downtown. These areas also provide some opportunity for expanding and revitalizing the core. For example there are numerous tracts along the western border that could be "in-filled," to create a stronger connection between the center and the boundary. It is also necessary to create a stronger link, both pedestrian and automotive, between the immediate western residential boundaries and the core.

To the north of the downtown core are two economic resources that are poorly connected to the core. The second largest unit in the Montana State University system is located roughly one mile north and is adjacent to the "hospital corridor." This corridor contains two hospitals and an assortment of specialized medical facilities and support services. The corridor is an expanse stretching from 27th Street North to 30th Street North and approximately five blocks toward downtown. Little has been done, however, to make these institutions physically more accessible to the core, nor to provide services that would cater to their needs.

Automobiles and Trains

The ecological model emphasizes that central city cores are located at the axis of transportation arteries. Because the convergence of transportation routes provides the most efficient means of linking interdependent activities, of importing and exporting goods, and providing access to a variety of opportunities for people, expansion and development of the city tends to be derived by development of the core. The reorientation of Billings' grid pattern inhibited the ability of the city's core to develop and to influence the economic expansion of the city. Instead of providing direct access to the central city, traffic is now diverted to the periphery of the core. Later decisions in the 1960s to implement one-way traffic control exacerbated this situation. One reason for the implementation of one way streets was to inhibit young people from "burning the point," a local phrase for cruising the streets in cars. The strategy was effective in stopping the practice; unfortunately, it was also effective in accomplishing an additional objective—to encourage people to move more effectively through downtown. With the conversion to one way streets the downtown core became friendly to automobiles, but not to pedestrians. People were encouraged to drive through downtown, but not to stop. When they stop, or attempt to stop, an additional impediment is encountered; parking.

The city's parking ramps are currently over 100 percent of capacity. Available on-street parking is not effectively distributed. Customers compete with business owners and their employees for parking spaces near businesses they wish to frequent. Coming after businesses have opened, customers typically lose out in this competition. A result is the perception that downtown is not a convenient place to shop, since it is necessary to walk long distances to access any particular destination. The compactness of the downtown core challenges this perception, yet the perception remains. As more than one informant noted, people often have to walk just as far in the sprawling parking lots at the mall and other large scale retail stores. At these locations, however, they can see their destination, which gives them a greater sense of proximity than they have downtown. In the current framework plan for developing the downtown core, this point is elaborated:

> Because psychological distances are great, walking a few blocks seems inconvenient and unpleasant. The result of an uninviting pedestrian environment is that people drive from one destination to another, thus depriving downtown the liveliness and interest of people on the move (Montana Telephone Authority and the City of Billings 1997, 21).

One informant emphasized that, if a place is attractive and people want to be there, parking is seen as being less of a problem. The lack of vibrancy and activity downtown minimizes the incentive to want to be downtown, contributing to the perception of a parking problem.

Negotiations during the mid-1990s between Philip Morris, the city, and Burlington Northern Railroad concluded with an agreement that the tobacco giant—in exchange for one million dollars for external restoration— could use the train depot as a part of its planned "Marlboro Train." While the proposed tourist train was scrapped in 1997, the depot was rejuvenated. This, in turn, inspired efforts to refurbish other buildings in what is known as the city's historical district. The district, just outside of the downtown core, represents the most assertive and successful attempt at revitalization and economic development outside of the West end or the heights. Restoration of this district also points to potential opportunities for the downtown core.

Trains no longer stop in Billings for cargo or passengers. The trains do, however, still run through the city, and this presents a rather ironic impediment to the development of the downtown core. Interstate 90 is directly accessible from 27th Street North. The railroad tracks still traverse the southern periphery of the core, running perpendicular to 27th Street. Unfortunately nothing has been done to make an overpass, either of the street over the tracks or the tracks over the street. Anytime a train runs through the city, it effectively cuts direct access to the modern mode of transportation, the highway. Since rail remains an important means of transporting agricultural goods and minerals in this part of the country, these disruptions are frequent, lengthy, and not entirely predictable. As a result it is difficult to plan a trip into or out of downtown in a way that avoids delays posed by the trains. Not only is interstate highway access severed, traffic within the downtown core is greatly disrupted with frequent and lengthy traffic jams one would associate with much larger metropolitan cities. The central core, in other words, is adversely affected by the very transportation mode that led to the city's founding. No previous or existent plan for downtown development has directly addressed this issue.

As highways emerged as the major mode of transportation—the Interstate Highway System in particular—major changes occurred with respect to the size and shape of cities. The ecological model recognizes that changes in forms of transportation can lead to a shift of the core, as the advantages of location to a new transportation form outweigh the advantages of a previous location. For Billings, completion of the Interstate Highway System is important to understanding recent development trends. Two major east-west interstates (I-90 and I-94) converge just to the east of the city. I-90 goes on to traverse the southern edge of Billings. Along this route, the eastern side of Billings is largely dominated by industrial (including two oil refineries) and ancillary businesses. The availability of open space is much greater in the western portion of the city. Proximity and more controlled access to the interstate have made this area the dominant location of economic expansion. It has not, however, resulted in a shift of the core. Resistance to controlled or planned growth, coupled with large open tracts of relatively inexpensive farm land, have lead to land intensive development. Typical of urban sprawl, this development is not centered. It follows along side the interstate and in adjacent areas away from the highway. Most of the city's large scale, land intensive shopping centers—including the Rimrock Mall—are located in this part of the city.

There is another feature of sprawl, both on the western side of town and in the heights, reflecting a trend that occurred during earlier bursts of growth and is a common feature of sprawl in other cities. It tends to be situated along heavily traveled thoroughfares, taking advantage of existing infrastructure. The first enclosed mall in Billings was also to the west of the city, in a largely undeveloped area directly accessible to downtown by a major east-west road (Grand Avenue). Westpark Plaza was built in the late 1950s. Instead of new businesses opening in the vacant area surrounding the Plaza, business expansion followed along Grand Avenue from the downtown core to the Plaza. Developers quickly bought surrounding property, and convinced the city government to change zoning codes from agricultural to residential. This nascent suburb filled in very quickly. The surrounding population densities, actually higher than found around the downtown core, and zoning codes, choked off any potential for this area to bifurcate into a competitive economic zone. More recent sprawl in the west end and in the heights follows a similar pattern, with business expansion occurring adjacent to existing streets. Infill tends to be residential, with intermittent instances of mixed use business/residential areas. Every major thoroughfare between downtown and its sprawling competitive areas is characterized by this mixed use pattern and non-adjacent residential infill.

Population and Housing

Conditions of downtowns and other economic zones are influenced by the distribution of socio-demographic attributes of the populations around them. This section examines the distribution of key socio-demographic data in one half-mile bands surrounding the three main economic zones in Billings. These bands increase incrementally to a distance of one and a half miles. The bands surrounding the downtown core are centered at a specific intersection (Broadway and 2nd Avenue North) that city officials consider to be the heart of the downtown core. The decision was made to "center" the sprawl on the western side of the city at the Rimrock Mall. This was the first business development in this section of the city, and the subsequent sprawl has developed north and—increasingly—to the south in the direction of I-90 where there is a greater availability of open space. The center of the sprawl in the Heights is situated at one of the main shopping plazas on Main Street (also a state highway), which leads directly to downtown, and is the traffic artery along which most of the sprawl is located.

Ecologically, the classical urban core can be depicted as having a rather well defined economic center surrounded by a concentration of industry and residential zones that are more densely populated, and having higher turnover rates and lower income populations. These characteristics tend to improve with increasing distance from the core, with densities declining, residential turnover receding, and income levels improving. Contemporary urban sprawl, by contrast, is depicted as having any absence of a center, and as lacking a mix of residential and economic uses. Moreover lot sizes tend to be larger in sprawl zones, creating a less efficient use of space than is found in the inner core, and, importantly, a lower density of usage.

These patterns are evident in Table 1, showing population densities from the 1990 census in areas extending from one-half mile, one mile, and one and one half miles from principal business locations in Billings. Figures for the year 2000 are derived from official U.S. Census estimates. There is actually a greater concentration of population within a half mile of the mall than there is to this extent around the inner city core. Beyond this point, however, it is evident that areas surrounding the downtown core are more densely settled than around the mall or in the heights. The population per square mile nearly trebles, from 2,445 persons within a half mile to 9,623 persons within one mile. Density increases to 17,860 within one and a half miles of the downtown core, the highest density of any of the areas mapped. Population density increases more slowly in areas extending from the mall, increasing from 2,643 persons to 15,783 persons per square mile in the outer zone. The lowest population densities are recorded in the heights, reflecting the large geographic area of open space that has encouraged sprawl in this part of the city.

The downtown core does not gain any advantage from the surrounding population densities because the population base is declining, housing values are lower, and residential turnover is higher. The dynamics of change during the 1980s point to a reasoned decision to leap-frog outside of downtown during the decade. The overall population base surrounding the core declined sharply during the decade, with the steepest declines in the inner and outer zones. This pattern has been replicated during the 1990s, though the losses are not of the same magnitude.

The inner two zones surrounding the heights recorded less severe population loss during the 1980s, and a pattern of growth in each zone during the 1990s. The region around the mall has been the most actively growing part of Billings for the last two decades. With the exception of the one mile zone during the 1980s, the mall region has experienced growth in each zone since 1980.

As noted earlier there are middle and upper class neighborhoods near the downtown core. However, median home values are the lowest in the core region. In fact, even at a distance of one and one half miles, median home values remain vastly lower than the home values in the inner zone surrounding the mall and in the heights. Lower housing values are also associated with a lower rate of home ownership. The maximum percentage of home ownership in 1990 in the core region is less than 40 percent, a proportion not even approaching the minimal level of homeownership for zones surrounding the mall or the heights. While there is a noticeable increase in homeownership anticipated for the inner zone of

Table 1: Demographic Characteristics Surrounding Principal Economic Zones

	Downtown Core			Rimrock Mall			
Population Density	**0.5 Mile**	**1 Mile**	**1.5 Mile**	**0.5 Mile**	**1 Mile**	**1.5 Mile**	**0.5 Mile**
1980	3,121	11,094	21,694	2,745	7,038	14,635	2,158
1990	2,445	9,483	17,683	2,785	6,858	15,773	2,015
2000*	2,204	8,915	17,294	2,926	7,502	18,930	2,061
Percentage Change							
1980-90	-21.7	-14.5	-18.5	1.5	-2.6	7.8	-6.6
1990-'00	- 9.9	- 6.0	- 2.2	5.1	9.4	20.0	2.3
Households (Total)							
1980	1,672	5,495	10,247	946	2,391	5,173	709
1990	1,248	4,669	8,864	1,108	2,730	6,267	836
2000*	1,187	4,485	8,205	1,212	2,979	7,748	884
Percentage Change							
1980-1990	-25.4	-15.0	-13.5	17.1	14.2	21.1	17.9
1990-2000	- 4.9	- 3.9	- 7.4	9.4	9.1	23.6	5.7
Housing Values							
Median Home	$33,069	$45,510	$47,685	$57,902	$60,047	$60,560	$54,360
Median rent	$ 203	$ 231	$ 247	$ 338	$ 358	$ 348	$ 289
Housing Tenure							
Owner, 1990	186	1,495	3,392	763	2,015	4,445	469
Owner, 2000*	262	1,464	3,222	859	2,153	5,159	533
Renter, 1900	1,062	3,174	5,472	345	715	1,822	366
Renter, 2000*	924	3,021	4,984	361	827	2,589	351

the core between 1990 and 2000, the percentage increase is based on small numbers. Moreover the numerical increase does not replace the decline in home ownership in the outer two zones. Declines in rental units in all zones surrounding the mall further illustrate the turnover and dwindling population base supporting the downtown core.

Socio-economic issues

Socio-demographic data such as employment status, income and education, and reliance on public assistance further reflect the diminished market base surrounding the downtown core. The bifurcation model frequently utilizes the proportions of white collar and blue collar workers as a key measure of population patterns (Allen 1983, 1997), measures that readily fit within the ecological model. Table 2 reveals that, even though there is an increase in the proportion of white collar workers as distance from the core increases, there are fewer higher status positions at a distance of one and one half miles than is found in the areas surrounding the mall. The heights falls between the core and the west end, but

Table 2: Socio-Economic Characteristics Surrounding Principal Economic Zones of Billings

Employment/Status	Downtown Core				Rimrock Mall		
	0.5 Mile	1 Mile	1.5 Mile	0.5 Mile	1 Mile	1.5 Mile	0.5 Mile
% White Collar, 1990	34.0	52.0	53.4	59.8	35.8	65.6	45.6
% Blue Collar, 1990	66.0	48.0	46.6	40.2	64.2	34.4	56.4
Income							
Median Family Income, 1990	$17,593	$20,288	$22,785	$28,901	$32,137	$32,805	$24,683
Median Household Income, 1990	$11,709	$14,589	$16,506	$25,532	$29,085	$29,314	$23,538
Education							
% 25 and Older Completed High School	63.9	71.6	74.9	84.2	85.6	86.6	80.6
% 18 and Older in College	10.8	12.2	12.5	7.3	7.5	7.9	8.7
% 25 and Older Completed College	13.9	16.9	19.3	17.3	20.9	20.9	8.6

even here the proportion of white collar workers is greater at each comparable distance than it is in the downtown area.

Family households typically have higher incomes than non-family households. This not only underscores the greater stability of the former, it contributes to a greater level of economic support for local businesses. Here, again, it is apparent that the three areas being examined have contrasting advantages. First of all, median incomes are higher for family households than for non-family households. What is startlingly apparent, though, is that in family households, incomes surrounding the downtown core are lower at every distance than median non-family household incomes are at any distance surrounding the mall or in the heights.

Human capital skills, such as formal education, are necessary for economic development. Contrasting the three areas, it is evident that the downtown core does have considerable problems, as has thus far been shown. Most dismal are the figures for the high school completion rates for the population 25 years of age and older. As with other socio-demographic measures the core falls well below the other two areas, with High School completion rates ranging from fewer than two-thirds (63.9 percent) in the immediate 0.5 mile zone to a high of 74.9 percent in the one and one half mile zone.

This contrasts with the comparable ranges of 80.6 percent to 85.4 percent in the heights and 84.2 percent to 86.6 percent surrounding the mall.

College enrollment figures for persons 18 years of age and older suggest a possible avenue of potential for the downtown core. The figures also reflect evidence of a brain drain that threatens to operate against such potential. On the positive side, the highest college enrollment rates are in the zones surrounding the core. This is due to the fact that Billings has two colleges, one public—Montana State University, Billings—and one private—Rocky Mountain College. MSU-Billings is the larger of the two and is located within these zones. Though the university is largely a commuter campus, there is a substantial portion of the approximately 4,000 student body who live on campus or in nearby neighborhoods. MSU-Billings is nearest to downtown, approximately one mile to the north. Rocky Mountain College is located one mile to the west of the university, but is still closer to the downtown core than to either of the other economic areas. It was noted earlier in the chapter that despite having resources such as these, and the nearby hospitals, so near to the core, there has never been any serious or concerted attempt to connect them to the downtown. Such connections should be physical—designing streets and walkways which make a more direct link and provide a more inviting atmosphere between these segments of the city. MSU-Billings, for example, is directly accessible to the downtown via North Twenty-Seventh Street. Rocky Mountain College is most accessible to the core from a road running parallel to the rims and intersecting with Twenty-Seventh Street. This thoroughfare is necessarily wide to accommodate the volume of traffic between I-90, the downtown core, and the airport. It does not invite a sense of connection between the colleges and the core. As an illustration of this point, an administrator at MSU-Billings admitted that he had visited Billings many times prior to his appointment. He had driven between the airport and downtown route via Twenty-Seventh Street, past the university, and never realized he had passed the campus. This may be partly a result of the university not making itself more visible, but it does reflect the absence of any connection between the campus and downtown, and the automobile friendly nature of modern cities.

To capture the attention and affection of the colleges and hospitals, it is also necessary to cater to the needs of these institutions. This is another deficiency of downtown planning. With the exception of bars, restaurants, banks, and government offices there are no enterprises that cater directly to the needs of these nearby populations that would draw people to the downtown.

The potential to link existing institutions to the core is less optimistic. When students graduate they are likely to move, not necessarily out of Montana or out of Billings, but between zones within the city. Thus creating a brain drain from the zones around downtown. Evidence of this brain drain is suggested by a comparison of the college enrollment figures with college completion rates of persons 25 years of age and older. Here the downtown core lags behind the zones surrounding the mall. With the exception of the one and one half mile zone, however, the core has an advantage over the surrounding zones in the heights.

Unfortunately, Montana's dependence on agriculture and mining and the lack of high skill occupations in the downtown core (and elsewhere in Billings) results in an out-migration of the more educated and highly skilled population from the state generally, and from Billings more particularly. There is a 'chicken and egg' dilemma to this issue: Why are there so few high skilled occupations in Billings generally and in the downtown core in particular? Because there is a dearth of highly educated, highly skilled persons in the immediate vicinity to draw upon. Why are there so few highly educated individuals in the area? Because of the paucity of employment opportunities to encourage the more highly skilled to remain, especially near downtown where the skills and incomes would be beneficial. Despite the many planning efforts by promoters of the downtown core of Billings, addressing possible ways of breaking the endless circle of this particular question has not been actively emphasized to any great degree. This contributes to the stagnation of the core. As has been emphasized in this section, the absolute decline of population, housing, home values and the lower socio-economic stature of areas surrounding the downtown core indicates the need to develop cultural, economic, and residential enticements in downtown.

Governmental Issues

On the national level it has long been recognized that federal policies have had a major impact on the decentralization of cities in the United States. The Interstate Highway System further reduced the friction of space between cities and outlying territory, permitting people, business and industry to move from the densely settled confines of urban areas to the open spaces beyond. The population shift was aided by the creation of federal entities such as the Veterans Administration and the Federal Housing Administration that offered subsidized housing loans requiring, lower down payments, and extended the time limit for paying off mortages (Palen 1995).

State and local governments have also developed policies that have contributed to the stagnation of downtowns and to the emergence of urban sprawl. Successful re-development must take these issues into account. Since the 1950s Montana has, as have other states, utilized tax incentives and annexation regulations to stimulate large tract development. Land is less expensive on the edge of city limits, it is more available, and developers can petition the various levels of government to provide the necessary infrastructural improvements that will facilitate business expansion—for the sake of new jobs and tax revenues. Montana's tax code has a forgiveness provision for new, expanding, and remodeled businesses. Remodeling can occur downtown in the many older buildings, and this occurs frequently in downtown Billings. New business and business expansion are more likely to occur in the areas peripheral to the city where space is more available. The forgiveness provision applies anywhere, but tends to favor non-core development. Businesses that meet the requirements of the provision may reduce their property taxes by ten percent for five consecutive years. After the fifth year property taxes increase by ten percent annually, providing businesses with a 10 year state tax subsidy. State regulators, as one informant observed, emphasize one side of the ledger—benefits—and ignore the costs involved in encouraging sprawl. These costs are not only direct, pertaining to the tax subsidies and the extension of infrastructure, they are less direct in that they encourage less intensive land use.

Sprawl in Billings is influenced by another provision in state law. The city is one of fewer than a half dozen in the state that are permitted to have what are known colloquially as "doughnut zones." These zones permit the expansion of city services such as streets, sewers, and water without annexation. These infrastructural extensions encourage decentralized business and residential development. There is a drawback to doughnut zones, in that questions are raised about the extent of city authority. Residents in these zones pay city taxes, for instance, without being a part of the city and without having any representative voice in city affairs. There is a trade-off between economic interests and political interests, and those whose interests are primarily financial see an incentive to locate in these zones.

Locally, state funds are also available to promote business development that creates at least 15 new permanent full time jobs, or that raise the wages of existing jobs to meet established guidelines. These businesses receive a job credit interest rate reduction of up to 2.5 percent as well as income tax credits. These incentives are available for any business development but, as one informant active in downtown development observed, they have had minimal impact on the core because they are available for growth and expansion in any part of the city, and downtown property owners and developers have not yet participated to any great degree.

Two major objectives of the current downtown development plan are to abolish some of the existing one way streets that impede access to the core and to promote greater residential use in the downtown area. Both of these objectives are met with political obstacles that have not been rectified. As was noted earlier, one way traffic control was implemented to deter cruising and to facilitate the flow of automobile traffic. City officials perceived a benefit for this proposal. The reversion to two way traffic flows would permit easier access to the downtown core from the thoroughfares that facilitate traffic flow past the core, along the north and south peripheries. City officials, in particular in the public works department, emphasize a more parochial issue that had been organized earlier; the cost of conversion. Though there is a general consensus that advantages may outweigh the costs, the city is—in this instance—the reluctant participant to come on board.

City reluctance is seen in another pressing area. Parking has been a perceptual impediment to downtown development. The Montana Avenue Historical District was granted a six month trial period for the elimination of parking meters. Instead of customers feeding the meters at regular intervals, parking regulators mark the tires of parked cars and ticket them after a designated (two hour) time limit. This policy, as one property owner noted, encourages a flow of traffic—people come and people go. Customers do not see parking as a major problem, as they do a few blocks away in the downtown core. Though the city has thus far let the six month experiment linger without challenge or assessment, there still remains resistance on the part of the city to abolish parking meters in the rest of the downtown area—because of the cost involved (meters generate approximately $4 million per year).

A third area that local ordinances can have an impact on downtown development pertains to housing. Virtually every informant stressed the need to increase the level of moderate and upper income housing. The issue is in the current development plan as well. A major impediment to the objective is a zoning ordinance that stipulates that a structure in the downtown area that is designated for one purpose, such as business, must be razed and constructed as new buildings, if they are approved as residential dwellings. Codes need to be changed, an informant noted, so that old buildings can be more readily converted into residential use. In Billings there is a precedent for this proposal in the medical corridor. This symbolic part of the city is also a legally defined area. As current use of a dwelling expires, usually upon change of ownership, the property is converted to medical use. This strategy has not been adopted by downtown property owners.

Development Prospects

Billings is in the early phases of implementing an action plan for the development of the downtown core. The plan has a comprehensive, community oriented title, "Everyone's Neighborhood." The title is reflective of the learning curve that city residents have hopefully had. The truth will be in the plan's implementation.

In the late 1980s city officials hired a consulting firm from Denver to create a development plan for downtown. Funding for the plan, and for its implementation, came from the creation of a tax increment district that encompassed the downtown core and adjacent businesses. Creation of the plan had a 1 million dollar price tag, which had to be paid whether the plan was carried out or not. That mistake on the part of city officials was compounded by a mistake of the consulting firm. During 1987 and 1988 the firm created its own vision of the downtown, neither consulting, including, nor inviting the participation of property owners, business operators, city officials or residents.

This "behind the curtains" approach had dire impacts that are still being felt. It was not until the public presentation of the proposal was exhibited that local residents were given a clear idea of what would be done and who would be affected. While the general idea of downtown development received widespread support, details of the plan split local interests. Some property owners and business operators whose establishments were not directly affected by the physical changes generally supported the plan because the overall development held the promise of improving their interests. Other owners who were not directly affected felt left out of the plan, while those owners whose establishments were to be razed or physically changed tended to resist the plan. The fissures among the various interests doomed the plan, which was never implemented. City officials were blamed for their agreement to pay for a proposal that did not need to be implemented. The subsequent animosities scuttled any comprehensive effort for downtown development for ten years. Recent development plans had to overcome these fissures, with wary property owners being the last to come on board.

A further consequence was a reduced ability to fund improvements in the downtown area. Prior to this aborted attempt at development, the tax increment district (TID) held a surplus of funds—tax levels were larger than the existing bond obligations. When local government entities, such as the school district and the city, saw a pool of unused tax money, they began to tap into it. Property values in the TID peaked in 1988 and have declined in every year since, as has the surplus, while the taxable value of the city as a whole has increased. At the same time, the proportion of the city's tax revenues generated by the downtown region has also declined (See Table 3).

In the early 1990s city officials made the decision to develop a quasi-governmental entity charged with economic development. Initially known as the Tradeport Authority, and currently known as the Big Sky Economic Development Authority, it has the responsibility of attracting and promoting new business. Its operations consist of a business incubator to help new businesses in their early operation; a small business development center, offering assistance in conceptualizing a proposed business, developing an operational plan, and assisting—but not providing—financial assistance. The responsibilities are largely tactical, not strategic. They are also more reactive—providing assistance for proposed business—than they are pro-active. Perhaps because of the failed development plan of the late 1980s, the tradeport has never been charged with developing any comprehensive development plan.

The Tradeport Authority is funded through a two mill tax levy. The levy made the Tradeport Authority a controversial and suspect entity, not only among some city residents but from other governmental entities, the county and city governments and the school district. The two mill levy did not represent a new levy, it represented a redistribution of existing tax money. All three governmental entities saw a reduction in funding levels. Some residents viewed the Tradeport Authority as being "just another bureaucratic layer" that was charged to do what others were doing. Despite this resistance the tradeport was created.

Because of the source of funding for the Tradeport Authority, its charge of economic development pertains to the city in general, not to the downtown area in particular. The minor exception to this is the Downtown Billings Association (DBA), a small entity within the tradeport that has a similar charge. Funding for the DBA, though, is minuscule ($60,000 annually). The lack of financial and human resources for the association has limited the potential of the DBA as an effective tactical or strategic asset for downtown development.

**Table 3. Value of Billings Tax Increment District
Compared to the City of Billings (Less TID) (1980–1997)**

Year	TID Taxable Value (000)	City of Billings Taxable Value	Year	TID Taxable Value (000)	City of Billings Taxable Value
1980	12,059	96,504	1990	15,171	103,287
1981	14,129	101,445	1991	11,538	105,757
1982	14,685	97,476	1992	11,699	107,736
1983	14,230	94,795	1993	12,015	115,977
1984	14,793	100,135	1994	11,681	117,391
1985	16,509	111,905	1995	11,619	119,970
1986	17,667	119,989	1996	11,676	122,535
1987	18,123	117,939	1997	11,376	124,986
1988	17,343	111,426			
1989	17,109	112,619			

The Historical District

It was noted earlier that the historical district, situated along Montana Avenue, had deteriorated into an area of mostly abandoned and dilapidated buildings, the principal exceptions being an upscale local restaurant and an art gallery. The initial promise of having a tourist train pass through the district, and the subsequent restoration of the train depot prompted property owners in the district to devise a plan to refurbish the area. The result is the most extensive development to occur in the downtown area in two or three decades.

How could an area that was one of the most blighted in the city become transformed, in the span of only about two years, from being a place mostly to avoid to being a thriving and vibrant area that people want to be in? One reason is the historical value of the district. Human ecology has been criticized for ignoring the distorting effects that cultural influences such as historical value can have on the evolution of cities. These influences can have an impact, but there needs to be an incentive for a historic impetus to emerge. Prior to the "smoking train" proposal there was an absence of such an incentive, because there was no clear idea around which people could organize.

With an incentive at hand, what other decisions and actions led to a successful revitalization effort? Two important distinctions between the downtown core and the peripheral historical district must be addressed. One distinction points to a key consideration for the success of any development of the core. The other distinction underscores a hurdle that must be overcome. The instigation for developing the historical district originated outside of local governments. The development plan for the historical district, however, was not created by outside interests, nor was it imposed on business operators in the district. Instead, business operators themselves developed the plan and enlisted the assistance of city officials and local development experts. This is quite the opposite of what transpired in the failed downtown development plan. As one informant put it, the restoration plan for the historical district was not shoved down the throats of business operators by city officials or anyone else. It began with the business operators in the district.

The second distinction involves differences between property owners in the historical district as opposed to the downtown core. In the historical district, business operators also tend to be the owners of the property they utilize. The downtown core, on the other hand, has a higher proportion of absentee property owners. Absentee owners are less apt to see or have an interest in problems and potential solutions, especially those that pertain to the broader community, and not simply their own more parochial interests. They are less likely to perceive any immediate incentive for comprehensive development, and, by their very absence, are far more difficult to actively bring into any planning project.

Seeing an immediate advantage, property owners and business operators in the historical district seized the opportunity. Their efforts went far beyond simple beautification improvements that thus far characterize the most visible development efforts of the core. Some of the city's oldest buildings are located in this district. No longer dilapidated and abandoned, they have been restored and occupied. Property owners actively pursued their own financing for improvements to their physical structures. They also petitioned the city to be designated as a special improvement district (SID). These districts are created when infrastructure improvements are necessitated, such as street and sidewalk maintenance and are similar to the principles discussed for creating TIFs as discussed by Burayidi and others in this volume. The request underscores the importance of having property owners involved in decision making—if not leading, at least actively participating. The initial request for SIDs development encompassed a small area, extending only two or three blocks in either direction from the train depot. SIDs require a levy placed on property owners who benefit from the infrastructural improvements, and are not popular in a tax aversion western state such as Montana. The potential benefits of the historical district development project, however, enticed property owners located an additional two blocks in either direction to request that they be included in the special improvement district. The restoration and infrastructure improvement now includes buildings on Montana Avenue that are a part of the southern border of the downtown core. Until recently a district inhabited mostly by prostitutes, their "Johns", and drug users, the historical district now represents the most vibrant social center near downtown. Its partially cobbled sidewalks, newly paved streets, beautification projects—such as hanging flowers, adopted in the core as well—create a historical and enticing luster.

Additional development is necessary, though, for the district to achieve its full potential. There still remain a few seedy establishments, and residential housing is non-existent. While there is a mix of business activity (restaurants, a national computer support service, an art gallery and a few small specialty shops), a greater diversity of land use is needed to increase the density of people in the area and enhance the district's emerging success.

Everyone's Neighborhood

Current efforts for developing the downtown core began in 1995, with two public meetings organized by both public and private interests. The second of these meetings, in May, 1995, was attended by 120 residents of the city who engaged in a two day workshop devoted to establishing the organizational framework for the creation and implementation of a new downtown development plan. The organization that resulted, known as the Downtown Billings Partnership, has four main components, or constituents. One is the Downtown Development Corporation, a non-profit entity administered by the Tradeport Authority. A second component is the Downtown Billings Association. The Parking Advisory Board was established as a third component, resulting from a task force created by the mayor to study parking issues in the downtown core. The fourth major component is the Property Owners Advisory Board, representing property owners and their interests.

It was noted earlier that property owners were the last representatives to support the current development effort. One reason for this is the city's ill fated attempt at downtown revitalization a decade earlier. A second reason is evident in the structure of the Downtown Billings Partnership. Three of the four constituencies are governmental and quasi-governmental entities. Even the pool of membership for the organization's board of directors provides property owners a lesser role. Board members are drawn from representatives of the tradeport, City of Billings representatives, and at large representatives. Despite the recognition that failure to include property and business owners at the outset had undermined a previous development project, and a successful plan to develop the historical district gave property owners a more central lead, the current planning project risks committing the mistakes of the past.

Two initial decisions of the DBPs steering committee were to develop a funding mechanism. The Billings city government contributed $150,000, with additional contributions coming from local businesses and property owners. A second decision was to establish a steering committee to serve as a central information gathering and planning agency.

Beginning in July, 1996 the steering committee commenced a series of 16 monthly meetings. The objective of each of these meetings was to sketch the outlines of a 'vision map' that would describe what the downtown should resemble, to assess the assets of the downtown area, to identify the issues needed to be addressed for the vision map and statement of values to be achieved, and to establish a framework diagram of how downtown landmarks could be better utilized to promote a sense of desirability to downtown and how to better connect the downtown core to the distinct adjacent districts of its borders, each of which is recognized as having a unique ambiance from the others.

A key decision made during the course of these sessions was to keep the emergent plan cohesive in its conceptualization, but flexible in its implementation. The cohesive elements include a goal of creating loft housing in existing buildings, attracting middle and upper middle class residents who have the potential to provide the downtown core with the socioeconomic boost that it is lacking.

These decisions provide a useful outline. The thematic development plan was presented two years later, in 1997. During the interim two years since "Everyone's Neighborhood" was submitted, the plan remains little more than a generic framework. An organizational structure was established to guide development, but once established could not reach any consensus about specific actions to be taken. In 1998, for example, two out of state proposals were given serious attention, by the Downtown Billings Partnership—neither of which have been officially eliminated. One was to develop a downtown mall that would necessitate the demolition of a block of existing businesses directly abutting the downtown core. The second proposal, is to develop a mixed use facility—including entertainment, residence, parking, and shopping. The proposed site, however, is located outside of the northern boundary of the downtown core. More critically, because it replicates a mistake made a decade earlier, the plan was proposed without input of the affected establishments.

Prospects

Billings' downtown has been shaped by the ecological conditions surrounding it, and by the anticipated and unanticipated outcomes of the decisions made about it. One informant described the downtown of Billings by way of analogy. "You can't have a body without a heart. If the heart is weak, the body can't be strong." The downtown core of Billings is the city's heart. It is weak, but it is not dead. It is also at a juncture of uncertainty. The comprehensive plan that has been adopted details the assets of the downtown core. It also addresses the different potentials that neighborhoods defining the downtown's borders provide, and how to better link these neighborhoods to the core. What is missing is an impetus, such as the depot restoration project in the historical district. Business owners, property owners, city officials, and city residents recognize the needs of downtown, but there is an inertia that has thus far kept the various interests from coalescing around any specific proposal. Contrasting the current efforts for the downtown core with the rather swift and successful restoration of the historical district reveals some of the complexities faced, even in small metropolises such as Billings.

The eight block historical district contains far fewer establishments than the downtown core. As was noted earlier, more business owners in the district own their establishments than is the case in the core. There are also fewer interests at stake. This made it far easier to come to an agreement about what to do and how to go about doing it. Property owners in the historical district also made a key decision that has proven fortuitous, and helped them coalesce around a single plan. Early on it was decided that they did not need a grandiose scheme — start simple and build upon it. It was also decided not to widely publicize the restoration efforts. Property owners deemed more important to implement the plan and see if it worked, instead of publicizing a plan that may not develop as anticipated. The strategy has been successful.

In the downtown core there is a sense of urgency that something must be done on a greater scale so the entire heart pumps faster. This has led to the consideration of large development projects like the downtown mall and the entertainment complex. Both of these proposals were given widespread publicity by city officials, tinged with a sense of inevitability, before all details for the plans had been addressed. When questions were raised about the advisability of the proposals, the response was to mute official discussions of the plans. This has resulted in a sense of suspicion and skepticism among city residents, business owners, and property owners. Most serious for the future of downtown redevelopment in Billings is the repetition of a decision that proved disastrous in the past. Failure to involve and inform all affected parties threatens to undermine a long, slowly developing, but deliberative process.

Planning in the historical district involved open meetings and had fewer factions and a smaller area to plan for. An important lesson for downtown development initiatives is that the design of the historic district's restoration plan was led by people with a vested interest in the process. Having similar interests and discussing ideas openly resulted in a design plan that had very few doubters or dissenters.

The planning process in downtown Billings has taken longer to evolve than was necessary in the historical district. It is still early enough in the process—at a point of deciding about design and implementation—that problems that have developed and mistakes that have been made can be rectified. The pieces of the puzzle needed for developing downtown Billings are apparent. There is an organizational structure. An overarching plan is available, one that identifies a vision map of the needs, possibilities, and assets of the downtown and surrounding neighborhoods. Funding sources for development have been identified. To be successful, however, the organizational structure needs to be as carefully designed as the plan. Decision making processes are inherently uncertain. Failure to more effectively design the structure and process by which the development plan is to be implemented has created more uncertainty and instability and threatens to result in current efforts taking the same path that previous development efforts have had.

References

Allen, Peter M. 1997. *Cities and Regions as Self-Organizing Systems Models of Complexity*. Australia: Gordon and Breach Science Publishers.

Allen, Peter M. 1983 "Self-Organization and Evolution in Urban Systems." In Robert W. Crosby (ed.), *Cities and Regions as Nonlinear Decision Systems*. Boulder: Westview Press, Inc., pp. 29–62.

Allen, P. M. and M. Sanglier. 1981 "Urban evolution, Self-Organization, and Decision Making," *Environment and Planning A* 13:167–183.

Beaumont, John R., Martin Clarke, Paul Keys, Huw Williams, and Alan G. Wilson. 1983. "A Dynamical Analysis of Urban Systems." In Robert W. Crosby (ed.), *Cities and Regions as Nonlinear Decision Systems*. Boulder: Westview Press, Inc., pp. 155–173

Berry, Brian J. L. and John D. Kasarda. 1977. *Contemporary Urban Ecology*. New York: Macmillan Publishing Co.

Crosby, Robert W. 1983. *Cities and Regions as Nonlinear Decision Systems*. Boulder: Westview Press, Inc.

Dendrinos, Dimitrios. 1983. "Epistemological Aspects of Metropolitan Evolution." In Robert W. Crosby (ed.), *Cities and Regions as Nonlinear Decision Systems*. Boulder: Westview Press, Inc., pp. 143–153.

Duncan, Otis Dudley. 1959. "Human Ecology and Population Studies." In Philip M. Hauser and Otis Dudley Duncan (eds.), *The Study of Population*. Chicago: The University of Chicago Press, pp. 678–716.

Hawley, Amos. 1968. "Ecology." in *International Encyclopedia of Social Sciences*. New York.

Jacobs, Jane. 1961. *The Death and Life of Great American Cities*. New York: Random House.

Montana Tradeport Authority and the City of Billings. 1997. *Downtown Billings Framework Plan: An Action Plan for the Future of Downtown Billings*. Billings: Montana.

Palen, John J. 1997. *The Urban World*. New York: McGraw-Hill.

_____. 1995. *The Suburbs*. New York: McGraw-Hill.

END NOTE

1. The author would like to thank Danette Carroll for her invaluable assistance.

CHAPTER 4

An Assessment of Downtown Revitalization in Five Small Wisconsin Communities

MICHAEL A. BURAYIDI

The case study of Billings, MT shows the importance of community involvement in any successful downtown revitalization program. In this chapter, we examine and assess the revitalization efforts of five Wisconsin communities. Our objective here is to evaluate the impacts that these strategies have had on the economic health of downtowns in these cities.

In 1971 an article in the Nation's Cities magazine described downtown Oshkosh in the following cataclysmic terms:

> Oshkosh has, like most other cities, suffered from sagging downtown trade. The Fox River which runs through the heart of Winnebago, the state's largest, has hardly helped lure the public into the retail district. Along its shores are empty warehouses, buildings for small and heavy industry, railroad tracks and other assorted not-too-attractive elements (The Oshkosh Daily Northwestern, April 4th, 1971; B4).

This characterization could well have been used to describe the downtown of many of the Fox cities, a number of small cities that straddle the banks of the Fox River in Wisconsin. The Fox cities form the largest urban area in Wisconsin and have been the fastest growth region in the 1990s. Much like other communities, the Fox cities have experienced a decline in the economic health of their downtowns. Over the past decade or so strenuous efforts have been made by these cities to revitalize their downtowns. As the Comprehensive Plan of the City of Appleton aptly justified the reason for downtown redevelopment:

> Appleton has too much at stake to allow a decline in its urban center. Downtown has only one percent of the City area, but five perecnt of the tax base. The largest non-industrial private investments in the City have been made Downtown. The largest non-transportation public investments are Downtown. The tax base of Downtown has, for many decades, helped fund the extension of city services and facilities to outlying developments. Downtown is an irreplaceable asset to the community. It is not possible to recreate the mixture of historic and new structures, the density of activity, the central location, and the

range of uses elsewhere for a comparable cost of continued maintenance and reinvestment in existing Downtown Appleton (The City of Appleton 1996, A20-4).

An organized attempt at addressing downtown decline at the state level probably started with the appointment of a Downtown Specialist in 1981 at the then State Department of Development (now renamed the Department of Administration). In the same year, the Wisconsin Downtown Action Council was formed to:

i) provide a forum for members to share knowledge, experiences and problems, and to develop educational programs concerning ways of improving downtowns;
ii) encourage development of more comprehensive legal and financing tools favorable to downtown viability;
iii) promote professionalism and career enhancement in the downtown management field; and
iv) increase public awareness of the benefits of having an economically strong downtown.

Then in 1987 the Wisconsin state legislature enacted statute 560.081 establishing a Mainstreet Program for the state to provide assistance to communities in their efforts to improve their mainstreets, focusing primarily on historic preservation and redevelopment. Other state programs that have benefitted downtowns include state Community Development Block Grants (CDBG)—for blight removal, the provision of public facilities, and economic development.

Besides these governmental efforts, there have also been quasi-public efforts at galvanizing support for downtown revitalization. For example, in 1987 the Iowa based North Central Regional Center for Rural Development organized a conference on Downtown Revitalization and Small City Development in Madison. One of the stated rationales for organizing the conference was to share information on the process of downtown redevelopment and to support efforts of cities to revitalize their downtowns. As stated in the conference proceedings, "There is a great deal to be learned about downtown revitalization through the systematic study of different aspects of the process" (Lenzi and Murray 1987, 3).

All said, despite efforts by these cities at downtown revitalization, there is as yet no comprehensive documentation of the outcome of these programs nor have the cities established benchmark indicators for reviewing their efforts.

Brief Background to Five Communities

The five communities selected for this study are Appleton (population of about 70,000), Fond du Lac (40,000), Green Bay (about 100,000 population), Oshkosh (population of about 62,000), and Sheboygan (51,000). With the exception of

Sheboygan, which is located on Highway 43, the other four communities are all located along US 41. Green Bay is the northern-most of the five communities and lies 30 miles northeast of Appleton. Appleton is 20 miles north of Oshkosh and 39 miles north of Fond du Lac. Sheboygan lies 39 miles east of Fond du Lac.

There are strong functional linkages between all five communities. For example, in 1990 the Census Bureau reported that about 25 percent of residents in Outagamie county in which the City of Appleton is located worked outside the county, usually in the nearby counties. Similarly, 19 percent of residents in Winnebago county in which the City of Oshkosh is located worked outside the county.

The five communities were selected for study because; they all lie on or near a major highway that has disrupted the economic health of their downtowns, and for several years these cities have embarked on a concerted effort to revitalize their downtowns. Since many communities have been impacted by highway development, the experience of these communities will provide valuable lessons for other communities as well.

APPLETON

Incorporated in 1885 as a village, Appleton's economy was built on lumber and paper mills. By the turn of the century, a number of paper mills and related industries had sprung up along the Fox River which offered ready access to transportation. College Avenue, the major arterial road to the downtown was dotted with commercial activity. By the end of World War I, Appleton had become a city of 28,436 people with a trade area of ten miles radius and a population of 75,000.

The city of Appleton is surrounded by three cities (Kaukauna, Menasha and Neenah), three villages (Combined Locks, Kimberly, and Little Chute) and three townships (Grand Chute, Greenville, and Menasha). These communities have a total population of about 180,000. Like the other communities in the region, Appleton had a healthy and buoyant downtown right up to the 1960s. Herein was located a rich mix of retail, finance, insurance, and real estate (FIRE) and business offices. However, business decentralization in the post war years began to take a toll on the downtown.

The opening of the Valley Fair Mall to the south of the city in 1954 started a trend of retail relocation from the downtown to the ouskirts of the city. Northland Mall to the north of the city also opened in 1969 further drawing business away from the downtown.

Other factors that contributed to business decentralization from the downtown include the widening of US 41 into four lanes in the 1950s and the expansion of College Avenue into a four lane in 1974. These arterials became favorite locations for hotels, restaurants, shopping centers, auto dealerships, gas stations, and banks, thus further weakening downtown's position as an economic hub.

What may be regarded as a major blow to downtown Appleton's economic health was the opening of the Fox River Mall west of US 41 in the town of Grand Chute in 1984. The mall attracted such department stores as Sears, JC Penney, Prange Way, Dayton, and Target. Many of these stores relocated to the mall from downtown Appleton.

FOND DU LAC

Fond du Lac owes its origin to the lumber industry in the nineteenth century. The city grew and prospered from the lumber industry becoming the second largest settlement in Wisconsin in 1870. Downtown Fond du Lac was the hub of city activity prior to the 1950s. City government, offices, and grocery stores were all concentrated in the downtown area. With the exception of manufacturing activity along the Fond du Lac River and west of the downtown, there was no outside competition to the downtown commercial district. Thus in 1955, Mainstreet boasted 252 retail stores, providing all types of merchandise trade.

The construction of US 41 to the west of the city made this area a prime location for business and industry and had an impact in decentralizing economic activity from the downtown. Several businesses that were previously located in the downtown moved to the highway location. These included the Shreiner's Restaurant in 1953, Super Value store in 1964, the Gateway Transportation Company, the Johnson Bus Company on Morris Street, and the American Bank that opened on West Johnson Street in 1968.

The opening of Forest Mall in 1973 dealt a severe blow to the economic health of the downtown. Built along US 41 and West Johnson street, the mall attracted such stores as Montgomery Ward, J.C. Penney, and H.C. Prange. The mall also attracted other business locations to the area; in 1979, Kmart opened a store in the area, followed by Sears in 1978, and Shopko in 1985. Then, in 1989 Fond du Lac Plaza Shopping Center, with more than 91,000 square feet of retail space, opened on West Scott Street.

The trend towards economic decentralization continued in the 1990s. Pioneer Plaza opened in 1990 along Pioneer Road and South Main, followed by Play It Again Sports in 1991, Play Outlet USA, Wal Mart, and Sergros Mexican Bar. In 1992, several other stores such as Target, Toys R Us, Payless Shoes, JoAnn Fabrics, and Red Lobster opened along Pioneer Road and US 41.

While economic activity was booming in the outskirts, the downtown was suffering due to many businesses folding up. The Northern Casket Company closed in 1965; Dais Jewelry closed in 1978 after fifty years of operation in the downtown; Ma and Pa Store closed in 1980; and Kresge in 1981. Other stores that closed included Beer Hut (1986), O'Brien's Dry Goods (1986), Guilmores Liquor Mart (1988), and Brickles Tavern (1990). Broadway Chevrolet-Buick Inc. relocated from South Main to North Rolling Meadows. Popcorn Lady on North Main closed in 1991 and Merwin's Fashion closed in 1994. Although the downtown saw some new activity, it was primarily in the form of governmental services and office-type businesses. For example, the Fond du Lac Savings and Loans Association opened in the downtown in 1975, Bank One in 1990, and Valley Bank in 1993.

GREEN BAY

Green Bay was incorporated as a city in 1854 with a population of about 2,000. Until 1815 Green Bay served mainly as a trading post for fur traders. Because of the city's location at the junction of the Fox River and Lake Michigan, it served as an important port for the fur trade. Paper products, power shovels, cranes, and canned and processed foods are the major manufactured goods produced in the city. The city is also famous for being home to the NFL's Green Bay Packers team.

The city of Green Bay is surrounded by one city (De Pere), four villages (Allouez, Ashwaubenon, Bellevue, Howard), and three townships (De Pere, Fort Howard, Green Bay, and West De Pere) for a total population of close to 176,000. Downtown Green Bay was the center of commercial activity right up to the 1960s. However, several retail and commercial clusters started to emerge outside of the downtown in the 1960s, especially along the intersections of major thoroughfares such as US 45 and Interstate 43 as well as along US 10 and US 41. Other locations that competed with the downtown for business location were the business corridors along Oneida Street, Military Avenue, West Mason; the business corridor of the Village of Ashwaubenon; and the Oneida Indian reservation. Thus, between 1972 and 1995, the number of businesses located in downtown Green Bay had declined by 39 percent (Green Bay Economic Development Authority 1995).

OSHKOSH

Like other communities in the region, the City of Oshkosh had a booming downtown prior to the 1950s. Oshkosh's economy was built on the lumber industry. Located on the Fox river, the city benefited from access to water transportation. The city is surrounded by the towns of Black Wolf, Algoma, Oshkosh, Nekimi and Vinland.

Up to the 1950s, downtown Oshkosh accounted for up to 75 percent of all economic activity in the city. The decentralization of economic activity away from the downtown began in the 1960s precipitated by the construction of US 41 to the west of the downtown. The highway offered convenience and easy access to potential customers and became a good location for business and industry. The opening of Copps Food Store near the highway in 1962 started a chain of events leading to a cluster of businesses along the highway.

The Park Plaza Mall, which was constructed and opened with much fanfare in 1970, was expected to provide the much needed catalyst for improving the downtown's economic health. It was hoped that the 450,000 square foot shopping center would draw customers from Winnebago, Fond du Lac, and Outagamie counties that had a total estimated population of about half a million people at the time. However, stiff competition from the Fox River Mall in Appleton and US 41 to the west of the downtown weakened the plazas drawing power as the anchor shops moved to new locations near the highway.

A peculiar contributory factor to downtown decline in Oshkosh was the difficulty of traffic circulation. The railroad line which in the early years of settlement had been a contributory factor to the city's development had now become an obstacle to business retention. As the train passed through the downtown, it created a backup of traffic stretching several blocks. This became a major nuisance and inconvnience for merchants and customers. This inconvenience further compounded efforts at downtown economic recovery.

SHEBOYGAN

Sheboygan is located fifty miles north of Milwaukee, Wisconsin's largest city. The city is located at the intersection of the Sheboygan River and Lake Michigan. The city's residents have deep multi-generational roots in the community stretching from the early days of the first German and Dutch immigrants in the nineteenth century. Sheboygan is known for its high quality of life. In 1997 Reader's Digest named Sheboygan the number one best place in the nation to raise a family. The magazine noted the community's family friendly atmosphere, observing that in this city "supermarket shoppers leave their car doors unlocked [and] preteens walk home alone after dark from soccer or hockey games" (p.3). The city has also been listed for five consecutive years by Money Magazine as one of the most livable cities in the United States.

Prior to the 1980s, downtown Sheboygan was blighted and neglected. The construction of the Kohler and Memorial Malls at the fringe of the city and along US 43, essentially sapped the economic life out of the downtown—many businesses moved out to these malls. Furthering the decline of the downtown was a recommendation made to the city by a Portland-based consultant; close downtown streets and turn them into pedestrian malls. While such a strategy worked well in warmer communities, the effect was disastrous for Sheboygan. The policy further precipitated the decline of the downtown.

By the early 1980s, industrialists in the community began to complain about their inability to attract top level personnel to the community partly due to the ill-health of the downtown. "Potential employees were shown everywhere else in the city but the downtown. It was a place to shy away from" commented Richard Meyer, manager of the city's downtown Harbor Centre. The public had a low esteem of the downtown and avoided going there.

These problems prompted a retreat to be called in 1984 for the purpose of discussing downtown redevelopment concerns. A public-private effort was suggested as a means for revitalizing the downtown. An aftermath of the retreat was the formation of a City Development Corporation for the purpose of raising money and making proposals for the development of the downtown.

Interpreting Downtown Decline

The decline of the economic health of downtowns in the five cities became obvious by the 1970s. We have already alluded to some of the obstacles and problems that hindered the prosperity of the downtowns—the proximity of the highways, parking and circulation problems, as well as leadership neglect. This section further outlines the key bottlenecks that impeded the development of the downtowns of these cities. It forms a precursor to a discussion of the downtown redevelopment efforts of the cities discussed in the sections to follow. The major contributory factors to downtown decline in these cities were accessibility, convenience of highway locations, cost of business expansion, and restrictive rules and regulations.

ACCESSIBILITY

Very often, downtowns are congested because streets were not designed to accommodate large traffic volumes and because parking in the downtown is either limited or available at a premium. Access to shopping areas in the downtown posed a problem to shoppers in all five communities. Since their downtowns were built prior to the automobile era, they lack the accessibility that is available to businesses located near the highways. The enclosed malls, often located in undeveloped land at the fringe of cities, offers convenience in shopping and protection from inclement weather conditions. So contentious was the issue of parking availability in downtown Oshkosh that the local newspaper once lashed out in an editorial:

> In April, 1967, they campaigned against the city manager form of government, charging that the downtown business area had been allowed to deteriorate. And now, these same vocal opponents of progress are opposed to city acquisition of off-street parking sites—a measure to help the downtown area remain vital. *Our downtown business center cannot grow unless there is more parking.* And a strong retailing area is vital to the growth and development of Oshkosh. It becomes very clear that public parking lots are not merely a sop to the merchants. They are an investment in the future of our community (*The Paper*, February 23rd, 1968, A4).

Parking and accessibility to downtown shops remain a perenial problem for downtown redevelopment in the five communities under study.

CONVENIENCE

Closely related to the problem of accessibility is the effect of highway development on business location decisions. When Congress authorized the Interstate Highway Program in 1956, it aided in the decentralization of economic activity away from the downtown to areas along the highways. The highways provided visibility and easy access to shopping. Highway locations thus became prime location areas for business. It is no coincidence that the decline of the downtowns in the five cities started about the time that the highways were completed. Thus, the 1973 Comprehensive Plan of the City of Oshkosh noted that, "the completion of US 41 to freeway standards and the westward growth of residential development could eventually result in pressure for the development of a major freeway-oriented shopping center. If the regional CBD shopping complex is to succeed, there must be adequate auto access to the central area" (The City of Oshkosh 1973, 24-25).

This prediction came true with the proliferation of several shopping centers along Highway 41, west of the downtown. The highways became a major competitor with downtowns for business location. Except for specialty shops, most shops have preferred the highway location to downtown.

COST OF BUSINESS EXPANSION

The downtowns of the five cities are already built up. This poses problems for businesses that want to expand. Assembling land for business expansion is expensive and tedious for several reasons. Some downtown locations such as the Universal Foundry and Radford industrial sites in Oshkosh are brownfields that are riddled with environmental contaminants and require clean up before the land is developed. Secondly, land parcels are usually owned by different people and this makes the acquisition of such property difficult because some land owners may not be willing to sell. For example, the construction of Park Plaza in Oshkosh in 1967 required the elimination of rail lines and the clearing of 22 buildings from the site. Also, the construction of the Paper Valley Hotel and Convention Center in Appleton involved the acquisition of 16 businesses and an expenditure outlay of $6.2 million. Sears moved from its downtown location in Appleton, where it occupied 63,000 sq. ft., to the Fox River Mall, in part, to avail itself of a larger store area of 107,700 sq. ft. This expansion may not have been possible or it may have occurred at a significant premium to the company had it remained in downtown Appleton.

RULES AND REGULATIONS

Because downtowns are already built up, they fall under several local restrictive ordinances that stipulate what one can do in those districts. Chief among these restrictive rules are historic district ordinances. Such ordinances often specify density, set back requirements, design features, and architectural styles that developers often find to be expensive and limiting. Besides the cities of Oshkosh and Fond du Lac, the other three municipalities have historic districts that specify the types of development that can take place within these boundaries.

Redevelopment Strategies of Five Communities

Downtown deterioration was beginning to take a toll on several aspects of the cities, including the ability to attract new businesses and to promote tourism. By the 1970s, it became obvious that the economic health of the cities was closely tied to the economic health of their downtowns. In an editorial piece, the *Oshkosh Daily Northwestern* personalized the cost of downtown deterioration in the following way:

> A moribund central business district means an added burden on the other taxpayers of the city. There can be no arguing that. But how much that can mean to the average taxpayer is something not easily related [..........]. Oshkosh's sister on the lake, Fond du Lac, has, by most any standard of measure, a downtown in a terminally ill state. So much of its central businesses have moved to the periphery of the community that the Main Street is - well, lonesome-looking. A reassessment came after the departure of the business center to the outskirts of Fond du Lac, and the tax burden was redistributed. A home at the modest value of $23,000.00 had to pick up an additional tax of $120.00. Slip that onto your own tax bill and see what interest you have in seeking the revitalization of the downtown (*Oshkosh Daily Northwestern*, March 13th, 1976, p.12).

Realizing something had to be done to improve the health of their downtowns, the communities adopted several pronged strategies for revitalizing their downtowns. These included the formation of downtown redevelopment committees, demarcation of Tax Increment Finance and Business Improvement Districts, appointment of downtown managers, and the implementation of special programs and events to draw people to the downtown.

Organization and Planning

Organization and planning were key first steps to downtown revitalization in all five cities. In Sheboygan, one of the most successful downtown revitalization stories, the city held a retreat in 1984 to discuss the redevelopment of the downtown. Community leaders realized from the onset that a joint public-private effort was essential to addressing the problems of the downtown. The retreat resulted in the formation of a City Development Corporation composed of both private and public sector organizations in the city. The corporation raised $1 million in seed money to study and make proposals for the development of the downtown.

In addition, funds were raised from the public sector; a $6.5 million federal money was obtained and used for the construction of a bridge, and the State Waterways Commission also gave Sheboygan $3.2 million for the city's waterways project.

In Green Bay, a downtown summit was held in 1994 to discuss the redevelopment of the downtown. Earlier, the Citizen Group for the Development of Greater Green Bay was formed in 1956, in part to promote downtown business. The group helped launch the first major downtown project in 1965—the Beaumont Ramada Hotel.

A similar approach in Fond du Lac and in Oshkosh led to the formation of the Fond du Lac Downtown Council and the Downtown Oshkosh Committee in 1975. Appleton also formed an Appleton Downtown Inc.—all aimed at helping to revitalize their downtowns.

Besides organizing, however, the five communities took concrete steps to see to the realization of the ideas generated at the group sessions.

Formation of Tax Increment Financing Districts

The state legislature adopted Wisconsin Act 105 establishing a Tax Incremental Finance (TIF) enabling legislation in 1975. TIFs are financial instruments that municipalities use to pay for the provision of public amenities, infrastructure, and to help stimulate development, or redevelopment, in blighted areas that would otherwise not occur. TIF revenues help pay for the cost of infrastructure by utilizing revenues generated from value increment of property in the district. Tax Increment Finance districts can be created for two purposes: a) to help promote industrial and commercial development; and b) for purposes of blight removal. As shown in Table 4, all five communities have created TIF districts, some of which, are in the downtown.

Creation of Business Improvement Districts (BID)

Wisconsin Act 184 created a financial tool that allows a municipality to levy a special assessment on property owners within a defined business improvement district upon petition of those property owners. The property owners in the BID district then use the assessment resources to maintain and enhance their business environment. Many downtown revitalization efforts have included a revolving loan program for businesses in the BID to undertake building façade improvement, provide signage and awnings, and expand business.

In Sheboygan, a BID district was created in 1992 with special assessment on property owners, and used the revenue generated to maintain and enhance business in the BID. As of January 1, 1998, total BID revenues were estimated at $40 million in private investment. The downtown BID is estimated at $27,165,500 and the Riverfront and Lakefront is estimated at $13,574,600.

Table 4: Value Increment of TIF Districts in Fox Valley Cities

City	Number of Active TIFs	Number in Down-town	Gross Base Value *	Total Current Value	Total Increment
Appleton	4	2	$124,942,900	$221,232,200 (1998)	$96,289,300
Fond du Lac	5	2	$5,657,500	$54,484,400 (1997)	$48,826,900
Green Bay	2	1	$40,364,200	$48,918,800 (1999)	$ 8,554,600
Oshkosh	10	6	$36,679,400	$116,777,300 (1998)	$80,097,900
Sheboygan	10	1	$77,444,800	$143,927,00) (1997)	$64,482,200

* These values represent a combination of the base values of TIFs created in different years and are a gross over-simplification. Since the dollar values were not inflation adjusted, they do not represent the real base values for the districts.

The only types of businesses within Sheboygan's BID district is that of retail trade. Other types of uses such as construction, manufacturing, utilities, and wholesale trade are all located outside of the BID. Although some residential properties lie in the district, it is limited to very few. These properties are considered run-down and are in need of improvements. The BID Board consists of thirteen members, seven of whom are property owners within the district. The board is appointed by the mayor and approved by the city council. Board members have a staggered term as designated by the council. In addition, board members are representative of different areas within the district, as well as large and small businesses.

Some of the projects undertaken by the BID committee included the development of Harbor Centre to promote the city's historic features—the lakefront, river front and downtown. The BID board undertakes promotion, recruitment, and service provision in the district.

The BID district has a set of goals that are designed to create a positive business climate in Harbor Centre, the downtown district. In order to meet this goal, a professional board member has been appointed with responsibility for among other things, recruiting business to the district, coordinating downtown activities with other development groups, acting as a clearing house for information, interacting with city government, and coordinating special events.

The Board of Directors coordinates activities with the Sheboygan Chamber of Commerce, the Sheboygan Development Corporation and city government. The board also undertakes promotion and marketing of the Harbor Centre.

Oshkosh created a BID in 1987 for the purpose of improving and ensuring the vitality of downtown and businesses located in the district. A ten member board currently administers the BID operating plan. Since its formation, the BID has engaged in marketing and promotion of downtown businesses, provided loans for façade improvement, promoted quality occupancy of downtown vacant space, and encouraged professional management. In 1998 BID revenues totaled $98,444.18, of which $82,425 was raised from the district's special assessment.

Green Bay also created a BID in 1995 for the purpose of redeveloping downtown Green Bay and bringing life back to the city. The BID board hopes to re-energize downtown businesses through such programs as façade improvement grants, streetscape improvement, and community gardens in the downtown. In 1999 the BID board raised $185,000 from tax assessment of businesses, received $60,000 from the city of Green Bay and $30,000 from businesses in the city. There are currently about 450 businesses in the BID.

Fond du Lac and Appleton do not have BIDs. However, Fond du Lac has a Central Business Council and Appleton has a downtown organization, the Appleton Downtown Inc. These two organizations through various programs promote and enhance business development in the downtown. For example, the Fond du Lac Downtown Business Council developed and implemented a business crime watch program, and helped pass a loitering ordinance. Appleton Downtown Inc. has been instrumental in recruiting and retaining businesses in the downtown. The organization has also helped local businesses to undertake historic preservation, streetscape, and façade improvements.

Appointment of a Downtown Manager

Regardless of whether a city has a BID or not, with the exception of Fond du Lac, the other four cities have appointed professionally trained downtown development managers and put them in charge of running programs for downtown improvement. This is an acknowledgement by the cities of the professional nature that downtown redevelopment has taken. All the downtown managers have a close working relationship with downtown businesses and with the cities' chambers of commerce. A typical job description for a downtown manager includes responsibility for business recruitment and retention, assistance of downtown businesses with management and marketing of their business, promotion of commercial rehabilitation and streetscape improvement, and developing and marketing the downtown to the public.

Special Events

Besides the efforts mentioned above, the five cities have also undertaken special programs geared primarily at increasing pedestrian traffic in the downtown. One such program common to all five cities is the farmers market. A farmers market, usually held on designated days of the week during the summer provides agricultural produce to residents. This helps to stimulate other businesses by creating the opportunity for nearby merchants to also increase their sales. Other promotional events include a downtown musical event, such as the Waterfest in Oshkosh, that features several musical groups every Thursday in the summer, and the Octoberfest in Appleton that features ethnic foods, music and cultural shows. In Sheboygan the annual fourth of July celebration and fireworks, Coho Family Weekend, and Lakefest draw thousands of people to Deland Park on the lakeshore. The community also holds free community concerts in the downtown in summer as well as sidewalk sales and carriage rides.

Measuring the Impact of Downtown (Re)development Programs

Given the several and sustained efforts displayed by the five cities to revitalize their downtowns, it would stand to reason that these cities would have a tracking devise for measuring progress in their downtown redevelopment efforts. Tracking the performance of downtown redevelopment programs is important from an economic and political perspective. Politically, tax payers from whom cities raise at least some of the money to undertake downtown improvement programs need to know whether their tax dollars are being put to good use and why they should continue to support such efforts. Economically, cities need to evaluate their programs in order to determine which programs measurably work. This is important because it will enable the cities to identify the programs on which to focus much of their efforts.

Anecdotal evidence exists to suggest that in some of the cities, downtown revitalization may be occuring. For example, in Sheboygan the city has witnessed the return of retailers from the fringe shopping malls back to the downtown. Even so, in all five cities, no systematic data gathering process is in place to help measure downtown redevelopment efforts. As a result, the cities lack hard evidence to show how their efforts are making a difference in the health of their downtowns. Some of the indicators that could be used to measure progress in downtown revitalization efforts include the following: a change in the tax base of downtown property; change in real property investment in the downtown; change in office space occupancy; change in population density; change in downtown housing values; change in downtown employment figures by employment sector; change in the size of the residential population living downtown; and change in the number of downtown businesses. These indicators and the potential sources of data for measuring them are provided in Table 5.

Table 5: Indicators for Measuring Downtown (Re)Development

VARIABLE	INDICATOR	SOURCES OF DATA
Tax Base	$ Value of Property	Tax Assessor's Offices
Change in Real Property Investment	$ Value of Annual New (Re)Development	Tax Assessor's Offices Departments of Community Development Chambers of Commerce
Change in Office Space Occupancy	Office Occupancy Rates	Chambers of Commerce Downtown Development Associations Departments of Community Development
Change in Number of Businesses in Downtown District	Number of Businesses in the CBD over Two Time Periods	Chambers of Commerce Departments of Community Development
Change in Population Density	Number of Persons Per Square Mile	Census Bureau Reports City Directories
Change in Size of Residential Population Downtown	Number of Residents in Downtown by Income Groups	Census Bureau Reports City Directories
Change in Downtown Employment by Sector	Number of Employed Persons in Each Sector	Census Bureau Reports Chambers of Commerce

As noted earlier, none of the cities have kept systematic data on any of the indicators suggested in Table 5. Where data exists, it is often uncollated. Compounding the problem is the elusive ways in which downtown boundaries are defined. For example, CBD, BID and TIF districts are usually not coterminus with each other. Also, while the Census Bureau usually reports data according to census blocks or block groups, downtown boundaries are often not aligned with the Census Bureau demarcations. Given these limitations, only two types of indicators could be reported for the downtowns of the five cities—property value changes, and change in the number of firms in the downtown. This data is displayed in Tables 6 and 7. Where downtown boundaries are either not defined or where data for the downtown are unavailable, the data is reported for the TIF districts that fall in the downtown area. This was the case for Sheboygan and Fond du Lac. Also, since the base years differ for each city, inter city comparison of changes in downtown property values over the same time period is impossible. Conclusions can, however, be made about the change in property values for each of the cities.

Tables 6 and 7 show that the changes in downtown property values have not been uniform for all of the cities. While Appleton and Sheboygan have recorded increases in property values within their downtowns, the same cannot be said for Oshkosh, and Green Bay. Infact Oshksoh experienced the worse case of downtown property decline between 1987 and 1998 primarily due to business flight from downtown Park Plaza. Green Bay also saw property values drop by 7.4% between 1990 and 1994. Residential property values in Fond du Lac increased by 26% between 1990 and 1998, but the city also saw a decline in property values in its TIF 2 district. In Green Bay and Oshkosh, where comparative data were

Table 6: Property Values in Downtown Districts

CITY	BASE YEAR	ENDING YEAR	INFLATION ADJUSTED VALUE	% CHANGE VALUE
Appleton	$23,972,586 (1992)	$74,352,400 (1997)	$64,654,261	169.7%
Oshkosh	$33,563,600 (1987)	$23,111,500 (1998)	$16,161,888	−51.8%
Green Bay	$100,258,900 (1990)	$97,176,000 (1994)	$84,500,870	−7.4%
Sheboygan				
TIF 1	$42,473,600 (1984)	$64,364,200 (1996)	$43,197,450	1.7%
TIF 2	$20,092,900 (1992)	$28,694,900 (1996)	$25,620,446	27.5%
Fond du Lac				
TIF 1	$17,793,800 (1978)	$46,275,100 (1997)	$18,965,205	6.5%
TIF 2	$ 4,525,700 (1981)	$ 6,874,900 (1997)	$ 3,928,514	−13.2%
Downtown Fond du Lac Residential Property Values	$24,218,100 (1990)	$38,732,800 (1998)	$30,498,268	25.9%

available, downtown retail businesses declined by more than two percent
between 1987 and 1998 for the city of Oshkosh, and between 1980 and 1999 for
the City of Green Bay.

Table 7: Number of Businesses in Downtown District

CITY	BASE YEAR	ENDING YEAR	PERCENTAGE CHANGE
Appleton	Unavailable	249 (1998)	N/A
Fond du Lac	Unavailable	223 (1998)	N/A
Green Bay	461 (1980)	450 (1999)	–2.4%
Oshkosh	141 (1987)	137 (1998)	–2.8%
Sheboygan	Unavailable	Unavailable	N/A

Conclusion

Two issues arose in assessing downtown revitalization efforts in the five Fox
cities; one is procedural, the other is substantive. Process wise, the cities have
had no clear definition of their downtowns. The variety of definitions that are
used in reference to the downtown such as CBD, TIF and BID confound efforts
at data collection and reporting. Therefore, it is important that cities clearly
define the boundaries of their downtowns as a prerequisite to evaluating downtown redevelopment programs. The vagueness with which downtown is defined
complicates attempts at assessing revitalization efforts.

Substantively, cities have not kept data on the effects of their redevelopment
programs. There is therefore a need to begin keeping and tracking data on downtowns. Preferably, this data should be organized according to the subject areas
suggested in Table 5. This will enable them to identify the most effective programs and accentuate them for downtown revitalization.

This study also identified a lukewarm support for downtown redevelopment
programs. Inadequate political and public support and confidence in downtown
redevelopment programs presents one hurdle to efforts at revitalization. The pre-
seumption among some community leaders is that investing money in downtown
is "throwing good money after bad money." The decline in the downtown is seen
as an inevitable process of urban development and, as such, it is reasoned that not
much can be done to stop this process from occurring. To overcome this perception, downtown managers and city planners will have to embark on a sustained

and vigorous public relations effort to sell the downtown both to the public and to political leaders.

Finally, downtown revitalization requires adaptation rather than adoption of programs that have worked in other communities. Since each community differs from others, the problems of downtown decline and the measures that need to be taken to revitalize downtown are unique to each city. For example, location, political culture, economic development history and financing options all differ from one community to the other. As a result, programs that work in one community are not necessarily transferable to other communities. Thus, while there may be lessons that cities can learn from each other, there is a limit to the replicability of downtown redevelopment programs.

References

City of Oshkosh, 1970. *Central Business District Plan*, Oshkosh, WI. Prepared for Chamber of Commerce by Sandstedt-Koop-Yarbro.

City of Oshkosh. 1973. *Comprehensive Plan.* Oshkosh, Wisconsin.

Green Bay Economic Development Authority, 1995. *Green Bay Central Business District: Business and Employment Study.* Green Bay, WI.

City of Appleton. 1996. *Vision 20/20: Comprehensive Plan.* Appleton, Wisconsin.

The Paper, "Development of New Parking Sites is Investment in City's Future." (February 23rd 1968): A4.

The *Oshkosh Daily Northwestern*, 1976. "Dead Downtown Costs Everyone." March 13th: 412.

The *Oshkosh Daily Northwestern*, 1971. "Pioneer Inn, Park Plaza's Story is Told Nationwide." April 27, 1971.

The *Reader's Digest.* 1997. "Exclusive Poll: The Best Places to Raise a Family." April 1997.

Lenzi, Raymond C. and Bruce H. Murray 1987. *Downtown Revitalization and Small City Development, Conference Proceedings.* (April 13–15 1987). Madison Wisconsin.

CHAPTER 5

Downtown Redevelopment in Selected Oregon Coastal Communities: Some Lessons from Practice

JENNIFER R. KLEBBA, MINDEE D. GARRETT, AUTUMN L. RADLE, and BRYAN T. DOWNES

A viable downtown is important to the economic and social health, heritage, and civic pride of a community. It is a critical area in any community no matter what its size or location. This is one reason why so much effort has gone into attempting to revitalize downtowns across America in the last few decades. It is an effort to reverse the economic, social, and physical decline that has occurred in the downtown areas of so many communities. The scenario usually goes something like this: buildings deteriorate; shops move to malls; crime rates increase; entertainment, community, and cultural activities leave; and so on. Hardt and Burayidi have shown in the previous chapters that this is a scenario encountered in large central cities as well as small towns.

Downtowns represent a tremendous investment. Their buildings, roads, utilities, and parks have been evolving since the nation was founded. Their businesses and industries generate much of America's economic capital. Downtown housing and recreational areas provide an array of places to live and find entertainment. Moreover, downtowns are usually the site of government offices, providing a framework for our society and its laws and opportunities.

A community's downtown also symbolizes its heritage and its people. Downtowns impart community history and traditions to residents and visitors alike. Buildings and public spaces are a living part of that heritage. From the humblest storefront to the most imposing courthouse, they are living reminders of our past.

Thus, downtown revitalization is important for many reasons. But, how is it accomplished? This study examines downtown revitalization processes in five small Oregon coastal cities: Newport, Lincoln City, Cannon Beach, Astoria, and Seaside. On-site interviews were conducted with city officials. Questions that were asked included: What downtown revitalization projects have been undertaken? What were the goals of the projects? What was accomplished? What key challenges and obstacles were encountered? and, What were the lessons learned?

Before turning to the case studies, we briefly review the history of downtown development in the United States; some of the reasons communities decide to undertake revitalization efforts; various prominent approaches to downtown redevelopment; and redevelopment strategies that have proven particularly effective. This provides a context for understanding both the case studies and the lessons from practice discussed in the conclusion.

History of Downtown: A Review of the Literature

Historically, downtowns emerged as the center of urbanized regions. Downtowns often represented a region's economic core. Traditionally they have also been at the center of community activity, and represent a city's principal image.

Downtowns have evolved over the decades in response to changing technologies and socio-economic patterns. This is evident in both small and large communities. For example, during the 20th century, significant changes occurred in the mix of downtown functions and in the utility of downtown to the typical metropolitan resident (Robertson 1995). In the early 20th century, American downtowns shaped by pedestrian traffic and mass transit, particularly the electric streetcar were at their zenith (Muller 1980). The major economic activities in early 20th century downtowns were retailing, offices/finance, and entertainment. In larger cities, these functions established separate, often contiguous downtown districts. In smaller cities these activities were all located downtown.

After reaching its pinnacle during the 1920s, however, the American downtown steadily declined. Continuous decentralization shifted downtown functions to the surrounding suburbs, particularly since World War II. Freeway construction and rising automobile use enabled activities and people to move away from the downtown district to the suburbs.

This shift of downtown activities, together with urban renewal and other policies enacted during the 1950s and 1960s, produced downtowns in many larger central cities vastly different from those of the early 20th century. Densities decreased significantly as core blocks were raised, while development increased on the periphery. Distances between activities increased making downtowns less pedestrian friendly; sidewalks narrowed as streets were widened to make room for more cars; walking became more dangerous from both heavy traffic and increased downtown crime; and reduced on-street activities made walking less pleasurable. Downtowns became characterized increasingly by dead spaces, "uninteresting parking lots, ramps, vacant buildings, and blank-walled office buildings. Finally, as fewer people commuted by mass transit, downtowns' influence faded" (Robertson 1995).

Downtowns in the five small rural coastal communities studied have also been going through transitions, brought about largely by economic and social changes. Historically Oregon's coastal communities have been dependent economically on the fishing and timber industries. These industries are in decline and the economic base of rural coastal communities in Oregon is changing.

Retail trade, tourism, and catering to the needs of retirees and second (vacation) home owners have become primary economic activities. The mix varies from community to community as does the remaining role of the timber and fishing industries. But the economies of some of our study communities have undergone fundamental change with high paying jobs in fishing and timber being replaced by low paying ones in the service industry. New groups of people have moved to town. Particularly evident are retirees and families owning second vacation homes. The population is also aging as young people leave seeking opportunities in large cities or in other states. Social problems, such as alcohol and drug abuse as well as spouse and child abuse have often become more acute as workers and their families try to adapt to this new economic situation. Relocation of business or new retail trade developments, oftentimes outside the downtown core, have both had serious consequences for downtown viability.

Why the Decision to Revitalize Downtown?

Faced with its fading influences, local officials confronted the challenge of trying to rebuild downtown and make it the center of the community again. Downtowns are seen as critical to overall city vitality, so cities of all sizes, and in all regions, are committed to successful downtown redevelopment. Yet despite three decades of continuous redevelopment polices and projects, most American downtowns still have serious economic problems and are perceived, particularly by suburbanites, as inconvenient, obsolete, and even dangerous places (Robertson 1995).

Why do community leaders and citizens decide to revitalize their downtowns? Palma and Hyett (1997) discuss several reasons. Downtown officials are beginning to realize that spenders' count, having distinct niches help, as do private/pubic partnerships. In addition, community leaders are finding that by combining these aspects, as well as using the tools of business, the entire community benefits. Overall then the primary motivation for downtown revitalization is most often economic. However, revitalization efforts do not come easy. There needs to be a clear shared vision of a downtown's future. Community leaders and citizens need a realistic understanding of downtown retail and office market opportunities in order to formulate a definitive vision and define appropriate courses of action.

Although it is true that American downtowns at the end of the twentieth century face many economic, social, and image problems, this acknowledgement need not imply a bleak future for them. On the contrary, the contemporary downtown has many attributes and amenities offering promise for its future. For example, looking toward the twenty-first century, downtowns need to develop a distinct identity. What is unique about downtown? Downtowns should develop attributes not found in the suburbs, or elsewhere, such as waterfronts, historic areas, and cultural facilities. For most American downtowns, the potential to establish a distinctive sense of place, especially within metropolitan areas or regions, is very high, if city officials take advantage of the qualities that set downtown apart from its surroundings. Robertson in this book and elsewhere (1995) has offered several recommendations for building stronger downtown identity and for identifying unique downtown assets.

Approaching Downtown Revitalization and Change

During the past decade, several approaches and many strategies have emerged in the effort to revitalize downtowns. Although not specifically designed for smaller communities, local officials can adapt and combine the various strategies to create an approach best suited for their downtown. A popular general approach combines public-sector incentives with private-sector organizational capacity and leadership. Further, Wagner, *et. al.* (1995), have identified two distinct types of approaches. One approach, for cities with strong economies, labeled a "catalyst" one, uses a major new or rehabilitated development project as a catalyst for revitalization. A second, for communities with weaker economies, is the "incremental" approach; one which emphasizes small scale, long term investment in buildings, public improvements and businesses. Key attributes of this approach are land use and design controls, including historic preservation ordinances; a comprehensive promotional campaign; professional downtown management and a downtown organization with an effective board of directors.

Given these all-encompassing approaches, the Downtown Research and Development Center has identified the following more specific strategies for downtown revitalization. The individual strategies are not meant to be utilized independently of each other, but are designed to be used in combination with one another for successful downtown revitalization.

Financial Strategies

The purpose of these strategies are to increase the economic health of the downtown, in other words to revitalize the economy. These include small business loan assistance, rehabilitation loans, grants and investment tax credits (RITCs), tax abatements, and tax increment financing.

The key is to increase the community's economic base. A community's economic base influences the success of the downtown revitalization program. Specifically, communities that have an economy based on manufacturing, higher education, and/or government have been more likely to have successful commercial rehabilitation programs than agricultural communities. This is the only factor that is outside public or private sector control.

Furthermore, revitalization programs funded primarily through local funds (public or private) achieved a higher degree of success than those depending on outside funds. The main reasons for success include: (i) they can be better targeted because local leaders are more familiar with the community needs; (ii) state and federal restriction on the use of funds may limit their usefulness for communities; (iii) local funders are generally more active in monitoring performance actions closely and responding quickly to changes; and (iv) local funders have a stake in the program's success because it is their own money.

Physical Improvements Strategies

The aim of physical improvement strategies is to revitalize the aesthetics of the downtown, so that it looks more appealing to residents as well as tourists. This includes: design assistance to businesses that intend to improve their properties; improving the streetscape by constructing and installing sidewalk benches, trees and shaded areas; and revitalizing and restoring the historic district.

The most successful programs were comprehensive ones that addressed a community's physical and economic issues. For example, sixty percent of the communities that emphasized activities such as physically improving buildings, recruiting developers, offering building construction and rehabilitation financing and promoting downtown improvements were successful.

Functional Strategies

Functional strategies are one of the most important for revitalizing downtowns. This includes: Coordinated downtown promotions by all businesses to "sell downtown"; coordinated store hours between businesses to increase cohesiveness of the downtown; free parking and special transportation for residents to increase traffic to downtown shops and businesses.

Other strategies focus on ensuring continuity and cohesiveness among downtown businesses. This might involve creating a business owners association, creating an awards program for businesses that excel in promoting downtown, and training business owners and merchants about how to run a successful business. Important also are survey and market studies to ensure customer and business satisfaction, as well as, staying in tune with the market.

Local Government Strategies

Full cooperation of the city, township, and/or county governments is important. This enables innovative zoning in the planning of the revitalization effort and ensures successful business representation. Using existing infrastructure, so as to not add more costs to the development efforts, can also be very important. The focus should be on increasing diversity in both the shops and overall appearance of the downtown. Also, look for best practices and use the programs that other downtowns have employed. These programs include: the Main Street Program of the National Trust for Historic Preservation, a downtown development authority program, and tax increment financing. Various local programs established by city governments or merchants associations can successfully address unique downtown needs.

Downtown revitalization programs must build a widespread base of community support to be successful. Without widespread support, there will be little public interest in the program. This will cause financial supporters to withdraw from the program.

Communities that regulated the downtown tended to be more effective than those that did not. The most powerful tools for improving the character and economic mix of a central business district were zoning, building code enforcement, design controls, and historic district ordinances. The final key to success is the need for a promotional program. Communities that conducted comprehensive promotional programs, special events, public relations campaigns, and retail sales events as part of their commercial revitalization programs tended to have a higher rate of success than those that did not do so.

The National Main Street Center suggests similar such strategies for downtown revitalization (Smith 1991). It stresses the importance of a comprehensive approach to downtown revitalization. The Center offers a four step approach to downtown revitalization: Design involving the improvement of the downtown's image by enhancing its overall physical appearance; Organization of the community by building consensus and cooperation among groups that play roles in the downtown; Promoting the downtown's unique characteristics to shoppers, investors, new businesses, tourists and others through effective marketing strategies; and, Economic restructuring by strengthening the existing economic base of the downtown while diversifying it. We now turn to a discussion of our five-city case studies bearing in mind the suggested strategies for downtown revitalization.

Five Case Studies

The crux of downtown redevelopment planning is effective implementation of the various approaches and strategies discussed in the previous section. As we shall see in the discussion which follows, this is no easy task. There are various factors in each of the case study communities which either facilitate or obstruct successful redevelopment efforts. Unfortunately, oftentimes missing are the ones critical to success.

NEWPORT, OR

Newport is located on Oregon's central coast region in Lincoln County. The 1997 population of Newport was 9,960, an 18 percent increase since 1990 (OEDD 1999). Retail trade employs the largest number of total residents. However, the largest single employer is Ocean Beauty Seafoods which is also the city's largest private manufacturing company with 500 employees. The principal industries of Newport are lumber, fishing, and agriculture, while the city has targeted the industries of forest products, high tech and software for increased economic diversification (OEDD 1999).

REVITALIZATION GOALS AND EFFORTS

The most important goal of Newport's revitalization efforts centers on attracting tourists off Highway 101 and into one of the City's three main districts: downtown, Nye Beach and the Bayfront. Highway 101 is the main coastal highway in Oregon. It runs north and south through Newport. In order to draw tourists into these districts, however, the city recognizes the need to connect these neighborhoods, particularly through pedestrian traffic. The impetus to pursue this goal came from the Newport Peninsula Urban Design Plan, commissioned by the city and conducted by Demuth Glick Consultants between 1991 and 1994. The report emphasizes the importance of making Newport pedestrian friendly, on both sides of Highway 101.

Newport has received funds for downtown revitalization projects from Measure 50, a recent ballot initiative. Currently, the city is constructing a one way couplet between Abbey and Angle Streets in order to slow traffic and encourage motorists to park their cars and explore the shops and other attractions in that area. The city is also in the process of buying a right-of-way at Fifty-Second Street so that a light can be placed at the intersection to adjust traffic and help get tourists out of their cars.

CHALLENGES AND OBSTACLES TO REVITALIZATION

Absentee Owners

While Nye Beach and the Bayfront are actively pursuing the overarching goal of increased connectedness between the neighborhoods, it is a greater challenge for the downtown city center. Absentee owners predominate in downtown and are less inclined to invest in the physical improvements or social capital of a community in which they do not live, or live for only part of the year. Tenants do not have voting power on needed bond issues and are likewise unlikely or unable to make commitments to revitalization efforts. Comparatively low rents downtown further reduces the likelihood that investments will be made in property upkeep, thereby creating a holding pattern, in which one owner cannot accomplish needed change without others joining in the effort.

Lack of Public Participation and Stakeholder Involvement

Residents' expectation that the government should solve the problems in Newport impedes revitalization efforts as well. One city official interviewed indicated that residents have been reluctant to take ownership of the revitalization process. Consistently low attendance at public meetings hampers cooperative problem identification and solution brainstorming, which typically results in plans that do not reflect the public's needs and are henceforth destined for failure. Residents' attitude that revitalization costs should be borne by the city and not fall directly on home and business owners, combined with fear of debt from marginal businesses, both impede the City's efforts.

Outside Agency Interactions
According to one city official, the Oregon Department of Transportation (ODOT) presents a challenge to downtown revitalization because they largely determine how traffic flows on Highway 101. ODOT is seemingly hesitant to listen to the city's ideas for changing traffic patterns so as to encourage travelers to pull off Highway 101 and experience Newport's side streets and gain access to downtown, Nye Beach and the Bayfront. Local officials are currently fighting an ODOT proposal to better synchronize the traffic lights through the city that would further dissuade drivers from stopping in Newport. Lack of monetary investment from property owners in revitalization efforts related to traffic is detrimental to this already strained relationship, because ODOT is hesitant to establish working partnerships when a commitment is not apparent on both sides.

Land Use Decisions Affecting the Economy
Nye Beach and the Bayfront act as the social hubs for local residents and tourists, respectively. Downtown Newport, however, does not offer many tourist shops, social establishments, or other attractions, which increases the tendency of motorists to drive along Highway 101 without stopping, given that there is apparently nothing of interest to draw them out of their cars. Moreover, although downtown remains the focus of government offices, there are few services that cater to these employees. They are, thus, forced to leave the city center for errands, thereby further depressing the economic life of downtown. The siting of Wal-Mart, a big-box retail store, just north of Newport directly off of Highway 101, has likewise diverted business activity from downtown merchants.

LESSONS AND RECOMMENDATIONS

Building Involvement and Partnerships
Many of the obstacles facing Newport's revitalization efforts derive from a lack of public participation and investment in the overall process. The city official interviewed appeared prepared to relinquish responsibility and slip into complacency in understandable frustration. Instead the city needs to be proactive and continue seeking greater involvement. Property owners associated with the downtown need to understand that a partnership with the city is crucial to the success of not only their individual business or residence, but to the community

as a whole. A productive alliance between the city and property owners ought to mitigate the discord between Newport and ODOT as well. Currently many residents see the city center as nothing more than a stretch of highway; they do not identify with the downtown district. It is up to the city to garner enough public buy-in to create an achievable vision of a walkable community with a thriving social and economic life for locals and tourists alike.

Learning from Past Mistakes

The priority that's given to new super-stores that are not invested in the city's overall social or economic welfare, over long-established local businesses reflects and perpetuates a history of poor planning decisions that are not unique to Newport. Nationwide cities desperate for a quick economic fix continue to welcome similar businesses without the foresight of how their downtown will be affected as commerce and social activity are drained to the outskirts of town.

Removal of Wal-Mart is not feasible. However, attracting businesses to downtown that will serve both locals and tourists, as well as stronger design review and zoning amendments to reduce the acceptance of future big-box intrusions, are fundamental to revitalizing Newport.

LINCOLN CITY

Lincoln City is located along the northern coast of Oregon in Lincoln County. The population of Lincoln City was 6,785 in 1997 a 15 percent increase from the 1990 population (OEDD 1999). The principal industries in Lincoln City are tourism, marine research, and commercial fishing, whereas the industries targeted for economic diversification are forest products, software, and high tech. Retail trade employs the highest total number of residents, while Chinook Winds Casino is the largest local employer, with approximately 650 workers. The two largest private manufacturing firms in the city are Starkor Manufacturing Company, followed by News Guard, Inc. Prior to the 1960s, Lincoln City was separated into five distinct cities strung out along Highway 101: Cutler City, Nelscott, Taft, De Lake and Ocean Lake. These cities merged shortly after the passage of the Clean Water Act in the 1960s in order to receive funding for sewage treatment operations. Disagreement existed between the cities prior to the consolidation. Although efforts were made to improve relations by creation of one cohesive identity, the result reduced opportunities for viability within the individual downtown areas.

REVITALIZATION GOALS AND EFFORTS

Smart Development: Nodes, Pedestrian Access, and Aesthetics

Lincoln City's revitalization efforts range from rudimentary sidewalk additions along Highway 101 to pursuing Smart Development principles in the context of a grant from the State Transportation and Growth Management (TGM) Program. During the summer of 1998 Lincoln City received a TGM grant for local planning. With the help of Shapiro and Associates, the city is addressing several issues and projects related to revitalization. These include, but are not limited to: code assistance, the feasibility of adopting mixed use guidelines which are currently forbidden in the city's zoning requirements, and possible implementation of a design review process that would make the five distinct downtowns more economically viable as well as aesthetically pleasing. The Smart Development principles Lincoln City is employing, revolve around the aforementioned issue of reestablishing the identities of the five original downtown centers. At the time of our interview with the Lincoln City official there had been three workshops with the Planning Commission regarding their Smart Development goals as well as a presentation of resultant project proposals, and public hearings concerning amendments to the city's zoning ordinances. The process has been well received by both the Planning Commission and the business community.

The preliminary plan calls for the creation of nodes—beginning with the former cities of Nelscott, Taft, and Ocean Lake—in a mixed overlay zone. Node design is intended to encourage pedestrian access by installment of a full complement of sidewalks and by keeping all main-street retail and hotels no more than 1,000 feet apart (the standard for acceptable walking distance). The incentive, or carrot, for a property owner is greater flexibility through mixed use allowances as well as relaxed parking requirements. The trade-off, or stick, is the elimination of parking in front of buildings if the building is located directly on the main street of downtown. In areas where redevelopment is possible, the plan recommends a reorientation of buildings, particularly, hotels and condominiums, so they no longer act as visual barriers to the waterfront. This would allow the value of the ocean to reach farther back into the heart of the city's neighborhoods.

URBAN RENEWAL'S CONTRIBUTION

Lincoln Citys Urban Renewal Department is working jointly with the Planning Department in using the funds from the TGM grant. Attention is currently focused on Ocean Lake and Taft. The input and design phase will begin in July 1999 for Ocean Lake. Taft will simultaneously receive funds for work on projects such as façade improvements, rehabilitation loans, changing traffic patterns, parking, extension of the Bay Walk, replacing street lights with historic lamps, and changing the present overhead utility lines to underground systems.

MERCHANTS' ASSOCIATIONS

The Bay Area Merchant's Association (BAMA) is currently concentrating its efforts on aesthetic projects such as adding flower baskets to street lamps, creating an archway over Fifty-First Street at the intersection of Highway 101, and placement of a memorial flag to commemorate the victims of bay drownings.

Although BAMA would like to undertake more ambitious projects such as burying utility lines, they cannot proceed without anticipated funds from the Urban Renewal Department. Ocean Lake Merchants Association (OLMA) is similarly waiting on urban renewal funds to be allocated for building upgrades. Of greater importance to them, however, are traffic and parking issues rather than aesthetic improvements. OLMAs long-term goals include construction of a pedestrian walkway system behind their stores to further buffer visitors from traffic on Highway 101.

CHALLENGES AND OBSTACLES TO REVITALIZATION

Highway 101: Parking and Traffic

Several challenges exist to the node plan as well as overall revitalization efforts in Lincoln City. As with other coastal Oregon cities, Highway 101 is both a blessing and a curse. Traffic flow and parking are both contentious issues in the city. Parked cars in front of businesses on Highway 101 create a physical and psychological safety buffer for pedestrians and allows customers to more easily access businesses. From an aesthetic perspective, however, it would be more advantageous to have parking in the back of the buildings. Even greater than this disagreement, however, is the argument over creation of left-hand turn lanes to avoid further traffic congestion. Under staunch objections from merchants, parking on either side of these lanes would be eliminated. In an effort to alleviate the objections of merchants, a compromise was proposed to only locate left turn lanes in critical congestion areas, thereby preserving a greater amount of parking in front of businesses.

Aesthetics

Signs present a challenge to revitalization efforts as well. Although ordinances exist to curb the size and occurrence of signs, enforcement is rare. Countless signs, thus, beset Lincoln City, each vying to out-compete the next in size and garishness. Attempts to invite tourists out of their cars and onto the quainter side streets of Lincoln City are considerably hampered by the visual offensiveness that abounds on Highway 101. In addition to this inattention to aesthetic planning, Lincoln City is also challenged by a lack of design review and adequate development standards that would prevent, in the words of one city official, more of the "schlock" that currently exists.

Animosity Between Communities

Interviews with representatives of the Bay Area and Ocean Lake Merchant's Association identified several of the aforementioned challenges to downtown revitalization, while also emphasizing the persistent enmity between the communities of Taft and Ocean Lake. While BAMA identifies itself as independent from Lincoln City's government aside from funding opportunities, OLMA charges that BAMA, and Taft in general, are receiving additional monetary benefits because the new city council includes two Taft residents. The interviewee representing OLMA asserted that their downtown is for residents—"people live here", whereas they claimed that Taft caters to "visitors only". The relationship between the merchants' associations is, thus, explicitly adversarial, and their relationships with city officials are strained at best. Indeed, the Urban Development Department interviewee noted that there is a lack of public participation in open meetings due to the fact that residents are irritated with the current situation.

LESSONS AND RECOMMENDATIONS

Development Standards and Design Review

More stringent development standards would assist Lincoln City in its efforts to target certain types of areas for development. Combined with the enactment of design review, most of the aesthetic challenges facing the city can be rectified or averted as well. Neither of these efforts, however, will be effective without the full support of all stakeholders, including the City Council, Planning Commission, Urban Renewal Department, and the cooperation of an empowered public that has been included in each step of the process.

Building Partnerships with the Public

In addition to the lack of public inclusion, the city must also contend with the divisiveness between the five distinct communities within the city limits, particularly Taft and Ocean Lake. The tension between BAMA and OLMA necessarily impedes revitalization efforts by contravening public participation and setting communities at odds with each other rather than building alliances for a greater common good. Moreover, the attitude that residents become involved in revitalization and other community issues only when they are upset is a self-fulfilling prophecy. Regardless of historical or contemporary participation trends, successful revitalization depends on active engagement of residents, particularly business and property owners. From issues such as parking and traffic flow to aesthetic improvements and urban renewal fund disbursement, the city is remiss if it does not tap the latent expertise of its citizenry.

CANNON BEACH

Cannon Beach is located along the Northern Coast of Oregon in Clatsop County. The city experienced a 17 percent population increase between 1990 and 1997, concluding the seven-year period with a total population of 1,425 residents (OEDD 1999). The principal industries of Cannon Beach are fisheries, lumber, and tourism, while environmental services, forest products and tourism have been targeted for economic diversification. While the greatest total number of city residents are employed in the retail trade sector, the largest local employer (located in Seaside) is Hallmark Resorts with approximately eighty workers. The two largest private manufacturing firms are Bell Buoy Crab Company and Phillips Candies, both located in Seaside, Oregon.

REVITALIZATION GOALS AND EFFORTS

By the close of the 1960s Cannon Beach was a dilapidated town at the end of an historic dependence on the logging industry. However, the beginning of the 1970s brought new life to the city as "hippie entrepreneurs" established a lively arts and crafts market. Major structural redevelopment occurred in the latter portion of the decade, including refurbishment of the Coaster Theater, which became the city's primary cultural anchor and visitor attraction.

PLANNING AND DESIGN REVIEW

Unlike the other case study cities, Cannon Beach is not located directly on Highway 101, and therefore does not face the same challenges with traffic congestion and parking except when tourists arrive during the summer months. The city included in its comprehensive plan a commitment to minimize development along Highway 101, to which it has generally adhered and has, thus, forestalled the aesthetic disaster common to other coastal Oregon cities. Cannon Beach is unique for this and other foresighted planning decisions over the last three decades. The official interviewed in Cannon Beach alleged that the city does not have a specific plan per se that has allowed them to maintain a viable downtown. Instead they rely upon a rigorous design review process that has received hearty support from the city council since the mid-1970s as a critical element of their land use program.

In addition to requiring buildings to have a better visual appearance and coherence, thereby creating a more unified downtown, design review has also enabled Cannon Beach to refuse permit requests from big-box retail stores and fast-food chains who cannot or will not conform to the city's higher development standards. Design review also promotes pedestrian scale and circulation, requires a 20 percent open space allotment, and encourages seating areas, plantings, and other amenities. All design requirements are privately funded, and according to the city official interviewed, these expenses are viewed by property owners as reasonable investments in the community's viability. Cannon Beach is currently considering expanding their design review process by creating a design guidebook for property owners to refer to in their building and refurbishing activities.

DEVELOPMENT STANDARDS AND THE ECONOMIC MARKET

According to one city official, the magic of the marketplace has also helped Cannon Beach create an economically viable and aesthetically pleasing downtown. People are apparently willing to pay considerable amounts of money for a desirable place to live, which conveniently allows the city to demand a higher standard for development. Downtown Cannon Beach is intended to attract and accommodate tourists. The community's economy is consequently flourishing thanks to success in carving out a niche in the competitive coastal tourism industry.

CHALLENGES AND OBSTACLES TO REVITALIZATION

Stakeholder Leadership
Leadership for Cannon Beach's downtown revitalization comes primarily from the city and the chamber of commerce. There is no downtown business association because, according to the city official interviewed, it is difficult to build leadership from small businesses who are often on the edge of economic survival and generally burnout before significant contributions can be made.

Services for Residents
Creating a desirable place for tourists does not come without costs. The city official interviewed admitted that residents of Cannon Beach are necessarily negatively affected by skyrocketing residential and commercial rent. Most local services such as grocery stores, pharmacies, and hardware stores have been forced out of business replaced by tourist-focused establishments. Seaside, eight miles away, is the nearest basic service provider for Cannon Beach residents.

Maintaining Success
In addition to the aforementioned task of ensuring local residents can afford to live in and access basic services in Cannon Beach, the other notable challenge facing the city is, ironically, how to cope with too much success. As a preferred place to live and visit on the Oregon coast, the city is confronted with increasing numbers of residents and tourists each year. Associated with these population surges are numerous project proposals that threaten to intensify current land use and increase building sizes beyond their current scale. Maintaining stringent design review and averting a loss of coveted village character will be a struggle in the wake of escalating development pressures.

LESSONS AND RECOMMENDATIONS

The city official interviewed considered the lack of services available to residents and the rising rental rates acceptable compromises given the city's overall success. However, the true merit and desirability of a community that no longer serves its residents is suspect. Cannon Beach must find a balance between catering to tourists and serving its residents or the cost of living and maintaining a business in the city may become so exorbitant that full-year residents will be driven out and only wealthy vacationers can afford to stay there. The cost of that success far outweighs its benefits and is not a worthy goal of revitalization.

LONG-TERM VISION

Cannon Beach is the most successful of the case study cities in terms of economic prosperity, design coherence and aesthetic appeal. The city has a self-proclaimed philosophy and tangible history of prudent planning decisions over the last three decades. Moreover, the community has resolved to avoid the hazard of seizing the illusion of the quick fix. Instead, Cannon Beach consistently resists the temptation to accept the first seemingly profitable offer and understands that the fruits of their foresighted efforts will not bear instantaneous results. City officials comprehend that each decision they make can alter the historical tone they have set for their community and are aware that shortsightedness and passivity will set Cannon Beach on the course of other struggling coastal Oregon cities.

ASTORIA, OR

Astoria, Oregon is the oldest American settlement "west of the Rockies." It was founded in 1811 by John Jacob Astor as a fur trading post. Located 95 miles west of Portland, at the northern-most point of Oregon's coast, Astoria has a population of 10,110 (ODOT 1997). Astoria is bordered both by the Pacific Ocean to the west and the Columbia River to the north. Highway 101 runs north/south through Astoria, branching into Highway 30, running through the center of town. Astoria's economy has been dependent historically on fish and timber. Today all the large mills and canneries are gone.

REVITALIZATION GOALS AND EFFORTS

Finding A Vision

The city of Astoria has had to face the hard reality that it is no longer the regions retail-trade center as it was in the 1920s. Facing this loss of identity, Astoria has decided to return to its roots, and embrace its rich historical past. The process of becoming a historical coastal town began with a petition to have Astoria's downtown area placed on the National Register of Historic Districts. In May of 1999, the request was approved and their effort was rewarded.

Astoria is now taking steps to make its historical status apparent to all those who visit, and to restore a sense of pride among city residents. Astoria has started by attempting to make its downtown area more aesthetically pleasing. To this end, the city, along with local downtown area merchants have undertaken several projects such as aesthetically enhancing the sidewalks with sod restoration, the installation of the city's original street lamps, and finishing the Riverwalk.

Riverwalk

The Riverwalk plan includes beautification and revitalization of the riverfront and a five-mile, landscaped and paved trail leading from downtown to the waterfront. The Riverwalk project is an attempt to "reconnect" the downtown retail district to the waterfront, making it pedestrian friendly through easier public access. The riverfront formerly housed large fish canneries, lumber mills, and log shipping operations.

Historic Goals

One of Astoria's main goals is to return the city to its historic roots. According to one city official, the city has never been a tourist town, and will not become one anytime soon. The city has made some moves in the right direction, but according to the same individual, projects undertaken to-date have been mostly "sluff." One of the goals is to begin making more strategic investments to realize the historical vision for Astoria's future, and to get professional help in doing so. Oregon's Downtown Development Association is willing to assist, but has stipulated that in order for things to proceed, there must be some form of unified merchants group with landlords and residents involved to cultivate a shared vision for the future. According to one city official, involving landlords in the process will be challenging, due to the number of absentee owners in Astoria.

Astoria has a Downtown Historic District Association that is financed through dues and surcharges on business licenses. However, this group is not entirely committed to this vision. Part of the vision includes developing a sense of pride in the city's history.

Astoria is also trying to create more demand for services in the downtown area. While some towns initially create more supply and then expect the demand to follow, the City of Astoria feels that by first creating a demand for services, the city will be able to tailor the downtown area to specific needs. Astoria's goal is not to recruit businesses that will ultimately make the downtown successful, but to first make the downtown a place people enjoy. City officials hope to accomplish this by getting more reputable businesses to relocate downtown. In addition to the restoration of the historic houses adjacent to Astoria's downtown, there is a need for more housing which will increase the number of residents spending their time downtown, and add to its atmosphere.

CHALLENGES AND OBSTACLES

One of the obstacles confronting Astoria is persuading residents and merchants to buy into the historic vision. In addition, large businesses in Astoria are finding that in order to expand they must move elsewhere. Safeway and Astoria's Clatsop Community College, are making plans to move to the outskirts of Astoria or to the neighboring town of Warrenton.

Safeway, whose current store is located in the downtown area, has plans to build a mega-store, which cannot be accommodated at the present downtown site because of space restrictions. A relocation of Safeway from the downtown would be a serious detriment to the downtown. Clatsop Community College is also considering expansion of its campus, including relocation to the outskirts of town. City leaders in Astoria would like to see the college relocate downtown, envisioning a scholastic atmosphere with the college buying up vacant buildings for classrooms and housing.

Parking is another of the major obstacles to a thriving downtown. The downtown area does not have adequate space to deal with the kinds of parking that a community college or other professional business would need.

Adding to these obstacles is Astoria's neighboring town, Warrenton. Warrenton can provide Astoria's businesses with the space they need to expand and relocate. It is also close enough to serve all residents of Astoria, which it has begun to do through a large shopping mall development adjacent to Astoria's city limits.

While most city officials and merchants in Astoria think that the overall vision of historic restoration and revitalization is a good one, many are not willing to do their part to make it a reality. In addition, the vision has not been made "official" in any way, which may be one reason merchants and residents do not feel comfortable buying into the vision completely.

The City of Astoria has offered monetary incentives to merchants in an attempt to secure more business relocation downtown. Local landlords were also offered monetary incentives to build housing in the downtown area, in order to draw more residents downtown. However, most landlords are still unwilling to build downtown, fearing its poor public image will cause any housing built there to remain empty. Downtown Astoria's poor reputation and vacancies resulting from that reputation are the main reasons why most residents find it undesirable in its present condition.

CHALLENGES AND OBSTACLES TO REVITALIZATION

Overcoming Reputation

Many residents view the downtown area as undesirable because of its controversial past. Strip bar establishments attracted a clientele that made the local residents feel very uncomfortable after dark. According to one city official, these seedy strip joints were involved in more than just selling alcohol and created an unsafe environment. Astoria's police eventually closed these businesses.

The closing of the strip bars has done wonders for the downtown in terms of its atmosphere. Downtown is safer, which has encouraged the return of some local residents and tourists. There are now more cafes and reputable businesses downtown as well. Even with these improvements, progress has been quite marginal. Although large numbers have yet to head for the downtown area, signs of growth and recovery are emerging. Slowly, merchants and residents are returning to downtown Astoria.

A Vacant Downtown

The city is not surrendering to the threats of flight of major businesses. Astoria's city officials have called in a quick response team offered by the State of Oregon, to deal with the Safeway challenge. The quick response team is comprised of architects and urban planners who have come to Astoria to work with Safeway and the city, and to try to develop a compromise. Unfortunately, Safeway's proposal requires acres of land that would necessitate zoning changes, demolition, and a rearrangement of the city's street pattern. Adding to the challenge is Safeway's tie to the community. Safeway has long been considered an anchor of the community, drawing residents of Astoria downtown. Moving Safeway to Warrenton would create more vacant space and remove one of downtown Astoria's only remaining social hubs.

Astoria has made a commitment to its residents. Astoria's city official's conscious decision to develop the historic aspects of downtown rather than promote tourism, may increase pride in the city and make residents feel good about living in Astoria. City officials believe this will ultimately lead to a stronger and more sustainable downtown area. City officials have also written grants which have been instrumental in facilitating Astoria's success thus far. Funding from grants has enabled Astoria to proceed with projects such as Riverwalk.

Patient, steady leadership is one of Astoria's greatest attributes. Having someone like Astoria's Community Development Director, who realizes that change takes time, and who does not become disillusioned by setbacks, has allowed Astoria to keep working towards its historic vision. He has developed patience and persistence. Both will help the city overcome obstacles. He realizes that successful revitalization takes time and that a positive attitude can help eliminate perceived obstacles such as lack of funding and cooperation. The Community Development Director will not be able to revitalize downtown Astoria by himself, however, he will need the cooperation and assistance of other city officials and residents in order to complete a successful downtown revitalization.

LESSONS AND RECOMMENDATIONS

Astoria plans to further pedestrian access by improving intersections across Highway 30. The city has been promoting a bypass project for almost twenty-five years with limited success. Once again the city is frustrated by actions of the Oregon Department of Transportation (ODOT). Those who have been consulted tell city officials that a bypass will lead to the ultimate demise of Astoria's downtown. City officials feel that a bypass would enhance downtown, making access to the riverfront easier for pedestrians who would no longer have to contend with log trucks and speeding cars heading through the middle of town. The city is forced to wait while the state conducts an environmental impact study. However, at this time the city does not have the capital funds to undertake a highway project of this nature, and city officials feel ODOT opposes a bypass project.

Highway 101 also bisects Astoria separating downtown from the waterfront. Astoria's transportation focus is making Highway 30 safer for pedestrians crossing from downtown to the river. Highway 101 is not a pressing concern for Astoria at this time.

It appears to city officials that downtown Astoria is improving both socially and economically. Those involved feel that one key is attracting professional businesses and keeping a watchful eye on the city's vision as progress resumes. The process of revitalization in Astoria is a slow one that will require patience and knowledge that nothing happens overnight. In addition, it seems helpful to have an attitude that welcomes change and encourages a sense of ownership in the vision.

FUTURE REVITALIZATION

Currently, one of Astoria's bright spots appears to be a local nonprofit group that would like to renovate Astoria's historic Liberty Theater into a performing arts center. The group has consulted architects from Portland to plan this revitalization of the old theater. This group is very dedicated and enthusiastic, and if they are successful, their efforts could greatly enhance and benefit the surrounding businesses and indeed the entire downtown.

OWNERSHIP OF HISTORIC VISION

The city official interviewed discussed a significant lack of ownership in the historic revitalization vision, on the part of residents, merchants and city officials. Creating a vision and mission statement and more specific historic goals for Astoria could be one way to eliminate confusion and create ownership. Involving key stakeholders in this process is critical to achieving a consensus and the necessary actions to realize the overall historical vision.

SEASIDE, OR

Seaside, Oregon is located 79 miles west of Portland along the north central coastal region, seventeen miles south of the Washington border. Seaside boasts of being a quintessential beach resort community with a population of 5,750 (ODOT 1997). The official end of the Lewis and Clark Trail,[1] the city is nestled in a region full of historic sites, historic forts, and museums. Retail trade employs the majority of Seaside residents, which also has a large retirement community.

REVITALIZATION GOALS AND EFFORTS

Seaside's revitalization efforts began in 1984 under the state's urban renewal legislation. The program was funded by the Seaside City Council through tax increment financing and state grants. The overall themes of the early revitalization were to increase the city's tourist capacity and appeal. Increasing the city's capacity for tourists required adding new water and sewer lines to the downtown area, as well as the reconstruction and enhancement of sidewalks, pedestrian crossings, and several downtown building foundations. Seaside also increased the number and condition of restrooms accessible to the public. The city's existing public restrooms were remodeled and new restroom facilities were built at several additional locations.

Once the city was able to accommodate a larger number of tourists, the focus of the revitalization effort shifted to transforming the downtown from a place where tourists simply visited for the afternoon to a place where they wanted to stay. Initial beautification of the downtown area included pedestrian kiosks, benches, flowers and trees—places where people would sit down, relax and enjoy themselves. This beautification effort also included the creation of stairways and paths to the beach, in an effort to make the beach a part of the downtown.

CHALLENGES AND OBSTACLES TO REVITALIZATION

Learning from Participation and Experience

One of the major obstacles to revitalization was a lack of experience. Several of the challenges encountered by the city provided learning opportunities for further revitalization efforts. Some of the city's lessons were learned the hard way, through trial and error. The city found that citizen involvement is crucial to advancing effort. Once downtown merchants were involved in the planning process through weekly meetings over breakfast, the atmosphere became more cooperative and the city was able to move forward with revitalization in a timely manner.

Seaside also encountered challenges in finding a cost effective yet trustworthy construction bid process. Forced to take the lowest bid by State mandate, the city was not aware that the bidders could be prequalified before the bidding actually began. This lesson was a costly one for the City of Seaside, since it is now faced with replacing poor quality work done by unqualified bidders. Careful planning can also mean saving vital dollars. During the city's downtown revitalization efforts, the city attorney missed an important city ordinance prohibiting the construction of any structure that would obstruct the view of the ocean at the end of the downtown's promenade. The city built a new public restroom facility at the end of the promenade and was sued by local property owners, who won the suit. Removal of the restroom facility combined with legal fees cost the city an estimated $100,000.

Citizen Involvement

The chairman of the city's Urban Renewal District from 1984 through 1992, indicated that citizen involvement is key to any revitalization effort, especially when merchants or other property owners are concerned. According to him, weekly informational meetings at the Pig n' Pancake Restaurant saved a great deal of time and effort. Letting people know what's going on is the key to reducing disagreements.

Interactions with the State

According to one city official, the city is now discussing plans with the Oregon Department of Transportation to create a traffic loop around Seaside. The traffic loop will be instrumental in eliminating the need for residents to cross Highway 101, the main north-south highway along Oregon's coast. City officials are not concerned that the traffic loop will dissuade tourists from entering downtown, since Seaside's downtown currently lies several blocks west of Highway 101. The city official indicated, as did officials in other study communities, that ODOT is often an obstacle rather than a partner in solving transportation challenges. Whatever the outcome, future efforts will be financed through the city's tax base in an effort to limit ODOT's involvement.

LESSONS AND RECOMMENDATIONS

Success

Of its many efforts, Seaside considers Quatat Park as a major success. Quatat Park was built on the Necanicum River next to the city's new convention center. It continues to be one of the most popular revitalization projects. Citizens and tourists alike find the park a nice place to enjoy concerts, picnics and other functions sponsored by the Seaside Chamber of Commerce. The park requires low maintenance and has raised valuable dollars for the city over the past ten years.

Projects for the Future

In recent years, the City of Seaside has witnessed a decline in the social and economic health of its downtown. According to the city's interviewee, most Seaside residents avoid the downtown area for a number of reasons. Seaside's downtown area currently has primarily tourist-type shops that are of little appeal to Seaside residents. The city is also having trouble retaining downtown merchants. Larger, upscale, retail chains that offer a wider selection of goods are coming to Seaside and locating outside the downtown area, drawing business from downtown. Adding to what might be considered urban sprawl, a large discount mall outlet was recently built towards the north end of Seaside several miles from downtown.

Currently, the city's focus is on its bridges. All five of Seaside's bridges over the Necanicum River need to be replaced or repaired. Replacing the city's bridges will also aid in keeping Seaside resident-friendly by increasing traffic flow.

Social and Economic Health

Seaside's downtown has several vacant buildings and the beginnings of a "run-down" atmosphere. According to city officials, out-of-state landlords charge extremely high rent for downtown building space. High rental rates and absentee landlords can be two reasons why there are vacancies downtown, giving it a blighted appearance. The social and economic health of Seaside's downtown needs serious attention from the city council and from the city's residents. Recognizing a failing downtown is the first step in dealing with its social and economic problems. The citizens of Seaside enjoy participating in the city's revitalization efforts, and their involvement may be critical to finding a solution to the downtown's failing health.

Seaside also has trouble with vandalism. Seaside draws a younger crowd that has become very unruly during school vacation. Greater police involvement could make the downtown area more user-friendly and safer for its residents. Residents joining with police can create crime-watch groups or community policing programs to maintain a safe downtown. The first priority should be making the downtown area more user-friendly and safe for residents.

Conclusions

The challenges faced by these small rural Oregon cities are not unlike the challenges encountered by other cities across America. So many are in transition due to economic, social, and other changes. Unfortunately this transition process frequently has negative consequences for a community's downtown. It is unfortunate that there is no readily available information designed for use by smaller cities interested in downtown revitalization. Much existing information focuses on larger cities with populations in the hundreds of thousands to millions. There is a general lack of documentation of downtown revitalization processes in smaller non metropolitan communities, regardless of success or failure. Whether it is possible to develop a best practices model applicable to the small city downtown redevelopment context from such information is a question which has yet to be answered empirically. In addition, in small towns there is also a general lack of available resources in the human, fiscal, and organizational capacities, in particular, to assist in the successful application of whatever we do know about "what to do" and "how to do it".

As presented earlier in this chapter, we have some very good ideas about *what* needs to be done in order for successful downtown redevelopment to take place. Critical are widespread involvement; a consensus over vision, mission, and goals among key stakeholders; and the willingness *and* ability to undertake the actions necessary to achieve successful implementation of redevelopment strategies. What we lack is guidance about *how* best to accomplish these tasks.

For example, what is usually missing is any discussion of leadership. Clearly, in most communities catalytic leaders are needed to help facilitate con-

sensus building among divergent interests and the development of working partnerships (Luke 1998). Catalytic leaders are also needed to build support for
action and to motivate key stakeholders to undertake agreed upon strategies, to
evaluate results, to learn from success or failure, and to continue the process.
According to Luke (1998), catalytic leaders assist communities in dealing with
one of their most critical challenges: How to provide effective leadership to
address interconnected problems with a reduction in fiscal resources, a lack of
consensus on options, and involvement of many diverse, independent minded
stakeholders? This is the key challenge in most community problem solving
efforts and as our cases indicate, a very critical one in dealing with the issue of
downtown redevelopment.

Development of the skills necessary for effective catalytic leadership would
be a useful intervention in most small communities, assuming, of course, interest. In Oregon, Rural Development Initiatives is one nonprofit organization
which has tried to develop such capacity along with assisting communities with
strategic planning. What they have learned, of course, is that most small communities not only lack leadership capacity but also the financial and organizational capacity to undertake actions agreed upon in their strategic planning
process in a manner that leads to effective problem solving. We have seen this
repeatedly in the case study cities with the notable exception of Cannon Beach.
Hit-and-miss, discontinuous incrementalism characterizes most city efforts in the
downtown redevelopment area. There have been lots of ideas, implementation of
some, and, lots more to do, but no consensus on what to do or how to proceed!

One of the key reasons for this approach is the lack of consensus on an overarching future vision. Communities need a longer term perspective, such as sustainability, to help them integrate and guide problem solving actions. One that
motivates action toward a critical future goal. According to Nozick (1992), the
goals of sustainable community development include: (i) building communities
that are more self-supporting and which can sustain and regenerate themselves
through economic self-reliance, community control, and environmentally sound
development; and (ii) building communities worth preserving because they are
grounded in the life experiences of people who live in them and in the natural
histories of specific regions. Catalytic leaders can assist communities to develop
such a vision and also to undertake the action necessary to assure its achievement. It is an ongoing process that requires looking at a community holistically;
integrating environmental, economic, and social concerns; and not undertaking
actions in the present which put future generations at risk (Downes 1995). It is a
process that views downtown redevelopment as one very important component
of a much larger, sustainable community development process.

References

Downes, Bryan T. (1995).*Toward Sustainable Communities: Lessons From the Canadian Experience.* Willamette Law Review 31,2: 359-401.

Luke, Jeffrey S. 1998. *Catalytic Leadership: Strategies for an Interconnected World.* San Francisco: Jossey-Bass Publishers.

Muller, Edward K. 1980. "Distinctive Downtown." *Geographical Magazine*, 52, 8: 747-755.

National Trust for Historic Preservation. 1988. *Revitalizing Downtown 1976-1986.* Washington, D.C.: National Trust for Historic Preservation in Association with the Urban Institute.

National Trust for Historic Preservation. 1987. *Mainstreet Guidelines: Public Improvements on Main Street.* Washington, D.C.: National Trust for Historic Preservation.

Nozick, Marcia. 1992. *No Place Like Home: Building Sustainable Communities.* Ottawa: Canadian Council on Social Development.

OEDD, 1999. www.OregonEconomicDevelopmentDepartment.or.us.

ODOT, 1997. www.OregonDepartmentofTransportation.or.us.

Palma, Dolores and Doyle Hyett. 1997. Born again: Downtown Revivals Offer Salvation for Cities. *American City and Country* 112,8: 26.

Robertson, Kent A. 1995. "Downtown Redevelopment in the United States: an End-of-the-Century Assessment," *Journal of the American Planning Association* 61,4: 429-438.

Smith, Kennedy. 1991. *Revitalizing Downtown.* Washington D.C.: National Trust for Historic Preservation.

Wagner, Fritz W., Timothy E. Joder, and Anthony J. Mumphrey, Jr. 1995. *Urban Revitalization: Policies and Programs.* Thousand Oaks: Sage Publications.

Wagner, Richard, Ted Miller and Paul Write. 1998. *Revitalizing Downtown: 1976-1986.* Historic Preservation Forum: National Trust for Historic Preservation.

Winterbottom, Bert. 1997. Maybe Your Downtown Needs a Report Card,? *Public Management* 79, 6: 12–19.

END NOTE

1. The official Lewis and Clark National Historic Trail is approximately 3,700 miles long, begins near Wood River, Illinois, and passes through portions of Missouri, Kansas, Iowa, Nebraska, South Dakota, North Dakota, Montana, Idaho, Washington, and ending in Oregon.

CHAPTER 6

A Multifaceted Approach to Downtown Revitalization in Brandon, Canada

WILLIAM R. HORNE

The City of Brandon, like its counterparts in the U.S. has witnessed the flight of businesses from its central core to the fringe. As a consequence, the city adopted a multifaceted approach to try and revitalize the downtown. In this example, the local merchants organized as a Business Improvement Area (BIA) and identified eight areas of concern which needed to be rectified to revitalize the downtown. This chapter examines the activities of the BIA between 1987 and 1999, identifies some of the successes and discusses the organization's shortcomings.

Brandon, Manitoba was selected because it is typical of free standing cities across the Great Plains. The city has a 1999 population of just over 40,000 with a surrounding agricultural population of about 60,000 in its primary service area. The closest larger cities are Winnipeg (655,000), 120 miles to the east, and Regina (200,000), 220 miles to the west. Brandon is the second largest city in Manitoba and there are no other cities over 30,000 in the province.

Brandon's history has similarities with many other North American cities, thus the solutions discussed here may be of value in other locations and are presented with this end in mind. The author has resided in Brandon for the past ten years, thus this report benefits from personal observation as well as the referenced material, much of which was supplied by the BIA.

Background

A detailed history of the city can be found in Welsted, Everitt and Stadel (1988). Brandon was founded in 1881 by the Canadian Pacific Railway as a divisional point on the trans-continental railway. The railway follows the south side of the Assiniboine River valley. The town site was a rectangle south of the tracks. Pacific Avenue runs parallel to the tracks between two previously surveyed township road allowances which run north-south, one mile apart. These were designated First Street and Eighteenth Street. Even today, the only bridges across both the tracks and the river are on these two streets. The rail yard was built east of First Street. The fourth side of the rectangle was an existing east-west road allowance, Victoria Avenue, about half a mile south of Pacific. The rectangle was then divided into 85 blocks with 16 additional north-south streets (Second to Seventeenth Streets) and four additional east-west streets (Rosser, Princess, Lorne and Louise Avenues).

The community grew quickly as a trans-shipment point for wheat from the surrounding agricultural area. Within a decade, it was known as the "wheat city" and it became the major service center in the southwestern corner of the province (Lehr 1997). Pacific Avenue was lined with grain elevators, warehouses and industrial buildings. One block south, Rosser Avenue developed as the main commercial street. The station was at the foot of Tenth Street and the corner of Rosser and Tenth became the peak value intersection. The original city hall, court house and fire hall were built a further block south on Princess Avenue. Large homes developed south of this, particularly along Victoria, with working class housing filling in the southeast and southwest corners of the rectangle. By the turn of the century development was approaching the edges of this rectangle.

Some early institutions were built outside of the rectangle. A large Mental Hospital was constructed east of First Street on the North side of the Assiniboine River in 1891. Brandon College (now Brandon University) was built on the west side of Eighteenth Street at Lorne in 1901. In 1910, a fire at the hospital led to the construction of a building on the Exhibition Grounds which were over a mile south of Victoria between Thirteenth and Eighteenth Streets (Refvik 1991). This later became the site of the Keystone Centre, the largest sports and entertainment facility in the city. Railways in competition with the Canadian Pacific Railroad (CPR) built lines just south of the city with yards east of First Street. This encouraged industrial and residential growth between Victoria Avenue and the Exhibition Grounds.

The construction of six miles of streetcar lines which operated between 1913 and 1932 encouraged expansion of the city (Welsted *et al* 1988). The city took on the characteristic 'T' shape of many railway towns, east-west along Rosser Avenue and north-south along Tenth Street (Lehr 1997).

The city grew slowly during the depression and war years but after 1947, as with many cities, the arrival of the motor car led to further spatial expansion. The city had expanded about a mile east, south and west of the original rectangle by 1960. To the east of First Street development was primarily industrial activities and working class housing. The area south of Victoria Avenue was a mix of industrial, commercial, and mixed residential areas. West of Eighteenth Street the majority of the development was middle and upper middle income housing. Growth to the north was slowed by the river valley until the Trans-Canada Highway by-pass was constructed in 1958 just over two miles north of Pacific Avenue. Victoria Avenue, First and Eighteenth Streets provided connections from the highway to the city. Eighteenth Street became part of the provincial highway route to the United States border, while Victoria Avenue and First Street formed a business loop for the Trans-Canada highway.

As early as 1967 a report described the downtown as "showing signs of decay and obsolescence which reduce its effectiveness and threaten to stifle its future growth and very existence" (Underwood, McLelland and Associates 1967, 69). Typical of many cities, the desire to cater to cars had created a poor environment for pedestrians, yet such a design also failed to meet the parking and delivery needs of vehicles. Further, it was clear the buildings were expensive to upgrade to modern building standards.

During the next decade there was considerable discussion about downtown renewal but little action. An overly ambitious 1971 proposal called for Rosser Avenue to be covered over from Sixth to Tenth Street and rooftop parking to be provided. No action was taken on this plan as no developer could be found (City of Brandon 1971).

The following year, a proposal for a multi-level, multi-functional mall with cultural facilities, a hotel, apartments and offices in addition to shopping and parking was made (Hlynski 1972). This proposal did not result in any action either. Even when a consulting firm came up with a similar proposal to counter the problems of too much surface parking, too many vacant lots, and too many empty buildings creating too dispersed a commercial area that looked rundown and neglected, no action was taken (Damas and Smith 1975).

It was not until 1980 that a downtown mall, known as the Brandon Gallery, finally became a reality. Located on Rosser between Seventh and Ninth it had retail space and above ground parking but none of the extras that had been envisioned. The project came about only after the city assembled the land and leased it to the developers for $1 for 99 years (Welsted, *et. al.* 1988).

During this same decade, suburban commercial development was booming. A K-Mart and grocery store mall was built at Victoria and Thirty Fourth Street in 1971. Car dealerships, service stations and hotels also lined this section of Victoria. A major suburban mall, the Shoppers Mall, was built south of the Exhibition Grounds and on the opposite side of Eighteenth Street in 1972. Over the next decade Eighteenth Street south of Victoria became two miles of strip commercial development with a full range of services. Commercial activity on Eighteenth north of Pacific and along the Trans-Canada highway developed later in the decade and was primarily highway oriented hotels and restaurants along with car, truck, and farm vehicle dealerships.

A business driven city council sent mixed messages. While a new city hall was built in the downtown and other government buildings developed, a performance theater was built next to Brandon University and the Keystone Centre was developed. Suburban commercial growth particularly on Eighteenth Street and Victoria Avenue also continued and was spurred on by new housing developments in the south and west of the city. Indeed, in 1972, the city expanded its boundaries north and south to capture the industrial and commercial growth taking place in the urban fringe (Welsted *et. al.* 1988).

The City of Brandon Development Plan identified similar problems and called for the downtown area to be restricted in size, physically upgraded, and improved with government and residential development. At the same time, it called for restriction on suburban commercial development, both in size and type, including a moratorium on new malls until 1994. The Plan also recommended a development committee funded by business taxes.

While the city council passed these laws it ignored the spirit of them. The city built a new Sportsplex pool and rink north of the Assiniboine River in 1979, approved expansion of the Keystone Centre in 1981 and constructed a professional baseball stadium in the river valley in 1984 (Horne 1998). The council also allowed a significant addition to the Shoppers Mall in 1981 and construction of a significant number of strip commercial developments throughout the decade. These were under the designated size limit of the zoning laws and were mostly along Eighteenth Street and Victoria Avenue. Most of these housed national franchise outlets.

The 1977 Plan envisioned the development of the downtown to continue with redevelopment of the two blocks west of the Gallery by 1991. This was to be followed by development of the Rosser to Pacific blocks between Seventh and Tenth Streets. Other surrounding blocks would then be developed. The developments west of the mall did not happen and other proposals fell behind schedule. All of this development relied on the efforts of private capital which did not have confidence in the potential return.

In 1985 the city council decided to make a concerted effort to revitalize the downtown. The council had planned to apply for federal grants available to assist with main street redevelopment design and to ask the province for funding. However, it was discovered that Brandon was not eligible for the necessary provincial grants. Manitoba's capital city, Winnipeg, which is 17 times larger than Brandon is considered by the provincial government to be the only city that qualified. Brandon could therefore only apply for grants available to rural communities. However, the city was too large to use these grants effectively. Although the city was prepared to designate its tax funds for downtown development, without external, provincial, financial aid the redevelopment could not happen. After twenty years of discussion the downtown had seen limited development and was still at risk due to continued growth of suburban shopping, new recreational facilities and more distant residential subdivisions (Maggiacomo 1998).

Organizing the Merchants

The downtown merchants were, however, unwilling to see the redevelopment idea die. They independently organized themselves as a Business Improvement Area comprising the original 85 block area of the city. Each business in the area became a member of the BIA including retail, wholesale, industrial and professional service firms. A Board of Management composed of six members elected for a three year term and two appointed city councillors was constituted. The manager of the Brandon Gallery, President of the Chamber of Commerce, and President of the Economic Development Board were made ex officio board members. Recognizing that much of the area had non-commercial activities, membership was opened to representatives of other groups as non-paying members, including: 18 agencies of the three levels of government that have offices in the area, 46 non-profit organizations from those with a small office such as the Arthritis Society to the YMCA with its large pool and sports facility, and the 10 churches in the area. The BIA also encouraged the formation of resident associations in the apartment buildings and neighborhood areas within the BIA and offered membership to these groups. In this way, the BIA included everyone who lived or worked within its boundaries. This gave the BIA a much louder political voice to push for its needs over those of other parts of the city (BIA 1997a; BIA 1998a).

The BIA oversees the Business Improvement Area Revitalization Plan the goal of which is to improve business opportunities by marketing the downtown and by making improvements to the physical environment. This latter objective involves financing the improvement of public space and assisting private developers in improving their properties via advice and assistance in obtaining available grants. These objectives can be further broken down as will be discussed below. The BIA recognizes that a multifaceted approach to the revitalization of the downtown is needed and that these efforts must be coordinated. An office manager and support staff were hired. Ongoing surveys of members on a wide variety of issues are used to prioritize activities (BIA 1998i; BIA 1998j).

Financing this activity was the first concern. The BIA began by arranging for the municipal government to give up a portion of its tax revenue. BIA business members now pay 2 percent of their business tax assessment, which is based on square footage, towards this project. The 450 paying members contribute from $10 to $4,000 annually. The total contributions are about $150,000 annually. To add to its funds, the BIA has lobbied the provincial government to change legislation so that they can apply for more substantial grants (Maggiacomo 1998). The following sections detail the various activities of the BIA, their successes and failures.

Marketing Efforts

The BIA began its program with an effort to promote awareness of the downtown and thus bring shoppers back to the area. One of the members of the BIA is the local daily newspaper. Using its facilities and distribution network, the BIA produces a tabloid flyer in March, August and November (Maggiacomo 1998). Originally a sixteen-page, two-color product, it has been changed to eight pages in full color. Issues usually have a theme related to upcoming events. Space is also devoted to news of business changes in the area. All issues provide a list of BIA members by type of service offered. The circulation is estimated at 35,600 across the city's trade area (BIA 1998j). This ongoing publication is supplemented by other informational material.

Special Events

Creating events to draw people to the downtown was the next step. This began
with the re-establishment of the Santa Clause Parade. The major problem is the
weather. Even in late November the temperatures can be well below freezing.
Therefore, there are no bands and the route is short. It begins at Victoria and
Sixth, goes north to Rosser, west to Thirteenth and back to Victoria. This event
now brings an estimated ten thousand people into the downtown. The parade is
financed through the sale of Santa hats (BIA 1997c; BIA 1998h).

Working on this success, the BIA organized a fall street fair. Many of the
small towns in the area have corn and apple harvest festivals. Brandon wanted
something similar yet unique. The BIA created the International Pickle Festival.
This event began in Princess Park and has expanded into the neighboring Gallery
and onto Tenth Street and Rosser Avenue, with six blocks now closed for the
weekend. Events include the traditional fall fair; judging of baked goods and
vegetables including relishes, games for children including pickle putting, live
music, displays and demonstrations, and outdoor food including "a pickle for a
nickel". Most of the events are free of charge and prizes and gifts are given away.
Not surprisingly, significant funding for this event was obtained from Bick's
Pickles (BIA 1996a; BIA 1997d; BIA 1998f).

Many stores use the opportunity for sidewalk sales. The closure of the streets
allows pedestrians to wander about freely and see the new stores that have
opened. It also encourages a park and walk mentality. A survey showed retailers
like the increase in traffic due to the Pickle Festival and would like to see it
expanded further. Some businesses which did not participate in 1998 indicated
they would participate in 1999 (BIA 1998g) A merchant committee has been
formed to co-ordinate business participation and coordinate activities on each
block.

The purpose of these downtown events is to generate customers and the BIA
would like to have staff volunteers in each business to keep the BIA aware of
what is happening. For example, a BIA survey indicated that more washrooms
and after event cleanup were concerns. Another survey showed strong support
for more events (BIA 1998g). The plan for the future is continued growth of
existing events and the introduction of a new signature event (BIA 1998i). Any
new event would probably take place in the spring.

Streetscaping

Once people have been attracted to the downtown they must have a positive experience if they are to return. The first element of that experience is a pleasant environment. A major undertaking of the BIA has therefore been the redevelopment of
the public space in the downtown. The aim of this streetscaping is to make it more
attractive and pedestrian friendly, and secondly to create an image for
the area.

This project began with the planting of up to nine mature trees on each block along the main streets. Beginning in the center of town, over a number of years all of Rosser and Princess Avenues and those north-south streets which did not have any existing trees were completed. Most of the primarily residential blocks have existing mature trees. In addition to improving the aesthetics, the trees also provide shade on the sidewalks and reduce the wind speeds at ground level, a common problem in plains cities.

It was then decided to develop a heritage theme in the core area. Street signs along the length of Rosser and Princess Avenues were replaced with slightly larger signs in green and yellow, the city colors, with a wheat sheaf, the city emblem, on each sign. Rosser Avenue from Eleventh to Sixth Street received further improvements. The standard concrete sidewalks were replaced with decorative concrete with a wheat sheaf pattern. Some parking spaces were replaced with wrought iron benches. Matching garbage containers, fencing and antique fire hydrants were installed. The streets were then resurfaced. Low level heritage street lamps were installed. The lamp posts are designed to support hanging flower baskets in summer, and banners, ribbons and Christmas lighting in colder months. The BIA is responsible for these seasonal decorations (Maggiacomo 1998). In 1995 Brandon won a national award for "enthusiastic and innovative street scaping" from *Communities in Bloom.*

Vacant land on Princess and Tenth was converted to Princess Park in 1970. In 1997 this was improved with the construction of a fountain and seating. In 1998 the construction of a performance stage utilizing heritage stone and incorporating a mix of seating added to the attractiveness of this space (BIA 1998d). Improvements to residential streets are next on the BIA's list of projects. A further purpose of these improvements is to attract private investment into the area and to encourage existing land owners to improve their properties. This was the next concern of the BIA.

Storefront Improvements

The improvement of public space had to be linked to improvements in the private space. The BIA obtained provincial government funding for a ten-year Storefront Improvement Program during which 71 businesses improved their façades. The BIA encouraged merchants to use its heritage theme and continues to offer design advice on structures and materials to encourage further development of this. A building which makes up about half of the seven hundred block of Rosser Avenue, for example, has had a heritage brick façade constructed which harmonizes the stores and offices it contains (BIA 1997f). Work on Tenth Street continues almost a decade behind the original plans, slowed by an inability to attract new tenants to the ground floor commercial space. Further from the center of town, two large derelict "heritage" buildings on Rosser have been condemned but have not been removed because the owners can not be found. In

1999 the City Council organized a heritage committee to identify and catalogue all of the heritage structures in Brandon with the intent of identifying those worth preserving and developing heritage tourism (Molnar 1999).

In 1998 merchants were encouraged to put up Christmas lighting and decorate their windows. The best display using the products of the business in a Christmas theme was offered a prize of 250 words about the store in *Discover Downtown Brandon* and one hundred dollars towards a staff party at any downtown restaurant (Maggiacomo 1998). In summer, businesses are encouraged to add hanging plants to their walls.

Sign regulations controlling sandwich boards, overhanging signs, murals, and canopies have been produced (BIA 1998c). Generally, these call for small, plain signs which do not overpower the streetscape, or block neighboring stores.

Traffic and Parking

Parking is always a problem in downtowns. Working with the city and Police Service, the BIA continues to accept comments about parking, loading zones, bus stops, and safety issues (BIA 1997b; BIA 1997c). As part of the new streetscaping, a number of parking spaces had been removed and others were converted into fifteen minute loading zones so that on-street parking was reduced. The closure of the railway station allowed the BIA to obtain a large lot at Pacific and Tenth Street. The city encourages downtown workers to park here and has installed plug-ins for car heaters during cold weather. A number of small vacant lots on Rosser and Princess were purchased by the BIA and developed into off street lots closer to the shops. These have been paved, fenced, and planted to fit into the streetscaping. All of the main blocks have back alleys and local merchants have been encouraged to make similar improvements to the lots behind their properties to increase parking spaces. People tend not to use this space because the unimproved visual appearance suggests that it is not safe. This request has met with limited success except for a small number of businesses which have included such improvements as part of building developments. The city persuaded the downtown mall to stop charging for parking in its two floor arcade and this made a significant improvement to the parking situation. The city also agreed to make the remaining on-street parking free after four o'clock on weekdays and all day on weekends and to remove 65 parking meters on the downtown fringe. The parking enforcement officers have been instructed to be polite (Maggiacomo 1998).

Still to be developed is a municipal bus station. At the moment, the first block of Eighth Street is closed to traffic and all city buses stop along it but the drivers do not like this. The BIA is facilitating discussions between the drivers and local merchants to identify alternatives.

Street Safety

Despite the rundown visual appearance of the downtown area, serious crime has never been a problem. A survey of local merchants indicated that their main concern about safety was panhandlers. A storefront police station has been opened at the bus station. The new street lights greatly increase the brightness of sidewalks after dark. Burned out lights, broken tree branches, and the build up of snow in the winter were mentioned by merchants as things which they felt worked against a safe atmosphere.

Business Development

Once consumers have been attracted to the downtown, there must be something for them to purchase. Merchants have expressed concerns about the mix of activities in the downtown and their target markets. What exactly is in the downtown and whether or not it is desirable is difficult to ascertain. For example, ground level and upper level uses are often different. Table 8 provides a listing of business types and their proportion in downtown Brandon.

Table 8: Downtown Businesses by Sector

Type of Business	Proportion in Downtown	Type of Business	Proportion in Downtown
Retail	20%	Media/Printers	8%
Government	18%	Automotive	8%
Prof. Services	11%	Entertainment	8%
Financial	9%	Churches	3 %
Medical	8%	Contractors	2%
Restaurants	8%	Others	1%

Source: Author

This table does not provide information on the non-commercial uses, including residential property, schools, and parkland. Most of this use is outside of the downtown core but it has effects on future expansion. Most of the houses on Ninth and Tenth Streets have been converted to commercial activities and similar changes could occur on other blocks. Schools and parks provide barriers to such change in the southwest and south east corners of the BIA area. This data may also exclude home based businesses in the area.

The merchant lobby has been able to persuade the city to restrict yard sales and put heavy licence fees on craft fairs and home based businesses. Local music teachers were one group who protested strongly against this restraint of trade.

As mentioned earlier, there is a considerable amount of vacant land in the BIA area. Some of this is used for unimproved parking. These areas need to be either improved or developed.

The table does not also reflect the industrial and warehouse land uses, especially along Pacific Ave. These activities reflect the historical development of the city and some feel they are inappropriate to a modern commercial area. This is a situation typical of many cities whose early growth was influenced by the railway. The BIA hopes to see some of these buildings converted to commercial uses (Maggiacomo 1998).

Within the retail category there are a number of concerns with respect to the mix. Merchants want complementary services in neighboring stores. They also want businesses which attract higher income shoppers and shoppers from more distant locations. Commercial vacancies and too many businesses which cater to the low income resident population are seen as less desirable. Vacancy rates at the Gallery have generally been higher than at the Shoppers Mall. In contrast to business desires, many local residents do not want to see drug stores and discount clothing stores replaced by craft shops and boutiques.

A BIA survey indicated 70% of respondents had located in the downtown because it met their locational requirements. Among the reasons given were that they felt their client base was already there and they felt it was a central location providing good visibility and accessibility with walk-in traffic. In addition they were close to other services that complimented their business. Some mentioned owning their own building, finding affordable space and liking the heritage theme (BIA 1998j). These results reflect the differences between merchants with local market areas and those with large ones. It also suggests that the BIA investment in street scaping has had some effect.

The automotive businesses mentioned in the table are mostly parts suppliers. Service stations are located along the edge of the BIA area on First and Eighteenth Streets and Victoria Avenue.

The three levels of government have provided capital investment in new buildings and continue to provide a considerable amount of employment in the downtown area. This in turn supports the large number of restaurants. However, they take up space which separates the commercial businesses. Two blocks of provincial and local government offices along Ninth Street divide the Rosser-Princess commercial area from that along Victoria Avenue.

The BIA supports both businesses and property owners in maximizing use of downtown land and buildings. At least five inquiries for space per week reach the office. Most are looking for space, new business ventures or property to buy (BIA 1998j). The BIA also links businesses and entrepreneurs to agencies that assist business development in the form of financing and business plan support services such as the Economic Development Board, Manitoba Department of Industry, Federal Business Development Bank, and Community Futures program (Horne 1989).

Merchants surveyed (BIA 1998j) would like to see a healthy mix of upscale specialty stores to offset the growth of bargain and discount stores. Four grand openings in the fall of 1998 were typical of the types of businesses being attracted to the downtown. Impressions and Party Supplies, Contract Solutions, a new pharmacy and McGilligan's Books are all new independent businesses. There is a lack of upscale franchise stores particularly in the clothing sector. In the downtown mall, Zellers, the anchor discount store, was converted to Best Value, a store that sells discount clothing and housewares.

The BIA obtained a vacant store and converted it into an incubator unit to encourage home based businesses to become retailers. Entrepreneurs considering going into retailing can obtain a small amount of floor space on a short term lease to try their idea. Provision for the sharing of office equipment has been made. When Prairie Lanes opened in 1998 it contained twenty small businesses primarily selling specialty goods and gifts.

The announcement that the largest store in the downtown, Eaton's, would close in the summer of 2000 created serious concerns. This is the anchor store for the Gallery mall, which in recent years has been suffering from a high vacancy rate. A 1999 account reported a 48% vacancy rate and revealed that Best Value had a clause in their lease that would allow them to pull out if Eaton's closed (Nickel 1999a). The Eaton's decision, as with the closure of Zellers, was made by corporate headquarters to meet company objectives and did not reflect the success of the local stores or their importance to downtown Brandon. One of the downtown movie theaters was also closed in 1999 to be replaced by a multiplex at the Shoppers Mall. This is an ongoing problem over which the BIA has no control or influence.

New businesses on Eighteenth Street opposite Brandon University have recently opened. Although these are within the BIA area, they appear to be more of an extension of the strip commercial activity along this street than part of the downtown development. Of note, the architecture of the buildings blends in well with neighboring residential buildings.

Residential Development

The BIA supports the concept of increasing the residential population of the area. Two new senior citizen homes have been built at either end of Rosser Avenue by local service clubs and a third is located on the east side of First Street at Victoria, just outside the BIA area. These add to two existing government seniors' buildings and have significantly influenced the composition of the population in terms of age and income. Young singles, including university students tend to live in houses converted to flats on Sixteenth and Seventeenth Streets. Unlike many North American cities, Brandon did not go through a period of significant gentrification, thus upper income housing in the BIA area is quite limited. A walking tour of the residential area highlighting these homes has been developed.

Thus the BIA would like to encourage improvements to the visual appearance of the residential streets. Efforts to improve the second stories of downtown buildings to increase residential development have seen little success as yet as the costs are generally prohibitive. A proposal to convert an old factory, on the corner of Pacific and Eighteenth, into condominiums, fell through when the developers could not get provincial grants similar to those which they had obtained in Winnipeg (Nickel 1999b).

A Part of the Community

The BIA has not tried to isolate itself from the remainder of the city. The city has entered the national Communities in Bloom Competition each year and the floral displays on the streets and buildings of the downtown are an important part of this city-wide event. The BIA offers a "Best Bloomin' Business" award (BIA 1998b). In 1998 the city won a special mention for community involvement from *Communities in Bloom.*

Each summer, the Travellers Day parade is a major local event. It begins on Rosser Avenue and winds its way south to the Keystone Centre fair grounds as part of the summer fair. The BIA has also been supportive of efforts to improve the Assiniboine River valley as a major recreational area. This parkland is just north of the downtown. A pedestrian bridge over the Assiniboine at Eighth Street was opened in 1998 potentially improving communication between the residential area north of the river and the downtown, at least in the summer months (Wallace 1996).

Conclusion

After twenty years of indecision, the merchants were organized into a Business Improvement Area with an elected management board. The BIA was able to obtain the support of the city to finance improvements via business taxation. A redevelopment program was established to improve the public property. The BIA attempted to assist private developers to bring their property up to the standard of the revitalized public space.

The BIA has been able to significantly improve the appearance of the downtown streets making it a pleasant place to shop. These improvements have also given it a more unified image and atmosphere of safety. Improvements in parking have helped to overcome one of the major advantages of suburban shopping areas. People are willing to come to the downtown for special events such as parades and the Pickle Festival.

Much of the public work has been completed. Thus most of the remaining improvements are in the hands of the private sector where the economic return on such improvements must be considered. Despite the physical changes, the downtown has had limited success in providing new shopping opportunities. Many of the stores are local operations and there is a lack of big name national chains to draw in customers from suburban and rural areas. This is a problem because the downtown residential population is both small and primarily low income. Decisions by such companies are made outside of the local area and are largely beyond the control of the BIA.

The unique position of Brandon within the province as the second largest community and yet not eligible for certain provincial grants given to the largest city has added to the problem of attracting new enterprises. The BIA acts as a lobby group for changes to this legislation but to date has had limited success, although it has been able to attract some federal money into the community.

The area immediately adjacent to the BIA has increased in commercial activity, especially the south side of Victoria Avenue and Tenth Street north of Victoria. Although the chair of the BIA was in favor of expansion of the BIA area to include this growth, the idea met with concern from the membership that this would spread the resources of the existing downtown area too thin (BIA 1998a). It must be hoped that this internal difference of opinion does not reduce the effectiveness of the BIA.

The degree of competition from the suburban area is another related factor. At the time of writing, the Shoppers Mall on Eighteenth Street was looking to expand again and two other developers have asked the city for approval to construct new malls at other locations on Eighteenth Street. Smaller developments continue to appear along Victoria Avenue and Eighteenth and this must be a worry for the BIA. The City Council, which is organized on a ward basis, has more members from the suburban area than from the downtown and continues to be reluctant to oppose the desires of higher income voters.

Improvements to the Keystone Centre in 1996 and the opening of a multiplex theater at the Shoppers Mall in 1999 further accent the limited entertainment facilities in the downtown. The closure of most downtown stores by six o'clock provides opportunities for suburban locations, which are generally open until nine o'clock, to obtain and potentially keep customers. Attracting customers to the downtown is therefore an ongoing challenge.

The deterioration of the downtown and the growth of suburbia is in no way unique to Brandon. The efforts to overcome this problem which this case study demonstrate may, therefore, be of interest to other communities. It is clear that unorganized redevelopment will meet with limited success. The bringing together of local merchants as a unified voice is important. The inclusion of other stakeholders in the area, such as the three levels of government, non-profit organizations, and residential associations increases the likelihood of success. Capital investment by such groups in the area will assist redevelopment.

This organization will only be successful if funding is available. Contributions by the municipal government, by returning a portion of taxes collected in the area to the area, may be the easiest source, but there is also a need to lobby for funds from upper levels of government. The presence of these funds should increase the probability of private sector investment in both improvements to buildings and the opening of new commercial establishments. A small staff, including someone with lobbying skills, will be required by the business association.

The downtown must compete with suburban malls. Thus it must look attractive, safe, and unified. It must also have adequate parking and smooth traffic flows. To a large extent such physical requirements involve the development of public space. Again, this will only happen if local tax payers are prepared to see their money spent in this manner.

The growth of suburban competition may be controlled better if the city council is elected at large rather than by wards. Growth beyond the municipal boundaries is more difficult to control although it may be of less significance in small, free standing cities than in large urban agglomerations.

Advertising and attractions are important in drawing people back to an area which they may not have considered a shopping destination for some time. Informing people of new stores which have opened is to the benefit of all of the merchants in the area. The BIA needs to employ someone with skills in advertising and marketing.

Another potential role for the merchants association is assisting new businesses to start up. This may include helping independent entrepreneurs find financing and providing data to support applications for franchise outlets. A good mix of stores is required to make the area a commercial success and this is often a problem.

Downtowns are generally viewed as the heart of the city, a heart in need of corrective surgery. The ideas presented here demonstrate that with proper planning and cooperation, action can be taken to prolong the life of the downtown.

References

Business Improvement Area. 1996a. "International Pickle Festival." *Discover Downtown Today.* V2.1.

_____ 1996b. "Young Entrepreneurs." *Discover Downtown Today.* V2.1, 4-6.

_____ 1997a. "BIA Announces Election of Executive Officers." *Discover Downtown Today.* V3.1,2.

_____ 1997b. "Downtown BIA Makes Bold Parking Changes." *Discover Downtown Today.* V3.2, 3.

_____ 1997c. "Downtown Parking." *Discover Downtown Today.* V3.2, 9.

_____ 1997d. "International Pickle Festival." *Discover Downtown Today.* V3.2.

_____ 1997e. "Let the Magic Begin." *Discover Downtown Today.* V3.4.

_____ 1997f. "Polsky Block Gets Facelift." *Discover Downtown Today.* V3.1,2.

_____ 1997g. "What Is Downtown?" *Discover Downtown Today.* V3.2.,3.

_____ 1998a. "BIA Board Elections." Downtown Alive. p2.

_____ 1998b. "Communities In Bloom." *Discover Downtown Today*. V4.1.

_____ [1998c]. "Design Ideas For New Signs In Downtown Brandon."

_____ 1998d. "Golden Shovel Event." *Discover Downtown Today*. V4.2, 9.

_____ 1998e. "Grand Openings Galore." *Discover Downtown Today*. V4.3, 2.

_____ 1998f. "International Pickle Festival." *Discover Downtown Today*. V4.2.

_____ 1998g. "Pickle Fest Survey Results." Downtown Alive. p3.

_____ 1998h. "Santa Parade '98." *Discover Downtown Today*. V4.3.

_____ 1998i. "What Does the BIA Do?" *Discover Downtown Today*. V4.3, 3.

_____ 1998j. "What Does Your BIA Do?" *Downtown Alive*. p3.

City of Brandon. 1971. "Rosser Avenue Mall Project." Brandon: City of Brandon Industrial Commission.

Damas and Smith. 1975. *Brandon Downtown Redevelopment Program*. Brandon: City of Brandon

Horne, W. R. 1989. "A Pre-feasibility Study for an Entrepreneurial Centre for the Wheatbelt Region." Unpublished report. Brandon: Westarc Inc.

Horne, W.R. 1998. "Economic Development Via Hallmark Tourism." Paper presented to the Canadian Institute of Planners. Winnipeg.

Lehr, John. 1997. "Western Interior: Transformation of a Hinterland Region." In *Heartland and Hinterland* 3rd ed., edited by Larry McCann and Angus Gunn. 269-329. Scarborough: Prentice Hall.

Maggiacomo, Carol. 1998. Personal Communication. Manager; Brandon BIA.

Molnar, Wendy. . 1999. "Heritage Tourism and the Westman Region." *Discover Downtown Today*. V4.3, 4-5.

Nickel, Rod. 1999a. "Best Value has Option to Exit Gallery." *Brandon Sun*. June 4.

Nickle, Rod. 1999b. "Developer scraps Condo Deal." *Brandon Sun*. June 28.

Refvik, Kurt. 1991. *A Centennial History of the Brandon Asylum*. Brandon: Brandon Mental Health Centre.

Underwood McLellan and Associates. 1967. *City of Brandon Urban Renewal Study* Winnipeg: Underwood McLelland and Associates.

Welsted, John, John Everitt, and Christoph Stadel, ed. 1988. *Brandon: Geographical Perspectives on the Wheat City*. Regina: Canadian Plains Research Center University of Regina.

Part Two

Urban Design and Infrastructure Redevelopment

CHAPTER 7

Re-engaging the Public in the Art of Community Place-Making

WENDY MCCLURE and FRED A. HURAND

Main Street was once the center of public life in small American towns. Unfortunately, these centers have lost their prominence in many communities. Several factors have contributed to the decline of downtown districts, but, foremost, is the lack of collective responsibility for their well being. The process of creating and maintaining meaningful public spaces is a shared responsibility requiring a culture of support from a diverse cross-section of the community including design professionals. According to Kuntsler (1993, 273):

> The culture of good place-making, like the culture of farming or agriculture, is a body of knowledge and acquired. Indulging in a fetish of commercialized individualism, we did away with the public realm, and with nothing left but private life we wonder what happened to the spirit of community.

As a culture, we have abdicated our collective responsibility for the public places that nurture community spirit. Citizens no longer assume the role of caretaker because it is not an ingrained cultural expectation. To restore economic well being and preserve historic continuity of downtown districts, it is necessary to first restore a culture of support. One strategy to nurture that custodial spirit is to engage citizens and civic leaders in the process of downtown design decision-making. This chapter will discuss the importance of citizen participation in the downtown revitalization process. Through case study examples specific strategies to involve citizens in downtown design and planning will be presented.

What is Participatory Design?

Participatory design, according to Fredrik Wultz is an umbrella term used to describe a variety of strategies for user involvement in design decision-making. Stages of involvement according to Wultz are lodged "between the poles of expert autonomous architecture (or planning) and user autonomous architecture (or planning)" (1990, 42). More traditional forms of participation place the professional designer clearly in charge of design decisions. For example, participants may be invited to review and comment on alternative design proposals prepared by professionals. In these cases participants play a relatively passive role in design. Concepts for participatory design outlined in this chapter are based on more radical user involvement and autonomy, strategies Wultz (1990) terms co-decision and self-decision or, as Altschuler notes (1970) planning with people rather than for them.

Community projects vary in scope from land use planning to individual building design. Participatory strategies can be successfully implemented for a variety of project types, requiring different resolutions of decision-making ranging from broad-based visioning to detailed, prescriptive solutions.

Why is Participatory Design Important?

A participatory design process serves a variety of valuable functions. Most importantly it enables citizen activists and civic leaders to build a broader base of support in the community. By participating in the design process citizens have more realistic expectations of project outcomes. Participants learn to believe in their town's potential. They also learn that well constructed visions for downtown improvements require strategies for phased implementation and sustained commitment (McClure, 1997). According to Texas Main Street architect Dick Ryan:

> There has been a long history of miracle approach failures-urban renewal, modernizing whole towns with slipcovers, streetscape improvements-any concept that meant all we had to do was one thing, and our problems would be solved. Now when we go into a community to assist them, they already realize they are entering a never-ending project and will have to work on hundreds of goals, not just one (Ryan1997, 27).

The importance of community participation in vision building cannot be overemphasized. "The out-of-town expert", usually an architect, landscape architect or a planning consultant, is too often hired to create a vision for the community when that vision, if it is to be supported by local citizens over the long haul, must be generated by the community itself. An architect for a downtown revitalization project in Desert Hot Springs California reaffirms the importance of citizen participation to avoid mismatched expectations between community clients and design professionals.

> The actual design of the project was a distant second to the requirement for participation and long-lived commitment by the locals. Our job really was to use pictures to give a vision and then get the community leaders to take that vision and make it their own (Hoenstein and Young 1987).

Visual Tools: Why Are They Important?

A participatory design process, to be effective, must be supported by tools that help citizens visualize problems and opportunities. Consultants trained in community design have the expertise to select appropriate participatory strategies and associated graphic material to enhance the general public's capacity for visualization.

During pre-design stages, visual information helps citizens to analyze their downtown's assets and liabilities and better define its character. For example, topically organized photographic surveys of the downtown area help clarify design issues. Historic photographs describe community context and provide a point of reference for interpreting changes over time. During design phases visualization tools can be tailored to support the needs of a particular phase of design from broad based visioning to specific improvement projects.

Since all graphic material represents an abstraction of reality, it is important that design consultants provide visual support that is structured for community use. Visual tools should be readily understandable to the layperson, enhance capacity for spatial thinking and be appropriately matched to the stage of design. During visioning phases design professionals can play a valuable role as the community's pencil (or model builder, or computer) by creating graphic material to help citizens visualize their ideas before committing to a particular course of action.

Case Studies

The following case studies will present several strategies for involving citizens in the revitalization of community places that focus on downtown districts. The downtown design processes for two small Eastern Washington towns, Colville and Colfax, with populations of 4360 and 2713 respectively, will be the center of the discussion. These projects not only required strategies for broad-based visioning but also for specific implementation action plans as well. They represent citizen participation at different stages of the design process. The Colville case involved long-term visioning associated with an overall downtown redevelopment and revitalization process. The Colfax project was more prescriptive in its outcome requirements and time schedule because it was an adjunct to an impending Washington State Department of Transportation highway improvement project. Citizens were to make specific recommendations concerning the allocation of funds for sidewalk improvements along Main Street.

Colville, Washington: Development of a Downtown Design Plan

PROJECT PURPOSE

The purpose of the Colville project was to provide a group of local business owners, the Revitalization Advisory Committee, with a process for developing its own downtown design plan. Committee members wished to strengthen their position in the regional trade market and compete effectively with a new Wal-

Mart store located at the northern edge of town. The physical extent of the project included the downtown historic core and the more recent strip commercial development at the edges of downtown. The committee lacked sufficient funding for extensive design consulting services and implementation phases thereby necessitating a self-help process. Our role as consultants was to design this process and facilitate its implementation. This gave us an excellent opportunity to use participatory design processes that would help the committee visualize specific outcomes.

THE SETTING

Colville, Washington is a timber community located in rural northeastern Washington. The community's economic health is boosted by its proximity to the Canadian border, and its position sitting astride one of the major north-south highways between southeastern British Columbia and Spokane, Washington, the major metropolitan center in the region. Canadian shoppers not only view Spokane as a major shopping center but also shop in the border towns in the United States to avoid some of the taxes on goods in Canada.

The highway from Canada to Spokane bisects Colville and serves as the spine for the downtown business core. The geographic center of town contains late nineteenth and early twentieth century brick buildings featuring classic revival and art deco styling. The once compact and square configuration of the town's commercial district has become elongated reflecting changes in commercial development patterns. Businesses have located along the highway corridor to gain exposure. New auto-oriented businesses have propagated at the northern and southern edges of town where larger parcels of land provide better support for the demands of contemporary commercial development. At the edges, large parcels can be subdivided to contain stand-alone businesses flanked by large parking areas. Aggregation of much smaller parcels in the historic core to build similar development would be difficult.

THE PROCESS

This project was our first attempt as consultants to design a process to teach design to laypersons. We utilized some of the techniques used in studio courses for planning and architecture students. Our goals for the design process were to empower the committee to think critically and visually about their environment, become advocates for their design plan, promote their plan to the community at large and act on their design recommendations. To accomplish these goals, the process was choreographed into three phases: goal setting, visual analysis and plan development. A brief summary of each phase follows.

Phase 1: Goal Setting

We scheduled two meetings with the committee to reduce the costs of completing the project. The first meeting focused on the first phase of the project.

Through a series of interactive small group discussions the committee established several broad goals for the design plan: create unity and connections between the core and the strip development at each end of the town; create unity within a diverse district without imposing a theme on downtown development; improve on existing streetscaping plans that were already under way; and reach a broader audience of business owners.

At the first meeting we used the same tools that have proven effective with our design students to orient committee members to critical design issues. A slide show illustrated typical problems as well as successes in similar towns. After viewing the slides, committee members were taken on a walking tour of downtown Colville to help them identify similar problems and assets in their own community. At the conclusion of the first meeting, participants were given homework assignments that became the foundation for the second phase of the process.

Phase 2: Visual Analysis

Committee members were organized into three teams to complete their homework assignment, a visual analysis of downtown Colville. Each group was assigned a specific category of physical elements to explore: (i) streets, sidewalks and landscaping, (ii) signage and (iii) buildings. Using photographic documentation, each team was asked to record positive and negative examples of its assigned categories.

At the second two-day meeting, teams were asked to share their findings with the other groups. Results of the visual survey exceeded our expectations. Instead of presenting a pile of photographs for discussion, each team created a display board featuring labeled photographs with brief explanations of design issues. On their own initiative, the groups met during the interim to compare notes and check on one another's progress. This gathering stimulated competition between the teams resulting in more intensive investigation and better organized visual information than we had expected from untrained designers.

The two-day workshop began with each team presenting their analyses. There are several benefits to having the citizens conduct their own visual assessments. Participants develop a visual understanding of problems by photographing them. They learn to recognize features that contribute to visual unity and to identify intrusive visual elements. This process also allows them to quickly isolate critical issues. For example, even though members of the revitalization advisory committee were largely unfamiliar with architectural language, they recognized the value of maintaining the rhythmic qualities of cornice lines in the historic core and the sense of scale that structural bays give to building façades. During the presentation of the " buildings" group, several members suggested that a lost sense of scale could be recovered by restoring pilasters that had been masked by awnings or other newer façade treatments. This discovery led, in later discussions of design guidelines, to guidelines that prescribed design characteristics for new construction that reflected these older building forms.

After reviewing the visual assessment materials, the committee defined specific objectives and actions. Based on their critiques of the existing downtown environment, each team spent half of the day developing specific design recommendations. Although they lacked drawing skills to delineate their recommendations, participants were able to express their ideas in visual form using representative photographs and rough sketches. The committee elected not to use photographs of their own downtown to articulate problems and solutions fearing that they would alienate other business owners.

At the conclusion of the workshop, each team prepared a display of their work and installed it in a local bank. The bank became the setting for a public open house for citizens that evening and the next morning. Committee members hosted the open house and stood by their displays to answer questions. Guests were encouraged to review the design objectives, make comments and select their preferences for specific design objectives by placing dot stickers next to those actions they preferred.

Phase 3: Design Plan Development

Based on the work generated by the committee and reviewed by the public at the open house, we then developed the written portions of the plan and the computer manipulated images of downtown Colville designed to illustrate key design objectives. The final plan summarizes key findings by the advisory committee and defines design objectives based upon the three areas of investigation: streets and sidewalks, signs and buildings. The plan was then presented to the committee for their approval and has become the guidepost for making downtown development decisions.

THE RESULTS

The successful development of a self-help process requires that consultants provide participants with the tools to analyze their own design problems. The photo displays enabled committee members to visualize opportunities and problems in the downtown area. Committee members also used the boards as an educational tool to build broader community support for the design plan. Their role as educators sparked enthusiasm among committee members and strengthened their ability to act. For example, a year after the adoption of the plan by the committee, they were able to secure a small grant from the U. S. Forest Service to help individual business owners with façade and signage improvements. Since funds were limited, businesses were required to submit proposals for a competitive review. Although we were asked to assist in this selection process, the committee members become jurors for their own review process. They responded by dusting off their visual assessment boards and reviewing design criteria they had established for downtown improvements. Empowered by their participatory process, the committee ultimately made appropriate decisions without much assistance from us. They exhibited the capacity to integrate their acquired design expertise into the decision-making process. The committee has since been invited to share their self-help process with other communities and at conferences sponsored by the Washington State Department of Community, Trade and Economic Development. Members remain active and committed to the guidelines in the plan.

Colfax, Washington: A Downtown Sidewalk Improvement Plan

The Washington State Department of Transportation (WDOT) scheduled a highway widening and re-paving project for the main street of downtown Colfax. In concert with the highway project, the City of Colfax voted to improve sidewalk conditions and make streetscape improvements along the highway. Since the state of Washington mandates a public process for highway improvements, the city, through a competitive process, selected us as facilitators. We worked with the Downtown Revitalization Committee, a group of citizen volunteers and business owners, to develop design recommendations for sidewalk improvements. We then summarized the results in a report to WDOT and the engineering consultants selected for the construction phases.

THE SETTING

Colfax is located in southeastern Washington. It is a vital agricultural community, county seat and a regional hub for agricultural equipment sales. The town is bisected north to south by a major highway that connects Spokane with Pullman, Washington, the home of Washington State University, and other cities in southeastern and south central Washington. Thus, Colfax merchants service the local farm community as well as truck and traveler traffic along the highway.

Sited in a tight canyon along the Palouse River, Colfax has historically been a linear city confined by its topography. The core of downtown consists of three parallel north-south streets and ten cross streets. Main Street, the major highway, features a dense cluster of turn of the century brick buildings along its three central blocks. Strip commercial development continues northward along the street to the edge of downtown. Residential areas, located on the steep slopes of the canyon, flank the downtown district.

The Main Street corridor, eighty feet wide from building face to building face, was not planned to accommodate four lanes of modern truck traffic. People who park along Main Street worry about losing the mirrors off their vehicles to passing trucks. To avoid this calamity, they often park with two inside wheels up on the sidewalk. During the negotiations with WDOT the city suggested removing one foot of sidewalk on each side of the street. WDOT responded by recommending four feet on each side. They compromised at three feet on each side.

Although most of the revitalization committee members were convinced the improvements would be positive, we as consultants were concerned about their failure to see the impact to pedestrian traffic and adjacent buildings by this widening. Any improvements would have to abate the negative impact created by the reduction in sidewalk width. Committee members were divided into two camps over the street widening. Those in favor were largely business owners who perceived economic benefits, and those opposed, mostly non-business owners, feared a negative impact on the historic character of downtown. Thus, it was important to design a process that would allow the committee members to visualize the outcomes of their design decisions and reach a consensus concerning final recommendations.

THE PROCESS

Our three-workshop process helped participants to: explore opportunities and limitations afforded by the street widening; sharpen their visual understanding of the downtown environment and the impact of the project on the sidewalks and adjacent properties; and establish priorities and formulate recommendations for publicly funded projects in the right-of-way.

Community Workshop 1: Goal Setting

At the first workshop participants were divided into small groups and asked to brainstorm answers to several broad questions: what do you like about your downtown, what don't you like, and what would you like to see happen? Each group of participants recorded their responses on sheets of flip chart paper. After completing their assignments, all the groups reconvened in one room and shared their results with the other groups. Each participant was then given a small number of dot stickers and asked to place their dots next to his or her most important concerns and favorite idea. These votes were then reviewed by all of the participants. The results of this process became the foundation for establishing community design goals.

Community Workshop 2: Orientation and Homework

Utilizing what we had learned from the Colville process, the second meeting began with a slide show and walking tour and ended with a homework assignment. The slide show depicted a series of street and sidewalk improvements made in other communities. To help committee members experience the impact of the proposed street widening and better understand the design constraints associated with the street widening, we drew a chalk line on the sidewalk three feet from the curb along an entire city block and had them walk inside of this constraint.

Since the Colville visual investigation was such a success, we concluded the workshop by dividing the committee into three groups to investigate the physical character of downtown just as in Colville. Although the committee's charge was limited to the formulation of recommendations for sidewalk improvements, we felt it was important for the participants to interpret other critical physical features of the downtown district to establish an appropriate context for design decision-making. Teams were asked to prepare presentations about their results for the next meeting.

Community Workshop 3: An All-Day Design In

The all-day workshop consisted of four sequential activities. The day began with homework reports. Each team presented its visual assessment boards for their assigned topic. Although each team researched a different topic, many of the examples overlapped. One team titled their board "the good, the bad, and the ugly of Colfax" humorously articulating perceptions commonly held by all the members of the committee. Another group graded buildings from A to F giving a similar account of their survey. The results of these surveys were strikingly similar recognizing the destruction of the physical character of downtown by the selection of inappropriate façade materials and previous improvements to the street.

The second activity involved creating a set of specific design objectives. Using the boards as a tool for discussion, the committee developed a broad set of design guidelines to help structure design decisions in subsequent activities.

The third activity was a photo portfolio sort. Each team was asked to create a poster board of images that closely represented ideas they would like to see implemented from sets of photographs of downtown improvements in other communities. The photo packets included scenes from downtowns with different types of character as well as various types of street furniture, lamps and landscape elements. The activity stimulated discussion about the desired ambiance for downtown Colfax as well as preferences concerning specific design choices in support of that image.

It was particularly important for committee members to recognize the design constraints and tradeoffs dictated by the reduction in sidewalk widths. To incorporate any of the streetscape improvements identified in the last activity, it would be necessary to sacrifice parking, a sacred cow to many participants, and perhaps trade-off a parking space to include spaces for trees, benches, drinking fountains, building awnings, or pedestrian bulges.

To demonstrate this, the fourth activity was a design-in built around a "kit of parts." Each team was given a map of a typical city block and a kit containing examples of scaled sidewalk bulges, trees and other street furniture. They were then requested to design a typical block in plan view by cutting and taping these elements to the map of the street.

Each of these exercises required a progressively more specific level of design decision-making. The more exacting design exercises were more difficult for each team to complete. Internal negotiation intensified as members wrestled with tradeoffs between perceived parking needs and desired amenities. The resultant plans were quite similar, suggesting bulges at intersections to accent pedestrian crosswalks and the provision of pedestrian amenities that could be accommodated by smaller bulges at mid-block. Several groups created crude representations of their ideas by sketching changes on tracing paper covering photos used in previous exercises.

Although this was the final scheduled design workshop, the committee wanted validation from a broader cross-section of the community. Committee members created a one-page questionnaire containing the suggested improvements. This questionnaire was distributed to businesses and residents of the city by including it in their water bills. Each respondent was asked to select the five most important suggestions for sidewalks, landscaping, signs, and buildings. Eighty-eight surveys were completed providing valuable feedback for community leaders and the design consultants.

Development of the Plan

The final step in this process, to summarize design recommendations by the committee and create the graphic support for their ideas in a report to the City of Colfax, was our responsibility. Using computer-imaging software, we manipulated photographs of alternative design concepts for sidewalk and crosswalk improvements and ground level building improvements. Additionally, images of the impact of the street widening and varying degrees of project intervention demonstrated the negative effects of the widening and means to abate these effects. We also created images to reflect the conceptual split in the committee over the importance of parking. Some business owners were convinced that parking spaces should not be sacrificed to accommodate design improvements. Others believed that the overall aesthetic impact of design improvements afforded by sacrificing parking spaces would encourage a more pedestrian-oriented downtown and actually improve business conditions.

Results

Since the State of Washington mandates a participatory process for all public works projects, there is some danger that other government agencies will pay lip service to the results. In the case of Colfax, the summary report and design recommendations we submitted to the city were turned immediately over to the consulting engineering firm in charge of design development and construction documentation for sidewalk improvements. Unfortunately the city manager at the time suggested to the consulting engineer that the study was a mere formality and that he need not pay attention to the results. However, recognizing the importance of community endorsement, the engineer did take the study into account for the final design.

Recently we interviewed the consulting engineer for the sidewalk improvement, who has completed numerous public works projects, about the relative success of the Colfax project. His response validated our participatory process. When asked how influential the design recommendations were to his firm and consulting landscape architecture firm's final solution, he replied:

Very helpful! But I'm not talking about details. The design detail of a project, like sizes of bulges and number of trees don't matter, in fact they changed several times throughout the course of construction documentation. What you did was get the town to believe in the project. By the time we came on board the community was ready for us. Those people wanted the improvements to happen—it was their project, not one that some outside consultant shoved down their throats. Too often we run into opposition from the community over dollars spent on sidewalks and trees—but not on this project. You made our job easy (Larry Hodge 1999).

Since the sidewalk improvements are in final phases of construction, as of this printing, the verdict is still out concerning the relative success of the process. The revitalization committee does continue to meet regularly to plan other improvements in the downtown area, indicating that a participatory process helped to mobilize the community. By participating in the process committee members were convinced that: successful downtown revitalization will require sustained commitment; improvements are not limited to the public sector but must involve the private sector as well; change will happen, not as the result of a single project, but through a series of projects large and small; design changes are good for business; and historic resources are an important component of community character.

Conclusions

Our experiences in Colfax, Colville and a variety of other small towns throughout the Pacific Northwest support the following conclusions about citizen participation in downtown revitalization. First, citizens can design appropriate solutions for community problems under the guidance of a community design consultant. It is important to emphasize, however, that our approach does not eliminate the need for a design professional. Instead, we contend that the traditional role of design consultants for downtown revitalization projects must change from creator to facilitator. In Colfax and Colville, we choreographed opportunities for users to make their own design decisions rather than creating a plan for their approval. Several strategies enabled participants to make decisions independently. However, we did not advocate a user autonomous, self-decision process. Ultimately we influenced design outcomes by structuring the decision-making process itself.

Second, a participatory process must be fortified with tools to stimulate visual thinking. Visualization techniques help focus discussion on specific design issues and features. By brainstorming the possibilities and then visualizing results participants are empowered to make recommendations with confidence. Design consultants should offer guidance in selecting visual tools that are legible to community users and appropriately matched with the particular stage of design.

Finally, participatory design is an empowering process enabling participants to set goals and develop creative solutions for functional and aesthetic problems. As co-designers, participants have a stake in the final outcome and have more realistic expectations. They become effective ambassadors to sell design ideas to the greater community and mobilize support for a project. Most importantly participants realize that positive place-making is a shared responsibility and that each member of a community is a stakeholder in a healthy downtown. Thus, community participation creates a sense of ownership in design outcomes, allowing citizens to become their own place-makers, reinforcing the notion that "the public realm is the physical manifestation of the common good" and the private individual has a responsibility to this public realm.

References

Altschuler, Alan A. 1970. "Decision-Making and the Trend Toward Pluralistic Planning." In *Urban Planning in Transition*. edited by Ernest Erber. New York: Grossman Publishers, pp. 183-186.

Hodge, Larry. 1999. Personal inteview.

Hoenstein, H. and R.Young. 1987. " Desert Hot Springs: A Balancing Act." *Proceedings of the Conference: Aesthetics of Rural Renaissance*. San Luis Obispo, California: California Polytechnic State University.

Kunstler, James Howard. 1993. *The Geography of Nowhere*. New York: Simon and Schuster.

McClure, Wendy. 1997a. "Computer Visualization: Implications for Community Planning." In *The Rural Town: Designing for Growth and Sustainability*, edited by Wendy McClure. Moscow, Idaho: Center for Business Development and Research, University of Idaho, pp. 39-46.

Nelessen, Anton C. 1994. *Visions for a New American Dream*. Chicago: Planners Press.

Ryan, Dick. 1997. "Rural Communities in Transition." In *The Rural Town: Designing for Growth and Sustainability*, edited by Wendy McClure. Moscow, Idaho: Center for Business Development and Research, University of Idaho.

Wultz, Fredrik. 1990. "The Concept of Participation." In *Participatory Design: Theory and Techniques*, edited by Henry Sanoff. Raleigh, North Carolina: Bookmasters.

CHAPTER 8

Towards a Typology of Urban Design Problems and Solutions for Downtown Revitalization

Some Evidence from the Mayor's Institute on City Design

SIDDHARTHA SEN and MATTHEW J. BELL

Planning literature on small and rural towns is dominated by discussions of economic revitalization (Glasmeier 1991; Glasmeier and Howland 1995; Hibbard and Davis 1986; Malizia 1986). Usually, very little attention is given to the role of design in urban revitalization. As Daniels *et. al.* (1995) point out, visual quality of small towns can be an economic resource and a draw for visitors and new businesses. To cite another example, Arendt *et. al.* (1994) recognize the importance of aesthetics, form, and design in maintaining small town character. In practice, the Main Street approach, sponsored by the National Trust for Historic Preservation, emphasizes the role of design in downtown revitalization of small towns (Robertson 1995). A careful analysis of the general literature on downtown revitalization also suggests a relationship between urban design and downtown revitalization. Robertson (1995), for example, points out that pedestrianization, historic preservation, and waterfront development are among the major redevelopment strategies for downtown revitalization. Certainly, all these strategies require an element of urban design. Others (Gratz *et. al.* 1998; Barnett 1995; Halpern 1988; Paumier *et. al.* 1988) have also emphasized the importance of design in downtown revitalization.

This chapter further explores this relationship through a review of the literature and an analysis of case studies on small cities of northeastern and southeastern United States. The case studies are based on a study sponsored by a National Endowment for the Arts grant that the Graduate Program in City and Regional Planning at Morgan State University jointly held with the School of Architecture at the University of Maryland from 1993 to 1998. The grant was sponsored by the Mayor's Institute on City Design, Northeast. The Mayor's Institute was set up by the National Endowment for the Arts in 1986 to develop a multi-disciplinary dialogue by encouraging constructive debate to improve the understanding of the design of American cities and the mayor's role in the design process. It consists of a series of small forums where participation is limited to twenty people: half are mayors and half are urban design experts. Each mayor presents a design problem from his or her city. Each case is analyzed by the mayors and design professionals, who working together, discuss how an appropriate design process can help solve the problem.[1]

Here we limit our discussion to cases that deal with downtown revitalization, although the problems that the mayors brought to this forum were not just limited to this issue. However, downtown revitalization through urban design did emerge as a predominant theme in the Institute. A total of 28 cities[2] attended the Institute. Here we limit our discussion to five.

The cities that attended the various Institutes are predominantly small urban communities. The smallest cites which participated in the Institutes were cities like Newburgh, NY and Easton, PA, with populations of 27,700 and 26,276 respectively. Larger cities such as Brockton, MA and New Bedford, MA had populations of 92,788 and 99,992 respectively. Cities like Greenville, SC, with a population of 58,256 and Oldbridge, NJ, with a population of 56,475 were somewhere in between. Not all cities were concerned about the need for downtown revitalization. For example, there were affluent cities such as Bowie, MD which is primarily a white collar bedroom community with a median household income of $72,142. At the same time we did have cities such as New Bedford, MD, which have lost their economic base due to industrial restructuring and who have a median household income of $22,674. We limit our discussion to the type of cities which have lost their economic base and are in need of downtown revitalization.

The chapter first presents a review of the literature on the relationship between urban design and downtown revitalization. A typology of design related downtown revitalization problems and solutions emerges from this discussion. We then present specific examples from the cities that attended the various Institutes to illustrate how design solutions are applicable to these cities. A brief discussion on demographic, economic, and, historic characteristics of the cities are also presented in the section. Finally, we examine how history may have played a role in creating today's downtown revitalization problems. This is followed by concluding remarks.

Review of the Literature

A brief definition of contemporary urban design serves as a good prelude to the discussion that follows. Contemporary urban design emerged sometime in the 1960s and was born out of a search for quality of urban form (Moudon 1992). It constitutes the interface of architecture, urban planning, landscape architecture, surveying, property development, environmental management and protection, and a host of other disciplines (Oc and Tiesdell 1996). This search for quality urban form continues to date, focusing on urban environments that have both functional and aesthetic appeal to those who inhabit them. From an initial predominately aesthetic concern with the distribution of building masses and space between buildings, it is now primarily concerned with the quality of urban public realm, which is both social and physical. Let us now turn to literature on the relationship between urban design and downtown revitalization. According to our interpretation of the literature, there are two predominant design principles on revitalizing downtowns. These are: (a) pedestrianization of downtowns and (b) reclaiming "lost spaces" or "cracks." Both principles are discussed below. As we shall see, these two principles are applicable to most types of design oriented revitalization strategies such as waterfront redevelopment, historic preservation, and main street revitalization.

Although pedestrianization played a key role in the design of suburbs since Radburn was initiated in late 1920s,[3] the importance of the pedestrian street in the vitality of urban life resurfaced in the 1960s with the work of social scientists such as Jane Jacobs (1961). Urban designers such as Kevin Lynch added to the resurrection of the social and symbolic function of the street during the period (Ellin 1996). The 1960s and 1970s also saw a wide variety of literature on pedestrianization of malls (Brambilla and Longo 1977; Rubenstein 1978). However, the interest in this type of research has declined with the decline in construction of such malls (Robertson 1990). The 1980s saw the continuation of publications that dealt with pedestrianization and the role of streets in urban design (Appleyard 1981; Moudon 1987; Whyte 1980, 1988).

However, the most influential design paradigm dealing with pedestrianization and urban design in the 1980s and 1990s deals with suburban design. This was developed by the "new urbanists" or "neotraditional urbanists" (Calthrope 1991; Duany and Plater-Zyberk 1992; Kelbaugh 1989; Krieger 1991; Katz 1994). The two most popular variations of the theme are Traditional Neighborhood Development or District (TND) and the Transit Oriented Development (TOD) or Pedestrian Pockets (PP). The TND is a new development that is designed with an emphasis on pedestrians. Developed by the architectural firm of Andreas Duany and Elizabeth Plater-Zyberk, it is based on a grid of straight streets and boulevards which are lined by buildings grouped by architectural styles. The PP, developed by architect Peter Calthrope entails retrofitting of existing suburbs along with some new growth to concentrated pedestrian pockets around public transportation hubs. Ideally, PPs should be located along strategic points of a regional transit system, such as light rail. They are mixed use communities with an average of one fourth mile walking distance to the transit stop. As we shall discuss later, some of the design principles for pedestrianization proposed by the new urbanists are also applicable to downtowns.

Let us now turn to the typologies, policy and design guidelines for pedestrianization of downtowns. A review of the literature (Barnett 1995; Gratz, et. al. 1998; Paumier et. al. 1988; Robertson 1990, 1993a, 1993b; Whyte 1980, 1988) suggests that there are four deterrents to pedestrianization. This literature also suggests that making downtowns more pedestrian friendly increases the image of the downtown, which in turn will promote economic vitality, especially for declining downtowns. The four deterrents to pedestrianization are best summarized in Robertson's terminology. These are: (i) low priority given to pedestrian transportation in comparison to the automobile. To cite one example of low priority for pedestrians, traffic lights are generally timed for efficient movements of automobiles, and not pedestrians. Given such priorities, the pedestrian usually finds it difficult and dangerous to cross busy streets; (ii) increasing distances between destinations, which makes walking unattractive. Even in relatively dense downtowns, the vast amount of space devoted to automobiles in the form of parking lots and ramps, deep landscaped set backs of newly constructed office buildings that occupy entire blocks, and expansion of downtown activities beyond the core, act as a deterrent to walking; (iii) street furniture such as traffic signs, parking meters, traffic signal poles, telephone poles, street lights, mailboxes, trash cans, and newspaper machines, not only take up pedestrian space, they also make walking an unpleasant experience; (iv) Poor quality of the pedestrian environment. Among other factors, people choose to walk only if the route offers high levels of interest and aesthetics in terms of people, activity, and architecture. Many downtown blocks are dominated by blank walls of modern office buildings, shops with no direct access from sidewalks, parking ramps and lots, abandoned buildings which prompt the pedestrian to walk by quickly rather than enjoy the walking experience. Parking lots, in particular, break the continuity of building façades. Often fear of lack of safety in such environments deter people from walk.

Specific strategies for pedestrianization of downtowns include widening of sidewalks, discouraging automobile traffic, climatization of the pedestrian environment, improving safety and security, increasing attractiveness of sidewalks, improving the quality and quantity of sitting spaces, changing zoning ordinances, and segregating pedestrians from vehicular traffic.

Among these strategies, widening of the sidewalks is the simplest one. Policies to discourage traffic could include reducing the number of parking spaces, increasing the cost of parking, and placing more restrictive time limits for parking. Climatization techniques include climate controlled underground concourses, skywalks, heated sidewalks, and covering of sidewalks with canopies. Strategies for improving safety include better lighting and foot patrols by police officers.

The attractiveness of the sidewalks can be improved by including colorful storefronts, outdoor exhibits, attractive landscaping, and encouragement of kiosks, fruit and vegetable stands, sidewalk cafes, outdoor eating, and artists and street performers. The quality and quantity of sitting spaces can be improved by orienting the seating toward sun and improving the view from the seating by facing it towards heaviest pedestrian flow. In addition to traditional benches, other forms of seating such as moveable chairs, wide ledges, and steps should be encouraged.

Mixed use zoning should be encouraged to promote residential activity in the downtowns. Zoning changes should also encourage deep setbacks from side-walks to interrupt the continuous street walls which is not conducive to walking. Zoning that requires high parking ratio should also be discouraged. While it may not be possible to replace all parking lots with garages, it should be possible to zone most important street frontages in such a fashion that at least a narrow one story building is constructed along the street side of parking lots. Another design solution is to allocate the ground floors of parking garages as retail space to maintain the continuity of the street. Keeping the sloping portion of the garage away from the street frontage is yet another design element to keep the continuity of the street façade.

Underground concourses, underground transit systems, skywalks, and grade level pedestrian malls are most common methods of segregating pedestrian and vehicular traffic. As pointed out by Robertson, three types of pedestrian malls have commonly been implemented in the United States. The first type consists of traditional pedestrian street designed for exclusive pedestrian use. The second type is the shared mall that permits limited automobile use such as one lane of one-way traffic. The third type is the transit mall which accommodates both pedestrian and transit use. A skywalk consists of a network of skybridges over streets, second story corridors within buildings and various types of activity hubs.

The new urbanists have also proposed several pedestrianization strategies. Although most of these strategies are directed towards pedestrianizing older sub-urbs or designing new pedestrian friendly ones, some of the design principles are also applicable to downtown situations. For example, the suggestion that streets should converge into common visible destinations such as core commercial areas and parks is applicable to downtowns. As suggested, they should frame vistas of public buildings, parks, and natural features. The suggestion to discourage the use of any particular street for vehicular traffic only is also applicable to down-town situations.

The new urbanists also suggest that architectural character, sidewalks, street trees, and on street parking could enhance the pedestrian friendliness of the streets. Certainly these are design principles that are applicable to downtowns. As suggested, aesthetically pleasing architectural character of the streets should include: proportionate relationship of building heights to right of ways, variety of scale and space within streets through landscaping, adequate interface of arcades, porches, stoops, stairs, balconies, eaves and cornices, loggias, chimneys, doors, widows, quadrangles, courtyards, and patios to ensure life on the streets, and adequate design block and lot sizes and shapes. The new urbanists suggest that block dimensions should be between 250 feet to 600 feet and blocks should be square, rectangular or irregular in shape. Such dimensions and size allow buildings to reach to the edge of blocks, thereby forcing parking away from undesirable locations such as the sidewalk, to desirable locations such as underground in the middle of the block or on the street. Lots should vary in widths to allow for a variety of building types.

Specific recommendations on street trees suggest that they should be required on all streets and should be placed no further than 30 feet apart in planter strips or tree wells between the curb and the sidewalk. Choice of trees and planting techniques should create a unified image for the street, and provide an effective canopy. The new urbanists also make some specific recommendations for commercial areas. They suggest large sidewalks to accommodate larger volumes of pedestrians and seating.

Their suggestion of encouraging on street parking is applicable to downtowns. They suggest that redevelopment and infill sites should be retrofitted to provide on street parking and landscaping. According to this school of design thought, parking garages are acceptable if their ground floor is at the sidewalk and used for pedestrian related activities. Absorption of parking and servicing loads by alleys should be encouraged in order to free up the outer faces of the blocks for pedestrian traffic.

Other pedestrianization strategies proposed by new urbanists that are applicable to downtown situations include minimized block radii to slow vehicles at intersections; landscaped medians to reduce apparent street widths, narrower street widths, two-way streets to improve pedestrian crossing safety, properly designed curbs, and accommodation for the handicapped. Some of Appleyard's (1981) recommendations for traffic control devices for pedestrianization are not only valid today, but also applicable to downtowns. The devices that can be used outside residential areas include speed limits and narrowing streets, traffic signals and cross walks, street bumps and humps, raised crosswalks and platform intersections, entrance gates; narrowing of streets, traffic circles and islands, semi-diverters, and diverters.

Imposing speed limits is a simple means of traffic calming. Appropriate use of traffic signals and crosswalks can ensure pedestrian safety at intersections. Speed bumps and humps can be employed as effective traffic calming devices. Rumble materials that make a noise or cause vibrations, are likely to slow down traffic. Platform intersections and raised crosswalks give the impression that they are pedestrian territory, and hence are likely to slow down the traffic. Entrance gates create an impression to the motorists that they are entering a community territory and may prompt them to slow down. Techniques for narrowing street widths include physical reduction of street widths and corresponding increasing of sidewalk areas; promotion of on street parking, and provision of green strips and trees or play spaces. Traffic circles and islands also provide some reduction of speed. Semi-diverters are physical barriers that permit traffic only in one direction. Diverters are physical devices placed diagonally across four way intersections to turn them into cul-de-sacs. These can range from temporary ones such as iron railings, concrete blocks, bollards, and wooden poles, to permanent ones such as parks or landscaped termination to streets.

Let us now turn to "cracks" and "lost spaces" that we believe act as deterrents to downtown revitalization. The terms are attributable to Lokaitou-Sideris (1996) and Trancik (1986). Lokaitou-Sideris (1996) defines cracks as gaps in the urban form, residual undeveloped places which are under-used or deteriorating, physical divides that purposefully or accidentally separate social worlds, spaces which have been bypassed by development or where new development has created fragmentation. She points out that freeways and highways superimposed over the American city have not only asserted their dominance in the human-made and natural landscape, but also created numerous cracks by segmenting urban form, dividing urban parts, and creating "gray zones" along their embankments and ramps.

Trancik's lost spaces are not that different from Lokaitou-Sideris' cracks. He defines lost spaces as undesirable, ill defined urban areas that make negative contribution to surroundings or users. Lost spaces fail to connect elements in a coherent way. Trancik, also cites the automobile as a major cause of these lost spaces. He points out that the construction of highways from the 1940s created lost spaces by isolating neighborhoods, replacing the avenue with the artery, and making the street lose its social meaning as a multipurpose place. Cracks or lost spaces can also be seen along other channels of transportation amenities such as surface parking lots and edges of freeways. Facilities that were abandoned with the advent of the highways such as waterfronts and train yards are also the cause of lost spaces in the city.

According to Lokaitou-Sideris (1996), these cracks can be filled by urban design. At the building level one should consider how the buildings should relate to the street, the orientations of entrances, the type and articulation of ground floor uses, the relationship between open and enclosed spaces, and the hierarchy between public, semi-public, and private spaces. She continues that design elements should reinforce bonds of public space to the rest of the urban structure. Public spaces should become connectors rather than buffers between areas. Public spaces should be linked to surrounding districts through block walkways, arcades, paeseos and through integration of streetscape.

Cracks such as empty lots, river banks, parking lots, freeway leftover space, and abandoned railroad lines should be reclaimed through urban design. Trancik's (1986) suggestions about lost spaces are similar. He sees lost spaces as opportunities for design. According to him, we should reclaim these spaces by transforming them into opportunities for redevelopment by infilling such spaces into the historic fabric of the city. Dysfunctional and incompatible public plazas, streets, and parking lots can be transformed into viable open space through urban design.

Towards A Typology of Urban Design Problems and Solutions for Downtown Revitalization

Pedestrian unfriendliness and cracks or lost spaces are primary types of design problems associated with the downtowns of the cities that attended the Institutes. Most cities have the simultaneous existence of pedestrian unfriendly streets and cracks or lost spaces. The discussion below illustrates the simultaneous existence of these typologies and their design solutions with specific examples from the cities. However, it is to be noted that during the Institutes, the design problems and solutions that we discuss here were not couched in terms of the literature on pedestrianization, lost spaces, and cracks. Our analysis and reflection on the design issues and solutions indicated this connection. It is also to be noted that the solutions were actually developed during the Institutes by the panel of experts (including us) and the mayors themselves. We have connected them to the literature in this chapter.

Cracks, Lost Spaces, and Pedestrian Unfriendliness in Waterfronts

Waterfront revitalization emerged as the major design problem that the Mayors brought to the Institute. Many of these waterfronts have lost their original use and have become cracks or lost spaces that are not pedestrian friendly. We discuss the cases of New Bedford, MA, and Wilmington, DE as examples.

New Bedford, MA

The city of New Bedford, Massachusetts, is 20.14 square miles in area and is located on the northeastern shore of the Acushnet river.[4] According to the 1990 census, it had a population of 99,922 and a median annual household income of $22,674. In terms of ethnic composition, 84.4 percent were White; 3.5 percent Black; 6.7 percent Hispanic; and 5.4 percent were of others races. About 74 percent of New Bedford's economy is made of small businesses. More than 71 percent of all businesses employ less than 10 employees and less than 2 percent employ over 100 employees. Services, retail, and apparel production industries employ the majority of the population at low wages.

It is useful to examine how the city's history may have contributed to downtown revitalization problems. The city's origins can be traced back to the year 1602 when the English landed off New Bedford's shoreline. Agriculture became the main stay of early colonists. Bedford village's ship building industry was started in 1760, and numerous other craftsmen came to the village to work in the associated industries. Whaling was also introduced around the same time period and Bedford Village was on its way to prosperity. New Bedford's maritime industry stayed at standstill until well after the War of 1812. By 1859, New Bedford's industry had turned from a mainstay of whaling to textiles. Although the gold rush in California and the discovery of oil in Pennsylvania drew many of the workers away, by the mid-1800s, wool, cotton, and iron industries were booming in New Bedford. The twentieth century saw the development of oil refineries, glass, copper, and silver businesses.

The textile industry continued as New Bedford's strongest economic producer particularly after the start of World War I. Later, financial mismanagement and other related problems including competition from other States and countries caused the demise of the textile industry. Thus, New Bedford is a typical example of "a restructured economy." Textile manufacturing, fishing and port-related activities had provided the region with a diverse economic base. When New Bedford's mayor attended the Institute in 1994, most of these industries had declined. This was despite efforts made by private industry and the local government to revitalize the economy through development of a privately owned industrial park, growth of port facilities, fishing and other waterfront activities, and related business. At the time of the Institute, the city was focusing upon its potential as a tourist destination given its rich historical heritage, in order to revitalize its economy. In fact, with the relative success of the Waterfront Historic District, tourism in New Bedford was on the rise at that time.

DESIGN PROBLEMS

The design problem of New Bedford presented by the mayor was to reclaim a crack or lost space by reconnecting the waterfront district with the downtown. With the rise of tourism, attractions such as the Whaling Museum and the Custom Houses had become popular tourist sites. These recent successes in New Bedford had refocused attention on the relationship between the working waterfront and the downtown areas. The recent New Bedford Heritage Park Plan was created to continue the efforts begun by the remaking of the Waterfront District. This plan recognized the need for the city to re-establish its historic link with the port and continued efforts focused upon the possibilities of tourism, industry and history which the site offers. Urban renewal efforts of the recent past created a lost space, or a crack, in the form of a physical rift between New Bedford's downtown and the waterfront. John F. Kennedy Highway, built to connect the downtown area with the neighborhoods and the ferry terminal to Nantucket to the south, had physically separated the waterfront from the town in concept and in detail. Several east-west streets of the historic district currently dead ended into concrete barriers along the edge of John F. Kennedy and the actual road bed of the highway was elevated several feet above historic streets at that time. Access across the highway from the downtown areas occurred in two places: on an elevated pedestrian bridge at Rodman Street; and further south at the intersection of Kennedy Highway and Union Street. Clearly, pedestrian access to the waterfront was a key to future development of both the historic district and the port area at the time of the Institute. In fact the Heritage Plans called for increased visibility of a pedestrian crossing at Union Street with landscaped medians, streetscape patterns and traffic signals.

DESIGN SOLUTIONS

The overall design goal is to reclaim cracks and make the connection between the waterfront and the downtown. The specific recommendations made during the Institute are discussed below.

It was suggested that if elimination of Kennedy Highway was not a possibility, then the city could consider closing the downtown portion of the highway one day a week to be used for a street festival or other public activity connected with the port and the historic district. The city could investigate the incorporation of MacArthur Drive into the new Kennedy Boulevard. Slowing down traffic along Kennedy Highway by decreasing the width of the vehicle right of way and adding possibly a public park or some similar long landscaped area adjacent to the historic district would be desirable. Investigating the possibility of tapering the then two lanes of south bound traffic to one lane on Kennedy Highway from a high speed highway to an urban boulevard was also highly desirable. However, the city could retain the ramp at the North Water Street from Kennedy Highway. This would facilitate easy movement into the historic district and into the adjacent parking garages. The city could investigate the possibility of another at grade crossing with a traffic light for pedestrians at Rodman Street. Facilitating the flow of traffic with timed lights was desirable. The city could also consider the long range possibility of lowering Kennedy Highway to the same level as the adjacent Front Street. This might make the connection from the water front to the historic district more apparent. In addition, the city could consider the elimination of a large portion of the grade parking on the wharf area and redesign the space with programmed activities and place for pedestrian gathering. Finally, the city could consider confining automobile traffic to a perimeter drive with parallel parking and an open space in the center of activities. Clearly, these recommendations are connected to the literature on pedestrianization, lost spaces, and cracks.

Wilmington, DE

Wilmington's waterfront is another example of a pedestrian unfriendly environment with cracks and lost spaces. Again industrial restructuring has resulted in such spaces. Before we discuss the history, it is useful to note that the City of Wilmington is 10.5 square miles in area and is located in the vicinity of the Brandywine and Christina rivers. According to the 1990 census, it had a population of 71,529 and a median annual household income of $32,510. In terms of ethnic composition, 42.1 percent were White; 52.4 percent Black; and 5.5 percent were of other races.

The city's origins can be traced back to 1638 when Swedish settlers constructed Fort Christina just west of the intersection of the Brandywine and Christina Rivers. Later the Fort was captured by the Dutch, who then expanded the settlement by building the town of Christinaham to the west of the Fort. In

1791, the name was changed to Wilmington and the population began to expand steadily. The early economy was based on milling industries on the Brandywine River, shipping and trading on the Christina River, and agriculture in the surrounding regions. Residential development was concentrated near Lower Market Street and on the higher ground to the west known as Quaker Hill.

Industries and manufacturing continued to expand during and after the Revolution War, and again after the War of 1812. As they grew, so did the working class population in the town. Many were housed in brick row homes built on the east side of Wilmington within walking distance of Christina River and the adjacent industrial areas. During the Civil War, the manufacturing of ships and railroad cars grew rapidly, along with the production of other material goods needed for the war. The founding of the horsecar line in 1864 aided the development of suburban neighborhoods by providing transportation for wealthy businessmen to the downtown manufacturing centers.

As the twentieth century began, the population of Wilmington increased by several hundred percent, due in large part to continuing immigration. Industry and population expanded throughout the first and second world wars, but began to decline in the 1960s and 1970s. Automobile travel made suburban living more attractive to those who could afford it, and several areas of the city were cleared for construction of new highways. In the 1980's, banking, finance, and insurance replaced manufacturing as the leading businesses in Wilmington. Clearly, Wilmington's waterfront has become derelict as shipping, trading, and milling industries that sustained the waterfront became obsolete. Lower Market Street district, which was the residential, commercial, and cultural center of early Wilmington had deteriorated when the mayor attended the Institute in 1994.

DESIGN ISSUES

At the time of the Institute, Wilmington's design issues consisted of lost space or cracks that act as deterrents to revitalization of the Lower Market Street district. This residential, commercial, and cultural center of early Wilmington, was now characterized by cracks consisting of deteriorating buildings and underutilized resources. Lower Market Street was now a Registered Historic District, but its image suffered from building vacancies, demolition for installation of parking lots, and unsympathetic renovations to buildings occupied by local businesses. Although access to the area was easily gained by bus, car and train, its appeal was somewhat dampened by the presence of a lost space in the form of a multi-lane Martin Luther King Jr. Boulevard, which fed directly to Interstate 95, and an elevated Amtrak train viaduct. Both of these elements physically divided Lower Market Street from the open waterfront to the South of Christina River at the time of the Institute. The city had recently renovated the streetscape of Market Street from Third to Fourth Streets with new street lights, new paving materials installed in both street and side walk surfaces, and buried utilities. Delaware Technical Community College is located to the west of Market Street. At the time of the Institute, a new retail and entertainment project called Riverview Plaza was being proposed to the south of the Amtrak viaduct. The proposed project would include several levels of structured parking and a multi-theater movie complex. Adjacent to the project area was the historic Pennsylvania Railroad Train Station. To the west is the Delaware project for the Arts and several renovated warehouses that were serving as office buildings. This new project would utilize a vacant site which was bordered by the Christina River to the South, the Amtrak viaduct on the north, the modern Amtrak train station at the east, and the Market Street bridge on the west.

DESIGN SOLUTIONS

The overall design goal is to reclaim cracks and make the connection between the waterfront and the downtown. The specific recommendations made during the Institute are discussed below.

Development along the waterfront could help retrieve this area. The city could try to develop a long range planning effort to redesign M. L. King Jr. Boulevard to accommodate pedestrian traffic. It was suggested that the traffic pattern should be redesigned to avoid high speed ramps which allow traffic to travel at a speed that is unsafe for downtown areas. Large turning radii which lengthens the time required for the pedestrian to cross the street should be avoided. Considering a continuous recreational amenity, such as a bike trail, along the river's edge would be useful. In the downtown area, the city could consider the use of building height limitations which would encourage smaller scale development and avoid the need for larger surface parking lots, which were certainly creating cracks in the urban form. Market Street should be seen as a connector stretching between the two rivers, and the city should continue to pursue efforts to preserve the historic architecture of lower Market Street and seek its revitalization. An overview such as this might broaden the conception of what constitutes the downtown of Wilmington and help to underscore the importance of the Christina Riverfront. Other connections from outlying areas could be studied. These access routes could be maintained by the introduction of pedestrian paths or bicycle paths. Low rise residential complexes could be considered for the waterfront with pedestrian paths and other active and passive public activities along the river's edge.

Cracks, Lost Spaces, and Pedestrian Unfriendliness in Main Streets

Although there were only a few cases of Main Street revitalization projects brought to the Institute, discussing at least one case study dealing with the issue is instructive since Main Street revitalization is indeed a salient revitalization strategy for small towns (Daniels *et. al.* 1995; Robertson 1995). The cases indicate that main streets of small towns that attended the Institutes have lost their original use and have become cracks or lost spaces that are not pedestrian friendly. We discuss the case of York, Pennsylvania as an example.

York, PA

The City of York is 5.8 square miles in area and is located west of the Susquehanna River. According to the 1990 census, it had a population of 42,192 and a median annual household income of $21,812. In terms of ethnic composition, 71.1 percent were White; 20.7 percent Black; 7.1 percent Hispanic; and 1.1 percent were of other races.

Here too it is useful to examine how the city's history may have contributed to the decline of its main street. The city's origin can be traced back to the year 1741. By 1787 business was flourishing and construction of elaborate homes had begun. York became a city in 1887, almost a century after its incorporation as a borough.

The first train arrived in York in 1838. The link to Baltimore had a great impact on York's development, resulting in a population and business boom. By the turn of the century, wealthier residents were relocating from downtown to newly planned communities to the northwest. These new developments required convenient transportation to the center of the city and by 1907 virtually the entire county was linked to York by electric street railways.

An early manufacturing center, York owes much of its growth and development to its industrial heritage. Like many cities of similar size, the city experienced a surge of expansion after World War II. However, later suburban developments shifted a large portion of the population out of the older neighborhoods. As a result, York's downtown retail district, especially the main street, experienced a sharp decline.

Like many cities of its size, the City of York saw the appearance of cracks in its downtown area from the 1950's through 1975. Department stores closed and businesses moved to the suburbs followed by downtown residents. From the mid-1970s through the early 1980s, significant revitalization efforts resulted in the city's rebirth and proportions of the center city took on new life. When the mayor attended the Institute in 1995, parts of the Main Street in York remained derelict, despite the city's effort to attract business to the downtown.

DESIGN ISSUES

At the time of the Institute, York's design related deterrents to downtown revitalization were cracks, lost spaces, and pedestrian unfriendliness of its main street, known as George Street. A one-way street over most of its length at that time, George Street had a mixture of houses to the south of College Street and businesses to the north. The businesses on it included auto parts store, drug stores, beauty parlors, barber shops, and dry cleaners mixed with a few upscale clothing and antique stores in the immediate downtown area. A modest streetscape effort was done in May 1995. Several cracks such as old abandoned buildings had been renovated, and a segment of the Victorian row homes had been renovated into moderate income rental units. Despite these efforts, George Street did not yet have a vibrant feel. One of the deterrents to pedestrianization were new lost spaces in the form of commercial-strip style buildings set back from streets behind parking lots. In addition, the one way street pattern resulted in several sections of five-lane, one-way traffic, which made the street pedestrian unfriendly.

DESIGN SOLUTIONS

Drawing from the literature on strategies for pedestrianization, lost spaces, and cracks, several specific strategies can be developed to solve the problems of George Street. The ones developed at the Institute are discussed below and certainly relate to this literature.

A variety of scale and space changes within George Street and appropriate landscaping could enhance its pedestrian friendliness and attractiveness. Since the street passed through several different neighborhoods, the design of the street should relate to the different neighborhoods and their different activities. A uniform treatment of the street would not appropriately reflect its varied character. Trees could be planted to reflect the changing character of the street. For example, trees may be better suited to the residential zone than the commercial zone. Other landscaping strategies such as medians and plants within the street in selected areas would not only create special places along the street, but also slow down the traffic. "Broken" medians might work in conjunction with other markers to provide a sense of progression into the heart of York.

Simple pedestrianization strategies such as changing to two-way traffic; creating "bulb-outs" or changing materials at traffic intersections; minimizing the left turn lanes; and widening of sidewalks were also suggested during the Institute. It was also suggested that safety of pedestrians at crossings should be ensured through proper use of signage and signalization. For facilitating pedestrian crossing at mid bloc, raised or mounted pedestrian islands could be employed. The quality of the walking experience could be further improved by intermittently placing benches against the buildings so people could sit down and enjoy watching the active street life. The city could also manage loading times for businesses and consider traffic-management strategies to accommodate rush hour traffic. Consideration should be given to establishing a plan to make alleys accessible to service vehicles within the next twenty to thirty years.

Cracks, Lost Spaces, Pedestrian Unfriendliness, and Other Types of Downtown Revitalization Problems

A variety of downtown revitalization issues besides main street and waterfront revitalization were brought to the Institutes by the mayors. Despite the variety of these issues, pedestrian unfriendliness and cracks or lost spaces were still the primary types of design problems associated with these downtowns. We discuss the case of Easton, PA, and Reading, PA as examples of how pedestrian unfriendliness and cracks or lost spaces characterize the deterrents to downtown revitalization in situations other than main street and waterfront revitalization.

Easton, PA

The City of Easton is 3.8 square miles in area and lies at the junction of Lehigh and Delaware Rivers. According to the 1990 census, it had a population of 26,276 and a median annual household income of $26,365. In terms of ethnic composition, 84.3 percent were White; 9.3 percent Black; 4.4 percent Hispanic; and 2 percent were of other races. Easton's population peaked in the 1950s, and has stabilized at about 26,000 since then.

As with other cities, it is useful to examine how the city's history may have contributed to the design problem presented by the mayor. Easton was chartered as a city in 1874. However, the history of the city goes back to 1752 when it was laid out as a city with a grid iron pattern streets and a public square at the center, known as Center Square. The space was modeled after squares designed for Philadelphia, with streets entering the space at mid-point of the square and surrounded by residential town houses and businesses. Between 1790 and 1890, the city's population had grown from 697 to 14,481. During Easton's expansion, one of the oldest farmer's markets in the United States was grounded in 1796 at Center Square. The farmer's market had operated continuously since then and was still operational when the mayor attended the Institute in 1997.

Easton developed a strong industrial base in the nineteenth century because of its location at the confluence of rivers and rail transportation corridors. The first industries to develop were iron ore manufacturing and railroad and canal shipping. Later, manufacture of building materials such as steel, slate, and cement became a staple source of the industrial growth of Easton and Lehigh Valley. The economy had diversified to include manufacturing of hosiery, machinery, chemicals, paper, and textiles. In summary, through most of its history, Easton's economic base has been primarily manufacturing and light industry. At the time of the Institute, Binney and Smith, makers of Crayola crayons and many other products, was one of Easton's largest and most well known companies. At that time, the city was trying to regain and maintain vibrancy by capitalizing on its historic past and emphasizing tourism.

Design Problems

At the time of the Institute, the primary design problem of Easton was pedestrianization of its public square and reclaiming cracks in the downtown. At that time, the city had been aggressively seeking to revitalize the downtown by developing tourist attractions such as the Two Rivers Landing Museum and the

Crayola Center, both of which had exceeded the expectations forecast for visitors. Relocation of City Hall to the Center Square area from a site some distance from the downtown was also a redevelopment agenda. The museum is located in the heart of downtown at the Center Square. However, many visitors entered by the rear entrance adjacent to the parking garage rather than the front entrance, which opens on to the Center Square. As a result, the retail spillover to Northhampton Street and the rest of downtown had been less than anticipated. Part of the visitor absence in the downtown was attributable to a perceived shortage of parking in downtown, although in reality there was ample parking, both on streets as well as in garages. Cracks in the form of vacant storefronts and a perception of decline also contributed to a sense that the downtown was not a place to shop. Although some restaurants and other attractions had opened around Center Square, questions remained about how much the new attractions could continue to help reinvigorate downtown Easton and the surrounding region. Deterrents to pedestrianization included the difficulty of crossing to the center of the square; the speed of automobiles negotiating the space; and the discontinuity of sidewalks and crosswalks.

DESIGN SOLUTIONS

The specific solutions discussed at the Institute are related to the literature on pedestrianization, cracks and lost spaces. These are discussed below.

It was suggested that the city consider using traffic calming devices such as stone paving to control the flow and speed of traffic around the circle of the Center Square. The use of Two Rivers Landing Museum to accommodate flexible needs and would also help. It was recommended that the corner quadrants of the Center Square should not be designed solely as parking. Designing them as small paved areas that could be used as parking areas on selected days and other uses on other days could promote pedestrianization. Simple landscaping strategies such as avoiding small, less useful patches of grass and curbing, and making sidewalks continuous in form and material were also likely to promote pedestrianization. To further improve the quality of the pedestrian experience, the city could consider a small kiosk that might help to "launch" visitors to other parts of the downtown. Other strategies to enliven the area include encouraging restaurants and stores to locate around the square.

Reading, PA

When the mayor attended the Institute in 1994, the City of Reading faced the problem of bringing shoppers that visit its famous outlet stores in the outskirts to a declining downtown. Before we discuss this problem it is useful to note that Reading is 9.9 square miles in area and is located along the Schylkill River. According to the 1990 census, it had a population of 78,380 and a median annual household income of $32,510. In terms of ethnic composition, 71.6 percent were

White; 8.8 percent Black; 18.5 percent Hispanic; and 1.1 percent were of other races.

As we have done elsewhere, we look at the city's history to examine how this factor may have contributed to the decay of its downtown. Reading was founded in 1748 and serves as the seat of Berks County in Pennsylvania. The city grew steadily over the first 100 years and was incorporated in 1847. Reading's location along the Schylkill River allowed it to prosper early in the industry as a supplier of cannons and rifles during the revolutionary War. Later, the Reading Railroad, became a symbol of Reading's importance in the nation's transportation system. The City also served as an early eastern center for the manufacturing of automobiles.

The city is economically better off than many of the cities that have lost their traditional economy. Located only fifty-five miles northwest of Center City, PA, Reading has easy access to established roads, rail, and air transportation systems of the northeastern corridors. This strategic location affords Reading an opportunity to not only promote it's own economic and industrial markets, but also tap the resources of other industrial and agricultural bases throughout the northeast corridor. Reading's local economy has been growing, especially in the service sector including engineering, finance, and insurance operations. However, the brightest spot in Reading's economy was its role as regional factory outlet center, attracting more than 12 million shoppers every year.

Despite these positive features, cracks and lost spaces characterized its downtown area. The traditional downtown had been unable to draw shoppers that came to Reading's well known retail outlets that lie on the outskirts of the city. There was a vast amount of "lost space" between the downtown and the outlets. Furthermore, redevelopment failures of the 1960s and 1970s in the central business district has resulted in the proliferation of cracks in the form of vacant lots and the general demise of the downtown retail district.

DESIGN PROBLEMS

As is apparent, the major design problem facing Reading, are cracks and lost spaces in the downtown area and the vast amount of lost space between the downtown and the outlets. At the time of the Institute, the mayor's main concern was how to draw shoppers to Reading's downtown. Many of these outlets were located in renovated factory buildings half a mile away from the downtown but in people's minds, a world away from downtown. Shoppers generally arrived by bus or car and did little walking beyond the outlets. This was despite several efforts by the city to revitalize the downtown area through projects such as the renovation and expansion of City Hall and a new Berks County services building.

DESIGN SOLUTIONS

Drawing from the literature on pedestrianization, lost spaces, and cracks, several specific strategies can be developed to solve the problems of downtown Reading. The ones developed at the Institute are discussed below and certainly relate to this literature.

There were two distinct themes on bringing the shoppers to the downtown. One was to establish a bus or trolley route between the outlets and the downtown using existing streets. Another was to establish low-cost or free shopper parking downtown and shuttle people from there to the outlets. Actions aimed at filling the cracks and lost spaces in the downtown should be considered in a broad context. For example, a proposed civic center and hotel could be a catalyst, but its design should be related to the rest of the city. These buildings should be pedestrian friendly by providing multiple entrances through Penn Street, a major downtown street. Avoiding blank façades along the front of such buildings was considered to be desirable. Nearby activities should include restaurants and specialty retail, which would compliment the outlets, but not compete with them. Dense development of housing was also to be encouraged throughout the downtown area. Significant visual elements of the downtown such as the Astor theater, across the street from the proposed civic center should be a key component of filling cracks. The vacant theater could be used as a neighborhood movie house or a diner theater. Other suggestions included preserving the theater's façade and using it as an atrium for an office building or as an entrance to an interior shopping arcade. Resorting the marquee of the theater would give image to the project.

Concluding Remarks

Perhaps, it may now be apparent that urban design can act as a catalyst for revitalization of downtowns of small urban communities. The review of the literature suggested that there are two design-related deterrents to revitalizing downtowns. These are: (a) pedestrian unfriendliness and (b) lost spaces or cracks. Our analysis and reflection on the design issues that the mayors brought to the various meetings of the Mayors Institute on City Design confirmed that this was indeed the case with the cities that had downtown decay. As discussed, a variety of downtown revitalization issues including main street and waterfront revitalization were brought to the Institutes. Despite the variety of issues, pedestrian unfriendliness and cracks or lost spaces were still the primary types of design problems associated with these downtowns. Most cities had the simultaneous existence of pedestrian unfriendliness and cracks or lost spaces.

If we were to generalize the solutions we developed, strategies for pedestrianization include: widening of sidewalks, discouraging automobile traffic, improving safety and security, increasing attractiveness of sidewalks, improving the quality and quantity of sitting spaces, changing zoning ordinances to promote mixed uses, segregating pedestrians from vehicular traffic, adequate landscaping, promotion of on street parking, and improving the architectural character of the street. Generalized traffic control devices for pedestrianization include: speed limits and narrowing streets, traffic signals and cross walks, entrance gates, changing of paving materials, and promoting street parking. In general, cracks and lost spaces can be reclaimed by design elements that reinforce bonds of public space to the rest of the urban structure. Public spaces should become connectors rather than buffers between areas. Public spaces should be linked to surrounding districts through block walkways, arcades, and through integration of the streetscape. Lost spaces such as empty lots, river banks, parking lots, freeway leftover space, and abandoned railroad lines should be reclaimed by infilling such spaces into the historic fabric of the city.

However, we need to keep in mind that there is a need to understand the history of the city to develop an overall design philosophy to arrest downtown decay. As our historical analysis revealed, there is indeed a relationship between the history of a city and downtown revitalization problems for the cities that attended the Institutes. If we were to generalize our findings on the historical relationship between downtown decline and urban design, we can sum it up as a "loss of image" of these cities. We discuss the concept below.

The type of small cities that have downtown decline were cities that came into existence because of industries such as fishing and manufacturing, or were dependent upon early modes of transportation such as the railroad. With global industrial restructuring, many of the industries which traditionally sustained these cities have now disappeared or shifted elsewhere, leaving a decreased economic base and a new demographic composition. The long history of such cities and the very reason for which they came into existence gave them an image. They were known as fishing towns, mill towns, steel towns, textile towns and so on. This association with a particular industry was an integral part of the image. The image was also associated with people's culture, architectural styles, and the town's layout. Sometimes the image or identity of the city was associated with a particular place in the town such as city square or the main street. There was often a strong relationship between the built form and the social, economic, and political reasons for which the city came into existence. With global industrial restructuring, and changed circumstances, this strong relationship has disappeared. The traditional image of the city as fishing towns, clothing outlet towns, mill towns, steel towns, and textile towns can no longer be sustained. With these changed circumstances, there is perhaps, a loss of self confidence about the image of the city among elected officials. More often than not, they do not know how to deal with this change.

In order to overcome this loss of image at this juncture of history, these cities need to redefine their relationship with the past. In other words the city officials as well as the residents need to be aware of: (a) what the city is all about currently; (b) where it has come from (i.e., its traditional image and its historical past); (c) what the city wants to be in the future (i.e. its future image)?; and (d) how this future image relate to the past or what can be done with its architectural heritage and built form to achieve this future image? Only when a city is able to redefine its "image" in today's rapidly changing social, economic and demographic conditions, can it implement a successful design-oriented downtown revitalization strategy.

References

Appleyard, Donald. 1981. *Livable Streets*. Calfornia, Berkely: University of Calfornia Press.

Arendt, Randall with Elizabeth A. Brabec, Harry L. Dodson, Christine Reid, Robert D. Yaro. 1994. *Rural by Design: Maintaining Small Town Character*. Chicago, Il: Planners Press, American Planning Association.

Barnett, Jonathan. 1995. *The Fractured Metropolis: Improving the New City, Restoring the Old City, Reshaping the Region*. New York, NY: Harper Collins.

Birch, Eugenie Lander. 1980. "Radburn and the American Planning Movement: The Persistence of an Idea." *Journal of the American Planning Association* 46: 424-439.

Brambilla, Roberto, and Gianni Longo. 1977. *For Pedestrians Only*. New York: Whitney Library of Design.

Burgess, Patricia. 1997. "The Expert's Vision: The Role of Design in the Historical Development of City Planning." *Journal of Architectural and Planning Research* 14: 91-106.

Calthrope, Peter. 1993. The Next American Metropolis: Ecology, Community, and the American Dream. New York, NY: Princeton Architectural Press.

Daniels, Thomas L, John W. Keller, and Mark B. Lapping. 1995. *The Small Town Planning Handbook*. second edition, Chicago, Il: Planners Press, American Planning Association.

Duany, Andres and Elizabeth Plater-Zyberk. 1992. "The Second Coming of the American Small Town." *Wilson Quarterly* (Winter): 19-48.

Ellin, Nan. 1996. *Post Urbanism*. Cambridge, MA: Blackwell.

Glasmeier, Amy K. 1991. *The High-Tech Potential: Economic Development in Rural America*. New Brunswick, NJ: Rutgers, The State University of New Jersey Press.

Glasmeier, Amy K, and Marie Howland. 1995. *From Combines to Computers: Rural Services and Development in the Age of Information Technology*. Albany, NY: State University of New York Press.

Gratz, Roberta B, with Norman Mintz. 1998. *Cities Back From the Edge: New Life for Downtown*. New York, NY: John Wiley and Sons.

Halpern, Kenneth S. 1988. *Downtown USA: Urban Design in Nine American Cities*. New York, NY: Whitney Library of Design.

Hibbard, Michael and Lori Davis. 1986. "When the Going Gets Tough: Economic Reality and Cultural Myths of Small-Town America." *Journal of the American Planning Association* 52: 419-428.

Jacobs, Jane. 1961. *The Life and Death of Great American Cities: The Failure of Town Planning*. New York, NY: Vintage.

Katz, Peter, ed. 1994. *The New Urbanism: Toward an Architecture of Community*. New York, NY: McGraw Hill.

Kelbaugh, D, ed. 1989. *The Pedestrian Pocket Book: A New Suburban Strategy*. New York, NY: Princeton Architectural Press.

Krieger, Alex, ed. 1991. *Andres Duany and Elizabeth Plater-Zyberk: Towns and Town-making Principles*. New York, NY: Rizzoli.

Loukaitou-Sideris, Anastasia. 1996. "Cracks in the City: Addressing the Constraints and Potentials of Urban Design." *Journal of Urban Design* 1, 91-103.

Malizia, Emil E.1986, "Economic Development in Smaller Cities and Rural Areas." *Journal of the American Planning Association* 52: 489-499.

Moudon, Ann Vernez, ed. 1987. *Public Streets for Public Use.* New York, NY: Van Nostrand Reinhold Company.

Moudon, Ann Vernez. 1992. "A Catholic Approach to Organizing What Urban Designers Should Know." *Journal of Planning Literature* 14: 123-133.

Oc, Tanner and Steven Tiesdell (1996). "Editorial: Re-emergent Urban Design." *Journal of Urban Design* 1: 5-6.

Paumier, Cyril B, with W. Scott Ditch, Constance C. Dimond, and Dina P. Rich. 1988. *Designing the Successful Downtown.* Washington, D.C.: The Urban Land Institute.

Robertson, Kent A. 1990. "The Status of Pedestrian Mall in American Downtowns." *Urban Affairs Quarterly* 26: 250-273.

Robertson, Kent A. 1993a. "Pedestrians and the American Downtown." *Town Planning Review* 64: 273-286.

Robertson, Kent A. 1993b. "Pedestrianization Strategies for Downtown Planners: Skywalks Versus Pedestrian Malls." *Journal of the American Planning Association* 59: 361-370.

Robertson, Kent A. 1995. "Downtown Redevelopment Strategies in the United States: An End-of-the Century Assessment." *Journal of the American Planning Association* 61: 429-437.

Rubenstein, Harvey M. 1978. *Central City Malls.* New York: John Wiley and Sons.

Trancik, Roger. 1986. *Finding Lost Space: Theories of Urban Design.* New York: Van Nostrand Reinhold Company.

Whyte, William H. 1980. *The Social Life of Small Urban Spaces.* Washington, D.C.: The Conservation Foundation.

Whyte, William H. 1988. *City: Rediscovering the Center.* New York, NY: Doubleday.

ENDNOTES

1. Until the Spring of 1998, there had been four Regional Institutes and a National Institute. The Southeastern Institute was generally held by Georgia Institute of Technology for this period, except for a combined Northeastern and Southeastern Institute in 1997. We organized a total of four different Institutes between 1993 and 1998.

2. These included: Reading, PA; Gorton, CN; Wilmington, DE; New Bedford, MA; Frederick, MD; Wheeling, WV; Hagerstown, MD; Freeport, NY; York, PA; Newton, MA; Parkersburg, WV; Orange, NJ; Bowie, MD; Cranston, RI; Danville, VA; Easton, PA; Greeville, SC; Kingsport, TN; Mount Vernon, NY; Old Bridge, NJ; Annapolis, MD; Brockport, MA; Camden, NJ; Middleton, CN; Newburgh, NY; Niagara Falls, NY; Northhampton, MA, and State College, PA.

3. Radburn was the brainchild of the Regional Planning Association of America (RPAA) that was formed in 1923 by a group of like minded architects, engineers, economists, and urban critiques such as Lewis Mumford, Clarence Stein, Henry Wright, and Clarence Perry (Birch 1980; Burgess 1977). The unique contribution of Radburn was the separation of pedestrian and automobile realms. In Radburn, large residential n-eighborhoods (known as super blocks) were outlined by arterial roads. These arterial roads acted as feeders to lanes that ended in cul-de-sacs, thereby creating a hierarchy of streets and eliminating unnecessary traffic in residential areas. The segregation of pedestrian and vehicular traffic in the Radburn plan became a salient feature of the American new towns ranging from those built in the 1930s to the latter day Columbia.

4. The socio-economic and demographic profile and the history of all the cities discussed in the chapter are based on the data provided by respective cities.

CHAPTER 9

Disaster Recovery in a Progressive Community: Santa Cruz, California

DANIEL J. GARR

Santa Cruz, California is a city of 50,000 located on the northern rim of Monterey Bay on the central California coast. Favored by both nature and circumstance, it enjoys a mild Mediterranean climate, a picturesque physical setting as well as proximity to Silicon Valley. In addition, its economy is bolstered by large employment bases in city and county government as well as by a University of California campus (UCSC) with more than 10,000 students. Until the early 1970s, politics in Santa Cruz were dominated by the pro-growth forces instrumental in attracting the UCSC campus to the community during the previous decade. In a sense, Santa Cruz was, in microcosm, a typical sunbelt community with most key decisions made by the chamber of commerce whose influence was strongly felt in city government (Parker and Feagin 1990). By 1989, the year of the Loma Prieta Earthquake, UCSC's impact on the local economy was measured at $373 million, increasing to $666 million in early 1999 (Doyle 1989; University of California 1999).

However, UCSC's impact on the community was not only an economic one. When eighteen year olds won the right to vote in 1971, the political landscape began to change and the repercussions of this turnabout still resound. The 1972 election gave rise to California's Proposition 20, an initiative which placed strict controls on coastal development and established a statewide commission to review all such applications. Not surprisingly, it catalyzed a growing environmental community both statewide and in Santa Cruz. Concurrently, development proposals by the Hilton Hotel Corporation threatened the city's scenic Lighthouse Field (adjacent to a legendary surfing spot), and, in response to this challenge, a coalition of environmentalists captured all three contested seats (out of seven) on the City Council. Additional proposals for a nuclear power plant ten miles north in the town of Davenport and for a "new town" of 10,000 homes at nearby Wilder Ranch (now a state park), gave the environmental movement further causes around which to rally. But, it wasn't until the 1980 City Council election that the old guard permanently lost its grip on the Santa Cruz electorate.

For more than a year, local organizers working with the Tom Hayden/Jane Fonda Campaign for Economic Democracy brought to Santa Cruz direct mailing techniques and an array of longer-term political strategies. Among these were ballot initiatives certain to bring out the student vote at UCSC. These included a measure to establish a commission to prevent violence against women and another calling for withdrawal of all U.S. military aid to the government of El

Salvador. The plan worked to perfection and a council majority, fueled by the UCSC student vote, had been achieved. But it wasn't only students who supported the council majority. An assemblage of environmentalists, neighborhood activists, members of the political left, and self-styled "socialist-feminists" all contributed to the mix (Robinson 1992d). Within a year, funding for human services and the arts jumped from $80,000 to over $1 million, and a sweeping change in the makeup of city department heads transpired with administrators who were prepared to carry out the new political mandate (Rotkin 1994).[1]

The vehicle for Santa Cruz's political makeup was the construction of a "progressive" coalition built on the popular idioms of environmentalism, opposition to the military-industrial complex, representation of neighborhood interests in city politics, and other more abstract causes that had broad appeal but lacked the potential to foment a backlash among local residents. One of those was the preservation of Greenbelt open space. While the student population at UCSC may not have had a strong interest in more complex local issues such as downtown revitalization, high profile causes such as ending repression in Latin America would draw them into the voting booth. The organization that perennially provides the glue for this progressive movement is the Santa Cruz Action Network (SCAN) whose mission statement includes; exhortations for "democratic, decentralized control over institutions that affect the lives of local residents" protection of the natural environment, protection for tenants against excessive rents and unscrupulous landlords, full civil rights for all people and strong affirmative action policies, a full-employment economy, the right of all workers to strike, and "democratically controlled development of the local economy" (Santa Cruz Action Network 1989).

In late 1998, SCAN claimed an array of progressive groups including itself, the Sierra Club, the Green and Peace and Freedom Parties, Central Labor Council, Service Employees International Union, Surfers Environmental Alliance, People Power, UCSC College Democrats, and the like, that could boast 20,000 collective members, or about 40 percent of the city's population. SCAN proclaimed its dedication to building "an involved and organized community" working together for social and environmental justice. In short, in SCAN's view, Santa Cruz has a large progressive community and an electorate that wants a progressive City Council. This is not a place where only money talks. It's no wonder those who would have Santa Cruz become a more typical place would have you seeing monsters (Spitzer and Belton 1998). Those exulting words, written in a Sunday newspaper commentary, suggest an organization flush with an electoral victory provided by an extremely broad base of support. Indeed, the November 1998 election moved the City Council still further to the political left, perhaps as far in that direction as it had ever been positioned. The question remains, have SCAN's social, economic, and political philosophies been equal to the challenges faced by Santa Cruz? Beyond that question, how did Santa Cruz cope with the Loma Prieta Earthquake of October 17, 1989, a temblor that measured 7.1 on the Richter Scale? Much of the downtown ultimately was destroyed, including its most significant historic buildings. City government performance could no longer be measured in terms of funding the arts and social services; its locus now shifted to rebuilding its structures and economic confidence in the wake of a terrifying natural disaster.

This chapter will evaluate the rebuilding of downtown Santa Cruz including the performance of its leadership, choice of recovery strategy, consequences of and adherence to that strategy, and outcomes attained thus far. In doing so, the social and economic situation prior to the earthquake will be reviewed, as well as, the city's performance in the areas of historic preservation and social service provision with specific reference to the homeless population. The sources for this paper will largely be drawn from the daily newspaper of record, the Santa Cruz County Sentinel (SCS), other accounts in the press, and from public documents.

An Economy in Decline: Santa Cruz, 1981-1989

The most salient characteristic of downtown Santa Cruz was its Pacific Garden Mall, a limited auto access and pedestrian downtown of the type that was fashionable in the 1960s and 1970s. At the time of its construction, it temporarily transformed an undistinguished street, Pacific Avenue, into a leafy and attractive thoroughfare, at least until the early 1980s. However, its continued viability was called into question by national sectoral and geographic shifts that had affected nearly every downtown in the country. Consumers were increasingly drawn to suburban shopping centers with ease of access and plenty of parking (Houston 1990). In Santa Cruz County, this competition materialized in the form of a formidable enclosed mall in nearby Capitola containing four anchor department stores and many smaller shops. The newest of these anchors, Gottschalk's, was less than five miles from a branch in downtown Santa Cruz. Its opening jeopardized the future of the smaller, less accessible, and older store once its lease expired, and served as an ominous warning to downtown that change was at hand.

Not surprisingly, a five year trend in sales tax figures for the fiscal years 1983-84 to 1987-88 showed the Santa Cruz economy lagging behind all other areas of the County. Although Santa Cruz retail sales increased by 2.5 percent, those for nearby cities such as Watsonville gained 21.6 percent, Scotts Valley 13.9 percent, and Capitola, with its refurbished and nearby enlarged mall, managed an increase of 11 percent. In addition, there was a failed attempt to build an auto plaza within the city limits in order to retain four dealerships; these later moved to Capitola, taking with them a fourth of Santa Cruz's taxable sales, or $500,000 to $1 million in lost revenues (Miller 1989c).

However, countywide and national economic shifts were not the only issues bedeviling downtown Santa Cruz. Socially, it was gradually becoming a place to be avoided. As early as 1975 an economic study prepared by Gruen, Gruen and

Associates probed the downtown's desirability; 71 percent of respondents said they would not consider living there under any circumstances (City of Santa Cruz 1982, 79). By 1982, transients were identified as an "undesirable aspect" of the downtown and citizens felt threatened by panhandling; many business owners concurred that this climate was not favorable for retail trade. The City's response was the assertion that, "These sentiments are balanced by concerns for every citizen's civil liberties" (City of Santa Cruz 1982, 106).

A more sanguine view of the situation was propounded by Karen Gillette, former director of the Homeless Day Resource Center and the recipient of the Santa Cruz Area Chamber of Commerce's 1995 Woman of the Year award. A former Grateful Dead follower and computer programmer, Gillette was twenty-three, homeless, jobless and, nearly broke when she arrived in Santa Cruz in the early 1980s. She described it as "'Disneyland for hippies.' I'd never known there was a town like the Rainbow Gathering" (Krieger 1996). But the business community was less entranced and in the spring of 1989, an open feud developed between the Chamber of Commerce and the progressive City Council. It was the chamber's view that shoppers were avoiding the downtown and would not return until an adequate police presence dealt with panhandlers and their drug and alcohol use. The response from progressive downtown bookstore owner (and future mayor and councilman) Neil Coonerty was that downtown Santa Cruz had "held its own" against Capitola and other competitors (sales figures notwithstanding), and that he would make a serious effort to get downtown businesses and city businesses to reconsider their support of the Chamber of Commerce. Coonerty also took umbrage with the chamber's view that the downtown was unsafe, and, where at times, street people outnumbered shoppers (Miller 1989e). It was also in 1988 that the police chief requested $279,000 from the City Council for a directed patrol that would put a more prominent police presence in downtown, but that was rejected by the City Council which was already facing a $1 million deficit (Miller 1989d).

The daily Santa Cruz County Sentinel editorialized that, with a general fund budget of $26.9 million, the city had little more than $2000 in contingency funds and had just shifted $100,000 from the general fund to support social service programs, noting that the previous year's budget required hundreds of thousands of dollars in midyear cuts (Santa Cruz Sentinel 1989a). Those problems were somewhat abated by a regressive tax on utility bills, but a new proposal to establish a streetlight assessment district was ultimately rejected (Miller 1989d). Yet, City taxing policies continued to be burdensome. Later that year, two traditional Santa Cruz events were cancelled due to excessive city fees. The Jaycees 19th Annual Band Review bowed out, and the Beach Street Revival, a parade of classic and antique cars, decided to move to Watsonville (Lasnier 1989a).

In addition to the economic and social deterioration of downtown Santa Cruz, another pivotal controversy surfaced. In 1987 a city building official had proposed an ordinance to require the seismic retrofitting of the many unreinforced masonry buildings in the downtown. However, the consensus seemed to be that the costs of doing this would be far too high and make the downtown even less competitive with the shopping mall in Capitola. Efforts were made to pass legislation at the state level to provide low-interest seismic loans, but the bill was vetoed by then-governor George Deukmejian (Robinson 1990a).

Finally, in the midst of these events a bizarre political scandal also raged. Despite denials to the contrary, three progressives on the city council had sent an obscene valentine to a political opponent. But, when their identity was revealed by handwriting analysis, one was forced to resign and an unlikely replacement was chosen who has since been re-elected twice. Katherine Beiers, a library official at UCSC, was named for her experience on various public commissions, most recently as chair of the city's planning commission on which she had served for a number of years. In her presentation to the City Council and subsequent questioning, she stated that she had no ideas about economic development in the city (Miller 1989a). This rather startling admission proved prophetic for it exemplified the tendency of Santa Cruz progressives to view economic growth as an irrelevancy far from the purview of the Planning Commission.

This section has provided an overview of the issues and ideologies in Santa Cruz during the first eight years of progressive government. With Santa Cruz in economic decline due to social and regional economic shifts, its historic core of unreinforced masonry buildings at risk, and a city council embattled by scandal and besieged by a badly divided community, the Loma Prieta Earthquake of October 17, 1989 would mark a traumatic end to an already difficult decade.

Historic Preservation and the Loma Prieta Earthquake, Oct. 17, 1989

At 5:04 p.m. an earthquake of 7.1 magnitude on the Richter Scale ruptured the San Andreas Fault in the forest of Nicene Marks, some eighteen miles from downtown Santa Cruz. The temblor cancelled a World Series game in San Francisco and wrought considerable damage in San Francisco, Oakland, Los Gatos (across the mountains from Santa Cruz in Santa Clara County), and in Watsonville, fifteen miles south. In Santa Cruz itself, half of the downtown's historic buildings were damaged and the entire downtown, some thirty-two square blocks, was, at one point, entirely within the perimeter of a chain-link fence (Santa Cruz Sentinel 1989b).

The City of Santa Cruz faced both the "euphoria of opportunity" and some grim realities. For one, it was in dire financial straits before the earthquake, and now faced bankruptcy in its aftermath. In a political culture hostile to economic growth, the chairperson of the Zoning Board observed, "The whole concept of development has been that it is a crime. The city's planning apparatus ran on the assumption that if you're going to commit a crime, you have to pay a very high fine. If you build housing then you have to build a school" (Lasnier 1989b). The earthquake necessarily marked the beginning of a new era of growth for Santa

Cruz, but how would it be achieved? Would pragmatism win out over ideology, and would progressives accept formulas for growth that had been successful elsewhere?

But before rebuilding could begin, a massive cleanup job awaited and some difficult questions had to be answered. Most specifically, these hinged on the fate of the city's treasured historic structures. The most notable of these was the Cooper House, built in the 1890s as the county courthouse but more recently converted to shops and cafes; it was named a National Register Landmark in 1972. Prior to the earthquake, its owner had reinforced it at his own expense with steel rods and, because of this, representatives from the National Trust in Washington, DC, not to mention many others, tried to stave off the unthinkable. However, a hasty decision was made and the Cooper House was demolished nine days later on October 26, 1989, a task made all the more difficult by the seismic retrofitting (Gibson 1998). Hundreds watched in an emotional state of disbelief as the building came down. By November 17, 1989, twenty-two structures had been demolished, two were scheduled for demolition, and nine were deemed unsafe or pending demolition.

One of these structures was the St. George Hotel, facing Pacific Ave. with Front St. as a rear access. Built in the 1890s and expanded and remodeled on various occasions, it served most recently as SRO housing as well as providing space to various businesses, including the old Catalyst club, which some have compared to those beacons of 1960s psychedelia in San Francisco, the Avalon and Fillmore ballrooms. The fate of the St. George was to be a controversial one. Zoning Board Chairman and architect Mark Primack declared it a rather shabby remodel of an old building (Perez 1990b). Although originally slated for demolition, the St. George was temporarily spared on March 18, 1990 when the City Council rescinded its demolition order so that it might be reviewed by the State of California's Office of Historic Preservation, a process that would take less than thirty days. With the National Trust for Historic Preservation leading the fight to save the hotel, the issue became one of feasibility and finances with predictably opposite views propounded by the owner and by preservationists (Bergstrom 1990a). However, when the city decided in July to go ahead with the demolition, appeals were filed in Superior Court to stop the action. The city countered with a demand that preservationists post a bond for further economic harm that the litigation would cause to forty-five business and property owners because the perilous condition of the St. George had required the entire street to be fenced (Bergstrom 1990f).

However, a few days later all was made moot as the St. George burned to the ground in a fire of suspicious origin. It had been known to the City Council that the structure had become a haven for transients and nothing was done to discourage them (Perez 1990c). Illustrating the deep divisions in the community, some believed business interests were to blame for the arson, while others felt the city was grossly negligent in its failure to secure the building (Krieger 1990).

Nevertheless, the conflagration symbolized the inability of the city to cope with its growing transient population, a recurring theme in both the 1980s and 1990s.

A debate similar to that of the St. George also raged around the Trust Building, on the corner of Pacific and Soquel Avenues. Unlike the St. George, there was little question of the structure's significance as it had been deemed eligible for inclusion on the National Register of Historic Places and was considered one of the finest remaining structures in Santa Cruz (Snyder 1992). But in March, 1992, it, too, perished in the same manner as the St. George. Continuing its lack of oversight, the City Council turned a blind eye to the fact that people had been seen breaking into the building and sleeping there (Robinson 1992b). Two other vintage structures would subsequently share the same fate, though they were not located in the immediate downtown.

The city's failure to protect its heritage had other implications. In November 1990, even before the demise of the Trust Building, a State of California Historic Preservation Officer had advised the city of her intent to petition the keeper of the National Register of Historic Places to remove the Pacific Avenue Historic District from its books. It was contended that "the qualities which caused the district to be originally listed were destroyed after the Loma Prieta Earthquake in 1989." As only sixteen of the thirty-four significant buildings remained, "in groups of twos and threes, separated from each other by noncontributing buildings," the area had lost its character (Perez 1991). Despite Santa Cruz's protests, the California Historic Resources Commission removed the Pacific Avenue Historic District from the National Register; it would be the first time in memory that an historic district would be delisted. Yet, the city persisted in preserving what remained of its heritage. For example, the façade of the former County Bank was saved, and the reconstructed Palomar Hotel on Pacific Avenue was in the process of being added to the National Register. Additionally, the Leonard Building on Front and Cooper Streets was in the process of seeking a listing, while the Veterans Memorial Building and the neighboring U.S. post office were already on the National Register (Musitelli 1992).

Earthquake Recovery, Historic Preservation and Downtown Revitalization: Santa Cruz and Los Gatos

Downtown Santa Cruz lost thirty-four buildings, including its three priority landmarks: the Cooper House, the Trust Building, and, (ultimately) the Flatiron Building at the confluence of Pacific and Front Streets. Estimates of damage to downtown buildings ranged from twenty million dollars to fifty million dollars, but rebuilding costs would be much higher (Doyle 1989). By April of 1993, eight buildings had been repaired, eight constructed and five were underway (Santa Cruz Sentinel 1993b). In contrast, in the Town of Los Gatos, twenty miles north on the Santa Clara County side of the mountains, 104 commercial buildings were damaged including the town's largest structure, the 27,000 square foot La

Cañada Building. But by October 1991, all had been rebuilt and the downtown business district was virtually complete and in tact. A commercial real estate broker observed;

> Los Gatos got right on the problems at hand as well as a town can get on the problems. Five years from now, I believe the earthquake will be the best thing that ever happened to Los Gatos. It finally allowed the remodeling and rehabilitation of downtown (Beebe 1991, A1).

Los Gatos believed that rebuilding had to proceed rapidly. The Sunday following the October 17, 1989 earthquake, the Town Council established a policy designed to expedite the recovery process. If a building is replaced as it had been, there would be a fast-track, no-fee permit procedure. In many cases, detailed plans were not required before a project commenced; instead, it was reviewed as it progressed. This was done in order to make the process as painless as possible and to encourage those property owners who were in a standby mode to get started. The town's chief building official believed that "success bred success." Government reached out to those attempting to rebuild, telling people, "Here's what we can do for you. Here's how it works." And it did work (Beebe 1991, A1).

While Santa Cruz tore down its much-beloved Cooper House in a matter of days and failed to protect its other damaged historic structures, Los Gatos had an altogether different policy: secure the building and get multiple opinions on whether it could be saved. Thus, La Canãda survived the disaster and was open for business thirteen months later. Its owner said, "Los Gatos would not have tolerated our tearing it down. We had said among ourselves it would be cheaper to tear the damn thing down. But it was an historic building and I'm sure they would not have allowed that." In the end, she recalled, "It was as if the project was on wheels. I can't begin to thank them enough." The owner of the Opera House, another landmark, observed, "I felt real fortunate. I don't know what I would have done if I were building in Santa Cruz" (Beebe 1991).

Two years after the quake, Santa Cruz was marred by numerous empty lots awaiting reconstruction. How did rebuilding and recovery proceed in a community whose leading political organization had repeatedly proclaimed its dedication to an involved and organized community? (Spitzer and Belton 1998). Shortly after the earthquake the City Council established a working group, Vision Santa Cruz (VSC), purported to represent a broad spectrum of the community and whose aim was, "to spearhead the recovery process and develop a plan that was expressive of the values of the community." In the spring of 1991, fifteen months after the earthquake, VSC produced its First Principles, whose focus was directed at form and character of new buildings within an historic townscape; building height, scale and character, and provisions to ensure that buildings do not shade key public open spaces; housing opportunities to be targeted throughout the downtown; accessibility that integrates access to ensure increased opportunity for the public to participate in commercial, governmental, residential, social and cultural activities; open space and streetscape to produce a strong network of public and private open spaces; circulation with an emphasis on pedestrian, bicycle, and transit access; and parking provision in a centralized manner to maximize shared use and minimize the quantity of stored vehicles (City of Santa Cruz 1991). VSC made no mention of the economics of rebuilding and summarily dismissed the "time is of the essence" dictum that underlies the real estate industry.

The First Principles also articulated the structure on which change would occur. This included the pattern of downtown streets and blocks; the pattern of public and private ownership establishing texture and grain to the downtown fabric; buildings of architectural significance which provide for a strong continuity of the past; and opportunity sites upon which the Plan can "exert influence" (City of Santa Cruz 1991). However, a more ominous view of downtown rebuilding was espoused in June 1990 by Bruce Van Allen, a former mayor and member of the Vision Santa Cruz Board of Directors; while praising the consensus that the group reached, terming it fulfilling, empowering, sometimes even magical, Van Allen warned the business community, "many citizens of Santa Cruz have insisted that their voices be heard, that no one is right just because they have title to land, or title to expertise. No plan for reconstruction of downtown will succeed without the participation of the public; no decision that affects all of us will be made exclusively in private board rooms or on the golf course." This, too, is as it should be, as the people of Santa Cruz expand the meaning of democracy further over the prerogatives of property, however disturbing this too may be for some (Van Allen 1990).

But despite consensus, Santa Cruz showed little progress in recovery. As Los Gatos proceeded apace, such was also occurring in Watsonville, fifteen miles to the south. An informal downtown recovery committee, referred to as a "kitchen cabinet," reported to the City Council that things were going so well that it was disbanding and that the formation of another committee would be redundant. One developer had three projects in the works and the owner of Ford's Department Store had proposed a new 75,000 square foot facility, displaying little enthusiasm for the return of his establishment to Santa Cruz. The daily newspaper, the Sentinel, lamented; "There's consensus all around, but nothing seems to be moving forward." Topics were rehashed for the umpteenth time and the business community was divided and stifled by uncertainty; Santa Cruz, with its habit of studying things to death, was making little or no progress (Santa Cruz Sentinel 1990a). By August of 1990, the president of the Downtown Association had resigned from Vision Santa Cruz, citing preoccupations with housing and social issues as opposed to commercial rebuilding (Bergstrom 1990e). In October 1990, a San Francisco newspaper described the mood in Santa Cruz as a dreamy sort of schizophrenia (O'Connor 1990).

In the midst of the consensus-building process, the Urban Land Institute (ULI), a non-profit organization composed of real estate professionals, developers and market analysts, had offered its gratis services. By March 1990, it had produced a set of basic recommendations centering on retail continuity in a compact district as well as retention or replacement of the two pre-earthquake anchor stores, Gottschalk's and Ford's (Bergstrom 1990b). This position was also expressed by consultants hired by Vision Santa Cruz who further stressed the necessity that the first phase of the rebuilding plan should be large, impressive and on an anchor site in order to set the tone that downtown is a viable shopping area. Both consultants also put a damper on the naïve expectation of many VSC members that a significant number of affordable housing units would be built downtown due to high construction costs (Bergstrom 1990c). Also viewed by many as unwelcome news was the consultants' recommendation that an aggressive recruitment program targeted to San Francisco Bay Area and national retail chains should be conducted (Sprague and Company 1991).

In the meantime, displaced businesses were housed in a group of seven tents, the Phoenix Pavilions, a venture funded in November 1989 by the Chamber of Commerce and the Downtown Association. The original objective was a six month hiatus until permanent retail space could be found, but the experiment lasted thirty-eight months, until early 1993. While some praised them as a lifesaver not only for the economic salvation of the downtown, but, in some ways, "the psychic salvation of the community." In the words of Mayor Mardi Wormhoudt, others viewed them as an excuse not to rebuild, indeed a lead weight on the rejuvenation of downtown Santa Cruz (Lasnier 1993). But, in the end, the consultant's exhortations fell on deaf ears and rebuilding languished.

Issues in Rebuilding Santa Cruz: The Risks of Having Faith in Us

Eighteen months after the earthquake Vision Santa Cruz met to take final action on a plan for rebuilding. Created by the ROMA Design Group of San Francisco, the plan called for a standard three story building height, with five allowed in certain locations. Ground floor spaces would be exclusively retail or restaurants with offices or residential uses above. One-way traffic would be directed to a planned parking garage, later the subject of bitter eminent domain disputes. Much of the planning process consisted of block-by-block meetings with merchants and property owners to integrate their views into the final plan. One common thread was the use of wider sidewalks at key intersections to support kiosks and art displays. Landscaping, however, was still undecided. One member of Vision Santa Cruz observed that there would be a struggle over what trees would be planted; indeed, "it would be an agonizing process." (Bergstrom 1991b; Pearson, Pepper and Rotkin 1991). All in all, six million dollars was allocated for streetscape, demolition, infrastructure, and consultant fees while construction costs for new buildings would be in the fifty million dollar range (Bergstrom 1990h; Clark 1991b).

By early 1991, only one new building had been constructed, a 3800 square-foot structure housing a clothing store on a side street, not on Pacific Avenue. In the meantime, a dozen additional projects had been approved by the city council; yet, none of them were associated with any of the key anchor sites despite consultant recommendations that the first phase of rebuilding should focus on important structures in crucial locations (Bergstrom 1991a).

Instead, more energy was expended on the Pacific Avenue landscaping than on locating anchor tenants. Mayor Jane Yokoyama, a survivor of the 1989 Valentine's Day scandal, stated, "I honestly think the landscaping will be the biggest hurdle because more emotions are invested in the landscaping." City officials rationalized the glacial pace of rebuilding as a natural outcome of a five year process, with the more difficult projects taking even a decade or more to complete. Another explanation was the engineering complications of building in an area prone to heavy shaking during earthquakes, while the state of the national economy was also cited for the lack of development downtown (Bergstrom 1991a).

However, local lenders disagreed with the city's analysis. Pacific Western Bank chairman Phillip R. Boyce observed that property owners are having difficulty raising the 25-30 percent equity needed to qualify for a construction loan. He affirmed that the bank's lending criteria had not changed in the past five years and that ample funds were available in Santa Cruz (July 1991). While owners had equity when their buildings were standing, they now owed debt on holes in the ground and therefore couldn't qualify for a loan, a dilemma left unaddressed by the city and VSC. Another objection that troubled lenders was the street, infrastructure and landscaping improvements interfering with construction and with access by the public. Mayor Yokoyama complained, "The city has done a lot to facilitate rebuilding. We've been handing out carrots. Maybe we'll have to start using a stick." She further complained that, "It's very difficult for the city to show good faith when there's a professional level of game-playing going on about when projects may come on line" (Bergstrom 1991a). But perhaps perceptions of the City Council by the private sector may also have been a cause for delay. "He knows the risks of having faith in us," is what Don Lane, Yokoyama's successor as mayor, would say of a developer a year later (Mendoza 1992a). Yokoyama was not specific as to what "carrots" were offered the private sector. Unlike Los Gatos, fast-tracking and waiving fees were not yet on the table.

Another obstacle to rebuilding was the inevitably higher rents required by new construction. With month-to-month arrangements plentiful in the Phoenix Pavillions, many merchants felt they could wait for rents to drop while others managed to find homes in lower rent repaired buildings. Thus, the Pavilions ultimately slowed recovery as construction financing required seventy to eighty percent of square footage be pre-leased and tenants were not materializing. Ceil Cirillo, the city's new Redevelopment Agency director, pointed out that while indeed the space is more expensive, it is also more efficient. In buildings with twenty feet of storefront and one hundred feet of depth, one quarter of a store would be "dead space" whereas new construction would be wider and shallower, offering more storefront per square foot of leased space (Fay 1991).

And a third limiting issue was the downtown social ambience. Larry Pearson, chair of Vision Santa Cruz's Rehabilitation Subcommittee, said that street people have for many years presented a knotty social problem for the city and have now become an economic barrier to reinvestment. He cited this as one reason Gottschalk's Department Store was going to abandon its damaged Santa Cruz site and concentrate resources in its new Capitola store, five miles away. Pacific Western Bank Chairman Phillip Boyce said a prospective office tenant's major concern was the street people problem and the perception that downtown Santa Cruz was overrun with anti-social and criminal behavior. Police Chief Jack Bassett was adamantly opposed to a garden atmosphere as recommended by VSC's design consultants. He added:

> I strongly disagree with the concept of formal garden areas, courtyards and out-door performance space unless these areas are private property and used for the intended purposes. Open public space will be abused criminally and will be a policing nightmare. The terms extended garden and intensely landscaped will in my mind require three to four times the staff to maintain basic public safety (Bergstrom 1991a).

Despite Bassett's comments, it should not be inferred that Santa Cruz officials were indifferent to this concern. Over the years, they invested significant sums attempting to address social issues throughout the city; in a later section these efforts will be discussed.

Downtown Rebuilding: The Costs of Crony Capitalism

Thirty-three months had passed since the Loma Prieta Earthquake and no anchor tenant was in view for any major downtown parcel. In hopes of igniting development, in 1992 the Santa Cruz City Council decided to offer up to one million dollars for the right project, a dramatic change for a city where economic development had never been a priority (Robinson 1992c). This section will discuss efforts to secure that anchor tenant and in doing so, will illuminate the extent of Santa Cruz's commitment to its consultants' recommendations as well as to the political cronies of the city council. Also to be discussed are the role of the public sector and efforts to build on the downtown's premier anchor site; that of the hastily-demolished Cooper House.

In November 1992, three downtown developers proposed competing multi-screen cinemas despite protests from local theater owners that even one would put them out of business; two of these proposals were located in the downtown, but the third was outside the core on the corner of North Pacific and River Streets

(Mendoza 1992b). Even before serious discussions began, the first concern of the city was the impact of the proposed complexes on film offerings in the community and how film distribution would be affected (Mendoza 1992c). In the early going, the proposal on North Pacific and River Streets had a substantial edge despite its marginal, non-core location. Former County Supervisor and Santa Cruz Action Network insider Joe Cucchiara had proposed a six to ten screen theater in a two-story building with retail on the ground floor. Ostensibly, no public subsidies would be needed (Mendoza 1992d). But a couple of months later it was learned that more than $600,000 would be needed to create a "critical linkage" across heavily-trafficked Water Street from the downtown core. Additionally, the Santa Cruz Metropolitan Transportation District was requested to route large numbers of buses to serve the theater (Mendoza 1993a). However, this project foundered because of procedural disagreements between the city and the exhibitor, United Artists (UA). Although Cucchiara's proposal called for eleven screens, one of which would be reserved for community use, UA indicated they only planned eight, and further stated, they would not be closing their four-screen, art deco Del Mar Theater, coveted by the city as a performing arts center (Edwards 1993a). Yet, a year later, the Cucchiara proposal rose from the ashes of failed negotiations, and the city council embraced the concept of "extending" the downtown further north and upping the ante on the "critical linkage" to the downtown core by another twenty-five percent to $750,000. The number of screens, one of which would be used for community purposes, and the question of the Del Mar Theater as a performing arts center were all as yet unresolved, but Mayor Scott Kennedy proclaimed, "The big negotiations are done" (Musitelli 1994d).

Two days later, everything changed. A nine-screen and retail complex was proposed in the downtown core on the former Gottschalk's site on Pacific and Locust. Although an earlier deal had stalled in 1990 when agreement with United Artists could not be reached, this time the Harris Theater Corporation and Blockbuster Music signed commitments, with a second retail tenant in negotiations, to occupy the remaining 18,000 square feet of ground floor space of what would be called the Cinema 9. The rival developer, Cucchiara, boldly stated, "It doesn't affect us at all. They are two completely different kinds of projects" (Musitelli 1994e). Three years later, Cucchiara was still proclaiming projects of this size just take time to amass the necessary tenant base. If construction had not begun by November 1997, the building permit would expire, requiring $22,000 in new fees, although the City Council would have the option of waiving them. And former mayor Kennedy suggested that the $750,000 in street improvements that had been promised now be reallocated to other downtown projects (Clark 1997a).

In May 1995, the Cinema 9 opened and single-handedly revived nightlife. On target to draw 700,000 people a year to its large screens, it proved to be the elixir that retailers and restaurants needed to advance their hours well into the evening. For example, the Pacific Cookie Company said forty percent of its business was done after dinner (Musitelli 1995d). In the first three weeks since the opening of Cinema 9, Natural Treasures, with its psychedelic candles, began to stay open to 11 p.m. on weekends and its business increased by fifty percent (McMillan 1995). The crowds on the streets were now substantial as new bookstores, coffee houses, and restaurants opened their doors. Russ Brink of Downtown Eugene, Inc., hired by the Downtown Association and the Redevelopment Agency to evaluate the changes, reported;

> There's a phenomenal amount of excitement and activity. It was jammed with
> people. It made me real jealous. Our downtown isn't like that at night. Yet
> (Musitelli 1995c, A1).

Another progressive County Supervisor would also play a major role in downtown Santa Cruz. In the fall of 1990, the city had amassed nearly half the cost for an $8 million parking garage on the corner of Locust and Cedar Streets. Councilman John Laird had successfully lobbied for a $2 million grant from the Economic Development Administration in Washington DC, the first time in a decade that funds had been allocated for such a purpose. The EDA agreed that the structure was crucial to revitalizing downtown as bigger buildings require more parking; the garage would provide 417 new spaces with as many as 250 needed to accommodate future employees of downtown stores and offices. Even so, the City Council was unconvinced of the utility of spending millions of dollars on a building that would house nothing but empty cars and some retail on the ground floor. The architect, perhaps with morbid humor, suggested the brick façade would be reminiscent of the old Cooper House in appearance.

The assembling of the land for the Cedar Street parking structure provides additional insights into the nature of progressive politics in Santa Cruz. The largest parcel on which the garage sits was owned by the family of Gary Patton, a five term county supervisor, and the most influential progressive politician in the county for more than two decades. In March 1991 the City Council voted to bring eminent domain proceedings against three property owners who controlled the remaining land needed for the new garage. When they were offered fifty dollars per square foot, they countered with eighty-five dollars, and cited recent land sales in the area of sixty to ninety per square foot. A Superior Court judge, however, ruled they were entitled to only forty-four per square foot (Rogers 1991). Seven years earlier, in March 1984, the Patton family had agreed to a ten year lease option with the city for their mid-block, 6,479 square foot parcel, priced as raw land. When the option was exercised in 1989, they collected $354,440 plus five years of lease payments at $60,000 per year, or approximately $101 per square foot.[2] Even allowing for inflation, the discrepancy between prevailing land values, the price paid for the Patton family land and that awarded in the Superior Court eminent domain suit, the question of cronyism and a level playing field cannot be dismissed.

The construction of the Cedar Street Garage, begun in 1991, can be seen as emblematic of the initial phase of rebuilding in Santa Cruz. More than two years after the earthquake, private sector participation was virtually non-existent in downtown. "We've been waiting for the private sector to come forward, but we can't wait forever and we're not waiting," lamented Mayor Don Lane. Indeed, the difference between new construction and empty holes in the ground was money, specifically, public money. Even in proposed buildings, city officials were lobbying state agencies such as the Coastal Commission to pre-lease office space, but no public tenant had yet materialized (Robinson 1992a).

There were four projects now underway, all of them heavily subsidized. The Cedar Street garage had already secured substantial federal funding. Second, the new St. George Hotel, affordable SRO's, had amassed nearly six million dollars in loans and grants from the public sector. Third, the McPherson Art and History Center on Front and Cooper Streets, a former County jail, had received a $2.5 million federal grant plus the structure itself was already in tact; it did need substantial rehabilitation, however. And fourth, the Mercado El Centro project of the Santa Cruz Community Housing Corporation (CHC) represented perhaps the most elaborate assemblage of public monies. This included nearly $1,500,000 from the State of California Rental Housing Construction Fund, about $350,000 from the City of Santa Cruz/Red Cross Housing Reconstruction Fund, $200,000 from the U.S. Department of Health and Human Services, $1,600,000 in Low Income Housing Tax Credits, and $250,000 from David and Lucille Packard Foundation (Robinson 1992a).

El Centro was the second undertaking of the CHC, a non-profit corporation created by the city council to develop affordable housing. The first, Neary Lagoon, was beset by problems, most notably the failure of its $3 million drainage system which polluted Monterey Bay on a number of occasions and prompted the California Regional Water Quality Control Board to require the city to obtain permits for any future discharges (Mendoza 1993b; Musitelli, 1994a; Robinson 1993b, 1993c, 1994). Despite these problems, which resulted from building on fill, the city made a finding of no significant impact on the environment for Neary Lagoon (City of Santa Cruz 1989). El Centro had its own problems, one of which stemmed from the relationship of the CHC to the Santa Cruz City Council. Two former mayors, Bruce Van Allen and Jane Yokoyama quickly found themselves in its employ. It will be recalled that Van Allen had set the tone for downtown in 1990 with his newspaper commentary, warning that the public would not tolerate decisions made in private board rooms or on the golf course and that Santa Cruz would expand the meaning of democracy further over the prerogatives of property (1990). By 1992, Van Allen had secured a position as the CHC's project manager for El Centro despite the fact he had no obvious background for the job, and his own business as a cabinet maker was "in shambles" (Robinson 1992d).

One of the goals of El Centro was to assist first-time business operators in forming food-related businesses congregated around a food court which would occupy about half of the 7500 square foot ground floor of the commercial/residential development. The upper three floors would contain fourty-four single occupancy rooms for low-income seniors, aged sixty-two and older. Completion of the $4.7 million project was anticipated in April 1993 (Lasnier 1992). That deadline would not be met. On February 5 of that year, the contractor stopped work after not being paid for several months. The Bank of America refused to disperse funds due to concerns about the contractor's dependability and the CHC's inability to manage the job. This in turn triggered further scrutiny by the State of California Department of Housing and Community Development, which had provided $1.4 million in funds; its interests also had to be addressed. The local press obtained a letter via the Freedom of Information Act which revealed that the bank demanded a new contractor and detailed reviews of project expenses, remaining budget, plans, specifications, and an updated completion schedule. Van Allen said at the time he could not remember the originally scheduled completion date or when the project would be completed (Mendoza 1993c).

The six month hiatus proved to be a costly one as work did not recommence until July, resulting in cost overruns of ten percent (Mendoza 1993d). A new project manager was brought in who had significant experience with publicly funded affordable housing development; and it was completed in December 1993, nine months late and $500,000 over budget (Edwards 1993). But problems with El Centro did not end there. Despite the fact that Santa Cruz is one of the most costly housing markets in the country, from mid-1995 through January 1999 chronic vacancies required advertising for tenants; presenting the ad would result in a month of free rent if a six-month lease were signed. Not surprisingly, the main street of downtown Santa Cruz was not a good location for senior housing. A sixty-six-year old El Centro resident complained of drug use, aggressive panhandling, screaming, and swearing; in one incident every buzzer for every room was pressed and obscenities yelled into the intercom. A year earlier, another senior complained; "The scene really gets moving around 11 p.m. and goes full tilt until all the bars close. The nightly menu consists of fights, shouting and screaming matches, men beating up their girlfriends, and car stereos played so loud our window frames shake" (Musitelli 1996). As for the food court, it was never successful, plagued by vacancies, sparse foot traffic, broken promises, rents which more than quadrupled, and the above-noted street ambience outside (Musitelli 1997). In January 1999, it was learned from a commercial real estate broker that the Mercado ground floor had been vacant for over six months and was available for leasing (McKendrick 1999).

But the most arduous chapter of downtown rebuilding would occur on the Cooper House site. Its location was the enduring symbol of both pre- and post-earthquake Santa Cruz. More than any other parcel, it embodied the spirit and centrality of the downtown and served as an icon of success or failure in the community's efforts to rebuild. By December 1989, plans were being discussed for a new structure whose neo-Romanesque design would be reminiscent of its universally-lamented predecessor. The first issues to be resolved were seismic in nature. Geotechnical studies suggested pilings to seventy feet would be necessary. Jay Paul, the owner of the former building for eighteen months prior to the earthquake, had been in the process of remodeling when the disaster occurred and had already completed seismic strengthening. In all, he had suffered a couple of million dollars in losses and did not anticipate any assistance from the city, but he remained optimistic about the future of downtown and his ability to find tenants and secure financing. He also dismissed concerns from California legislator Sam Farr that Santa Cruz would go the route of Carmel, whose high rents were driving small businesses out of town (Lasnier 1990).

But things remained stagnant for the next twenty-one months. By the fall of 1991 Paul's plans for the Cooper House had expanded to include an adjacent lot as the new structure was to include 100,000 square feet of retail and office space among its five stories. Discussions were being held with two restaurants for ground floor space as well as with a national children's clothing store and other shops. All the funding would be from private sources and it was expected that the City Council would approve the structure within the next month (Clark 1991a). However, another three and a half years would pass before further progress was manifested. In March 1995, Fractal Design, a rapidly growing software company, had signed a ten-year lease for 40,000 square feet of space, enough to put the project over the 70-75 percent pre-leased requirement so that financing could be obtained. Part of the synergy that reinvigorated the Cooper House was the progress made on the Cinema 9, which was to open in two months. It re-established confidence in Santa Cruz as a viable commercial center and triggered other building projects as well (Musitelli 1995a).

But the Cooper House was still stalled. Although the entry of Fractal Design was an encouraging development, city parking deficiency fees had to be paid. In September 1995, the City Council voted to provide $1.1 million in subsidies for 188 employee parking spots in three city garages at an annual cost of $118,440; Paul would have the option of securing an additional 92 spaces if needed. With that in hand, Paul said he would start construction immediately and finance the project himself. In addition, another high tech tenant, software imaging leader Live Picture, Inc., had agreed to a Cooper House lease (Musitelli 1995b). But problems with financing continued to plague the landmark site and Fractal Design backed out in favor of a new site in Scotts Valley, better known as home of Seagate Technology and six miles closer to San Jose and Silicon Valley (Miller 1996).

Maneuvering continued, this time with Cisco Systems. The computer networking leader had purchased Santa Cruz-based TGV Software in January 1996 and had expressed interest in a five-year lease, half the length sought by the developer. There were also issues relating to whether the city could provide incentives to Cisco in the form of subsidies to property taxes for its sophisticated equipment (Miller 1996). But a year later, Cisco was out of the Cooper House picture and with the commitment to subsidize parking fees about to expire, the City Council would have to renew its offer if there were to be any hope for new development on the site. Therefore, in April 1997 a six-month extension was granted which appeared to pay dividends as the $70,000 in building permit fees were finally paid in October, 1997; had those fees been delayed one day further, the parking subsidies would have been withdrawn. Linda Steinau, executive director of the Downtown Association, proclaimed, "I think we all know the old Cooper House was the heart of downtown. It's the real, final linchpin in our recovery" (Clark 1997c). But once again, the project foundered and the parking subsidy agreement expired. For the first time since the earthquake, city officials belatedly expressed in the press the belief that the Cooper House was indeed central to downtown recovery (Clark 1998a).

At least work was finally beginning on the other downtown anchor parcels. With the completion of the Cinema 9 in May 1995, four major sites remained vacant, including the Cooper House. But by early 1998, progress had begun on three: the site of the old Flatiron Building, completed in the summer of 1998; the old Trust Building, which had earlier succumbed to a blaze of mysterious origin; and the site of Ford's Department Store on which the University of California planned to build offices and student housing (Clark 1998c). But, a fourth key location, a 12,000 square foot plot on the southwest corner of Locust and Pacific, remained a weed-strewn eyesore.

Finally, in July 1998, development of the Cooper House was ready to begin and has in fact moved forward. This time the City Council offered a scaled back package of $950,000 in parking subsidies for ten years, the sum predicated on the property taxes to be generated by the project on an annual basis. But the Council did add a caveat to its deal, requesting that any ground floor retailers refrain from competing with nearby businesses. The chief beneficiary of this provision was bookstore owner and former mayor Neal Coonerty. This led councilwoman Cynthia Mathews to raise the issue of fairness, believing that the development was given too many cash incentives. Jay Paul, in the meantime, had put $3 million of his own money into the Cooper House. This was probably the last chance for the structure; if it had not moved forward, some believe it would not have been built in the foreseeable future (Clark 1998b). It is scheduled for completion in July, 1999.

Social Services, Street People and the Homeless in Santa Cruz

The deteriorating social ambience in downtown Santa Cruz, already a factor in the 1970s, had become a critical concern in the early 1980s, but nothing was done to address it until the year of the earthquake. Ironically, a task force was scheduled to meet on October 18, 1989, one day after the temblor. Nine months later, Vision Santa Cruz voted to take up the question but soon found itself in factions as to whether the street element should be allowed to participate.

Councilman and socialist-feminist Mike Rotkin, one of SCAN's founders, argued against the idea:

> What I understand this issue to be about is certain kinds of illegal and antisocial behavior. You're not going to go out and find a panhandler to serve on a committee. As far as I'm concerned, as soon as they identify themselves as panhandlers, they should be arrested. (Perez 1990b; A1)

A contrasting view was propounded by Mayor Mardi Wormhoudt who argued, "I cannot imagine they'd (VSC) be foolish enough to develop plans that affect people's lives without consulting them (Perez 1990a).³ Participation or not, the issue of street people in Santa Cruz had so transcended the local arena that the city was now a national magnet as homeless activists poured in from outside the county for a July 4, 1990 protest targeting the city's camping ban. In a countervailing action, a large number of area residents called for a "Take Back Our Town" demonstration at city hall, also on July 4. Lost in the emotions of the day was the fact that in 1990–91 the county budget had allocated more than $2 million specifically for homeless services such as health care, job placement, food and shelter, all on top of more than $80 million in related services from which the homeless could benefit. In addition, Santa Cruz was one of two counties in California to receive a federal supportive outreach grant for assistance to the mentally ill and others. The county was also one of 105 jurisdictions which received a Stewart B. McKinney grant to provide health care for the homeless and had just received another $182,000 to assist homeless individuals and families in the earthquake's aftermath (Santa Cruz *Sentinel* 1990).

Over the years, the homeless, street people, deadhands, and allied protestors have held center stage in downtown Santa Cruz. But even beyond that, a total of fifteen distinct agencies (or perhaps more) had been established to specifically cater to the homeless. They include: Santa Cruz Citizen's Committee for the Homeless, Community House, Homeless Community Resource Center, Homeless Garden Project, the River Street Shelter, Coalition for a Safe Place to Sleep, Homeless Day Center, Interfaith Satellite Shelter Program, Local Emergency Food and Shelter Board, New Life Shelter, Cabrillo Shelter Project, Free Meal, St. Francis Shelter, Homeless Person's Health Project, and Housing Options. While many of these have since merged or been superceded, it is by any standard an impressive array of infrastructure for a city of 50,000 and a county of 200,000. But since most of the county social services catering to the homeless are in or near downtown Santa Cruz, the bulk of the problem was in the city itself (Beebe 1990). And yet the homeless problem has persisted over the years, often flaring with seriously disruptive consequences for the downtown.

Confrontations between the street population and society have continued to persist in downtown Santa Cruz. Just before Christmas in 1993, a group of homeless occupied a strip of sidewalk in the name of their World Peace Vigil, receiving the support of Mayor Scott Kennedy. The manager of the Santa Cruz Coffee Roasting Company observed, "It seems really pointless that we put millions and millions into the downtown area." And the owner of Game-A-Lot Toys, said; "When I walk by in the morning, I can smell them a block away. I'm a big believer in human rights, but nobody likes to go where it stinks." Deputy Police Chief Jeff Locke said that although there had been an outcry from merchants, those conducting the Vigil were asserting their First Amendment Rights, but had not been caught sleeping in violation of the city's camping ban. Further, he offered; "It is tough for us to take any other position when you have the mayor going out and speaking for them"(Mendoza 1993e). The next night, rioters ran rampant as twenty stores had windows broken and five police officers were injured; $30,000 in damages were recorded (Mendoza 1994). But the World Peace Vigil continued, with participants cited for violating the camping ban. One of them had already cost the city $1,000 in police time and his citations filled three screens on the Police Records Office computer (Musitelli 1994b).

By now, even the progressive City Council was running out of patience. In March 1994 it approved what was believed to be the toughest anti-panhandling laws in the state, but dropped a requirement that beggars obtain a permit. They would be allowed to sit quietly, holding signs, but aggressive soliciting, blocking a sidewalk, following people, swearing, asking for money after dark, or near banks, vending machines or on buses was prohibited. Oddly, people asking for money were not allowed to misrepresent their reasons for doing so. Further, it was illegal to recline or sit on sidewalks; and other restrictions were based on public nuisance laws (Musietelli 1994c). The legislation precipitated continued conflict downtown with resistance both before and after dark. In May 1994, 300 protesters confronted police, breaking windows in four downtown establishments. Interim Police Chief Steve Belcher related, "One group had a party attitude, a few people were there for true civil disobedience issues, and a contingent was there just because they feel they have the right to do what they want whenever they want." Several council members expressed reservations as to how the demonstrators were treated, but Belcher insisted, "It was a very militant crowd. Police were continually taunted by people in the crowd and were hit by rocks, eggs, and bottles. There's a difference between civil disobedience and in-your-face-type of confrontation" (Marks 1994). In August, 1994, two local judges threw out cases brought for violating the Santa Cruz ordinance even though a similar set of laws had been upheld in Seattle by a federal judge (Santa Cruz County Sentinel 1994). Finally, by early 1996, when U.S. District Judge William Orrick withdrew his decision which upheld panhandling as a manifestation of free speech, the city's package of ordinances stood in tact, albeit with some modifications (Clark 1996a): Two years had now passed, consuming countless hours of council time and the downtown was still not at peace.

In February 1996, homeless activists occupied city hall's pleasant breeze-ways in a round-the-clock bivouac, leaving a trail of litter, human waste, and rats.

The City Council voted 5–2 in closed session to ask the City Attorney to obtain a court injunction against the campers whose actions sought to dramatize their wish that the city's camping ban be repealed. In the previous year, council members had sought to find a facility where homeless people could sleep during the summer when winter emergency shelter programs close but had little success (Clark 1996c). But a Superior Court judge refused to uphold the city's view and the chaos continued (Clark 1996d).

During the 1996 city council elections, downtown emerged as the key issue. "It isn't getting any better, it's getting worse," said Julie Hendee, co-owner of the popular women's store Cat N Canary. "It's getting more violent." The business had lost $300,000 in three years largely due to the transient element. Another candidate said; "Santa Cruz residents' may have arrived at the point that limits of tolerance may have been reached. The issue is who owns the street" (Clark 1996f, A1). The city was not without its own creative solutions. In 1994, Mayor Scott Kennedy wrote to Jerry Garcia of the Grateful Dead, asking for help to feed the hordes of the band's followers who regularly descended on Santa Cruz, inundating the city's soup kitchens. But a band spokesman replied; "There are lots and lots of people in Santa Cruz with long hair and tie-dyed T-shirts, and many of them are employed taxpayers. The last I heard, we weren't issuing identity cards to our fans" (Guara 1994b, A17). Three years later, a merchant-led campaign resulted in rising tempers. The goal of their "Real Change, not Spare Change" program was to offer the homeless names and telephone numbers of community resource groups. But Karen Gillette, executive director of the Homeless Community Resource Center, was less sanguine. "The cards will be an excellent gauge of what people really want" she said. "If you give someone a card and get responded to with a barrage of obscenities, that answers the question" (Clark 1997b; A1).

Thus, if legislative and community strategies had proven insufficient to address the long-simmering downtown social ambience, what contributions did the publicly-funded agencies add to the cause of homeless issues for a population estimated at 600 for the city and 2,000 in the county? The following pages will review activities at the River Street Shelter as well as the activities of the Santa Cruz Citizens' Committee for the Homeless (SCCH). The River Street Shelter, about a mile north of downtown, is administered by the Santa Cruz Community Counseling Center. A daytime correlate program, Pioneer House, is managed by the same agency; both are supported by a combination of local, state, federal and private funds with a combined annual budget of about $700,000. With its thirty beds the shelter typically provides about 11,000 nights of lodging per year to a client group that is typically white, male, 22 to 34 years of age, with little or no income and a history of psychiatric, drug or alcohol problems. In addition to a place to sleep, it provides shower and laundry facilities, two meals, storage lockers and coordinated drug/alcohol, mental health, job, and housing counseling (Beebe 1992). The Shelter has tough rules and regulations with a focus on treatment and rehabilitation. In 1995, eighty percent of the Shelter's population was addicted to drugs and alcohol and fifty eight percent was mentally ill. But the homeless population is not static, with nearly half having arrived in the previous eleven months. The perception exists that they were coming to Santa Cruz faster than they could be rehabilitated, if such were always possible. Nancy Houk, its program manager, called for the establishment of another shelter, suggesting that "downtown people need to become part of the solution by understanding what the homeless are all about" (Benson 1995, 5).

The second major force in homeless issues and advocacy was the Citizens' Committee for the Homeless (SCCH), founded in 1985. Its initial objective was to secure funding in order to purchase an acre of land adjacent to the River Street Shelter and build a low-cost housing facility to be known as Community House. This goal received an initial boost in 1990 with a $225,000 grant from the Red Cross as part of its earthquake recovery program. However, until Community House could be built, SCCH championed the cause of a legal camping facility on the site with facilities and services that could accommodate up to 150 people; this cause was joined by the Coalition for a Safe Place to Sleep and other organizations, allegedly some fifteen in all. Another goal of SCCH was the purchase of land for a permanent camp outside the city limits (Kostyal 1990). However, the city was not ready to support such a concept as it already was contributing to several other related programs and lacked funding for the necessary infrastructure improvements and a six-month operating budget in excess of $130,000.

Without a city-sanctioned campground, the site was used anyway for a number of years and a SCCH spokesman said, "It became a place where people bought and sold drugs, and we had to close it down and patrol it." Termed the Open Air Shelter, it was nevertheless backed by a number of social service programs. After breakfast, the campers would place their belongings in a tent and head out to jobs, classes, or treatment programs, while others would pursue their own agendas. Surrounding the campground is the year-round River Street Shelter, a small medical clinic, one public shower and 214 old bus station lockers. Although the campground costs $150 per night to run, it was a relative bargain in that by 1994 the City of Santa Cruz was spending more than one million dollars on homeless programs (Guara 1994a).

Although the campground had successfully offered lodging during the summer months for the past three years, in 1995 city officials sought to close it down for the rainy season, offering the National Guard Armory as an alternative. But the Armory did not allow dogs and imposed strict behavior standards. When the residents demanded the site be kept open on a year round basis, threatening to invade downtown Santa Cruz during the Christmas shopping season, the city relented. But after a downpour that lasted nearly a day, the low-lying site became a morass of foul mud, contaminated by three overflowing portable toilets and the feces of the twenty on-site dogs (Guara 1995). As an alternative, the city voted to accept ten donated trailers from Stanford University as a transitional housing program for forty-five people, refusing to allocate further funds until doubts about SCCH could be resolved. It was also sensitive to pressure from homeless service providers, who were now competing for city funds against the campers' demand for monies (Musitelli 1996a).

The closure of the city's campground paved the way for one of the most bizarre episodes in its long and costly history to aid the homeless. The encampment was moved en masse to New Brighton State Beach in Capitola with city funding and an unspecified amount of private donations. Councilman Mike Rotkin maintained that, "the group was not criminals and are basically living in a state campground like anybody else has the right to do, when we take the entire welfare, mental health and jail population for the county." Capitola and mid-County authorities were outraged, and Rotkin offered that County Supervisor Walt Symons had never before shown any interest in the homeless issue until then (Musitelli 1995e). By the end of the two week experiment, one-fifth of the campers had been arrested for substance abuse or inappropriate behavior. Nonetheless, it was later resurrected in March 1996. "This may be the stupidest thing we've ever done, but we've got a commitment to these people," said councilwoman Katherine Beiers. And George Cook, District Superintendent for the State Department of Parks and Recreation, disputed the appropriateness of residential use of campgrounds, and indicated legal action would be taken (Wildermuth 1996). Others urged members of the city council to house the homeless in their own yards. Councilman Scott Kennedy said that people who believe Santa Cruz wasn't doing enough to solve the problem should "adopt" a homeless person, saying he would take up the issue with his own family (Clark 1996b). But when only twelve people signed up for the State Campground program, it was quietly abandoned.

Ultimately it was thought the Stanford trailers would serve as the basis for the long awaited Community House; eight would be used as housing, one as a kitchen/dining area, and one for administrative staff. The construction phase of the project was expected to cost $250,000 with less than half of those funds already on hand, $83,500 was provided by the city's Community Development Block Grant Program and $50,000 from the Packard Foundation, but only 50 percent of that could be used for construction. Moreover, $300,000 per year would be required for operating expenses. The money for this came from a HUD grant which was designed to reward the best homeless programs in the nation. Community House would receive $662,000 in federal funds while the Homeless Community Resource Center, which provides services for those requiring immediate help, would receive $310,000. The grant was the culmination of the work of a consortium of twenty agencies with homeless programs located throughout the county. However, instead of the older trailers from Stanford, the city decided to buy eight new double-wides for a total cost of $360,000. With a construction budget estimated at $1.3 million, it was uncertain how all the funding would be amassed (Clark 1996e). That finally was settled in September 1997 when the city agreed to a loan worth $557,000 amortized over twenty years. It was assembled from another federal grant as well as from remnants of the Red Cross Earthquake Housing Reconstruction Fund; up to forty people would be housed at the facility (Santa Cruz Sentinel 1997).

However, just as it appeared Community House and the SCCH appeared to have righted themselves, an internal audit uncovered some disturbing findings; but even this did not satisfy the city since the examination was not conducted by an outside certified public accountant, which is required of all non-profits to which it grants funds. The SCCH had in fact not had such an audit for the past two years. It was found that the Community House project director had diverted the organization's funds to himself for personal reasons and not for reasons concerned with the business of Community House. As a result of non-compliance with city policies, SCCH was cut off from all funding until an outside audit was done. In addition, funds obtained from the Packard Foundation could not be properly accounted for (Gammon 1997).

The Page Smith Community House was scheduled to finally open on June 1, 1998, but that date was cast into question as more problems with SCCH began to surface. Although the organization was purported to be successfully managing its $721,000 budget, that was achieved largely because $300,000 in loans or misused grants were either forgiven or restructured. In addition, the formal outside audit had not yet been performed, SCCH had operated for a year without an executive director, and had been found to have had fifteen separate checking accounts, each requiring only one signature. In addition, it faced a wrongful termination suit from the employee who allegedly diverted organizational funds for his own personal account. A final vexing issue was the fact that the organization had no funds to hire an executive director for the 1998–99 fiscal year and had already spent all of the city's annual $50,000 commitment to help it run Community House. The problem of leadership may have been solved by merging with the Homeless Community Resource Center, but complications arose with the Resource Center's Director and the Board of SCCH (Clark 1998b). In the meantime, transients both downtown and in the neighborhoods, continued to be a problem. In the wake of the 1998 City Council election, which culminated in a sweeping victory for the left, re-examination of the city's camping ban became the first item of discussion.

Conclusion: Leadership, Planning and Urban Revitalization

Leadership is a crucial factor in addressing urban economic decline. Further, the capacity of that leadership to formulate and project a coherent strategy for coping with decline will determine the success or failure of the city's revitalization efforts. In Santa Cruz, nearly a decade after the Loma Prieta Earthquake, the downtown streetscape amply exemplifies the strengths and weaknesses of the city's political culture.

It is in public sector activities that Santa Cruz has excelled. Infrastructure for the rebuilt downtown was adequately funded from higher levels of government. Other areas of the civic realm were also amply supported, a reflection of the city's connections with public sector largesse. It was able to win grants for homeless programs from the Department of Housing and Urban Development, although one could question whether those were pursued as vigorously by other communities. Projects such as the Community Housing Corporation's Mercado El Centro SRO's received funds from many sources, especially Low Income Housing Tax Credits and State of California Rental Housing Construction monies. The Cedar Street Garage was subsidized by the Economic Development Administration, the McPherson Art and History Center secured $2.5 million in federal grants, and the St. George Hotel SRO's had amassed nearly $6 million in loans and grants from the governmental sector. Few communities could have equaled the magnetism of Santa Cruz in drawing public funds.

However, equally prominent in an evaluation of Santa Cruz and its political leadership is another more troubling factor: aversion to expertise. Certainly, a community ravaged by an earthquake that was already in deep economic distress should welcome all the assistance made available to it. But Santa Cruz does not trust outside expertise, especially in an area where it has little of its own. Bruce Van Allen, a former mayor and Vision Santa Cruz board member, warned that no one is right just because they have title to land or title to expertise. The advice of the city's own consultant and that of the Urban Land Institute were tossed aside with respect to where and how to ignite the rebuilding and recovery process. When urged to make a major statement on an anchor site, the city did precisely the opposite, backing the ill-conceived movie theater project of a political crony on a non-downtown site, and allocating $750,000 in scarce resources to support what would become a doomed venture. In doing so, it dismissed the concept of retail continuity that was also stressed by experts. Ironically, Van Allen, himself a failed cabinet shop owner, became the project manager of the Mercado El Centro, a $5 million project; he was eventually removed at the insistence of one of the project's lenders. Another ex-mayor, Mardi Wormhoudt, was appointed CEO of the Santa Cruz Community Credit Union without any background in business and finance, and that institution soon badly lagged its peer group on key measures of asset quality established by the National Credit Union Administration (National Credit Union Administration 1993). And Katherine Beiers, now serving more than two terms on the City Council, launched her career to elective office as chair of the Planning Commission, all the while admitting to having no ideas about economic development. A March 1999 election to decide whether city water should be fluoridated is another case in point. According to Councilman Mike Rotkin, who compared flouridation to nuclear power; "For those of us that came of age in the 1960s. I think more and more people from my generation feel there are reasons to question experts" (Wilson 1999; A1).

If leadership in an urban setting should set the agenda for development and build confidence for investors, in Santa Cruz precisely the opposite happened. Not only did Bruce Van Allen disparage expertise, land ownership and access to capital, but other Santa Cruz mayors repeatedly added to an uncertain investment climate. Don Lane said one developer already knew the risks of trusting us while Jane Yokoyama complained, however sophomorically, of "professional level game playing going on when projects may come on line." Since building confidence is essential to attracting investment, why would three mayors make statements in the press that would defeat that end? Were they merely loose cannons in a crisis situation or were their comments part of an overall real estate strategy to jawbone downtown land prices so that government or its cronies could bottom-fish real estate?

The issue of crony capitalism must also be weighed in an assessment of rebuilding in Santa Cruz. The failed, moribund non-downtown cinema is one case in point. The $100/sq. ft. paid to the family of another County Supervisor (Gary Patton) for the land for the Cedar Street Parking Garage must have roiled the downtown land market especially since adjoining property owners got less than half that sum. And the non-competition clause as a condition for the ground floor space in the new Cooper House was a thinly-disguised ploy to protect the interests of another mayor (Neal Coonerty) who owns the largest bookstore in the County less than one block away. Did the City Council violate its trust to further the public interest by unduly favoring certain individuals?

Other city actions still leave the observer perplexed. The failure to secure and preserve irreplaceable historic buildings, most notably the Cooper House and the Trust Building, still leaves the citizenry baffled. It would be difficult to imagine even a tiny minority in the city supporting the hasty demolition of the Cooper House, at least not without second, third or fourth opinions; this deliberative process insured that not a single historic structure was lost in Los Gatos.

The management of the homeless issue is another troubling aspect of Santa Cruz's leadership. Although in place for twenty-four years, the new Katherine Beiers-led City Council immediately brought up the possibility of the repeal or alteration of the camping ban. As past events have shown, unruly street behavior, and safe residential and business environments are not compatible. In a city that has probably done more for the homeless than nearly any other of comparable size, relaxing the camping ban could attract many more homeless; even socialist-feminist Mike Rotkin warned against loosening the ordinance, fearing that Santa Cruz would become a magnet for undesirables (Sanford 1999). In 1997 the Executive Director of the Downtown Association pleaded with the public to support the downtown and not be intimidated by what was termed "challenges to the social atmosphere on Pacific Avenue" (Steinau 1997). Indeed, as Santa Cruz's experiences have shown, one could argue that a significant portion of the homeless are intractable and unwilling to accept any help, preferring a disruptive pattern of behavior instead (MacDonald 1997).

Indeed, optimism for the future is slowly fading in Santa Cruz. The new President of the Chamber of Commerce, himself a veteran of the city's vast array of non-profit organizations, endorsed rebuilding efforts and the fact, that however belatedly, the City Council was focusing on what the city needed to do to create the economic environment needed for people to really thrive and that the people leading the City Council had some real insight and vision. And the Chamber's new CEO added, "But now we've got some new guys elected who are not living in the real world as far as the economic realities and the contribution business makes to the general fund" (Pittman 1999, D1). The city is at a turning point. A major anchor site is still a weed-strewn lot and other parcels remain vacant. The synergy spawned by the opening of the Cinema 9 is now fading into the past. Can the city continue on its recovery path, addressing the needs of business which provides the economic engine that funds the City Council's programs in human services and the arts? Can the council build consensus and confidence to continue the process? With a new radical leftist council led by former planning commissioner Beiers, such appears unlikely. "In politics," she said, "you don't really build consensus. It all comes down to the vote" (Jeannette 1999).

References

Beebe, Greg. 1990, July 12. "Police Chief Blasts Homeless. "Santa Cruz County *Sentinel* (SCS), P. A1.

_____ 1991, Oct. 17. Los Gatos Takes the Fast Track to Rebuilding." SCS, p. A6.

_____ 1992, Feb. 13. "Report on Homeless Shelter Profiles Typical User," SCS, p. A2.

Bergstrom, Mark. 1990a, March 18. "St. George Spokesman Blasts Stay of Demolition," SCS, p. A1.

_____ 1990b, March 26. "Plans for Mall Please Officials." SCS, p. A3.

_____ 1990c, April 10. "Downtown Rents May Nearly Double." SCS, p. A1.

_____ 1990d, May 8, "Mall Dilemma: Street People." SCS, p. A1.

_____ 1990e, Aug. 17. "Mall Vision Clouded." SCS, p. A1.

_____ 1990f, Sept. 25. "Appeal Filed in St. George Demolition." SCS, p. A2.

_____ 1990g, Oct. 3. "Downtown Parking Garage OK'd." SCS, p. A5.

_____ 1990h, Dec. 14. "Bankers Say Sensible Projects Will Get Loans." SCS, p. A3.

_____ 1991a, Feb. 3. "Here's the Rebuilding Projects OK'd But Only One Constructed." SCS, p. A1.

_____ 1991b, March 31. "Downtown Santa Cruz: the Mold is Almost Set." SCS, p. A1.

Benson, Maggie. 1995, July 20. "SC's Fort Homeless. Santa Cruz Metro, p. 5.

City of Santa Cruz. 1982. Downtown Area Plan: Existing Conditions and Issue Identification Report. Santa Cruz: author.

_____ 1989. "Notice of Finding of No Significant Impact on the Environment. Assessors Parcel

Number 4-071-05, Santa Cruz, California, August 7.

_____ and ROMA Design Group. 1991. *Downtown Recovery Plan.* Santa Cruz: author.

Clark, Karen. 1991a, Oct. 19. "Expanded Cooper House Planned." SCS, p. A1.

_____ 1991b, Dec. 12. "Streetscape Plan Goes Out for Bids." SCS, p. A2.

_____ 1996a, Feb 3. "SC's Panhandling Law Survives Judge's Reversal." SCS, p. A3.

_____ 1996b, March 27. "Homeless Camping Plan OK'd." SCS, p. A2.

_____ 1996c, May 16. "SC Lowers Legal Boom on Squatters." SCS, p. A1.

_____ 1996d, May 16. "Ban Puts City Hall Off Limits at Night." SCS, p. A1.

_____ 1996e, Sept. 17. "Homeless Projects Land Nearly $1 Million." SCS, p. A1.

_____ 1996f, Sept. 20. "Forum Takes on Downtown Issues." SCS, p. A1.

_____ 1997a, Feb. 25. "Developers Face Deadline on North Pacific Project." SCS, p. A3.

_____ 1997b, May 2. "Program Aimed at Downtown SC Homeless." SCS, p. A1.

_____ 1998a, Jan. 21. "Cooper House Loses Subsidy Pact with City." SCS, p. A1.

_____ 1998b, May 23. "Homeless Committee Faces City Scrutiny." SCS, p. A2

_____ 1998c, July 29. "City OK''s $1 Million Cooper House Deal." SCS, p. A1.

Doyle, Jim. 1989, Oct. 27. "Santa Cruz Faces Rebuilding." San Francisco *Chronicle*, p. A8.

Edwards, Katherine. 1993, May 12. "Cinemaplex Deals Stalls." SCS, p. A1.

Fay, John. 1991 May. "Waiting for Credit: How the Banking Crisis is Slowing Downtown Santa Cruz Development." *Santa Cruz Magazine*, p. 15.

Feagin, and R.E. Parker. 1990. *Rebuilding American Cities*. Englewood Cliffs, NJ: Prentice-Hall.

Gammon, Robert. 1997, Feb 1. "SC Unhappy with Non-Profit"s Audit." SCS, p. A1.

Guara, Maria. 1994a, July 12. "Summer Shelter for the Homeless." *San Francisco Chronicle*, p. A15.

_____ 1994b, Oct. 12. "Santa Cruz Mayor Asks the Dead to Help the Hungry." *San Francisco Chronicle*, p. A17.

_____ 1995, Dec. 13. "Homeless Evacuated from Flooded Camp," *San Francisco Chronicle*, p. A21.

Houstoun, Lawrence O., Jr. 1990, June. "From Street to Mall and Back Again." Planning, pp. 4-10.

Jeannette, Kim. 1999, Jan. 7. "Beiers lights the way in SC," Good Times, p. 6.

Kostyal, Mike. 1990, Aug. 28. "Homeless: aiming for an answer," Mid-County Post, p. 7.

Krieger, Kathy. 1990, Oct. 1. "St. George onlookers watched, wondered," SCS, p. A1.

_____ 1996, Sept. 8. "Rebellious saint: activist Karen Gillette finds a balance," SCS, p. C1.

Lasnier, Guy. 1989a, Sept. 27. "Santa Cruz band event in doubt," SCS, p. A1.

_____ 1989b, Nov. 19. "The growing pains are just beginning," SCS, p. A1.

_____ 1990, Jan. 7. "New, bigger Cooper House set," SCS, p. A1.

_____ 1992, Oct. 16. "Food court planned at El Centro," SCS, p. B5.

_____ 1993, Jan. 11. "Folding up the Pavilion saga," SCS, p. A1.

MacDonald, Heather, 1997, Nov. 17. "The Homeless Don"t Need Outreach," Wall Street Journal, p. A19.

Marks, Jamie. 1994, May 19. "Outside agitators," Santa Cruz Metro, p. 9.

McKendrick, Nance. 1999, Jan. 19. Phone interview.

McMillan, Carolyn. 1995, June 18. "The late show"s a hit in SC," SCS, p. A1.

Mendoza, Martha. 1992a, July 8. "Outlet center moving ahead on "good faith,"" SCS, p. A1.

_____ 1992b, Nov. 10. "SC developers compete to build new movie house," SCS, p. A2.

_____ 1992c, Nov. 10. "Further study for theater plans," SCS, p. A2.

_____ 1992d, Nov. 12. "The perils of project approval: veteran of county politics pitches theater project," SCS, p. A1.

_____ 1993a, March 7. "Theater site could be costly for taxpayers," SCS, p. A2.

_____ 1993b, March 23. "Surfers urge SC to clean up Neary Lagoon water," SCS p. A2.

_____ 1993c, March 26. "Resolution for standoff seen for CHC project," SCS, p. A1.

_____ 1993d, Aug. 27. "CHC scrambling to find funds for downtown El Centro project," SCS, p. A2.

_____ 1993e, Dec. 30. "Right at home on Pacific Avenue," SCS, p. A1.

_____ 1994, Jan. 7. "City, merchants plan safer avenue," SCS, p. A1.

Miller, Donald. 1989a, March 29. "Beiers picked for council," SCS, p. A1.

_____ 1989b, April 27. "Chamber, mayor disagree about downtown," SCS, p. A1.

_____ 1989c, May 4. "Holiday sales slipped," SCS, p. A1.

_____ 1989d, May 21. "Streetlight tax called unnecessary," SCS p. A2.

_____ 1989e, June 4. "Furor over the image of downtown," SCS, P. A5.

Musitelli, Robin. 1992, Feb. 7. "Another downtown aftershock," SCS, p. A1.

_____ 1994a, Feb. 12. "SC needs permits for ocean discharge," SCS, p. A1.

_____ 1994b, Feb. 17. "Santa Cruz police shut down vigil early," SCS, p. A3.

_____ 1994c, March 9. "Council passes panhandling laws," SCS, p. A1.

_____ 1994d, May 17. "SC theater deal signed," SCS, p. A1.

_____ 1994e, May 19. "More SC theater plans," SCS, p. A1.

_____ 1995a, March 28. "Rebirth of Cooper House near," SCS, p. A1.

_____ 1995b, Sept. 13. "Cooper House developer given parking subsidy," SCS, p. A3.

_____ 1995c, Oct. 8. "Day or night, the crowds come to SC," p. A1.

_____ 1995d, Oct. 8. "For Pacific Avenue resident, party is too long, too loud," SCS, p. A12.

_____ 1995e, Dec. 8. "Rotkin tells Capitola to quit whining about homeless camp," SCS, p. A1.

National Credit Union Administration, 1993. Financial Performance Report, Santa Cruz Community.

Credit Union, 1989-1993, Concord, CA: author.

O"Connor, John. 1990, Oct. 7. "Santa Cruz struggles to come back," San Francisco Examiner, p. B1.

Parker, R.E. and Joe R. Feagin. 1990. "A "Better Business Climate" in Houston," in Dennis Judd and Michael Parkinson, eds., Leadership and Urban Regeneration: Cities in North America and Europe. Newbury Park, CA, London and New Delhi: Sage Publications, pp. 216-238.

Pearson, Larry, Jim Pepper and Mike Rotkin. 1991, May 9. "Blueprint for recovery" Vision SC says yes," Santa Cruz Magazine, p. 9.

Perez, Steve. 1990a, June 12. "Task force examines mall street people," SCS, p. A4.

_____ 1990b, July 12. "SC Zoning Board votes to tear down St. George," SCS, p. A3.

_____ 1990c, Oct. 1. "Fire ravages downtown hotel," SCS p. A1.

_____ 1991, Jan. 17. "Delay sought in historical delisting," SCS p. A6.

Pittman, Jennifer. 1999, Feb. 14. "Business group will lobby for broad economic issues," SCS, p. D1.

Robertson, Kent. 1995. "Downtown Redevelopment Strategies in the United States: An End of Century Assessment," Journal of the American Planning Association, 61:4 (Autumn), pp. 429-437.

Robinson, John. 1990a, Feb. 6. "Lawsuit filed in quake death: landlords blamed for falling buildings," SCS p. A1.

_____ 1992a, Feb. 16. "Road to development paved with public funds," SCS, p. A1.

_____ 1992b, March 6. "Another landmark burns," SCS, p. A1.

_____ 1992c, July 1. "City holds out $1 million to hook developer," SCS, p. A4.

_____ 1992d, Sept. 27. "Rise of a political movement," SCS, p. A1.

_____ 1993a, June 30. "City accused of "dragging feet" on lagoon," SCS, p. A2.

_____ 1993b, Dec. 16. "City closes beach waters on surf season"s best day," SCS, p. A1.

_____ 1993c, Dec. 17. "Fouled beaches create an outcry," p. A2.

_____ 1994, April 21. "Lagoon outflow source of debate," SCS, p. A1.

Rogers, Paul. 1991, Dec. 4. "Santa Cruz wins suit on eminent domain," San Jose Mercury-News, n.p.

Rsotkin, Michael E. 1994. "Class, Populism and Progressive Politics: Santa Cruz, California,   1970-1982," University of California, Santa Cruz doctoral dissertation.

Sanford, John. 1999, Jan. 29. "Rotkin Warns City against campsites," SCS, p. A1.

Santa Cruz Action Network. 1989, September. Newsletter, n.p.

Santa Cruz Metro. 1996, July. "Unoccupancy factor," p. 8.

Santa Cruz County Sentinel. 1989a, July 13. Editorial, "Santa Cruz budget is a tenuous one."

_____ 1989b. 5:04 p.m.: The Great Quake of 1989. Santa Cruz: Santa Cruz Sentinel Press.

_____ 1990a, May 24. Editorial, "Untracking a recovery downtown."

_____ 1990b, July 2. Editorial, "Homeless not slighted in our area."

_____ 1993a, Jan. 2. Editorial, "Perilous slow rebirth of downtown."

_____ 1993b, April 23. Special Section, "Celebrating Downtown."

_____ 1994, Aug. 9. Editorial, "Council mustn"t weaken because of court rulings."

_____ 1997, Sept. 27. Staff report, "Loan approved for homeless program," p. A2.

Snyder, Martha. 1992, March 14. "Trust Building owners seek demolition," SCS, p. A2.

Sprague, Robert and Company. 1991. "Santa Cruz Retail Market Review," in ROMA Design Group, City of Santa Cruz Downtown Recovery Plan." Santa Cruz: 1991.

Spitzer, Skip and Bernice Belton. 1998, Nov. 15. "SCAN represents the people of Santa Cruz," SCS, p. A13.

Stanford Environmental Law Society. 1971. San Jose: Sprawling City. Stanford: Author.

Steinau, Linda. 1997, April 7. Letter to the Editor, SCS

University of California, Santa Cruz, Public Information Office. 1999. Website http://www.ucsc.edu/news/

Van Allen, Bruce. 1990, June 3. "New SC mall will be monument to consensus," SCS, p. A23.

Wildermuth, John. 1996, March 30. "Santa Cruz to house homeless in State Parks," San Francisco Chronicle, p. A19.

END NOTES

1. See Rotkin (1994) for a fascinating insider view of political and social change in Santa Cruz leading up to the elections of the early 1980s. Ironically, Rotkin is now viewed as a conservative pro-growth force on the City Council.

2. The documents relevant to this transaction may be found in the Official Records of Santa Cruz County, CA, Book 3692, page 599ff.

3. Wormhoudt was another politician who was provided for after she left office. Without any background in business and finance, she was named CEO of the Santa Cruz Community Credit Union in 1991. By 1993, her last year, the Credit Union was well below peer group standards on six of seven key measures of asset quality determined by the National Credit Union Administration. In addition, delinquent loans had increased by 449% (National Credit Union Administration 1993).

Part Three

Waterfront and Brownfields Redevelopment

Waterfront Planning as a Strategic Incentive to Downtown Enhancement and Livability

ZENIA KOTVAL and JOHN R. MULLIN

Historically, ports have provided a working gateway into many American communities. For those lucky enough to be situated along rivers, lakes, and harbors, small towns with waterfronts were easily accessed by explorers, travelers, and eventually industry. The working waterfront of past years was the heart of the industrial and fishing communities in a small town. As a result, the commercial centers of these towns developed next to the waterfronts as well. Today, the downtown areas in small towns typically can be found within a few blocks of the waterfront.

Over time, many of these waterfronts have ceased to be "working waterfronts." No longer are the shores lined with mills, warehouses and processing plants. Rather, in many communities, abandoned buildings litter the edges of rivers and lakes. The waterfront has become a derelict part of town, on which the community has turned its back. Several of these towns now face uncertain futures with the historical base of their economy no longer a viable option for the future. Where fishing and logging along the waterfront once supported the local economy, advances in technology, automation, and transportation seem to have diminished the advantage offered by waterfront access.

Large cities throughout America have discovered that waterfront areas can be unique assets in the revitalization of downtown districts. Baltimore, Boston, and San Francisco are great examples of cities that have capitalized upon their waterfront areas to provide unique shopping districts that attract millions of tourists annually. Smaller towns too, can benefit from looking to the waterfront when planning improvements to a downtown district. The proximity of thousands of small towns along the nation's oceans, river and lake systems make this a viable economic revitalization tool for many communities. Indeed, it is in these smaller communities that there is the greatest need for attention to the downtown-waterfront relationship and where there is the greatest pressure for change. These communities, to begin with, typically have volunteer government, minimum waterfront controls, weak waterfront management, and an attitude that the marketplace will best decide how their waterfronts and adjacent downtowns will be revitalized in the future. They also must bear the burden of handling disputes between, for example, fishermen and recreational boat people (who has priority?), land use decisions (primacy for waterfront dependent uses?), and environmental problems (how do you control smell and ensure proper waste disposal?). It is our position that these smaller ports are in great need of assistance. Unless careful attention is given to these waterfront communities, there will be a significant loss to our local and, indeed, national character.

This chapter discusses the critical factors facing smaller communities in their efforts to revitalize their downtown waterfronts and nearby shipping districts. It is primarily based upon our research and practical planning projects in New England, Michigan, the Canadian Maritimes, Upstate New York, Northern Ireland, and Portugal. In these areas, we have been involved with waterfront planning along inland lakes, rivers, bays, and the ocean. These experiences have been in ports as large as Boston, to smaller harbors such as Gloucester and New Bedford, MA to tiny waterfronts such as Menemsha (Martha's Vineyard) and Stonington, CT. The emphasis of the chapter is upon how these smaller communities have worked to revitalize their downtown waterfronts. The key word is *revitalization* for, in many cases, these port communities have been active from the middle of the 1600s! What follows is a set of guiding principles that hopefully will be of assistance to communities that are struggling to find means and methods to nurture and enhance these special areas.

The Principles

1) INTERNATIONAL AND NATIONAL POLICIES AND TECHNOLOGICAL CHANGES TYPICALLY HAVE QUICK IMPACTS ON WORKING WATERFRONTS. THESE POLICIES DIRECTLY IMPACT ON THE ECONOMIC HEALTH OF DOWNTOWN WATERFRONTS.

We know of no other industry where international policies and treaties have as quick an impact upon the economic health of companies as with fishing. For example, the ports of Gloucester and New Bedford have been devastated by fishing treaties concerning Georges Banks and the Grand Banks. International law now governs when, where, the quantity, and the type of fish that can be caught. The net result is that the fishing industry is in dramatic flux. A visit to these, as well as fishing communities in Canada and Portugal, shows countless vessels tied to wharves awaiting bankruptcy sales and/or the wrecker's torch. Given these controls, it is little wonder that there are heated exchanges at both the diplomatic levels and among fishermen of different nations at sea. In the meantime, investors, given this uncertainty, are less inclined to improve their downtown waterfront properties.

We would be remiss if we didn't comment on the end of the Cold War: On both sides of the Atlantic, the easing of tensions has led to a decline in the need for the construction of naval vessels and the maintenance of defense facilities. As a consequence, there is excess capacity. These areas represent tremendous potential when integrated into adjacent port facilities or as new public ports in their own right. We have noted this most recently in the concerns over the future of the defense installations located in the harbors of Portsmouth, New Hampshire, and Quonset Point, Rhode Island. The former facility, primarily a submarine base, remains active and open but only because of sacrifice on the part of the civilian workforce and political support. How long this operation continues is an open question. The United States is not building many submarines at this moment and the need for these ships in the future is a subject of sharp debate. The latter facility has been closed and is now in the process of conversion to civilian use. This port, given its location and infrastructure has tremendous potential. But, even here there are critical issues: Should it be modernized while the long standing port of Providence, approximately 20 miles away, receives nothing? The question of who gets and who pays must be answered.

Changes in technology are bringing new vessels to harbors and we must be prepared for them. We are noting increased use of catamarans, a rise in interest in cabotage (coastal shipping), short haul ferry operations, and the tour boat industry. Our planning must anticipate these new activities and types of vessels. This is no easy task. On one side, these smaller harbors are, for example, special places that are typically attractive to tourists. And yet, visits by a tour boat of 1,000 passengers can quickly overwhelm a downtown shopping area. We have recently noted that tour boats are, increasingly, visiting Martha's Vineyard. After being put ashore and purchasing a meal or a "T" shirt, this island offers little to the day-tripper. In fact, there are minimal comfort stations. Inevitably, there is great disappointment. We have consistently heard from day-tripping tourists to this island that the best part of the experience has been the boat ride to the ports! The key point is that simply welcoming new vessels is insufficient. Planners must take into regard the experiences that follow the docking of a ship. Issues ranging from the swift handling of customs, agricultural inspections, off-loading of luggage, and transportation of tourists inland must be faced. Moreover, the mixing of freight and passenger vehicles, the hours that shops are open, security, and even the ability of ships to quickly leave have to be examined.

Finally, one must respect the environmental movement along with its stringent regulations. One can understand the fact that garbage is a by-product of fish processing. One also can note that garbage attracts vermin and the risk of health problems. There are also issues dealing with the flushing of waste tanks on vessels and the filling of gasoline and diesel tanks. We have recently noted the criticality of these issues in the harbor village of Onset, MA. We expect that if environmental issues are handled in a "state-of-the-art" fashion, there will be reinvestment in the downtown. If they continue as they are, they will discourage investment. While more and more harbors are becoming more cognizant of environmental issues, there is still extensive work that is required. Moreover, great care must be taken to insure that sewer and/or combined sewer/storm water outflows are treated. Too frequently we have observed situations where the lack of treatment has created less than optimal conditions. Nothing illustrated the problems of sewage disposal in harbors so much as 1988 Presidential Candidate George Bush standing on a boat in Boston, MA, Harbor declaring it as America's most filthy port. The fact that he was running for President against the governor of Massachusetts at the time and that the federal government had not seen fit to grant clean-up funds was irrelevant. The port was filthy. Today, approximately ten years later, conditions have improved tremendously and the harbor is well on its way to recovery. The experience of Boston needs to be a lesson to all ports, regardless of size.

The environmental movement has also raised the consciousness of the public concerning the dredging of harbors. On one side, the depth of a harbor substantially dictates the size of vessel that can be welcomed. Thus, there is little mystery concerning why so many communities will endeavor to create deeper and deeper channels. On the other side, there are environmentalists who, justifiably, are concerned about the impact of this dredging on flora, fauna, and sealife. This conflict is difficult to resolve and requires extensive work on the part of all parties.

II) SUCCESSFUL DOWNTOWN WATERFRONTS TYPICALLY BUILD ON THEIR HISTORIC AND CULTURAL ASSETS.

Many harbor communities are rich in history and culture. Many have historic forts and castles right on the waterfront. Lighthouses, maritime museums and trading ports all add to the charm and attraction of the harbor. These historic and cultural structures draw tourists and help with the educational aspects of harbors as well. The maintenance and management of these elements are important to harbor planning and marketing. The presence of Tall Ships, the "Blessing of the Fleet," active aquariums, and colorful boats are examples of these elements.

In larger cities, these attributes are typically well protected and promoted. We have seen the progress of Boston's efforts to create a walking trail along its waterfront and the marvels of Baltimore's Inner Harbor and New York's South Street Seaport. All have enhanced the retail base of the waterfront areas. In smaller ports, they are too frequently ignored. Indeed, ports with long histories such as Point Judith, RI, and Stonington, CT, make it extremely difficult for the pedestrian to observe and participate in the waterfront experience. What is most distressing is that gaining access to these historic and cultural facilities is not, typically, a costly endeavor. With careful planning, they can be enjoyed by downtown business owners, workers, residents and tourists.

III) GIVEN THE COMPLEXITY OF GOVERNMENTAL INSTITUTIONS INVOLVED IN DOWNTOWN WATERFRONTS, MASTER PLANNING IS ESSENTIAL BUT DIFFICULT AND TIME CONSUMING: WHO IS IN CHARGE?

One of the strategic steps to having a successful harbor is to have a long-range harbor plan and comprehensive zoning regulations to reflect and enforce it. In order to maximize the potentials for the harbor, it is important to determine the use and character that the harbor will serve. Harbors must be planned with the water as a unifying element. In fact, we urge harbor communities to first emphasize water dependent and water related uses. Once these are satisfied then other uses could be considered. It is equally important to coordinate planning efforts. Many communities have created port authorities who are responsible for a physically defined area. These agencies often totally control all aspects of the port including operations, management, financing, and planning. They, in effect, serve as a governmental entity in their own right. When this happens, relations between the municipality and the authority can be contentious: The agendas of each may be quite different.

Harbors should be integrated inland as extensively as possible. The daylighting (the opening up of these water bodies for public viewing) of channels, canals, rivers, and streams can add value to communities and, perhaps more importantly, can integrate the harbor more fully into the fabric of the community. No where can this be more vividly noted than in the City of Providence, where the city has recently changed the direction of its river (three miles from the Atlantic Ocean) and created one of the most vibrant city centers in the nation. The river is used for festivals and ceremonies throughout the year. There are elegant bridges and pedestrian walkways along its edges as well as open picnic areas that tie in the shopping areas, hotels, office buildings, and the state capital. It has totally transformed the city. While Providence's river corridor has been comprehensively planned, as part of a major revitalization effort, the Ipswich River through Peabody, MA, is being integrated into an existing downtown fabric. This river had been long forgotten. It was simply a small stream that flowed behind the downtown shops and institutions. Approximately five years ago, the city cleaned the river and created walkways along its banks. Today, many buildings are re-orienting their entrances to focus on both the riverside and the city's Main Street. It is following the example of the nearby town of Ipswich which has long integrated the river into its downtown with many shops having openings on both river and land sides.

Furthermore, harbors must plan for 24-hour operations. Those ports that are dependent upon tidal flow or accustomed to a shortened operational day will be at a disadvantage. Moreover, the longer a vessel stays in port, the more expensive the cost of operations. Given that shipping companies have choice, the rapidity of off-loading is a decided asset. Part of "planning for time" means that shops must be open when the customers arrive. Nothing represents a missed opportunity than a tour boat arriving on a Sunday when the shops are closed. Harbor planners can learn a lesson from airport planners who insure that shop operations coincide with the arrival and departure of commercial aircraft.

There should be recognition of the need to plan for multiple publics. The downtown areas adjacent to harbors are likely to attract different types of people all through the day. For example, from 5:00AM to 8:00AM, the typical waterfront may be full of fishermen, repairmen, women, and other laborers. From 8:00AM to 9:00AM, office workers will be on the street. From 9:00AM to 12:00PM, it will be tourists, followed by the lunch crowd. From 2:00PM to 5:00PM, tourists again will be commonplace. At five, the "night crowd" begins and continues until after midnight. While no two waterfronts will have the same mix at the same time, the fact remains that they all will have to cater to mixed publics. Workers, boat owners, business people, tourists, families, night-lifers, and the like all have different requirements that need to be met.

IV) DOWNTOWN WATERFRONTS CAN BE SUCCESSFULLY REVITALIZED WHEN THE PROBLEMS OF MIXED USES ARE RESOLVED.

Waterfronts must be planned for multi-use activities to include fishing, fish processing, recreational boating, boat building, and repairs and tourist activities. Furthermore, these uses are not mutually exclusive of each other. A working waterfront can co-exist with a recreational harbor if it is well planned and managed. In fact, mixed uses might actually complement each other. Such is the case in Portland, ME where the authorities, using municipal zoning powers, have limited recreational boating to certain places where there is no threat to the fishing industry. We have also noted in poorly planned areas where the lack of careful planning has led to conflict between fishermen and recreationalists. When this conflict exists, it is apparent, given present economic conditions, that the fishermen suffer. In Westport, MA, for example, we have noted that the harbormaster (not the planner!) has had a difficult problem in meeting the needs of fishermen and recreational boaters. Who should have priority on the dock? The problem has been exacerbated by the fact that there are fewer and fewer fishermen and, thus, less need for providing the working boats their own space. The recreational boats, in the meantime, are expanding. Here, the harbormaster is faced with the dilemma of maintaining tradition or changing with the times. As he grapples with this decision, shoreline commercial uses are likely to be impacted. With careful planning and flexibility, the Westport problem can be overcome. On the other hand, the small harbor village of Menamsha on Martha's Vineyard, for example, has overcome this problem by maintaining a small area on the dock, immediately adjacent to the fish stores, for the working boats. In the meantime, it has been able to expand outward into the harbor to meet the needs of the recreationalists.

While Menemsha has managed to meet the needs of both groups by expansion, there is often resistance to too much expansion. Such was the case in Stonington, CT, when a group of developers attempted to convert a working factory along the water's edge, adjacent to downtown into condominiums. (Those of you who saw the movie "Mystic Pizza" may recall the character of the area.) While harbor residents were saddened by the idea that the factory would be closed, they understood that it had become outmoded and that the condominiums could fit in with the community character. However, the residents became incensed when the developers proposed the creation of "documiniums" that would be linked to the condominium units. In other words, a person purchasing a unit in the building would have the option of also buying dock space in the harbor. The residents felt that this would overcrowd the harbor and organized to fight the proposal. They were successful! The teaching point here is simply that the relationship between competing uses must be planned with care and flexibility and that there are, often times, limits concerning the carrying capacity of harbors.

There is a place and need for the working harbor. Not only does it provide jobs and tax base for the community, it serves a locational niche for water-related industries and supporting businesses. Furthermore, a safe, well maintained and managed section of the working harbor can actually be a draw for tourists curious to learn and observe the working of various industries. A shipping fleet ready to go out to sea or returning with fresh catch could be an entertaining and learning experience. The small fishing pier at Provincetown, MA, is illustrative of this point. Tourists can walk along the town's highly colorful and unique shopping street, past monuments, institutional structures, restaurants and parks to the whale-watch boats and the harbor cruise vessels to the fishing vessels and, ultimately, at the end of the pier, a commercial museum that focuses on the wreck and partial recovery of the Wyadah, a seventeenth century pirate vessel that foundered along Cape Cod. All of the above are tightly integrated and safely walkable. There is little wonder that this town is popular with school groups from across New England. There is something for everyone.

Museums, aquariums, and teaching programs would certainly be a draw for tourists and residents alike. As well, teaching and research programs would be highly beneficial to the harbor related industries. A research laboratory for a specialized trade could make the harbor a special destination for professional groups as well as students. The federally funded "Sea Grant Program" provides resources for American universities to become involved in such activities. For example, faculty from the Massachusetts Institute of Technology are currently involved in aquaculture experiments in Quincy Harbor. Further, hundreds of school children each day visit Boston's Aquarium and its "Tall Ships" (The U.S.S. Constitution and The Beaver). Similar activities can be found on Chatanooga's riverfront and in Baltimore's Inner Harbor. New Bedford is staking a large part of its commercial future on the tourism/education components through its proposal to create an aquarium/hotel/conference center along its waterfront.

v) WORKING WATERFRONTS ARE AT RISK. SPECIAL ACTIONS ARE NECESSARY TO PROTECT THEM WHILE THE NEARBY DOWNTOWN IS UNDERGOING REVITALIZATION.

Given the problems of international fishing and the market sensitivity of boat making, these waterfronts, in many cities, appear to be quite fragile and could easily switch uses. We urge planners to ensure that the potential for recovery remains as a critical planning principle. We have noted this tension in New Bedford and Gloucester, MA. In New Bedford, one of the most successful harbors in the nation, current planning efforts are focusing upon the aforementioned building of a new aquarium, hotel, and other tourist/conference facilities. As well, the harbor area has recently been declared a national historic park. One can only wonder about how a working port with its chaos, smell, truck traffic, and relatively low cost structures can co-exist with these new activities. In Gloucester, Rogers Street is at once the major distribution point for the fishing industry and a focal point of tourism activity. Moreover, the blue collar, hard living qualities of a working port often do not match the expectations of guests from far away. Junger, in his best selling story entitled *A Perfect Storm*, characterizes Gloucester's waterfront as being anchored by three bars that form the city's "Bermuda Triangle." These places clearly have a place in a working port. However, they could be considered offensive, or less welcoming, to tourists. It is important to remember that a working harbor provides jobs, private investment, tax benefits and a colorful contribution to everyday life. Junger (1997, 35) describes the relationship between the working harbor and tourists in Gloucester as follows:

> The boat repair yards "are surrounded by the famous galleries and piano bars of Rocky Neck. Tourists blithely wander past machinery that could rip their summer homes right off their foundations." Conflict!

VI) HARBORS THAT INCLUDE EDUCATIONAL INSTITUTIONS AND PROGRAMS ADD VALUE TO THE DOWNTOWN WATERFRONT.

The Wood's Hole Oceanographic Institute, MA is significantly involved in activities along Falmouth's harbor in Buzzard's Bay. Within hundreds of yards one can move from a quiet, bucolic campus through laboratories and research facilities to a village shopping center to the Knorr (one of the National Oceanographic and Atmosphere Administration's research vessels), to the hustle and bustle of the Massachusetts' Steamship Authority Terminal. The teaching activities co-exist nicely with both working and recreation functions due to the scale and organization of space. However, it is important to remember that they have very different needs and serve primarily very different clientele. Serious scientists and curious day-trippers rarely have common purposes! If harbor uses are mixed, special attention needs to be given to each element such that one doesn't negatively impact the others. For example, salvage operations, scrap ships or dilapidated industrial structures, unless carefully integrated, would not contribute much to the recreational experience and curious tourists might hinder the needs of the working harbor. The Port of Portsmouth, NH, has accomplished this quite nicely. Across from the city's best hotel is one of the largest scrap yards in the Northeast. It is active and colorful while still messy. Tourists are able to observe what is happening through open fencing and are able to gain a sense of the activity without interference. In a final analysis, regulations clearly need to address possibly conflicting issues.

VII) TOURISM CAN PROVIDE A SIGNIFICANT ECONOMIC BOOST TO OLDER WATERFRONT AREAS.

Visitors tend to support ancillary activities such as specialized shops, restaurants and bars, and even hotels and conference facilities. As well, other related activities and amenities such as marinas, boardwalks, parks, bandstands, swimming, and fishing activities can be used by local residents. If the harbor is to serve as a tourist attraction, it is important to keep in mind services and amenities that are necessary for tourists. Information kiosks, telephone booths, public restrooms, benches and trash receptacles need to be provided and be well marked. Interestingly, in America's ports, it is the lack of public restrooms that typically are problematic. Whether it is a security cost or liability factor, American cities do not provide enough comfort stations or public toilets. And yet, the presence of these facilities can be a draw in itself. Traveler after traveler across America will stop at McDonalds or Burger King because, in part, they have clean restrooms and changing facilities. While using these facilities, they will inevitably spend money at the restaurant. We know of one business complex that was approaching bankruptcy until it placed a sign outside the building advertising "clean restrooms." The business completely recovered.

It is also essential to remember that the tourism experience is intended to be unique and special. For this reason, ports that create a special atmosphere can gain an advantage. Historic preservation, architectural guidelines, period street lighting, and/or different street patterns (e.g. cobblestones) can all add flavor to the experience.

Finally, there is the issue of maintenance. It is all well and good to create a wonderful design scheme and/or to provide amenities. It is a disservice, however, if these features and facilities are not well maintained. Every implementation scheme must include a maintenance scheme. Nothing is so illustrative of this point as a visit to the Marginal, the extraordinarily beautiful walkway along the Tagus River between Lisbon and Cascais, Portugal. As one walks, one sees the beautiful buildings on the shore side and the powerful tide crashing against the rocks on the seaside. And yet, the memory that one takes away from the walk is of untreated sewage. Thankfully, this problem is now being corrected.

VIII) THE RECREATION POTENTIAL OF HARBORS HAS DRAMATIC POTENTIAL IN THE COMING DECADE.

Harbors are considered to be wonderful recreational amenities for communities. The potentials for boardwalks, marinas and swimming areas are certainly considered to be assets for both the local residents and tourists alike. A recreational harbor also acts as a catalyst for other tourist related activities such as specialty shops, restaurants, hotels, marinas/boat rentals and aquariums. While there are hundreds of examples of this in the planned resort areas of the United States (e.g. Florida, California), there are far fewer smaller communities where harbors combine activities. The placing of these activities in ports of transition can be costly, time consuming, and risky. However, even in these areas, small city after city is endeavoring to combine these activities within the port. Such has been the case, for example, in Newburyport, MA, Portsmouth, NH, Wickford, RI and Port Jefferson, NY. In all of these instances, there is no one feature that stands out. It is the balanced combination of activities that has led to success.

IX) CAREFUL ZONING, HISTORIC PRESERVATION, ARCHITECTURAL AND SITE PLANNING REGULATIONS CAN ADD GREAT VALUE TO DOWNTOWN WATERFRONTS.

Zoning regulations, architecture and design controls and site planning regulations are all important to ensure that historical, cultural and aesthetic attributes as well as the optimal juxtaposition of uses at the harbor, is well coordinated. Design, color, lighting, and the festive nature of a place are definite draws. These elements enhance the feeling of security, vitality and bustle. In terns of design, there is a strong case for maintaining a sense of harmony, scale and "cultural feel" with the historic waterfront. While one should not get carried away and recreate a stage setting ("ye olde port"), it is important to respect the evolutionary character of the harbor. Part of this will relate to the use of color. Harbors tend to have backdrops of dark colors on the land side and shades of blue and white on the seaside. It is the land side that typically needs to be brightened. While color inevitably adds to a positive aesthetic environment it also contributes, along with lightening, to the creation of a strong sense of security. The walking public must feel totally safe when walking through the port. The key word is "feel." If there are psychological feelings of distress then, regardless of fact, the chances of public use of this space will decline. As Porter (1995) has noted, one of the most important elements of urban revitalization is a total sense of safety and security. Given that waterfronts often are considered dank, and the homes of the derelict and dangerous, the need to change this image must be a priority. Moreover, the transitional areas between harbors and downtown are equally problematic.

Festivals attract people. People like to see and be seen. Events ranging from the "taste of downtown" and "chowdah" fests to the blessing of the fleet, the "tall ships" regatta and yacht races can add value to the waterfront and downtown. So can dinner cruises and whale watching opportunities. We have seen these activities add value to smaller downtowns across New England. However, we have also noted one key problem; too often, the events are not coordinated with the downtown merchants. The crowds come when the businesses are closed, the participants block out regular customers or the streets are blocked such that deliveries cannot be made. We can illustrate this with a recent case when a Lollapalozza Concert was held at Quonset Point. The crowds were so huge that virtually no normal business could occur. The sponsors gained a profit but a significant number of local businesses actually suffered.

The downtown environment at the street level can play a significant role in the successful revitalization of a downtown. Traditional streetscape programs that incorporate overall signage programs, street furniture, and unique paving patterns can take on a water characteristic in downtowns with active waterfront communities. Bringing aspects of the water such as color, symbols, and waves can all serve as a reminder to shoppers and visitors that the water and its activities lie just beyond the edge of the downtown. These aspects of the water can be incorporated in the signs used to identify the downtown district, on signs for individual businesses, in the paving patterns of bricks used in parks, and along the sidewalks. We have noted where special signs (e.g. a pipe for a pipesmith, a barber pole) have added character to an area. We have also noted where bricks and cobbles announce to tourists that they are in a special area.

Urban design controls must call for a "stepping down" in the height of buildings. Too frequently, the views of harbors are blocked by high-rise buildings. We urge communities to maintain a low-rise profile along the waterfront and, if necessary, to increase the height as one moves inland. This concept has been successfully adopted in Boston where high-rise structures have, on the whole, been kept well back from its working and recreational boating areas.

Furthermore, waterfronts belong to the public. And yet, too often access is denied by private interests or the practical everyday work that takes place. It is important, as a planning principle, that public access be emphasized. We urge walking/biking paths be developed as close as possible to the water. We recognize and respect private property rights. We also consider the waterfront as a people's place. Integrating these two potentially conflicting issues will be no easy task.

X) A PHYSICAL, SOCIAL AND PSYCHOLOGICAL CONNECTEDNESS MUST BE NURTURED OR DEVELOPED BETWEEN DOWNTOWN AND THE WATERFRONT.

In order for a community to begin capitalizing upon its proximity to a waterfront it must almost literally "turn around" and begin facing the water once again. Downtown districts have typically developed next to the water's edge with streets radiating out from the port of dock area. Buildings have built up along these streets with their backs to the water. From the water's edge itself, the downtown and community can appear almost closed off to travelers. From the street level of the downtown area, the water may not even be readily visible. Finding a way to re-connect with the water will be essential for any small town that wants to revitalize its downtown through waterfront development.

In order to maximize the potential of the harbor, there needs to be a well-defined connection between the harbor and the downtown area. As tourist harbors tend to be catalysts for growth in tourism related activities, the community as a whole can benefit through supporting businesses. Downtown stores, hotels, and restaurants can be an integral part of the tourist experience. Wide roads or large paved parking areas that disconnect the rest of the community from the waterfront will be less likely to attract tourists inward from the harbor. The issue of wide roads is particularly problematic. Throughout the 1950s and 1960s a period of great highway building, highway engineers typically chose flat areas that were less than vibrant as sites for their roads. Too frequently, they are located along the water's edge. In Boston, an enormous elevated highway, constructed in the 1950s resulted in the city's turning its back to the sea. (It is now changing this by tunneling the road under its waterfront—the infamous "Big Dig"). In Hartford, it is virtually impossible to walk from the center city to its riverfront— although it is less than a half mile distant. (It is only today, where, through the Adrian's Landing Project, that this linkage is finally occurring). Similar disconnections can be noted in Middletown, New Haven and Bridgeport, CT and Providence, RI.

When direct connections are not possible due to the historic layout of the harbor and the community, good signage and design elements (such as period streetlights or walkways and bridges) could offer direction and draw people from one area to another. This "connectedness" can be clearly noted throughout New Bedford's Historic Whaling District and Portsmouth's Strawberry Banke. In fact, the scale of these cities is such that there is little separation between the ports and the historic parts of downtown. Furthermore, there are constant efforts to expand the connections to other surrounding areas. One does not feel that the port and downtown are two distinct areas.

There is also a need to define the nature of the local market. Allowed uses at the harbor could be of concern to downtown businesses. This would certainly depend on the physical layout of the harbor in relationship to downtown. When the downtown area or retail business center is adjacent to the harbor, there is little distinction between harbor and downtown. However, when the harbor is separated from the downtown there is the potential for competition. This must be carefully watched. In Providence's case, harbor revitalization has helped to shift the market center of the city toward the river's edge. This has raised such a concern in the city that the Mayor required a recent "river's edge" developer, through a linkage agreement, to also invest in the traditional downtown as a condition for gaining building approval.

XI) DOWNTOWN WATERFRONTS BENEFIT SIGNIFICANTLY FROM OPEN SPACES SUCH AS PARKS, PLAZAS AND TRAILS: THEY ADD ECONOMIC VALUE.

The term waterfront project represents a wide range of options from bike and pedestrian trails to river and boardwalks to plazas, docks, piers, and market places. The scale and size of a waterfront project will be determined by many factors including available funding and the needs of the community. Before selecting a specific tool, a community should assess the specific needs of their downtown and identify the unique characteristics of their waterfront and downtown district. Does the downtown need a better mix of businesses, or do the buildings themselves need to be rehabilitated? Do people still use the downtown as a place for their primary shopping needs, or is it an area that is struggling to compete with a strip commercial center on the edge of town? Does the community want to promote a downtown that is used daily by its citizens, or is it a district that attracts tourists by providing specialized goods and services?

Finding answers to these and other questions can help determine the type of downtown and waterfront area desired by the citizens of a community. This information then can be coupled with the unique physical characteristics and natural beauty of the waterfront to select the best project for each town. Towns can choose from several types of waterfront projects that vary in size and purpose.

Trails can be situated along a waters edge and extend into the downtown area and beyond. This type of system links the water's edge, the shopping district, and nearby residential areas in a way that opens up the waterfront and downtown to children, parents, and tourists. We have noted them, for example, in Skinneatlis, NY, and Peabody and Ipswich, MA. The City of Portland, MI, a small town situated at the merging of the Lookingglass River with the Grand River in lower Michigan has created approximately four miles of river trails that provide year round entertainment for all members of the family. These trails provide spaces for roller blading, biking, walking, cross-country skiing, and take advantage of historical bridges crossing the two rivers. These paths wind along the river, through an existing city park at the water's edge, and pass through the downtown.

City parks provide a space near the water's edge that also allows a community to come together. These parks provide a reason for people to come down to the waterfront. While there, they are able to take advantage of nearby shopping and dining establishments. These city parks can provide outdoor spaces for recreational activities that involve water such as boat rides, or they can be an area for families to gather.

The community of Port Clinton, Ohio, is located in northwest Ohio on Lake Erie. This community has developed small city parks along the two streets running parallel to the main street of the downtown. These parks feature historic statues, as well as gazebo and gathering spaces for downtown shoppers and employees. Adjacent to the water the community has situated sports athletic fields that draw kids during the day for informal sports, and families during the evening for organized games during the summer months.

Boardwalks and riverwalks provide citizens of the communities as well as tourists a way to interact directly with the water. These walkways put a person directly on the water's edge and give the water prominence in the community. Today, these walks provide access to docks used for recreational fishing and sporting as well as larger boats and yachts. For shoppers to a downtown district they can showcase the downtown as well as the area's history.

The town of Grand Haven, MI, has been particularly successful in using this tool to revitalize its downtown.The main street through the downtown, Washington Street, radiates out from the water's edge. The street culminates in a plaza area that allows visitors to access the boardwalk. The two and a half miles of boardwalk was completed in 1984 and funded through an investment of over $30 million through grants and public funding (Farell 1999).

The boardwalk features access to shops, eateries, charter fishing boats, a miniature golf course, and scenic parks. As well, the boardwalk takes visitors past several prominent features of the downtown. Tourists are able to visit the Tri-Cities Historical Museum housed in the original railroad depot, the Waterfront Stadium, which seats 2,400 people and was built for viewing the "World's Largest Musical Fountain" that plays nightly during the summer months, and the William Ferry Landing, a plaza area that provides a brass replica of the Grand River, done to scale and imbedded in the cement walk area of the boardwalk.

The development of the boardwalk has led to significant reinvestment in the downtown area. One example of this is the Harbourfront Place, a recently restored grand piano factory. The Harbourfront Place now features several boutiques and specialty dining areas that serve as an anchor for one end of Washington Street. Connected to the commercial area is a portion of the factory that has been converted into residential units.

Plazas can provide a focal point for the waterfront and downtown areas of a community, as well as, provide a place for festivals, recreational activities, and informal social gatherings. These plazas can function independent of a boardwalk area or as part of a greater scheme. The most important aspect of the plaza for the downtown is physical and visual access to the space. If visitors and shoppers to the community cannot easily access the waterfront, the downtown will not benefit as greatly.

Petoskey, MI, is a small community that has gone to great lengths to develop a waterfront park area, Bayfront Park, that features the "Midway" promenade in addition to other smaller recreational uses. The Bayfront Park is physically accessible to the nearby downtown district known as the "Gaslight District" by means of a pedestrian tunnel passing under a busy thoroughfare. The Gaslight District is an approximately six-block area that is filled with small, independent shops that offer a unique shopping experience. Petoskey is situated off Lake Michigan in the northern part of the lower peninsula of Michigan at the intersection of two busy highways. The annual tourist industry brings thousands of additional visitors to the town each year to visit the historic downtown district as well as the waterfront areas. One of these busy highways lies between the water's edge and the downtown district.

To assist the tourists and citizens of Petoskey in accessing the waterfront, a tunnel has been created that allows people to pass under Highway 31. From the water's edge, the tunnel is clearly marked to show that the downtown lies just beyond view. From the downtown, the water is clearly visible from several vantage points, and the path to the tunnel is marked as well. The waterfront plaza development, is a bright, colorful place that provides access to fishing, baseball fields, playground equipment, a museum, and gathering spaces. The area is used by young and old alike, pedestrian, bicyclers, and roller bladers. Above all, these parks, plazas, trails, and bikeways must integrate the downtown and the port.

While one can argue that these amenities are expensive, there is a significant amount of evidence that they encourage investment and reinvestment and add value to neighboring properties. Once the link is accomplished there is inevitably great community pride. This is particularly valid in areas that celebrate local culture. In New Bedford, for example, the existence of the whaling historic district (now a National Historic park) has continued to spur interest in both the downtown and the waterfront. Its location, between the port and central business district is the "glue" to the city's revitalization strategy. In Springfield, MA, the city has long sought means and methods to move people from its Connecticut Riverfront (home of the National Basketball Hall of Fame) through its downtown to its complex of museums—a journey of approximately one-mile. It is now developing plans to link the areas through flags, unique lighting, and symbols related to Dr. Seuss (Theodore Giesell, author of the Dr. Seuss series, was raised in Springfield). In this case, the city is using its heritage (the founding city of basketball, famous author, its culture) to link the downtown to the water.

XII) HARBORS MUST BE COMPREHENSIVELY LINKED TO KEY TRANSPORTATION SYSTEMS AND ADOPT TRAFFIC MANAGEMENT POLICIES.

If rail systems or access to major roads is difficult, it will impinge upon the ability of a harbor to meet its optimal potential. We have noted harbors, for example, that require off loading on to trucks for a short journey where the products are then re-loaded onto rail facilities. This, inevitably, adds costs to the products. Similarly, if trucks must pass through crowded streets and/or there are outdated cranes or a lack of rail or "roll off–roll on" capabilities, then the harbor will be at a disadvantage. Nowhere have we noted this as much as at the Harbor at Quonset Point where the rail line is being converted for "double stacking" and a former local street is being reconstructed into an arterial highway. In short, the greatest weakness determines the greatest output.

Unplanned traffic circulation can be chaotic for both vehicles and pedestrians. Some separation or controlled traffic management is necessary regardless of the use at the harbor. This becomes more imperative if there are mixed uses. Adequate parking, well-defined walkways, (bike paths), and jogging trails need to be established. The need for managed circulation is a requirement not only for both the aesthetics and functionality of the harbor but also for safety reasons. Once again, if it is not possible to entirely separate vehicle traffic from pedestrians, strategies such as traffic calming or specific time limits for service vehicles would be beneficial. For example, Nantucket is considering requiring service vehicles to make deliveries before 10:00A.M.

XIII) MARKETING AND PROMOTION ARE REQUIRED IF THE DOWNTOWN WATERFRONT IS TO PROSPER.

Not unlike any other amenity, the harbor needs to be marketed and promoted. All aspects of the harbor need attention. The working harbor needs to be marketed toward water related industries and support services. The education aspects need to be marketed toward professional and trade associations as well as universities and other educational institutions and the recreational aspects need to be marketed and promoted toward residents and tourists alike. The harbor, along with all its functions, and the community itself needs to market and promote itself as a tourist destination. Depending on the nature of activities, it could market itself to different target audiences such as family tourists, the young college/university students, business travelers, the sports minded tourists, seniors, or people looking for a relaxing hide away. Above all, the marketing must be balanced. We know of no downtown waterfront success story that has narrowly defined its orientation: Balance leads to success. We also know of few successful downtowns that survive by orienting themselves to a short season (e.g. the summer months). It is very important that marketing specialists orient themselves to a multi-seasonal approach. This has worked quite well in the downtown harbor areas of Martha's Vineyard (Edgartown, Vineyard Haven, Oak Bluffs) where the marketing specialists have successfully expanded the "shoulders of the season" from April to December. Each year more and more businesses are expanding the length of time that they are in operation.

XIV) GIVEN THE SPECIAL NATURE OF DOWNTOWN WATERFRONTS, THERE IS A GREAT NEED FOR PUBLIC PRIVATE PARTNERSHIPS.

Management issues are crucial to the well being and success of the harbor. Given its varied functions and clientele, public/private partnerships are in order. Most likely there will be a port/harbor authority that will be in charge of overseeing the day-to-day running and management of the harbor. However, the authority needs to work closely with government officials to ensure coordinated and collaborative efforts. The Chamber of Commerce and/or the Tourism Boards will play a role in the recreational and tourist aspects of the harbor management. Other public service divisions such as police, Coast Guard, fire protection, and parking authorities will play important roles. Established merchants, associations, and recreational clubs will be involved along with special interest groups. Coordination and communication among all these various functions will be crucial to the management and success of the harbor and the community as a whole. There must also be a sharing of costs. Downtown waterfront areas are "high maintenance." They frequently require additional municipal resources (security, lighting, sweeping). We have found that the use of Business Improvement District arrangements is an excellent approach to resolving this issue.

Conclusion

Downtowns in small towns throughout America are struggling to maintain viability and compete with suburban commercial centers. As communities seek to revitalize their downtowns, towns with waterfronts find themselves in a unique position to offer something special to citizens and visitors. Finding ways to make the waterfront an essential part of the downtown is a challenge to small communities, but also a great opportunity to build upon their unique culture and history. This chapter has provided several examples of small towns that have each found a special way to meet the needs of their downtown by providing amenities at the water's edge. These waterfront developments have been successful in bringing more people of all ages to the community and to the downtown. They are special places.

References

Coughlin, W.P. 1992. Gloucester Sees Port's Rebirth, *Boston Globe*, 28 February: 17.

Farell, Connie. 1999. Chamber of Commerce Coordinator, Association of Commerce and Industry, Grand Haven, Michigan, Personal Interview. April 9.

Hoyle, Brian, editor. 1996. *Cityports, Coastal Zones and Regional Change*. New York: Wiley.

Junger, Sebastian. 1997. *The Perfect Storm: A True Story of Men Against the Sea*. W.W. Norton & Co. Inc.

Kennedy, Lawrence W. 1992. *Planning the City Upon a Hill: Boston Since 1630*. Amherst: University of Massachusetts.

Porter, M. 1990. *The Competitive Advantage of Nations.*, New York: The Free Press.

Porter, Michael. 1995. "The Competitive Advantage of the Inner City", *Harvard Business Review*. 73 (3): 55.

CHAPTER 11

Brownfield Restoration and Waterfront Redevelopment in Wisconsin's Fox Valley Cities

JAMES R. SIMMONS

We may be at a changing of the tide. The forty-year movement out of central cities—especially out of the older industrial cities of the frostbelt, with its attendant deleterious effects on those left behind—may now be in the process of changing. The relocation of primary industry from the central city to the urban fringe has been precipitated in part by the prospects of lower taxes, less regulation, accessible transportation, and the availability of cheap and uncontaminated green space. Recent changes in state legislation combined with innovative local plans for urban waterfront development may allow several north-central Wisconsin cities to reverse this all too familiar pattern of commercial flight.

A quarter-century ago, the conventional view of federalism was that states and localities were so politically corrupt, administratively inept, hostile to innovation, and captive to regional commercial constituencies that they were incapable of taking a serious role in environmental policy (Rabe 1997). Today, it is the central government's regulatory efforts that have come under severe criticism and now the new conventional wisdom sees in policy devolution the mechanism through which environmental solutions can be found when cities and states find creative ways to tailor remedies to local realities (Mazmanian and Morell 1992). Overcoming obstacles posed by contaminated urban brownfield and vacant industrial land tracts is a critical area in which all levels of government have sought innovative and cooperative techniques for restoring blighted municipalities.

This chapter examines the way in which several of Wisconsin's Fox Valley cities have begun to utilize their state's new Brownfield legislation and the natural advantage of Lake Winnebago and the Fox River to make use of their decaying shorefronts to promote civic environmentalism. My primary focus will be on the number and variety of the recovery efforts that such medium-sized municipalities like Green Bay, Appleton, Neenah-Menasha, Fond du Lac and Oshkosh have already attempted as well as the balance among and potential for these efforts. However, this study also examines the ways in which the state of Wisconsin might attempt to ensure the success of the current efforts of these cities through the further enactment of specific complementary enabling laws and strategies for land recycling. Finally, I will discuss sustainable development theory and suggest how a change in basic social values and the way community progress is measured might ultimately prove to be the best way to improve life in the valley.

The Contaminated Municipal Land Problem

Brownfields as defined by the U.S. Environmental Protection Agency are "Abandoned, idled or underused industrial and commercial facilities where expansion or redevelopment is complicated by real or perceived environmental contamination"(Ryan 1998, 2). Brownfields can take many forms, from a closed dry cleaning business or leaking underground gasoline station storage tank to the more obvious abandoned industrial site. The majority of such brownfields occur in the central area of cities (Greenberg *et. al.* 1983).

Vacant buildings and industrial sites contaminated by chemicals lay as a curse on older cities. Called brownfields (in contrast to unspoiled greenfield outside the city), they scare away investors and bankers. The Federal Comprehensive Emergency Response, Compensation and Liability Act (CERCLA) makes a new owner responsible for cleaning up a site even if the new factory or commercial development will make the property safer than it was before. Potential developers can't estimate beforehand future expenses for cleaning up the site. Even if they could there is no assurance that their efforts will satisfy the Environmental Protection Agency (EPA) or calm local citizen fears over the risk posed by the new land use. Thus, new development has fled to the fringe of cities to greenfields, which are uncontaminated and less expensive parcels of land.

The redevelopment of brownfields is one way to slow the urban sprawl that is occurring in many areas. The movement of people, business, and industry from the urban core has created losses in the general municipal tax base as well as an inner city with poor residents that have few options for employment close to their homes. The high price of cleaning up a contaminated site keeps investors away from sites where there is only a possible contamination problem. This leads to wholesale abandonment of large sections of the city's central core that continue to be unusable public eyesores in addition to posing a threat to public health. Even the discovery of minor contamination on a property can trigger federal enforcement and liability rules that ultimately inhibit owners from selling the site, securing financing, or proceeding with reuse (Mazmanian and Morell 1992).

Until recently, most of the efforts at brownfield remediation in Wisconsin have depended on three national contaminated land cleanup programs administered by the state's Department of Natural Resources (DNR). These three key federal initiatives are the Superfund Program, the Leaking Underground Storage Tank Program (LUST) and the Resource Conservation and Recovery Act (RCRA) Program (Bonderud 1999). Such federal programs have produced many small cleanups at sites with minor contamination but have had little success at the major industrial sites. Indeed, infamous cases like the Better Brite Plating Company chrome and zinc shops site in Depere have produced twenty years of litigation, a temporary containment cap, and a bankruptcy but no permanent resolution. The even more notorious polychlorinated byphenal (PCB) contamination of the Fox River near Menasha has seen fifteen years of negotiation during which local public officials and the paper mills have successfully stalled state and federal dredging projects, resisted an effort by EPA to impose a Superfund designation at six river locations and prevented disposal of excavated sediment in nearby county landfills (Culhane 1998).

Highly salient failures like these have caused state authorities to look for policy alternatives that produce less resistance and better results. In order to achieve this goal, Wisconsin joined several other states and two Canadaian provinces to create a Brownfields Project under the sponsorship of the Council of Great Lakes Governors. A Brownfields Regional Advisory Group (BRAG) was then formed that built on case studies of provincial successes to develop a framework for regional land recycling that had a long-term perspective on economic and environmental benefits (Pebbles 1999). BRAG's Brownfields Project Working Group ultimately designed a "state-of-the-state" blueprint for brownfield redevelopment that has come to be known as the Chicago Model (O'Brien 1998). Although the model's specific policy proposals are complex, the central idea is that while brownfields are a national problem, the right solution resides in the local experiences of stakeholders affected by these properties (Peterson 1997).

Adherents of the "model" insist that although no single "best" public-approach will resolve all brownfield issues, an integrated approach to land redevelopment would require a decentralized approach that emphasized state initiatives, local government proaction and private sector partnerships (Bartsch, Collaton and Pepper 1996). Centralized federal environmental policies frequently fail because they get in the way of remediation efforts by utilizing a single "one size fits all" strategy, emphasizing cost recovery (make the polluter pay) and by adhering to a confrontational orientation that treats business and investors as potentially responsible parties or likely malefactors. Therefore, what government needs to do in order to revitalize fallow industrial properties in older city sites is to intervene in ways that ease regulatory laws, reduce risk for potential developers, fill in the funding gaps, establish public subsidy programs, and bridge the other voids in the marketplace that hinder voluntary private cleanup and improvement of contaminated sites.

Armed with this cooperative plan, Governor Thompson established a Wisconsin Brownfield Study Group in 1997 and the legislature began enacting initiatives that address the issues that were uncovered by the studies. Strategies for brownfield legislation were to come not only from the joint Great Lakes Project but also state agencies, lenders, realtors, universities, federal agencies, businesses and non-profits. The end result of this combined effort are initiatives that complement the federal programs and state funds to speed up remediation and redevelopment. Many state land recycling efforts have been consolidated so that Wisconsin's DNR, its Department of Commerce, and several smaller agencies jointly administer brownfield policies. These complimentary programs fund part of the cost of state-lead remediation at privately-owned properties, sponsor redevelopment projects, reimburse municipalities for expenses incurred and partially exempt from liability the various parties who voluntarily participate in the cleanup process.

State Innovation

Wisconsin's public officials have found the cooperative institutional partnership idea embodied in the Chicago Model especially appealing. The state's Republican governor and legislature have found particularly attractive the perspective that views owners of contaminated land as potential redevelopment partners rather than reckless or irresponsible "bad actors." Equally appealing to the business community and conservatives is the idea that government's command-and-control regulatory efforts hinder urban development. Consequently, it should not be too surprising that Wisconsin has adopted more features of the "model" than any other state (see Table 9) and is well on the way to implementing and expanding them (Bartsch and Anderson 1999).

Along with programs that are administered by the federal government, the Wisconsin legislature has enacted several state initiatives which complement federal programs and provide additional remedies and state funds to help clean up contaminated sites. The Wisconsin Department of Natural Resources (WDNR) holds primary responsibility for administering the contaminated land investigation, cleanup, and remediation program, but the Department of Commerce administers the 1997 Brownfield Initiative program that provides grants that are used to fund the cost of redevelopment projects at abandoned, idle, or underused industrial or commercial facilities (Jarvis 1999). Furthermore, the Wisconsin Housing and Economic Development Authority (WHEDA) administers a site remediation loan guarantee program and the Department of Agriculture Trade and Consumer Protection operates a program for the cleanup of agricultural chemical spills (including those in urban settings).

The WDNR operates the State Funded Response Action Program. This program is similar to the Federal Superfund Program. Authority to clean up any site is given to this program, but it is mainly used for sites in a waste management facility like a landfill or a sewage treatment plant. Train spills and large industrial spills are also handled by this program (Bonderud 1999). As with other programs, the liable party is responsible for the cost of the cleanup or for whatever part they contributed to the contamination. However, if the responsible party cannot be found, the state pays for the cleanup. This differs from the Superfund program where one party, who only caused part of the contamination, may have to pay for the entire cleanup when no other responsible party can be located (Hird 1994).

Wisconsin government also provides liability exemptions to encourage voluntary cleanups. The 1993 Wisconsin Act 453 created limited liability for the purchaser of contaminated property. Under this Land Recycling Law, an Assurance letter or No Further Action letter is issued to remediated sites to assure

Table 9: Wisconsin Brownfield Programs

Targeted Financing programs	Voluntary Clean Up and Assurance	Private Investment Initiatives	Other Initiatives
Brownfield Grant program	Land Recycling Act (1994)	Development Zone Tax Credits	Brownfields Study
State Trust Fund Loan Program	Voluntary Party Liability Exemption	Business Improvement Districts (BIDs)	Innovatove Technology/ Competitive Bidding Waiver
Land Recycling Loan Program (DNR Priority List)	City Immunity and Development Corporation Liability Exemption	Sustainable Urban Development Zone Tax Increment Financing	
Redevelopment Loan Guarantees	Off-Site Discharge Property Immunity	Delinquent Tax Cancellation	
Brownfield Environmental Assessment Program (BEAP)	Lender Liability Exemption		
Dry Cleaner Environmental Response Fund			
Stewardship and Community Development Block Grant Funds			

Source: "Summary of Wisconsin's New Brownfields Programs and Initiatives," (WDNR RR-563-87, February 10, 1999).

the owners that they are legally protected from any further costs associated with contamination on the property (McGahren 1998). "The Act authorized purchasers of contaminated property to obtain an exemption from further remedial action of the property and prohibited the Department of Justice from commencing an action under the Federal Superfund Law if the purchaser takes certain actions to investigate and clean up the property" (Bonderud 1999, 2).

In 1997 Wisconsin Act 27 expanded 453 to include any voluntary purchaser of a property who did not intentionally or purposefully cause the leakage of a hazardous substance. Property owners who are impacted from contamination coming from a neighboring or off-site property are also exempt from liability or remedial action. The offsite exemption was created to assist property owners or prospective purchasers to clarify who is liable when the contamination occurs off-site. The law was designed to encourage remediation of properties but require the responsible party to pay for the cleanup (Giesler 1999). The process for the cleanup of off-site contamination is similar to the cleanup of all non-liable properties. As McGahren observed:

> Liability protection that reduces future environmental uncertainty for property purchasers and developers is an important incentive under brownfields legislation. State brownfield laws commonly include liability relief provisions that protect innocent purchasers or developers from liability if they agree to cleanup a site. Brownfield laws may also include a release of liability to future property owners who acquire the property after the site has been remediated (McGahren 1998, 18).

Liability protection was also established for the local governments and economic development corporations because those units obtained property in an unwilling manner. Past legislation requiring cleanup by parties possessing contaminated property included governments and development firms. The new land recycling law (Bangert and Giesfeldt 1998) and the 1997–99 state budget have removed such liability in order to create incentives for the redevelopment of property that was acquired in certain ways (Savagian 1998). Local governments are exempt from liability if the property was acquired in the four following ways: (i) through delinquency proceedings or as the result of bankruptcy; (ii) from another local government unit that acquired the property through delinquency or bankruptcy; (iii) condemnation or eminent domain; or (iv) for the purpose of slum clearing. An economic development corporation would be exempt if the property was used to further economic development (Bonderud 1999).

Although Wisconsin has attempted to consolidate and streamline its remediation and redevelopment program, several other state agencies also operate brownfields programs. The Department of Commerce (DOC), The Department of Agriculture, and WHEDA each administer separate but complimentary state policies. The DOC's Brownfields Grant Program is awarded to public or private projects for expenses including demolition, rehabilitation of facilities, investigation, and cleanups. Sites are limited to those in which the responsible party is unable to pay or can't be located. Award priority is based on the project's economic development potential in the area, whether the project will have a positive effect on the environment, the level and the quality of applicant support and the degree of innovativeness of the recipient's proposal for remediation and redevelopment (Amerson 1998). There are different levels of grants and different amounts that must be co-paid by the redeveloper. The grant amount pays 50 percent of the cost of a major project.

The program administered by the Department of Agriculture Trade and Consumer Protection (DATCP) provides funding for the cleanup of agricultural chemical spills. The responsibility of cleaning up agricultural chemical spills was transferred from the DNR to the DATCP in 1993 (Bonderud 1999). This program is relevant because many of these spills occur in urban areas where many such chemicals are stored and transferred. The final agency that manages a brownfield program is WHEDA. The agency runs the Brownfields Loan Guarantee Program which insures private bank loans for up to 80 percent of the principal for the redevelopment of a contaminated site (Amerson 1998).

Wisconsin's brownfield redevelopment program already has five success stories since its inception. These include successful cleanups at an industrial site in New Berlin where Cellular One received the state's first "certificate of completion," the City of Glendale's downtown Technology Center site, Milwaukee's abandoned Tannery, Manitowoc's former WCI Commercial Refrigeration Division in its Lake Michigan harbor area, and the construction of the Village of DeForest's Public Safety Building on what were four blighted downtown brownfield properties (Savagian 1998). By 1998, 125 sites had entered the program for voluntary party liability exemption and six received certificates of completion. Since its inception in 1996, thirty-three sites have participated in the Brownfield Environmental Assessment Program with two BEAP properties fully redeveloped and many others in process of completion. Last year, the first round of brownfield grants were awarded to fourteen projects, twelve new businesses, and seven expansions. In 1999, the state legislature was poised to add a substantial increase in funding targeted to land recycling.

Fox Valley Renovation Efforts

Wisconsin's new brownfields programs and initiatives have had special significance for the WDNR's Northeast Region. Although this region of the state has only six "official" sites on the EPA's National Priorities List (EPA 1998), it is a thriving regional center of industrial activity and undoubtedly houses a much larger number of unidentified sites that have yet to make the federal government's Superfund or the state's Priority List. Northeast Wisconsin is the most rapidly growing and urbanizing region of the state. The municipalities in the part of Wisconsin known as the Fox Cities are also home to many abandoned properties with suspected contamination problems where the owner of the property is insolvent or cannot be located and taxes are delinquent so the local community suffers (Greenberg 1996). The city services that are provided like police and fire protection, sewer and water services, among many others, are hurt because of the decrease in public revenues resulting from the reduction in the property tax base.

Brownfields are not a new problem to this area or to other parts of the state. Nevertheless, this is a rapidly urbanizing region whose growth is handicapped by the contaminating legacy of its industrial past. Many of the lumber mills, metalworking shops, and other heavy smokestack industries that once were the primary source of prosperity in these central Wisconsin cities have relocated or simply gone under. Thus, transforming the Fox River corridor from its historic manufacturing base into a more diversified service economy will require convincing existing industries all along the Fox River from Green Bay down to Fond du Lac to relocate to industrial parks. It will also involve persuading potential developers that sufficient market demand exists for commercial, recreational, or residential projects on the old urban industrial sites.

As indicated earlier, federal agencies have had little success with the valley's contaminated urban tracts. The EPA's Superfund program has produced lawsuits and limited preliminary actions at places like Ripon's old city landfill and Appleton's leaking N.W. Mauther Co. site, but little else. Wisconsin's land recycling law, on the other hand, was designed to transform the estimated 8,000 unusable and even abandoned industrial brownfield properties throughout the state into productive lands that contribute to each community's tax base. Despite the recent vintage of these land recycling policies, there are several examples of Fox River Valley brownfields that have already been cleaned up as a result of state initiatives or substantial modifications of federal programs.

One such property is the bankrupt Fred Rueping Leather Company Property located in Fond du Lac. The property has several areas of contamination. The first is an underground storage tank that was leaking petroleum, and the second is the non-isolated, subsurface soils contamination that contains arsenic, phenanthrene, several benzene compounds, and perylene. The groundwater was reported to contain arsenic, antimony, barium, cadmium, and chromium levels that were all beyond the safety levels established by the state (Nass 1998). Cleanup of the site was accomplished by installing a clay cap over the contaminated portion of soil. The groundwater by the underground storage tank was pumped and run through an activated charcoal filter to remove the gasoline that was present in the surrounding area. The phase I and II environmental assessment as well as much of the remediation were funded by the WDNR Brownfields Environmental Assessment Program. The city of Fond du Lac demolished the plant buildings and provided both the cap and the monitoring wells (Nass 1998).

The second brownfield success story is the American Quality Fibers Property located in Menasha. This is a small site that consisted of a warehouse and an additional building foundation. The property had been used for paper and plastic recycling, industrial drum recycling, and as a warehouse for a chemical company. Contamination was reported in the soil and the groundwater during the 1998 assessment. Completion of the project will involve pumping and treating the groundwater along with demolition of the buildings and the treatment of the soil. Winnebago County has waived the delinquent taxes on the property to assist with the cleanup (Amerson 1998).

Other actions involve three sites in Green Bay, Wisconsin. The Thomas Sherman Property was once a service and filling station. It houses a leaking underground tank and an area that was used as a slough for unwanted contaminated fill material. This property is important because of its close proximity to the Fox River. Brown County has acquired the property and deeded it to the city. The city plans to demolish the buildings and remove the structures to a landfill and remediate the rest of the site for use in a future development. Another remediated city brownfield property was the burned and abandoned WCI Commercial Refrigeration Division that was not a major contamination problem, but one that was underused. The property was close to the downtown Lake Michigan harbor area that the city is trying to convert to a commercial zone. Consequently, city officials decided to purchase the area and build a new library to replace a smaller one at a different location. By using a brownfield property, the city was able to buy the land at a low cost that enabled some projects that have lacked funding to be accomplished (Savagian 1999).

The City of Green Bay also has made plans to remediate another site along the west bank of the Fox River. The seven-acre property was used as storage for coal, salt, and other wastes from manufacturing and various industries. The site was purchased as a part of the city of Green Bay's master plan. It is located in a low-income neighborhood which is in need of improvement. Some preliminary work has been done to remediate the site. The coal and salt residue and the four underground storage tanks have been removed. All the city's efforts to investigate and clean up this third site is dependent on receiving money for the project in the form of state grants. City officials intend to market the restored property for an office complex, residential housing or possibly a museum (1998 BEAP Sites).

The final potential success story involves the City of Oshkosh. Within this city there are six different types of brownfields or potential brownfield sites. In total, there are 117 different properties with 148 different contaminated sites according to the Site Assessment Report prepared for the Oshkosh Planning Department. This number is only speculative since many brownfields are not known or, if known, are not reported. The most infamous brownfield site in Oshkosh is the Universal Foundry property. City officials purchased both the old foundry and the nearby Radford Building and created a new Tax Incremental Finance District to pay for building demolition and land clearance. Oshkosh will receive a loan and grant money from the state to fund site investigation, soil cleanup and capping. The city then intends to either lease the property to the

University of Wisconsin–Oshkosh for athletic fields and parking, or market it for mixed commercial business or residential housing and apartment development.

The City of Oshkosh Case Study

One of the most critical tests of the state's land recycling project will be the daunting task of redeveloping the brownfields along the riverfront near the city of Oshkosh. This particular central Wisconsin municipality provides an interesting case study for both an examination of a community with a legacy of severe environmental problems, as well as a sounding board for innovative ideas about land recycling and sustainablity in a medium-sized city. Oshkosh's environmental challenges are more serious than most cities its size because it is an old industrial city that has traditionally given environmental issues low civic priority (Ebert 1996). Local officials and business interests have generally been far more concerned with industrial and commercial development. They fear that any government action or even the public discussion of municipal environmental problems might dampen growth (Simmons 1997). Consequently, the "City on the Water" generally ranks water, air, and land issues low on the list in discussions about the quality of community life.

Oshkosh was once home to basic industries that pollute heavily, including paper mills, foundries, metal working firms, lumber mills, and match companies. Prior to the onset of environmental activism in the late 1960s, hazardous materials were simply dumped in local landfills, contained on site, or piped into streams, rivers, and lakes; where they settled to the bottom of these waterways. The city continues to attract to its industrial parks some firms that follow questionable practices. In addition, the metropolitan area is served by an aging water filtration plant, an old sewer system, landfills rapidly approaching capacity, and a large number of abandoned industrial sites. Furthermore, the city has many older neighborhoods with homes that house both lead-based paint and copper or lead pipes.

Sustainable development and civic environmentalism are theoretical concepts that have had limited appeal to local government officials. Former City Manager Bill Frueh, who managed Oshkosh from 1976 to 1996, was highly critical of what he called "charging environmentalists" and said that "such people should balance their environmental concerns with the costs of the solutions" (Mangan 1994). However, "balance" is precisely what most land recycling and sustainable development approaches promote. Because Oshkosh exemplifies the prototypical older city handicapped by unused industrial sites, it provides an excellent locale for studying the extent to which authorities have responded appropriately to alterations in their legal and physical environment. What follows, therefore, in this section is a brief inventory of the city's major environmental problems, an accounting of projected forms of remediation and a general discussion of applications of sustainable growth measurement and planning as a means for resolving locally contested political issues.

Environmental Problems Inventory

Nothing is likely to happen to resolve outstanding environmental problems—especially when they require expenditure of substantial resources—until the public reaches a high level of awareness. The following inventory is simply a listing of the major trouble spots that have generated substantial local media interest, government action and citizens group activity. The list does not encompass all environmental problems that have been identified locally or, for that matter, those that have yet to be fully identified.

WATERWAYS CONTAMINATION

Both Lake Butte des Morts and the lower Fox River have been identified as major sources of environmental contamination. The EPA and Wisconsin Department of Natural Resources have targeted several key sites on the river and lake for a major cleanup of polychlorinated byphenals. Paper mills used these waterways during the 1950s and 1960s to discharge PCB contaminated waste water generated through their efforts to recycle carbonless copy paper. The DNR is proposing damming up several of the most seriously contaminated water sites, dredging up 1,440 pounds of the contaminants from bottom sediment, mixing this material with ordinary municipal waste and disposing of the mixture in regional county landfills. A coalition of local governments, industry, and state agencies support this proposed action, but the Clean Water Action Council, a local citizens group, and environmentalists oppose the plan.

TOXIC CHEMICAL GENERATION

Several area companies and some of the city's largest employers have been identified as among the state's top waste releasers. Industry data show that Oshkosh Truck Corporation was the seventh-largest producer of waste (503,000 pounds) containing chemicals suspected of causing cancer. Pierce Manufacturing Inc. ranked ninth (397,000 pounds) in waste and Square D Company tenth by producing 338,000 pounds. Small and large generators of hazardous waste are registered for waste production that occurs on the site. The small generators produce 100–1000 Kg of non-acutely hazardous waste, while the larger produce more than 1000 Kg. Large generators have to ship the waste off-site to a disposal facility every ninety days while the small generators every 180 days. Any producer that generates less than five 55-gallon drums in five years needs no registration and proper disposal is assumed. Rockwell International is a large producer that has to dispose on site solvents used to degrease machinery equipment. Small generators of waste solvents in the city are firms like Gunderson Cleaners and the Tower Paint Company.

Wisconsin's Citizens Action Coalition has recommended legal changes that would require that companies go beyond reporting and set goals for reducing their use and disposal of such wastes. Current levels of toxic emissions and the absence of local waste-disposal facilities are also local issues. Industry representatives insist that most of these potential pollutants are highly controlled and are not emitted into the air or water.

WATER TREATMENT

Tough EPA regulations and DNR warnings are forcing the city to construct a new water filtration plant to replace its aging 85-year old water treatment plant. The existing facility has high operation costs, signs of structural failure, potential for water contamination in the event of accidents and a lack of adequate equipment or trained staff for dealing with chemicals. Current plant capacity is inadequate given the recent growth in the community's population that can lead to water use restriction on peak demand days. Higher water rates estimated at a 30 percent increase will be needed to cover costs of construction and a recently enacted federal government low-interest loan program will provide the necessary capital for the upgrade.

AIR POLLUTION

Gear Feed Inc. was forced to shut down its dairy livestock feed pellets plant and eventually close down operations altogether after neighbor's complaints caused city officials to threaten legal action. Although the plant had begun efforts to eliminate odors emanating from the facility, the City Health Department felt that the company's timetable for retrofitting was unacceptable. Gear officials would have been forced to close temporarily, in any case, because of a fire in the plant's dryer section unit. Excessive waste water emissions had already forced the company to inject highly concentrated wastes into the city sewers and nearby landfills.

Brownfield Contamination

The state DNR estimates that there are 454 known or suspected contamination sites in Winnebago County. Some 258 of these grounds are still open while another 196 are now closed. Many of the city's old and abandoned industrial plant sites are properties that cannot be developed because the cost of cleanup outweighs their value (Leasum 1995). Three of the most prominent and notorious local examples are:

i) Wisconsin Public Service is cleaning up coal tar contamination near Riverside Park on the Fox River. The tar contains a number of compounds—PAHs—that travel downstream and destroy the basic building blocks of the aquatic food chain.

ii) The bankrupt Universal Foundry is contaminated by barrels of unusable chemicals dumped on-site just south of the facility and leaking, underground, gas tanks. Furthermore, attempts to salvage the plant's collection baghouse system spilled hazardous waste in the form of heavy-metal dust containing high levels of lead and cadmium. This dust has since migrated into the storm sewers in the neighborhoods surrounding the plant.

iii) Another property on the State's Contamination List (SCL) is the Tower Paint Company. The contamination of the property consists of Toluene, Zylene, and paint thinners. The nearby Miles Kimball Company owns property that has the chlorinated solvent vinyl chloride in the groundwater.

Landfill Leachate

Two former city landfill sites are the focus of investigation as the origin of trichloroethylene contamination in local water. In 1994, the DNR issued a health advisory for drinking and cooking in a one-square-mile section south-east of Oshkosh and the Town of Algoma. Dozens of local wells were found to be contaminated by TCE, or arsenic, and shut down. The DNR forced the city to monitor groundwater and insisted that area residents shift to municipal water. The major active landfills north of the city have been given a clean bill of health but they are rapidly approaching capacity and efforts are being made to extend their life expectancy.

Nonpoint River Pollution

Some stretches of the Fox River flowing through Oshkosh are just barely passing water pollution tests. Tests for water clarity and floating sediments are consistently receiving poor marks. Sources of the increasing nonpoint pollution include erosion from agricultural lands, construction site spillage and storm water runoff from city streets, parking lots, and lawns. Fertilizers, chemicals, and other nutrients attach to sediments, contributing to excessive fertility in the water and dense algae blooming in the winter. Consequently, oxygen becomes scarce as algae die, frequently resulting in fish kills. A 1994 DNR study also revealed trace amounts of crytosporidia in the local water. Although, the results showed that these disease-causing micro-organisms posed no immediate health threat, the data did indicate that the incidence was increasing.

Ozone Restrictions

Preliminary data from DNR recordings of Oshkosh-area ozone levels may place the city and the surrounding Fox Valley area into one of the state's ozone problem zones. Winnebago is perilously close to being included with the eleven counties near Lake Michigan that are regulated by the U.S. EPA as official problem areas for periodically exceeding health standards. Industry representatives fear that such a move will drive businesses to unregulated areas.

Sludge Incineration

The City of Neenah, just North of Oshkosh, has leased four acres of a public park to Minergy Corporation which intends to build a facility that will use natural gas to burn paper sludge that would otherwise end up in the county landfill. This incineration will produce a glass aggregate and steam that will provide energy for Minergy's adjacent plant. A local citizens group has filed suit charging that this lease is misuse of a public lake and watershed but their primary concern is the potential air and ash pollution that are the byproducts of hazardous waste incineration. The plant suffered a rash of fires and other malfunctions after it went on-line in 1998.

LUST Sites

Winnebago County currently accounts for 197 of Wisconsin's 12,000 leaking underground storage tank sites (142 have been cleaned up and closed). This number greatly underestimates the contaminated sites that will ultimately be discovered and added to the DNR's cleanup list. Just twenty of these known gas sites pose a serious threat. While those places have produced contaminated water supplies as well as vapors that travel sewer lines and enter homes causing fires or explosions, at most of the known sites chemicals dissipate before they pose a health threat. Nevertheless, the price tag for the state's LUST program grows while the number of local state personnel declines.

Remediation Efforts

Despite the marked commercial orientation of public officials and local business interests, the city has undertaken a number of positive steps to remediate local environmental problems. Furthermore, the city's administration has taken the initial steps necessary to take advantage of the state's new land redevelopment programs. And, although none of these programs individually, or in combination, are driven by the underlying orientation of sustainability, they offer some hope that a more comprehensive strategy could be attempted. Their adoption also suggests that some of the prerequisites for a local sustainablity movement exist at least in embryo form.

WASTE AUDITS, REUSE AND RECYCLING

The government officials have initiated a large number of measures aimed at extending the local landfills and promoting concepts like source reduction, reuse, and recycling. Since recycling became law in Winnebago county last year, recyclables—generally plastics, glass and paper—cannot be dumped in Wisconsin's landfills. Residents are now confronted with sorting, rinsing and placing these items in blue bags for pickup and recycling. They will now also have to personally transport their unwanted appliances and some of their furniture to the land-fill and be charged a fee ranging from $13 to $23 each. The city and county land-fill will still pick up yard waste, brush, and organic material but at limited times. There are also new weight limits on pickup as well as costs for disposal for specific items.

COMMUNITY HEALTH

The city's Department of Community Development's Health Division is involved in activities related to environmental health services, nursing, and laboratory analysis. Over 1,200 inspections are performed by environmental staff relative to the 411 licenses issued by the city. Inspections are undertaken to ensure proper sanitation is followed by restaurants, taverns, markets, bakeries, confectioneries, hotels, motels, church kitchens, school cafeterias, and public swimming pools. The city's Public Health Nurses provide a variety of health assessment services to community residents and conduct monthly immunization clinics.

PUBLIC LANDS

The city's Department of Parks is primarily responsible for quality of life issues including the twenty-four public parks, forestry services, Riverside Cemetery maintenance, the zoo and 450 acres of public open space land. The Parks Division has a staff of fifteen employees and a 1999 budget of $1.5 million. The department's forestry division is responsible for the planting of all trees and plant materials on public lands. It is also responsible for various ongoing programs, such as insect control, terrace tree irrigation, storm or wind damage cleanup, fertilization, new plantings, and maintenance of downtown planters and green areas.

UNIVERSITY PROGRAMS

In 1994, the University of Wisconsin-Oshkosh introduced an environmental studies program that is intended to become an important resource in understanding and dealing with regional environmental concerns. The program will create a local forum for applied research, reflection and action (Taylor 1994). Current research and projects by university faculty and students focus on the larger Fox-Wolf watershed and the way decentralized environmental decision-making can make both citizens and public officials more aware of their responsibility for protecting critical habitats as well as the necessity for developing sustainable lifeways. Students collaborate with faculty involved in environmental research, remediation projects, and outreach activities, as well as, intern for local business firms and government agencies.

In 1998, the University also opened a Center for Community Partnerships in the city's downtown Park Plaza mall. This Center will enable the community to access resources and information from the university for business and governmental purposes (Grulke 1999). This latter cooperative effort by the university is intended not only to spur redevelopment along the river but to ensure that the institution's expertise will improve the overall quality of change in this urban center (Feinauer 1999). One of the first direct efforts by the university to act as the city's partner is UWO's proposal to lease the Universal Foundry brownfield site for use in student parking, sports, and recreation (Saiki 1998) .

WATER QUALITY LEGISLATION

The county's Land & Water Conservation Department allows landowners within designated "watersheds" to volunteer to control water pollution from sediment erosion, animal waste, fertilizers, and runoff from city streets. The costs of these preventive practices are then shared between landowners and the state. The DNR allows county governments to administer the grants and enforce the four prohibitions—manure overflow, unconfined manure, feedlot runoff, soil destruction by livestock—on all non-point or runoff pollution originating from farms. The county has undertaken a countywide inventory of water quality and has prepared a plan outlining pollution prevention and reduction priorities.

ENVIRONMENTAL ACTIVISM

A variety of local groups have sprung up to promote care of local lakes and rivers and to oppose locally unwanted land use. The Student Environmental Action Coalition is active in environmental awareness campaigns such as its Toxic Tour, informational forums, and protest activities. The Environmental Decade has located a regional chapter office in Oshkosh and is attempting to coordinate environmental activists groups and promote sustainable ideas like mass transit. Spontaneous citizens mobilization has been increasing locally over disputes like the efforts of the DNR to mix hazardous and municipal waste for disposal in the county landfill and Minergy's hazardous waste incinerator project. Opposition to Exxon and Rio Algom corporation's efforts to begin copper mining at Crandon in upriver Forest County has also resonated locally stimulating substantial citizen's activism.

WATER TREATMENT

Under EPA and DNR pressure, the city is moving ahead with the construction of a $30 million new water treatment plant to replace the 85-year old structure that currently serves the community. This facility should reduce operational costs and reduce the high levels of particulate matter in city water. Concerns over potential health problems should also be ameliorated following the highly publicized crytosporidium outbreak in downstate Milwaukee. The expense of the necessary revenue bonds, however, will initially bring about a substantial increase in user fees by residential water rate payers, commercial and business users.

STORAGE TANK CLEANUP

The DNR is responsible for the cleanup of the 284 leaking gas tank sites in Winnebago, Waushara, and Calumet counties. The agency itself now manages only the twenty most serious cases and allows private consultants to handle the remaining sites. Property owners are reimbursed for some cleanup costs through a Petroleum Environmental Cleanup Fund award, funded by a fee on each gallon of petroleum brought into Wisconsin. While local contaminated sites are constantly being added to the cleanup list and state funding has grown, the number of DNR staffers overseeing the cleanup projects has dwindled as a result of federal funding cuts. The state has responded by concentrating on sites with chemical discharges that potentially pose a serious health threat and by allowing remediation at certain sites to stop if it is ineffective (Seaborn 1995). In the latter case, drinking water restrictions are imposed until natural attenuation can be demonstrated to have dissipated the problem.

LAND RECYCLING

City officials have taken advantage of the municipality's limited liability under state's Land Recycling Act and its grant fund to acquire the unoccupied and contaminated 82-year old Universal Foundry Company property. Changes in the brownfields law enacted in 1998 by the Wisconsin legislature give the city government liability protection from being forced to pay full or triple damages for contamination caused by the previous property owner. Buoyed by the new rules, the Oshkosh Common Council moved forward with an ambitious plan to acquire the vacant foundry site and the nearby Radford Building plant. Funding for the land purchase and building demolition came from the state Commerce Department's grant dollars, tax incremental financing through a special "environmentally challenged" TIF district created in this part of the city for that purpose and surplus revenue from the municipality's Southwest Industrial Park. Officials plan to lease five acres to the University of Wisconsin-Oshkosh for a parking lot that will cap the most contaminated soil. The remainder of the property is targeted by the city's comprehensive plan for the promotion of commercial development, multiple-family rental housing units or an ice skating arena.

Although the city's government does not inherit the liability of "guilty party" by purchasing the property as it would have under the "deep pockets" theory of the old law, it will not be exempt from a legal challenge by a third party, such as an adjacent property owner who found contamination on his or her property that had migrated from the site. Critics like Caryl Terrell, legislative coordinator for the Sierra Club in Madison, wonder whether capping the property provides adequate long-term protection from groundwater pollution and argue that even when a municipality buys such a property, someone will have to clean it up (Trebon 1998). If a contamination problem were to arise, it would be assessed and placed on the state SCL list based on its relative severity like any other contaminated site. Although the city would not be considered a responsible party and, thus, liable for cleanup costs, state funding for such remediation is still minimal compared with the number of similar projects waiting for money.

The question of toxic risk makes matching up potential developers and landowners difficult but it is hardly the only issue. While officials recognize the riverfront as the city's number one asset, the Fox River's history as a manufacturing and industrial center presents another hurdle for the master plan to redevelop the shoreline for recreational and residential uses. Oshkosh Community Development Director, Jackson Kinney, admits that potential buyers and developers must be convinced of the commercial viability of the waterfront and the downtown if this grandiose long-term vision for a sustained Fox River renaissance is to succeed (Ebert 1996). This will mean that the city must initiate many more sustainable urban redevelopment zones than the one planners are currently working on at the foundry site since there is suspected contamination from the Bay Shore Drive area near Lake Winnebago and all along both sides of the river up to the shores of Lake Butte des Morts.

Toward a Sustainable Agenda

When civic boosters of Wisconsin's municipalities like Oshkosh talk about keeping the city "moving forward," they are usually simply vowing to continue population growth, expand commercial development, increase jobs, and attract new industry. Local leaders generally measure progress in terms of market activity in much the same way that national leaders use Gross Domestic Product (GDP). The normal indicators of economic well-being have always been problematic locally given the unusually low household income and decline in real wages in Oshkosh compared with other cities in this region of Wisconsin. Such data become even more dubious if we consider an alternative measure of community health called GPI (genuine progress indicator) which is now favored by some economists (Cobb *et. al.* 1996).

The standard index of local well-being emphasizes public and private transactions. It is also biased in the sense that growth (population, construction, industry, paving, etc.) is nearly always evaluated on the positive side of the ledger. Furthermore, major features of community life such as child and elderly care, home maintenance, crime, homelessness, voluntary neighborhood service, church and civic associations, political participation, and so on, are ignored. All these individual or group activities and social conditions are given a relative value of zero.

The usual measures make no distinction between those activities that diminish well-being and those that increase it. Even the breakdown of the social order and destruction of the natural environment are treated as gains. If arson destroys a home or a whole neighborhood and if the fire damage is insured, the resulting reconstruction falls under the heading of a "housing start." When local officials recently filled in major wetlands on the west side in order to create industrial parks to attract new industry, the activity was viewed in only a positive light. This is very much like keeping accounts using a calculator that has an "add" function but no "subtract" function.

Public officials, major local employers, and the Chamber of Commerce are fond of talking about the city's government as a "$40 million dollar business." Any actual business that kept its accounts this way would never know where it stood. Such a company would have an exaggerated picture of its condition and prospects. So it is with a city that relies exclusively on the price or market value of everything and has no other quantitative or qualitative measures of general community well being. This problem is especially severe in the case of the inventory of local environmental problems cited earlier since, by all accounts, the depletion of natural capital (assets) is treated as a current benefit. Nor is there any general accounting for the eventual expenditures that will be necessary for future environmental remedial efforts.

Efforts to examine the health of the local community have been attempted but most of this takes the form of popular magazine accounts, newspaper editorializing, or traveler's guides. A serious effort to establish a GDI for the city would have to include the following:

i) Fixing Mistakes and Social Failures from the Past: Cleanup efforts at old industrial brownfield sites are not real progress. They may create temporary jobs but they simply get the city back to where it was if they can restore the land to its prior condition. Reuse of the property for public or private projects after cleanup will generate employment but will also create future liabilities if the new owners abuse the property as the old tenants did. The local prison, three correction facilities, and a mental health center are another example. Forced confinement is a response to earlier societal failures to help people gain a valued place in the economy and community.

ii) Borrowing Resources from the Future: Winnebago county's impressive agricultural output is partially a product of enormous chemical use. Such usage occurs at the expense of depleted natural capital (fertile soil and clean water) and poses a present threat to community health through nonpoint chemical runoff from these farmlands. It also undermines recreational potential and presents real costs to future generations in the city.

iii) Shifting Functions from the Household to the Market: Daycare centers, baby sitters, nannies, and maid services substitute for parents as an increasing number of local households have two wage earners.

• Commercial yard care maintenance and agricultural pesticide delivery replaces family activity in land use.
• City sponsored use of public employees for recycling efforts and household hazards pickup replaces voluntary compliance.
• Grocery store sale of vegetables replace the household garden and fast food chains like Hardee's substitute for the family's kitchen.

• Police officers and burglar alarms substitute for the watchfulness of neighbors.

• TVs, the Internet, computers, VCRs, and video games substitute for interaction among family, friends, and neighbors.

In each of these cases, free services (free in the sense of absence of market compensation) have disappeared to be replaced by an established market relationship. In most instances, this shift represents a measurable gain in traditional economic terms but a decrease in the traditional fabric that holds the family and community together.

New measures of urban progress are needed. The old measures provide a false sense of well being. For example, pollution and hazardous waste are treated as a double gain since they are created as a byproduct of some commercial activity and are again counted as a gain when the city pays to clean them up. Several new measures of well being have been established (Cobb & Cobb 1994; Miringhoff 1994; O'Connor 1994) but the best indicator seems to be the Genuine Progress Indicator, or GPI developed by an organization called Redefining Progress in San Francisco (Cobb *et. al.* 1996).

The GPI starts with the same data that underlies GDP, but then it is modified with both additions and subtractions:

i) Weighted Income Distribution: GPI would not only account for an increase or decrease in total income in Oshkosh but also the way in which household and individual income is distributed. Highly inequitable distributions would depress the city's income gains or losses in the aggregate.

ii) Defensive Expenditures: Defensive individual expenditures (water filters, weapons, burglar alarms and other home security devices) as well as social expenditure (jails, police, sheriff, corrections, courts, litigation, etc.) which maintain public order would be debited since they don't represent real increases in well being.

iii) Natural Capital Depreciation: Environmental assets and natural resource consumption are subtracted. Items such as the public expenditure for air, water, and land pollution; loss of wetlands, farm acreage, and forest; depletion of natural resources at quarries, mines, fisheries, and so on, would be debited against normal economic gains.

The Genuine Progress Index is "conservative" in the sense that it does not go as far as it could in subtractions of negative factors. For example, it would not negatively account for the increased commuting time that urban sprawl produces, the "addictive consumption" of residents who use cigarettes, alcohol, and drugs or the number of Oshkoshians who are "overweight" through overconsumption of fast food. However, this indicator does get at important factors that enhance or devalue community life.

Summary and Conclusion

Much of what passes for innovative programs in Wisconsin and its Fox Valley can be loosely described as what DeWitt John labeled "Civic Environmentalism" (John 1994). For states and localities, this means a new direction in environmental policy-making in which regional authorities design and attempt to carry out their own initiatives rather than simply implementing federal regulations or acting as a laboratory for testing ideas designed by the national government. Specifically, civic environmentalists espouse a non-intrusive agenda in which state and local government officials attempt to induce commercial interests to participate in community redevelopment partnerships by utilizing non regulatory tools like economic incentives, risk assurances, grants, technical assistance, education, tax breaks, and liability exemptions. In Wisconsin at least, this approach has produced several notable accomplishments both for cities in the valley and those in other regions of the state.

Wisconsin's fledgling land recycling project is the latest in the sub-national governmental movement to harness market forces in redevelopment efforts by identifying, ranking and actively promoting commercial opportunities (Eisenger 1988). Such public sector entrepreurship is especially welcome in the Fox Valley because of the large number of distressed urban neighborhoods near old industrial sites along the rivers throughout this metropolitan area. Targeted pilot projects like Green Bay's Downtown Urban Design Plan and the Marion/Pearl Redevelopment Plan in Oshkosh must proliferate and prosper if the cities in this rapidly growing region of the state are to have any reasonable chance at regaining commercial viability for the many brownfields adjacent to their central business districts, major thoroughfares and river-fronts.

Despite some initial success, it is far from certain that Wisconsin's programmatic model for civic environmentalism will live up to its promise of a renaissance in the state's inner-cities. Thorough land recycling may require more money for financial inducements than the legislature is willing to appropriate and more risk and leadership ability than local officials have the capacity. Some public works projects and "dirty" industries may be lured to relocate in former brownfields by the state's mix of inducements, but far more projects are likely to be attracted to the relative safety of green farm fields or the proximity of exurban property to affluent suburbanites. Nor can we confidently project that public subsidies for innovation will produce a quick technological fix or a timely reduction in the immense expense of contaminated soil cleanups. Finally, absent regulatory diligence or a change in commercial values, the new sustainable urban development zones projected for Wisconsin's central cities might simply degerate into another form of corporate welfare.

The effort to address the civic environmental agenda, protect public health, and redefine Fox Valley cities like Oshkosh as sustainable communities will require more than can be generated by any of the region's modest efforts to remediate past environmental practices and redevelop old industrial sites for commercial purposes. This potential shift may reflect the maturation of environmental policy. As Bron Taylor, the Director of the UWO Environmental Studies Program, has argued "activities have shifted away from creating more recycling to a more sophisticated concern ... After all we could be recycling everything and our forests would still be going down and species becoming extinct" (Taylor 1996, A7). Locally, this means that efforts must be made to redefine the way in which the city measures community well being and how both public officials and private developers link these values with decisions about investments in the quality of community life.

Such a redefinition means learning more about the region's ecological and cultural relationships and how residential behaviors affect them. How driving, gardening, and consuming behaviors along with business activity and government developmental efforts alter the prospects for creating ecologically sustainable lifeways. Questions will have to be raised about how urban expansion eliminates agricultural and wild lands. We also need to discuss the way in which our infrastructure favors the automobile in ways that are hostile to mass transit, the pedestrian, and the bicyclist. Such rarely examined questions must be placed on the public venue if we are to become ready for environmental self-government.

Heightened citizen sensitivity to issues of sustainabilty will become necessary just to ensure that civic environmentalists aren't so enthralled by the prospect of public-private partnerships that advance urban cleanups and land reuse activities that they become inextricably committed to giveaways and bad deals.

Theories of urban sustainablity offer promise because they emphasize both what we should add and what we should subtract from our equations defining the quality of city life. There are encouraging signs of recognition of this perspective in central Wisconsin that extend beyond the university community and the many established environmental activist organizations. A variety of localized groups have sprung up to promote care of local lakes and rivers, as well as, to oppose unwanted land use. There is also a growing dissatisfaction with new suburban development or central city redevelopment that is unguided by any aesthetic or ecological considerations. More and more county residents object to the paving and commercial development of agricultural and wild lands. Nevertheless, it remains to be seen whether the sustainablity movement will take hold in the Fox Cities or whether their residents will remain mired in conventional counter-productive practices and continue to be content with modest efforts at repairing mistakes from the past.

References

Amerson, R. 1998. "Brownfields Environmental Assessment Program." (Wisconsin Department of Natural Resources (WDNR: June 1).

Bangert, S. & M. Giesfeldt. 1998. "Brownfields Redevelopment by Expanding Eligibility for Act 453 Protection." (WDNR: September 29).

Bartsch, C. & C. Anderson. 1999. "Matrix of Brownfield Programs by State." *Northeast-Midwest Institute* (January 20).

————, E. Collaton & E. Pepper. *1996. Coming Clean for Economic Development* Washington D.C.: Northeast-Midwest Institute.

Bonderud, K. 1999. *Contaminated Land and Brownfield Cleanup Programs.* Wisconsin Legislative Fiscal Bureau #62.

City of Oshkosh.1998. *Marion Road/Pearl Avenue Redevelopment Plan.* Dept. of Community Development: August.

————. 1998. *Tax Incremental Finance District #13.* Dept. of Community Development: August.

————.1999. *City of Oshkosh Annual Report.* Oshkosh, WI.

Cobb, C. & J. Cobb. 1994. *The Green National Product.* Latham, NY: University Press of America.

Cobb, C., T. Halstead, and J. Howe 1996. *The Genuine Progress Indicator.* San Francisco.

Culhane, E. 1998. "Making Waves," *Post-Crescent,* February 1, A1-2.

Ebert, K. 1999. "Fox River Cleanup: Floating an Idea," *Northwestern.* February 2, B 1.

————.1996. "A River runs through it." Northwestern, July 28, F1-3.

Edelstein, M. 1998. *Contaminated Communities.* Boulder: Westview.

Eisenger, P. 1988. *The Rise of the Entrepreneurial State.* Madison: University of Wisconsin.

Environmental Protection Agency. 1998. *Superfund: National Priorities List (NPL) Sites in Wisconsin.* October, 8.

Feinauer, D. 1999. "News Briefs," Center for Community Partnerships 1 (1), Spring.

Giesler, M. 1999. "Wisconsin's Remediation and Redevelopment Program." WDNR. Madison, Wisconsin.

Greenberg, M. 1996. "There Goes My Neughborhood." *Planning,* 62.

———— & D. Schneider. 1995. "Hazardous Waste Site Cleanup and Neighborhood Redevelopment." *Policy Studies Journal,* 23 (1), pp. 105-121.

————, A. Downs & K. Small. 1983. *Urban Decline and the Future of American Cities* Washinfton D.C.: Brookings.

Grulke, B. 1999. "The University and the City," *Northwestern,* February 2, B 12.

Harper, C. 1996. *Environement and Society.* New Jersey: Prentice Hall.

Heidenheimer, A., H. Heclo & C. Adams. 1990. *Comparative Public Policy.* New York: St. Martins, 1990.

Hird, J. 1994. Superfund . Baltimore: Johns Hopkins.

Jarvis, J. 1999. "Brownfield Initiative." Wisconsin Department of Commerce, April 1.

John, D. 1994. *Civic Environmentalism.* Washington D.C.: CQ.

Mangan, G. 1998. "Redevelopment Along the Fox River," *Northwestern,* March 7, A 13.

_____. 1994. "Frueh Defends City Water," *Northwestern*, November 22, B1.

Mazmania, D. & D. Morell, 1992. *Beyond Super Failure*. Boulder: Westview.

McGahren, J & W. Hatfield. 1998. *Brownfields: By the Book*. New York

Meyer, F. & R. Baker. 1993. *State Policy Problems*. Chicago: Nelson-Hall.

Miringhoff, M. 1994. *Index of Social Health*. Tarrytown, NY: Fordham.

Nass, A. 1998. *Fred Rueping Leather Company Property Report.*. WDNR, Madison, Wisconsin.

O'Connor, M. (ed.) 1994. *Is Capitalism Sustainable?* New York: Guilford.

O'Brien, J. 1998. "Chicago Model Lending Package." *Smartgrowth Network*, December 5.

Pebbles, V. 1999. "Brownfields Project." Council of Great Lakes Governors. July 30.

Peterson, E. 1997. *Lessons From the Field*. Washington D.C.: Northeast-Midwest Institute.

Pirages, D. (ed.). 1996. *Building Sustainable Societies*. New York: M.E, Sharp.

Rabe, B. 1997. "Power to the States." in Vig, N. & M. Kraft (eds.) *Environmental Policy in the 1990s*. Washington D.C.: CQ.

———. 1994. *Beyond Nimby*. Washington D.C.: Brookings.

Raber, J., R. Bruch & H. Liebzeit. 1989. *Winnebago Comprehensive Management Plan*. WDNR, Oshkosh, Wisconsin.

Ryan, K. L. 1998. Toxic Turnaround" Planning. Chicago. American Planning Association. December.

Saiki, K. 1998. "Campus Exterior Master Plan." Oshkosh: University of Wisconsin-Oshkosh.

Savagian, A. 1998. "Success Stories in Wisconsin Brownfield Redevelopments." WDNR, December 1.

Seaborn, T. 1995. "Leaking Underground Storage Tanks." Unpublished manuscript.

Schnaiberg, A. & K. Gould. 1994. *Environment and Society*. New York: St. Martin's.

Simmons, J. 1997. *"To Overhaul Oshkosh,"* The Small City and Regional Community. 12, P. Meyer & T. Lyons (eds.), Foundation: pp. 210-216.

Taylor, B. 1994. "Environmental Studies Project." *ES Newsletter* 1 (1), October.

———. 1996. "Environmental Studies: Getting Real." *Northwestern*, April 21.

Trebon, M. 1998. "Pollution Solutions." *Post-Crescent,* March 22, A 1.

Wright, T. & A. Devlin. 1998. "Overcoming Obstacles to Brownfield and Vacant Land Redevelopment." *Landlines*, 10 (5) September.

Part Four

Retail and Commercial Redevelopment of Downtowns

CHAPTER 12

Managing the Growth of Retail Space

Retail Market Dynamics in Lawrence, Kansas

KIRK MCCLURE

Many communities seek to preserve and protect their existing downtown shopping district or, if that district has experienced deterioration, they pursue various strategies to revitalize the downtown. A host of research is available concerning community redevelopment, focused particularly upon downtown revitalization (Black 1983; Frieden and Sagalyn 1989; Paumier 1988; Smith 1988; Urban Land Institute 1992). Communities across the nation have façade improvement programs, building renovation programs, and historic preservation programs designed to preserve their downtown shopping districts. While the programs all have their place, fundamental economic analysis of the retail market is often missing from these revitalization and preservation programs. A key component of any effort designed to preserve a downtown district is to ensure that the supply of retail space is supportable by the level of spending that exists within the market area.

Many factors must be addressed in the preservation of older downtown areas. The proper promotion of the downtown district is useful. Efforts to preserve the special architectural style or character that may be found there are needed. Solutions to parking problems, if they exist, should be found. Provision of needed capital to finance improvements, even at below market interest rates, may be required. However, they all are dependent upon the retail market achieving an overall balance between the supply of space and the available spending that can support that space. If the spending in the retail market is sufficient to support the stock of retail space, then the supply will be properly maintained and even prosper. If the spending is insufficient, then the retail space will suffer from revenues that do not foster proper maintenance and, if the situation continues, some of the retail space will become blighted. Clearing and revitalizing blighted areas is extremely expensive. Maintaining a balance between the demand for retail space and the supply of retail space is a low-cost means of preventing blight.

Planners have often ignored analysis of the fundamental economics of their communities. Planning tools have too often been limited to zoning and the provision of financial assistance for redevelopment. Zoning is a crude tool. It allocates uses over available land and hopes that the development industry responds in a manner that fulfills the community's wishes. Even this crude tool is often rendered useless as communities frequently zone excessive amounts of land for commercial space. This is done in a desire to attract the non-residential development that contributes to the city's property and sales tax income. Beyond zoning, communities often provide various forms of financial assistance to developers of new or redevelopment projects. These financial packages have their place as they can lower the cost of constructing or operating a development. This can make a marginally infeasible project viable, causing projects to be built that would not have occurred otherwise. Financial packages can attract development to a particular location, such as a revitalizing downtown, serving the community's objectives. However, neither zoning nor financial assistance can cause customer spending to occur within the downtown if the spending is not available in the community. Ultimately the spending within a marketplace is a function of the population that can be attracted to the market and the disposable income possessed by that population.

Planners need to make greater use of tools that perform basic market analysis. This analysis will answer questions such as how much retail space can the market support? Does the community have the right amount of retail space now, too much space, or too little? If the community wants to preserve its downtown, how much new space can be absorbed elsewhere in the community without reducing the downtown's capacity to survive?

This chapter examines these issues using a case study of a town in the Midwest, Lawrence, Kansas. Lawrence is a college town in northeast Kansas with a population of 75,000. The chapter explores the actions that the community has taken to assist its downtown. It examines the errors that the city has made in that process, and explores a tool that planners can employ to improve their actions in the future.

Background on Lawrence, Kansas and its Downtown

The downtown of Lawrence has a history of growth, decline, and revitalization not unlike many other communities. The downtown is a retail district along Massachusetts Street. Lawrence was settled by abolitionists from Massachusetts, and they named their "Main Street" for their former home. The downtown includes Massachusetts Street, a major street running south from the bridge crossing the Kansas River. It also includes the two additional streets, Vermont and New Hampshire Streets, running parallel and either side of Massachusetts Street. Thus, the downtown is comprised of these three streets running for five long blocks, about two-thirds of a mile, from the City Hall on Sixth Street to the County Court House at Eleventh Street along with the cross streets.

The downtown includes about 150 buildings total, over 100 of which were built prior to World War II, and about one-half are structures built during Lawrence's original development from 1860 to 1900. These tend to be two story brick buildings with façades flush against the sidewalks. Many of the buildings have received metal façade covers of varying styles over these years. Many of these façade covers have been removed, and the original brick walls with stone lintels have been restored to their original condition. Massachusetts Street itself was spruced up in the mid-1970s when it became tree-lined and landscaped with planter boxes, benches, and artwork.

The downtown has grown in size continuously over its history but has experienced rapid growth in the 1990s. The downtown retail space contained about 1.25 million square feet of leaseable area in 1997 plus additional offices and loft apartments. Despite peaks and valleys in spending activity, the supply of space has been larger in each successive year. In 1950, the downtown contained 860,000 square feet. In 1970, the downtown reached the 1 million square feet level. Several projects have been added each year for the last few years, including a fashion outlet mall, the conversion of a bank into two different clothing stores, and the construction of a book store through integration of an existing historical building with a new structure.

The downtown is just one of several retail districts in the city. Over time, the retail market has expanded in many directions. Many neighborhood centers have been developed at the intersection of the major arterial streets. Lawrence has also had its share of "commercial strip" development. In this regard, Lawrence's retail market is a prototypical case of "downtown versus perimeter growth." The downtown has more square feet under lease than ever before. However, the spending in the downtown has been a stable to declining share of the city's retail spending as a whole. The spending in the downtown district was $108 million in 1997, up from $90 million in 1993. However, the revenues per square foot downtown are very low, too low to sustain the space over the long term. Revenues in the downtown, at under $90 per square foot, are only about two-thirds of the citywide average and about one-half of the level found in the new retail space built on the perimeter of the town.

Recently retail developers have indicated that they need in excess of $250 per square foot in order to keep their projects viable (Lawrence Journal World January 9, 1999). Clearly, new space will need to command higher revenues than are typically found in the downtown in order to amortize the costs of the new construction. The differential is large between the threshold level of $250 per square foot new construction and the $80 to $90 per square foot that is being experienced by average properties. The needed new investment will not occur in the downtown area unless it can command revenues much higher than what is now typical for most downtown shops.

The retail space developed at the perimeter of the community has come in both small and large increments. While the small incremental additions have not generated much controversy, the large additions have been the subject of long and frequently heated debates. Lawrence fought over the years to avoid a "suburban style mall" on its perimeter and tried in vain to attract new retail developments to the downtown. The city pursued several ill-fated attempts to attract developers to the downtown area. Plans were prepared to redevelop various blocks of the downtown into large retail spaces, some with expansive parking garages. All of these plans failed to attract developers. One developer, the JVJ Company, sought to develop a suburban style mall on the southwestern edge of town. The proposal was denied planning permission, in part, due to the perceived negative impact that a suburban style mall would have on the downtown. The developer fought the decision, taking it to court. The city won, but the court was not the last word on the debate over development of freestanding retail stores at the perimeter of the city.

Over the decades, Lawrence allowed strip style development along Twenty-third street, an east-west artery running along the southern edge of the city. This commercial strip developed incrementally with each successive site being developed with its own curb cut, a lighted sign atop a pole, and no integration of building design with the adjacent buildings. The incremental development of this street began just west of the intersection of Twenty-third and Massachusetts Streets and moved westward. When the development reached Iowa Street, a distance of just over one mile, it turned south and continued unabated. Two large discount stores developed along South Iowa Street: K-Mart and Gibson's. A Wal-Mart store came along later. By 1990, the development along Twenty-third Street and South Iowa Street was beginning to rival that of the downtown with over 630,000 square feet of space.

Given the rapid growth of the perimeter retail district's space, the city chose to return to its plans for revitalization of the downtown with a retail structure of some type. If the private sector could not be attracted to any of the previous development proposals, the city opted to enter into a public-private partnership to create that space. The private partner would be a developer of retail shopping centers who would bring development expertise to the project. The city's contribution would be land, financing, and more, if needed to make the project feasible. The goal was simple, preserve the downtown by attracting retail shoppers with a fashion outlet mall that would "anchor" the downtown.

This public-private partnership sought to develop a fashion outlet mall on city-owned land just east of the City Hall. A city-owned garage would serve the mall. The mall building itself would be financed though the proceeds from the sale of revenue bonds. The mall building, opened in 1989, ultimately contained 145,000 square feet of retail space for about 70 different vendors ranging from full-sized stores of about 5,000 square feet to operators of small booths selling specialty goods.

The building itself cost about $16 million and was fully financed by the revenue bonds. The building was owned by the city during the ten-year life of bonds and reverted to the private developer when the bonds were retired. The building was leased to the private sector partner, Chelsea Development Group, one of the nation's leading developers of fashion outlet malls that became so popular during the 1980s. The lease rate charged for the mall building covered the city's debt service obligation on the bonds plus an amount equal to about 50 percent of the normal property taxes that would have been collected if the building were privately owned an⁴ ⱷperated. Thus, the building not only enjoyed 100 percent public financin₉, but it also benefited from a property tax abatement as well. The land on which the mall was built has been retained in city ownership. A parking garage of 510 spaces was built adjacent to the mall building for about $3.5 million, financed entirely through general obligation bonds. This garage also remains in city ownership. The mall made no payments to the city for the use of the garage. Except for a small fee paid by users, the parking garage was paid for by the taxpayers of the city.

It was not new for the city to invest in its downtown. During the early 1970s, the city extensively improved Massachusetts Street. New curbs, walks, angled parking, streetlights, trees, benches, and artwork were installed. The city has also built and improved parking lots at various times over the decades. These parking lots serve the downtown shops, being located "behind" the buildings along Massachusetts Street, accessible from Vermont and New Hampshire streets.

The outcome of the public-private partnership has been that the mall never succeeded as projected. This is not to say that it failed. The mall did pay its lease obligations to the city, and the bonds have been retired without default. In the early years of its operation, the mall was active and appeared to be fulfilling its objective to bringing shoppers back to the downtown. However, beginning very early on, the mall had occupancy problems. Many shops were vacant. "Phantom" vendors would be created to fill some of the empty stores to give the appearance of a fully occupied mall, and from the start, the mall was plagued with high turnover of its tenants. Eventually, this failure to attract retailers caused the mall to enter into a change of use of much of its space. The three-story mall building was forced to lease much of its lowest level as office space, becoming a "telemarketing" center for minimum-wage workers who sell products by telephone. The mall has been forced to run advertisements on local television and in the press reminding the public that it is still open for business. One advertisement reads, "Myth: The mall is closed, Fact: We're still open!"

Upon completion of the lease, the owner, Chelsea Development Group, offered the mall building for sale. It cost $16 million to build the mall in 1988. In 1998, it was offered for sale at a reported price ranging from anywhere from $6 to $12 million *(Lawrence Journal World,* December 29, 1998). A set of local businessmen have offered to buy the mall for a price rumored to be about $7 million contingent upon the city giving concessions on the use of the parking garage. Office use is anticipated. While office space is not an inherently bad thing, it clearly will not provide the retail space that can anchor the downtown as a retail district. In addition, office space will not generate the sales tax dollars that the city hoped would compensate the city for its contributions to the project.

During the same time period, one downtown retail project faltered. One block along New Hampshire Street, known as the Winter block after the family that owns it, was cleared to make way for a Border's bookstore at the north end of the block and a mixed-use retail and office structure at the south end. The bookstore was built and occupied as planned. However, the developer has been unable to find tenants for the retail space at the south end of the block. As such, the block sits as a vacant, unattractive site.

What happened? Why did the mall project fail to become the viable retail shopping development that it was projected to become? Why do other downtown projects struggle? The answer is that the city overbuilt fashion malls in particular and retail in general.

The city allowed too much fashion outlet mall space to be built when it approved the development of a second fashion outlet mall in 1993. This mall was located out of the downtown district, in the neighborhood known as North Lawrence. This second fashion outlet mall was located, as is common with such facilities, adjacent to an interchange along the interstate highway that serves the community. The Tanger Company, another of the nation's leading developers of fashion outlet malls, developed this center. When Tanger proposed this mall, it was to be much larger. The city called for development of the Tanger Mall in stages. Fearing that it could prove to be harmful to the city's existing Riverfront Mall, the city wanted Tanger to return to the city periodically for planning permission to build additional space. If the city's downtown mall was performing as expected, then the complete Tanger Mall could be built. If the Tanger Mall hurt the city's downtown mall, then the city could minimize the harm by limiting the Tanger Mall to just what had been built. The Tanger Company assured the city that the retail spending available in the market would be more than enough to support both malls, Tanger's and the Riverfront Mall, at full scale. However, Tanger acceded to building their mall in two stages.

Only one phase was ever built; the second phase was never completed. This first phase was built containing 96,000 square feet. One year after the first phase was constructed the Tanger Company proposed construction of the second phase. This second phase was to contain additional retail space. This proposal was subsequently revised to include only hotel and restaurant space rather than retail space because retail vendors could not be attracted to the second phase. Tanger also was unable to attract either a hotel or a restaurant to the site. Failing to attract vendors to this second phase of their mall, Tanger withdrew the proposal for the second phase. The first phase of the Tanger Mall, which continues to operate, is also struggling with occupancy problems. It has abandoned the factory outlet concept in an effort to attract tenants of any type.

The city also allowed too much retail space to be built elsewhere in the community, especially in the commercial strip areas along the south edge of the city. During the mid-1990s, the city approved the development of many "Big Box" retailers on sites at the perimeter of the city. A major decision was made in 1993 to allow these retailers to develop on South Iowa Street. Ironically, these large stores were built on the same site where the city had refused the JVJ firm permission to construct its "suburban style" mall. By 1993, the political climate of the city had changed. A majority of the City Commission favored the perimeter retail development, if not a majority of the Planning Commission or the planning staff. A heated debate was waged, and the city approved the development of large discount structures along South Iowa Street, costing the Director of Planning his job.

The K-Mart store had already been built in 1974 on a site along South Iowa Street, and Wal-Mart moved to a new 120,000 square foot structure just south of K-Mart, vacating its older building less than one mile to the north. Target opened a "superstore" of 96,000 square feet. The J.C. Penney Company opened a new 80,000 square foot store. It vacated its location on Twenty-third street, to which it had moved when it left the downtown area in the late 1960s. K-Mart chose to expand and redevelop its site adding over 35,000 square feet to its store along with development of a Kohl's store containing about 50,000 square feet. Along with a few other smaller stores and strip malls, over 700,000 square feet of space were added to the Twenty-third Street and South Iowa Street districts during just the years 1993 through 1997. By 1997, the retail stores in the West Twenty-third Street and South Iowa Street districts had expanded to contain over 2.3 million square feet of retail space, dwarfing the downtown area.

What has been the result of this massive retail construction campaign along the city's southern edge? The downtown has lost market share, attracting a smaller proportion of the city's retail spending. The downtown district's retail revenues per square foot continue to lag the market. The city has hurt its own downtown by overbuilding retail space in the districts outside of the downtown. By permitting this overbuilding of retail space, the city has threatened its own investment in Riverfront Mall.

How did the city let this happen? What should it have done to protect its investment in downtown? The city fostered the demise of its own mall and the downtown areas as a whole by failing to regulate the pace of growth of the stock of retail space. The city operated on the belief that its role need not go beyond direct assistance to downtown developments, such as the Riverfront Mall. The city reasoned that, if it helped the Riverfront Mall become an active competitor in the retail market, then the downtown could sustain itself through this competition and that the market would regulate itself, building only as much retail space as it needed. This belief in the self-regulatory nature of real estate markets has proven to be a mistake. The market for retail space has built more square feet of space than the local population's spending can support. This could have been prevented by carefully monitoring the scale of the spending over time and regulating the flow of new space so as to keep pace with the growth in spending.

Economic Theory of Retail Markets

The first principle of real estate market analysis is that supply follows demand. Supply does not create its own demand. Rather, supply responds to latent demand, that is, demand not satisfied in the marketplace. Alternatively, new space added to the total supply may capture some share of the existing available demand, taking it away from other suppliers. In this case, the new supply attracts spending to itself that previously was going elsewhere.

Developers of retail space know this principle very well. They avoid markets where the supply of space is growing too rapidly. In those markets, latent demand will soon be absorbed. Entering the market after extensive growth in the stock of space may make the last additions to the stock very hard to lease. Equally, developers avoid stable markets where demand is flat. If there is no increase in the demand for the retail space, it means that adding new space would create a surplus. A surplus lowers values and creates vacancies. Developers seek markets where demand is in excess of supply. This means that there is a shortage of space and that tenants can be found for the space as soon as it is built.

A second principle of real estate market analysis is that capital flows to investment opportunity with the highest return. When rents rise, signaling a scarcity of supply and surplus of demand, the return on investment in that market rises as well. This attracts new capital to the market. The new capital translates into new development responding to the higher return on investment. When rents fall, signaling a surplus of supply, return on investment falls and new investment slows or stops.

If the demand is in excess of supply, the retail space will become a scarce good. When this happens the rents on retail space will rise in real terms, that is, faster than inflation. This hurts profitability. Weaker firms cannot survive if they must pay excessively high rents for retail space. Vacancies will fall in the retail space. This means a reduced capacity for retail vendors to expand. It also means a reduced capacity to permit entry of new firms into the retail market. It may also mean that spending may leave the community for other markets. If the public cannot spend its money within the community, as it wants, it will find retail facilities elsewhere.

Economic theory suggests that this system is self-correcting. Developers respond to rising rents and falling vacancies with new development. When developers see the revenue that retail space can earn is sufficiently high, they will build new space. The new space should ease the pressures created by high and rising rents. Once sufficient new space is built, the rents will become lower and vacancy rates will increase to a level that permits a normal amount of turnover.

The market should work in the opposite direction as well. The supply of retail space may be in excess of the available demand for that space. Where this is the case, the return on investment in that space may become inadequate. The value of retail property falls. The investor's response may be to disinvest, or at least, to invest no further. This takes the form of maintenance plans being reduced or halted. Parking lots, signs, and storefronts fall into disrepair. This surplus of space means that property owners cannot easily attract new tenants, thus they focus on capturing the maximum share of existing tenants possible. Landlords compete for existing tenants within the community. "Tenant robbing" becomes standard practice within the marketplace. This process finds owners of one retail building or mall attempting to attract tenants away from another as each property owner has an incentive to keep its own space afloat. Older retail space is often the least popular. It tends to be in locations that are less desirable, thus, it fails first. Too often, this older space is in the downtown district, and the new space is located in the perimeter, commercial strip.

If the supply of retail space is in balance with the demand, then good things happen. Maintenance spending is adequate to keep the stock in good condition. The parking lots are repaired when potholes occur, and periodic resurfacing takes place. The signs are fixed when parts break. Improvements are made as needed and according to a long-term investment plan. The storefronts are refurbished periodically and new roofs are installed as needed. The return on investment is adequate to attract and hold investors because of the stable prices that exist in a balanced market.

This system should be self-correcting. There should be no need for any government intervention to regulate the process. Some markets are effective at self-regulation with no government intervention. For example, the market for single-family housing tends to be good at this process of self-correction in response to price signals. This is true because of the small scale of operation of most local homebuilders and the short timeframe within which they work. They can easily adjust their scale of output from one season to the next, and they will not build so many units at any one time so as to take the market out of balance. If the last few homes built sold very quickly, then the homebuilder can build a few more next season. If the last few homes sold slowly, then the homebuilder can construct fewer homes next season. This keeps the market in balance. Rarely will the supply of single-family housing in a local market be far out of sync with the demand for that housing.

In contrast, the retail market is not good at self-regulation. This does not mean that the market for retail space is incapable of self-correction. The retail market does correct itself, but it does not do so as well as the market for single-family housing. The supply of retail space is often out of sync with the demand for that space, and there is a general tendency to overbuild. This has become a widespread problem of some considerable proportions threatening investments in retail malls in markets throughout the nation (Downs 1997; Benjamin *et. al.* 1998).

Why do retail markets tend to overbuild? The factors that contribute to an answer to this question are many. First, there is a long lead-time that runs between the time that the developer reads the signal calling for additional supply and opening the development for operation. The signals that spawned development can change dramatically before the development is completed. It takes time to acquire land and to get the necessary zoning changes in place before the construction can begin. It takes time to build the building. Finally, it takes time to market and then lease the new retail space and get it into full operation. During the passage of all this time, the latent demand that the new space was designed to absorb can be captured by other space. The additional space being built becomes excess space that the market does not need. An example of this process in Lawrence would be the Tanger Mall. When it was proposed, the projections for demand indicated that the market could support the Riverfront Mall as well as the Tanger Mall. By the time the Tanger Mall went into occupancy, the new "Big Box" retailers along South Iowa Street had already absorbed much of the growth in demand for new retail space.

Second, additional retail space is built in increments of whole developments. Unlike the market for single-family housing units, which are built one at a time, retail space tends to be built in much larger increments. Some individual stores are built, but the most common increment for the development of retail space is a "strip mall" with thousands of square feet. Here again, the Tanger Mall is an example. Even though it was pared down to a "first phase" and a "second phase" at the city's request, the space that was built was 96,000 square feet. This is not a small undertaking for a community the size of Lawrence. A development this large represents a significant share of the market as a whole. The Tanger Mall is arguably a mistake in that it was added to the market that was later found to be unable to support it as expected. However, this mistake is an entire mall of just under 100,000 square feet that cannot be broken down into smaller increments or readily converted into other uses.

Third, owners of retail space will take any tenants and any shoppers. They are indifferent as to their tenants' prior location. The developer wants the new space occupied. The developer is equally happy if the tenant is a new retailer in the community or if the tenant relocates out of another development from within the community. This willingness to take tenants from elsewhere comes from a desire to grab sufficient market share so as to achieve the highest possible return on investment. This is not always a bad thing. Some turnover and filtering of tenants can be a good thing. This process allows firms to grow and expand. Older space must compete forcing owners of that older space to improve in order to remain competitive. New space is also willing to take shoppers away from existing stores. The primary concern of the owners of the new stores is attracting sufficient shoppers into its stores so as to make an acceptable profit. The owners of new stores are relatively indifferent to any harm that may be done to the stores losing those shoppers. However, if the new space raises the competition for tenants and shoppers beyond the level at which the older space can compete, the process can be destructive. This can create vacancies in existing retail structures. Older, less desirable locations and buildings may not be able to become occupied. In Lawrence, the Winter block serves as an example of this process. What should be a desirable site within the downtown, the south end of the Winter block, is unable to find a tenant. Rather than being built and occupied, this one-half block site in the middle of the downtown is sitting empty and blighted.

Fourth, retail shoppers are mobile and willing to take their dollars to other markets. Shoppers are quite willing to travel for a "better deal." New malls in adjacent towns can capture demand, reducing the amount of space that can be supported in the community. There is a constant tug-of-war for retail dollars. The supply of retail space may have been in balance in one community but becomes out of balance by the introduction of new space elsewhere within reach of a community's shoppers. This may be a factor in the common demise of the two fashion outlet malls in Lawrence, both the publicly sponsored Riverfront Mall and the private Tanger Mall. The town of Olathe, Kansas is a growing community on the southwestern edge of the greater Kansas City metropolitan area. It lies only 25 miles away from Lawrence. A large fashion outlet mall was built in Olathe, opening in 1998. It is unclear how much spending from Lawrence goes to this Olathe mall, but it is clear that, nationwide, fashion outlet malls have been built to excess (Kaufman 1999).

Strategy Taken by Lawrence

Lawrence chose to take an active role in furthering the development of its downtown retail district. It chose to enter into a public-private partnership to create a development, the Riverfront Mall. In doing this it chose to be "pro-active." It wanted to place the city in a position to get the downtown development that the community wanted. It did not want to wait for a developer to propose a mall in the downtown area to the liking of the city. This was a laudable effort by the city. It sought to take charge of the situation and guide development in a manner that served the goals of protecting and enhancing the downtown district. However, when the city entered into this partnership, it did not understand fully the dynamics of retail supply and demand nor the tendency for retail markets to overbuild. The city needed to monitor the balance between the supply of and demand for retail space throughout the community. It also needed to guard against the tendency for the retail market to overbuild. Had the city understood these processes fully, then it would have realized that it needed to carry its role in the development process one step further. The city needed to manage the growth of retail space elsewhere within the community. This could have prevented many of the problems that the city now confronts.

The city took no steps to limit the flow of new retail space into its market. It approved the Tanger Mall on the northern edge of the city and approved the "Big Boxes" on the southern edge of the city. This failure to manage growth elsewhere made the downtown project vulnerable. It did not manage the flow of other space into the market. Rather, it permitted the development of so much additional space that it virtually ensured the failure of the Riverfront Mall, a project in which it invested significant amounts of public funds so as to revitalize the downtown.

The city relied upon the market to be self-regulating, to build only as much space as it could support. This has been shown to be an unwise decision. The city should have adopted a mechanism to monitor the flow of space into the market.

A Tool for Growth Management

Communities need a tool to help them control the flow of new retail space into their markets. The tool should provide them with the means to maintain a constant real (inflation adjusted) level of spending per square foot in the retail space within the community. Such a tool certainly differs from the standard zoning and public investment mechanisms now used by planners. Monitoring the level of spending per square foot within a community's retail market would be new to most planners. It would require that they become actively involved in measuring and regulating the market conditions within their community.

Tools of this sort have been developed and used by market analysts for many years. Many tools used to measure the performance of an individual retail market focus on movement in rents and vacancy rates, rather than on sales price data (Eppli and Benjamin 1994). Fluctuation in rents or vacancy rates signal that the market is adjusting to changing conditions. A real rent increase, that is an increase greater than the rate of inflation, and a vacancy rate reduction signal that the market is tightening and that more supply may be needed. These signals do not necessarily ensure that more space is needed in the market because it may be moving from a condition of being severely overbuilt to one where the market finds a better balance between the amount of demand for retail space. Alternatively, a real rent decrease and a vacancy increase signal that the market is softening and that the market may have too much space. Here again, these signals do not necessarily ensure that the market is overbuilt. Rather, the drop in rent and the increase in vacancy may simply indicate a short-term adjustment to the entry of a new structure to the market. A new retail center may, temporarily, cause a market to have too much space. However, this surplus may be short-lived as new spending growth quickly absorbs this surplus.

Unfortunately, it is very hard to manage a market through monitoring fluctuations in rents or vacancy rates in retail space. Reliable data on rents charged for retail space and vacancy rates are hard to get. Usually the few individuals or companies who have such information view it as proprietary. Realtors and leasing agents do not want their competitors to learn of their own performance. As such, they will not publish or release information on the rents leveraged in their recent transactions. Even if they were willing to release such information, lease rates vary considerably. They generally include a base lease rent plus an overage taken as a percentage of the tenant's gross sales. This makes it hard to determine the lease rate at any one point in time. Lease rates need to be normalized over a period of years so as to include periods of both recession and expansion. In addition, the rent levels differ by location and by the responsibilities taken on by the tenant. For example, in most cases the retailers, at their own expense, provide all improvements within the retail space. However, in some cases, the owner of the property will provide some improvements but charge a higher rent to cover the costs of these owner-provided improvements. Given this point of negotiation between owners and retailers, it is difficult to find standardized data on the rental rates for retail space within a marketplace.

Data on the sales prices of retail stores sold could substitute for rent information in that the price a buyer will pay for income earning retail space should reflect the capitalized value of the net operating income of that space. While the sale prices of commercial building are frequently a matter of public record, such data are often scarce and hard to interpret. Relatively few retail buildings sell in any one market during any single year. Even when recorded sales are found, an individual sale price may reflect the value of a business acquired not just the value of the building. As such, it is difficult to make meaningful conclusions on the movement of building sale prices within a marketplace over time.

Just as rents and property sales data are hard to determine, true vacancy rates are also extremely hard to calibrate. While it seems that it should be obvious whether or not a space is occupied, it is often very hard to tell. Mall operators often fill a space just to keep it from looking empty. A retail space that is available for lease on a permanent basis may be occupied by a quickly set up operation, such as one selling souvenir tee-shirts or holiday decorations. If a permanent lease can be signed for the space, this hastily established shop can be shut down. It is generally better to have a shop occupied at a very low revenue level on a month to month basis than to be empty with no revenue. Some revenue is better than none, and empty shops damage the appearance of a shopping center. Shopping center owners often promise to create these "phantom shops" so as to protect the other tenants and as a marketing ploy to attract tenants.

Given these problems, what data are available? Data on the supply of space are generally available. The local property tax assessor has information of the amount of retail space that exists within the community. Generally, the tax assessor will know the gross amount of space within any retail structure as well as the amount of net square feet that can be leased. This smaller amount of net leaseable square feet will often serve as a better measure of the stock of space. Especially when examining older downtown buildings, much of the space in a structure may not be capable of earning any income because it is in a basement or an upper floor that will not attract customers. In such cases, the gross square footage of the building will exaggerate the scale of the structure.

Data on retail revenues are generally available from the state or local sales tax collector. States usually report sales tax revenues to cities at the vendor level. However, there may be confidentiality problems in acquiring these data. Full release of these data would permit competing stores to know exactly how much business each did during a certain time period. This could provide proprietary information to a competitor. However, the tax collector may be able to release the data aggregated at the level of a district or for the community as a whole. This aggregation of the data would prevent the problems of reporting information about individual vendors.

With these two data series, it is possible to calculate the level of spending per square foot within a district or a community through simple division of the two. This spending per square foot figure can serve as a very good indicator of the condition of the retail market. To make comparisons over time, the calculated level of spending per square foot needs to be adjusted for inflation. The Consumer Price Index (CPI) for a state or region can be used to make this adjustment. If the increase in the spending per square foot between two points in time is approximately the same percentage as the increase in the CPI for the same two points in time, then the real level of spending has been stable. However, if the percentage increase in spending per square foot is less than the percentage increase in the CPI, then the spending is falling in inflation adjusted terms. Alternatively, if the percentage increase in spending per square foot is greater than the increase in the CPI, then the real level of spending is growing.

It is possible to monitor this inflation-adjusted level of retail spending per square foot over time. If it is rising, then it suggests that the market is tightening and that more space could flow into the supply. If it is falling, then it suggests that the market is softening and the rate of additions to the stock should be reduced. It is important to note that this indicator is just that, an indicator; it is not foolproof. Any market can experience short-term fluctuations in its level of spending. Also a community may experience short-term reductions in general spending per square foot across the community with the addition of a new structure. These short-term fluctuations should not be interpreted as a need for public intervention into the workings of the marketplace. In fact, it has been argued that local retail markets are out of equilibrium more than they are in equilibrium (Benjamin *et. al.* 1994). However, long-term trends away from level spending do suggest a need for public intervention.

Application to Lawrence, Kansas

Although too late to protect its own Riverfront Mall, Lawrence has begun to monitor the fluctuations in the level of real retail spending per square foot. Lawrence does this both for the community as a whole and for the various retail districts of the city. Analysis at the level of individual districts permits more detailed evaluation of how the downtown is performing relative to the Twenty-third street commercial strip, the South Iowa Street "big box" district, or the miscellaneous neighborhood retailing centers.

Table 10 lists the data assembled for Lawrence's retail market for the year's 1992 through 1997. The data are listed for all retail districts combined and separately for each of the city's eight retail districts. For each district, the total amount of retail space is listed for each year. Also listed is the total amount of retail spending in the district in constant 1997 dollars, calculated by adjusting each year's actual spending level by the change in the CPI. These data permit calculation of the inflation-adjusted retail spending per square foot.

The recent history of Lawrence's retail market is interesting. On the supply side, the growth has been dramatic. By 1997, the retail market of Lawrence contained almost 4.5 million square feet of space. This is a 21 percent increase over a period of only 5 years. This means that the stock of space has been growing by about 4 percent or 170,000 square feet per year over the last five years. While this is impressive, it is actually only slightly more growth than was experienced during earlier years. Over the last 25 years, the stock has grown by 3.6 percent per year. On the demand side the growth has been even more impressive. In 1997, about $610 million dollars were spent in retail stores. Real spending has grown by 23 percent, or 5.3 percent per year during this four-year time period. The fact that the growth in spending has outpaced the growth in space suggests that the market is tightening, but the gross figures mask a great deal of fluctuation over the years.

The growth in the supply of retail space in a market will generally correspond to the growth in the population and income within a community. Assuming no significant changes in the consumers' propensity to spend a portion of their disposable income on retail goods and services, then trends in population and income growth will serve as good indicators of the trends that will occur in retail spending. In Lawrence, population growth has been steady at about 1.6 percent per year for the last several years (U.S. Bureau of the Census 1997). In addition, income growth has exceeded inflation. Income is up in the Lawrence area by about 4.3 percent per year while prices are rising by about 3.1 percent (U.S. Bureau of the Census 1999; U.S. Bureau of Labor Statistics 1999). As a result there has been real growth in incomes of about 1.2 percent per year.

However, if growth in population and income explained all of the increase in spending, the growth in spending should have been lower. If population grows at 1.6 percent per year and income grows at 1.2 percent per year after inflation, then this would combine to a 2.8 percent rate of growth in retail spending in any one year assuming no change in the percentage of income allocated to retail spending. However, the spending recently grew by about 5.3 percent per year indicating a net pull of spending into the market or changes in consumer preferences. For spending to grow by 5.3 percent over and above inflation when population and income suggests a growth rate of 2.8 percent means that consumers must be spending more of their consumer dollars inside the community than was true in the past. They might be spending more of their income on retail consumption than was true in the past. Alternatively, the community may be attracting more shoppers from outside the community than has been the case in the past. Whatever the source or sources of the spread between the actual spending and the spending that could be expected given population and income growth, there has been dramatic real growth in the spending level. The result has been predictable; the real rise in spending has attracted developers who have built large quantities of retail space.

What does this simultaneous growth in spending and growth in space mean for the market as a whole? How do they combine in terms of spending per square foot?

Despite the short time frame for which these data series are available, these five years cover a full business cycle from low growth, to high growth, and a

Table 10: Lawrence Retail Sales and Square Feet of Retail Space by District, 1992 to 1997 in Constant 1997 Dollars

District Name / Year Item	West 23rd St	South Iowa	East 23rd St	Downtown	North Lawrence	W. 6th St. & Hillcrest	Neighborhoods East	Neighborhoods West	All Districts
1997									
Retail Square Feet	665,141	1,236,708	136,237	1,298,902	278,045	557,461	135,747	168,750	4,476,991
Retail Revenue	107,883,100	196,579,800	17,520,600	107,865,900	37,048,600	87,695,400	36,583,300	18,693,600	609,870,300
Revenue/Square Foot	162.20	158.95	128.60	83.04	133.25	157.31	269.50	110.78	136.22
Change in Revenue/Sq. Ft	-2.00	-3.16	3.75	-1.82	-4.46	0.56	-9.48	4.20	-2.00
Change as a Percent	-1.22%	-1.95%	3.00%	-2.15%	-3.24%	0.35%	-3.40%	3.94%	-0.01%
Revenue Share of Total	17.69%	32.23%	2.87%	17.69%	6.07%	14.38%	6.00%	3.07%	1.00%
1996									
Retail Square Feet	665,141	1,216,350	136,237	1,278,902	276,725	536,727	135,747	163,425	4,409,254
Retail Revenue	109,213,451	197,182,984	17,009,811	108,535,463	38,108,001	84,135,763	37,869,791	17,417,933	609,473,197
Revenue/Square Foot	164.20	162.11	124.85	84.87	137.71	156.76	278.97	106.58	138.23
Change in Revenue/Sq. Ft	-4.16	7.47	17.45	1.56	2.89	7.30	1.96	-6.16	3.08
Change as a Percent	-2.47%	4.83%	16.25%	1.88%	2.14%	4.89%	0.71%	-5.46%	2.3%
Revenue Share of Total	17.92%	32.35%	2.79%	17.81%	6.25%	13.80%	6.21%	2.86%	100.0%
1995									
Retail Square Feet	665,141	1,210,350	136,237	1,264,277	272,675	536,727	135,793	143,963	4,365,163
Retail Revenue	111,977,603	187,167,714	14,632,191	105,317,653	36,762,095	80,216,152	37,615,970	16,229,926	589,919,304
Revenue/Square Foot	168.35	154.64	107.40	83.30	134.82	149.45	277.01	112.74	135.14
Change in Revenue/Sq. Ft	-4.22	-15.35	-8.44	3.42	28.93	18.38	40.65	85.92	4.81
Change as a Percent	-2.45%	-9.03%	-7.29%	4.28%	27.32%	14.02%	17.20%	320.42%	3.69%
Revenue Share of Total	18.98%	31.73%	2.48%	17.85%	6.23%	13.60%	6.38%	2.75%	100.00%
1994									
Retail Square Feet	659,571	1,040,122	136,237	1,264,277	272,675	536,727	135,793	110,947	4,156,349
Retail Revenue	113,825,289	176,813,076	15,782,479	100,991,249	28,874,333	70,352,547	32,096,229	2,975,101	541,710,302
Revenue/Square Foot	172.57	169.99	115.85	79.88	105.89	131.08	236.36	26.82	130.33
Change in Revenue/Sq. Ft	5.15	10.13	15.78	8.55	25.51	-2.74	-27.90	-26.35	5.68
Change as a Percent	3.08%	6.34%	15.77%	11.99%	31.74%	-2.05%	-10.56%	-49.56%	4.56%
Revenue Share of Total	21.01%	32.64%	2.91%	18.64%	5.33%	12.99%	5.92%	0.55%	100.00%

									Total
1993									
Retail Square Feet	659,571	954,100	136,237	1,257,633	265,311	521,355	135,793	47,489	3,977,489
Retail Revenue	110,429,468	152,522,693	13,632,501	89,703,122	21,325,675	69,765,984	35,884,545	2,524,654	495,788,642
Revenue/Square Foot	167.43	159.86	100.06	71.33	80.38	133.82	264.26	53.16	124.65
Change in Revenue/Sq. Ft	—	—	—	—	—	—	—	—	—
Change as a Percent									
Revenue Share of Total	22.27%	30.76%	2.75%	18.09%	4.30%	14.07%	7.24%	0.51%	100.00%
1992									
Retail Square Feet	646,691	788,427	134,505	1,257,633	169,811	508,475	135,793	47,489	3,688,824

return to low or no growth. During this period, the growth rates in supply and demand have risen and fallen together. The years of 1993 and 1994 were years on the upswing as the economy was rebounding from a recession. Both the additions to the stock and the growth of spending were vigorous during these years, although sales were slower to rebound. Growth in supply peaked in 1993, and growth in sales peaked in 1994. However after these peaks, both series began a decline to a valley in 1996 and 1997. Retail sales were actually flat from 1996 to 1997, meaning that the growth in spending grew only at a rate slightly greater than the rate of inflation. Retail space has continued to be added to the stock during 1998 and 1999 on the hopes that spending will rebound as well. The stock grew by over 8 percent in 1998 and just under 5 percent in 1999.

The combined retail districts of Lawrence seem to be enjoying spending levels of about $133 per square foot. However, the level of spending per square foot in constant dollars was below $125 in 1993. This figure rose rapidly to a peak of over $138 in 1996 but then fell back to a level of about $136 in 1997. Looking at individual districts, Table 9 indicates that two trends are at work. First, the trend of rising to a peak and then declining for the combined districts is generally true for each of the districts individually. With the exception of the West sixth Street and Hillcrest district, all of the others peaked in either 1995 or 1996 and declined afterward. Second, there are large differences in the scale of spending between the West Twenty-third Street and South Iowa Street commercial strips and the downtown. Even after the decline, the two perimeter districts enjoy average spending at about $160 per square foot while the downtown district captures only about one-half of that level at just over $80 per square foot. The downtown district pulls in only about 18 percent of the retail spending in the community, but it contains about 28 percent of the stock of space. This is not a healthy combination.

Table 11 also lists a set of alternative projections for the future. These projections are critical to the process of monitoring and regulating the flow of new retail space into the market. If the projections indicate that the spending per square foot will fall well below the long-term average, then the flow of new space should be reduced. If the projections indicate that the spending per square foot will rise above the long-term average, then even more supply can be absorbed into the market. If the projections indicate that the spending per square foot will stabilize around the long-term average, it indicates that the flow of space into the market is about right.

Projections are based upon assumptions about the growth of both the pace at which new space will be built and the pace at which retail spending will grow. The growth in the supply of retail space is somewhat easier to predict. The city knows the size and location of all retail developments that are either under construction or approved for construction. It is also aware of some major developments for which the developers have begun discussions with the planning staff of the city. It also seems likely that, for the next few years, construction of new

Table 11: Lawrence Retail Sales and Square Feet of Retail Space for the City as a Whole

Year	Square Feet Actual and Approved	Square Feet Projected (4.1% growth)	Retail Sales Adjusted for Inflation	Retail Sales Projected at 5-yr. Ave. 4.1%	Sales per Square Foot Actual	Sales per Square Foot Projected 5.3%	Sales per Square Foot Projected 4.5%	Sales per Square Foot Projected 3.5%
1993	3,977,489		495,788,642		124.65			
1994	4,156,349		541,710,302		130.33			
1995	4,365,163		589,919,304		135.14			
1996	4,409,254		609,473,197		138.23			
1997	4,476,991		609,870,300	609,870,300	136.22	136.22	136.22	136.22
1998	4,868,140			642,277,506		131.93	130.92	129.66
1999	5,070,814	5,070,814		676,406,761		133.39	131.34	128.84
2000		5,276,559		712,349,572		135.00	131.90	128.15
2001		5,490,652		750,202,307		136.63	132.46	127.46
2002		5,713,432		790,066,456		138.28	133.02	126.78

Projections based upon:

Average Growth in Square Feet: Five years 1995–99   4.1%
Average Growth in Retail Sales: Four years 1993–97   5.3%
Average Growth in Retail Sales Set at: 4.5%
Average Growth in Retail Sales Set at: 3.5%

Growth Rates (Actual and Projected) of Square Feet and Sales for All Districts 1993 to 2002

Year	Growth rate of Square feet Actual	Growth rate of Square feet Projected	Growth rate of Sales Actual	Growth rate of Sales Projected (5.3%)
1993	7.83%		1.30%	
1994	4.50%		9.26%	
1995	5.02%		8.90%	
1996	1.01%		3.31%	
1997	1.54%		0.07%	
1998	8.74%			0.07%
1999	4.16%			5.31%
2000		4.16%		5.31%
2001		4.06%		5.31%
2002		4.06%		5.31%

retail space will continue at a pace similar to that experienced during the last few years. The projections detailed in Table 10 are based upon the assumption that the retail space will continue to grow at the same rate experienced in the past. Over the five years from 1994 through 1999, the stock of space grew by 4.1 percent per year, and this five-year average rate of growth has been assumed to continue for the next few years, through the year 2002. This pace of growth suggests that the city will add a little over 200,000 square feet per year during each of the next few years. This certainly seems reasonable as it corresponds to the scale of the proposals that are being received by the city. A development proposal on the city's northwestern boundary calls for the construction of 165,000 square feet of retail space (Fagan, May 27, 1999). A development proposal has been prepared calling for another 250,000 square feet in the South Iowa Street commercial district (Fagan, June 17, 1999). Developers have submitted plans to the city proposing a total of 78,000 square feet of new retail space downtown (*Lawrence Journal World,* January 9, 1999).

The growth of retail spending, which is the demand side of these projections, is more difficult to estimate. Spending is more cyclical. It varies as a function of external forces. These include wage and unemployment levels within the community and retail competition from outside the community. However, it is possible to assume that the future growth in spending will reflect the past. The five-year average growth is 5.3 percent per year, and a projection has been made based upon this rate continuing. This is an optimistic assumption in that this pace of growth assumes that the boom years of the immediate past will continue, at least for the next few years. It is also possible that the growth in spending will subside, dropping to lower levels that more closely reflect the city's growth in population and income. For this reason, projections have been prepared assuming that the growth in spending slows to rates of 4.5 percent per year and 3.5 percent per year.

The projections are instructive. Table 11 indicates that the spending per square foot will fall below the five-year average level of $133 under all three alternative projections, at least through 1999. This is the result of the large quantity of space that has already been approved for development and is under construction. The years 2000 through 2002 are more problematic, however. If the retail market continues to enjoy 5.3 percent growth in retail revenues, then the spending per square foot will go above the five-year average. This suggests that the city can absorb even more space than the 4.1 percent annual expansion that has been assumed. However, at the other extreme, if the retail market experiences only 3.5 percent growth in retail revenues, then the spending per square foot will decline further for the next few years. This suggests that the retail market cannot absorb all of the space that has been built and will probably be built if the city approves all of the development proposals that are pending. The intermediate alternative is nearly ideal. This projection assumes 4.1 percent annual growth in the supply of retail space and 4.5 percent annual growth in the retail spending in the market. These combine to stabilize the spending per square foot indicator at approximately its five-year average rate. This pace of growth should result in neither a decline in revenues to the existing retail vendors nor provide them with a windfall by excluding new retailers.

What if demand slows even further? The slow-down in spending in 1996 and 1997 could continue. The two-year average growth in retail spending for these years was just 1.7 percent per year. If the next few years through 2002 continued at this pace, then the citywide level of retail spending per square foot would fall drastically to under $116 per square foot, or a 13 percent drop from the five-year average. This would strongly suggest an overbuilt retail market. However, such an outcome seems unlikely, and the years 1996 and 1997 seem to be exceptions to the rule. Only in 1992 did real spending actually decline, that is, the growth in inflation adjusted spending was actually negative. Of course, 1992 was the worst year of the last recession. Not since early 1980s has there been a three-year period with spending growing by less than 2 percent, and this occurred around the recession of 1982. Thus, it seems that this very pessimistic alternative is very unlikely to occur, especially as long as population, employment, and incomes all continue to grow.

The alternatives listed are all based upon variations in the amount of retail spending. This is, of course, a factor that is out of the control of the city. The city can take steps to regulate the flow of supply, but it can do very little to alter the level of aggregate spending within its retail market. The city can, however, approve none, some, or all of the development proposals that come before its Planning Commission. What if the supply grows even faster than the 4.1 percent per year that has been assumed based upon recent experience? This could happen very easily simply by the city approving all of the development proposals that have been proposed. If the city adds space at a rate of 6 percent per year, or about 345,000 sq. ft. per year, the projected spending per square foot drops to under $125 per square foot.

What do these projections suggest in terms of the city's policies? The projections indicate the importance of closely monitoring the level of retail spending within the community. It is clear from analysis of the projections that the overall health of the city's retail market depends heavily upon the sales continuing to grow faster than the combined rates of growth of population and income. As long as the retail spending continues at this rapid pace, the city will be able to absorb large amounts of new retail space each year. Even if much of this new retail space is located outside of the downtown area, the downtown appears to be following the same trend as the retail market as a whole. If the downtown can attract its share of the new stores, then it will probably be able to maintain its share of the overall retail spending. The downtown has captured a relatively constant 17 to 18 percent share of the retail spending over the last few years. However, if the overall level of spending in the city's retail market does not continue to grow at a pace in excess of about 4 percent, then problems will arise.

Retail spending growth at a rate below this level means that the city should reduce the flow of new retail stores into the market or risk becoming overbuilt. If the city becomes overbuilt, then the downtown district, which already suffers from low levels of spending per square foot, will suffer further. As the downtown disproportionately contains the older retail buildings within the market, it is likely to bear the brunt of the problems generated by an overbuilt market.

Evaluation and Implications

How can cities evaluate the strategies for the preservation and protection of their downtown districts? One of the most common approaches is to examine the costs and benefits of participation in downtown revitalization projects. The experience of Lawrence, Kansas suggests that there is value in a city entering into a partnership with a private developer to leverage the type of development that the city wants but will not occur in the absence of public intervention. Lawrence's experience also teaches the lesson that this type of public-private partnership in the retail sector requires that cities closely monitor and regulate the flow of space into the retail market or risk losing their investment.

Lawrence entered into a partnership to develop its Riverfront Mall. The costs of the city's participation in this partnership were significant and varied. Some of the costs of entering into this partnership were low. Other contributions were effectively without cost. The city could provide quick staff review and planning approval of the development proposal at no cost, although this expedited review would have value to the private sector developer. The city could also provide financing for the building through the use of revenue bonds. These bonds provide full, long-term, fixed interest rate financing which, again, comes at little to no cost to the city but is of great value to the private sector developer. Such financing eliminates the need for the private sector to find equity financing, and it eliminates the risk associated with a variable interest rate that is commonly charged by conventional real estate lenders. The tax abatement offered on the property generates no actual out-of-pocket expenses for the city as it foregoes taxes that may never have been collected anyway. The city does lose the opportunity to develop the site for other uses that may have generated more property taxes. Given the length of time that the site of the Riverfront Mall sat vacant, it seems doubtful that the city lost any significant revenues here. However, as before, this tax abatement lowers the private sector developer's costs of operation, and this has value to the developer.

Other costs encumbered by the city were significant. Public improvements made to the streets and utility systems serving the site did cost the city real dollars. The city improved streets and sidewalks adjacent to the mall as well as improved storm drainage systems around it. The funds for these improvements had to be found in current city budgets. The city also had to raise the funds to build the parking garage. This major capital improvement was financed through the proceeds of selling general obligation bonds. Thus, the parking garage, built at city expense, necessitated a long-term property tax levy sufficient to repay the bonds.

To offset the costs of leveraging the construction of the Riverfront Mall, the city expected to realize many benefits. Sales tax revenues were expected as the primary benefit. If the mall had been fully occupied and had attracted $250 per square foot in sales, then this would generate sales of $37.5 million per year. With a 1 percent local sales tax, the city would receive about $375,000 per year plus the unabated portion of property taxes. This would have compensated the city for the costs of the parking garage and the other capital improvements. In addition, some spillover effects were expected as well. The Riverfront Mall was expected to attract shoppers to the mall who would linger in the downtown area, spending still more dollars there. This would enhance the downtown as a shopping district as well as increase the sales tax revenues received from all downtown merchants. The reality is that the sales tax revenues have been meager. The mall never reached full occupancy, and now it is virtually empty. Empty space may pay some property taxes, but it generates no sales taxes. In addition, an empty hulk of a building becomes an eye-sore that does nothing to attract shoppers to the downtown. Rather, it may actually repel them.

The Riverfront Mall project had very real costs and few benefits to justify the city's participation. The city should have instituted a monitoring system that could have prevented this loss. It can use such a regulatory mechanism to prevent similar losses in the future. If the public sector is to become a player in the process of retail development, then it should also implement a system to regulate the flow of new space into the market. This system will work to the overall benefit of the market as a whole. However, such a regulatory system has its costs and benefits as well.

The real out-of-pocket costs of such a system are minimal. Relatively little staff time and effort are required to collect and analyze the sales tax and retail building data. There are, however, some costs that are less tangible. If the regulatory mechanism does slow the pace of retail development within the community, then there is a loss of that development opportunity. The city will be missing out on the property and sales tax revenues that would have been generated by the new development that is delayed or denied.

The benefits of such a system can be significant. The avoidance of blight can be of enormous benefit to a city. Blight is expensive. Blighted space generates few revenues, if any. When a community attempts to redevelop a blighted area, the private sector rarely offers much of a contribution. Generally, the private sector expects to be fully compensated by the taxpayers for their participation in a redevelopment process. Generally, the public sector is looked to as a major source of capital for the redevelopment of blighted areas and as a party that must minimize the risk of the other parties who participate in the redevelopment process. Beyond avoidance of blight, the city can benefit from a process that regulates the flow of retail space into its market by taking charge of the development process itself. A regulatory tool of this sort lets the city have a greater say in the development process. It expands a city's capacity to design the outcomes of the development process, rather than just responding to developer initiatives.

The Lawrence experience indicates that monitoring and regulating the flow of retail space into a market is a necessary step for communities to take. Planners can monitor the balance between the demand for and the supply of retail space. The marketplace cannot be relied upon to regulate itself. Experience shows that the retail development process is prone to excessive construction, saturating markets with space to the point that some will fail.

The public sector is uniquely positioned to serve in this capacity, preventing the costs of overbuilding and blight. This is true, not only because the public sector is the sole party with the capacity to regulate land use, but also because it is the only major player in the process with an interest in maintaining a balance in the marketplace. Developers of new space and owners of land in the path of commercial development favor little or no regulation on commercial expansion. Any regulation that slows or eliminates their plans is viewed as unfair and harmful. A chorus of builders and realtors often joins in with them. They argue that all growth is good and that the interests of the community are served by unfettered growth. In contrast, owners of existing space and lenders holding the notes on that space will frequently be on the opposite side of this debate. Their investments are at risk if too much new space is added to the market. Their return on investment can be enhanced if their space becomes a scarce commodity. They can profit from restrictions on future growth.

Unlike the other players in the development and management process, the public sector has an interest in a balanced retail market. If the market is overly restricted such that development leaves the community and goes elsewhere, then the community loses that potential revenue. Thus, the public sector has an interest in avoiding excessive constraints on the development process. If the market is not regulated, then overbuilding and blight can occur and the public sector will be confronted with the high costs of redevelopment and revitalization. Thus, the public sector has an interest in avoiding unregulated growth as it has its costs as well.

Unfortunately, communities too often believe the pro-growth advocates are correct that all growth is good and that blight is inevitable. Communities are often told that all competition is good and that it will force the owners of older properties to invest in improvements in order to compete for the consumers. Empirically we know that retail markets do not work that way. Blight is not an inevitable part of the development process that cannot be avoided. It can and will occur in any retail market left in an overbuilt state for too long. It can be avoided if supply and demand are kept in balance. Blight is the result of supply in excess of demand. When blight does occur, the public sector is looked to for solutions, usually at significant public expense. Blight can be avoided if the level of supply in a market can be kept in balance with the level of demand. Prevention of blight is much less costly than curing blight.

Communities can regulate the flow of retail space into their markets at very low cost. This growth management tool requires only limited staff time and effort collecting and analyzing data that is usually available to communities. Communities can achieve a balance between the supply of retail space and the demand for that space. Planners can monitor the condition of a community's retail market in general and the downtown district in particular. For downtown areas to survive, communities need to prevent excessive development of retail space that competes with the older downtown stores. Tracking the variations in supply and demand over time permits a city to assess the balance that exists between the supply of and the demand for retail space. It also permits analysis of the impact that new development will have on the market. This tool can be instrumental in guiding communities through the tricky process of preserving and protecting their existing downtown retail districts against the onslaught of proposals to build large retail outlets on the perimeter of the community.

References

Benjamin, John D., G. Donald Jud, and Daniel T. Winkler. 1998. "A Simultaneous Model and Empirical Test of the Demand and Supply of Retail Space." *Journal of Real Estate Research* 16(1): 1-14.

Black, J. Thomas. 1983. *Downtown Retail Development: Conditions for Success and Project Profiles*. Washington, D.C.: Urban Land Institute.

Downs, Anthony. 1997. "Retailing's Painful Evolution." *Wharton Real Estate Review* 1(2): 13-21.

Eppli, Mark J. and John D. Benjamin. 1994. "The Evolution of Shopping Center Research: A Review and Analysis." *The Journal of Real Estate Research* 9(1): 5-32.

Fagan, Mark. 1999. "Planners reject New Plans for Former Hospital Site." *Lawrence Journal World*. May 27, 1999.

————. 1999. "Home Depot anchors S. Iowa Development," *Lawrence Journal World*. June 17, 1999.

Frieden, Bernard J. and Lynne B. Sagalyn. 1989. *Downtown, Inc.: How America Rebuilds Cities*. Cambridge, Massachusetts: M.I.T. Press.

Kaufman. Leslie. 1999. "Outlets Slipping Out of Fashion; Traditional Stores Counter as Off-Price Malls Overreach." *New York Times*. January 15, 1999.

Lawrence Journal World. 1999. "Downtown Projects Hope to Lure Hungry Retailers." *Lawrence Journal World*. January 9, 1999.

Lawrence Journal World. 1998. "Simons-Led Group Buys Mall." *Lawrence Journal World*. December 29, 1998.

Paumier, Cyril B. 1988. *Designing the Successful Downtown*. Washington, D.C.: The Urban Land Institute.

Smith, Kennedy. 1988. *Revitalizing Downtown*. Washington, D.C.: The Main Street Center, National Trust for Historic Preservation.

U.S. Bureau of Labor Statistics. 1999. *Consumer Price Index for All Urban Consumers.*

U.S. Bureau of the Census. 1997. *Estimates of the Population of Metropolitan Areas 1990-1996*. Washington, D.C.: U.S. Bureau of the Census.

————. 1999. *Small Area Income and Poverty Estimates Program*. Washington, D.C.: U.S. Bureau of the Census.

Urban Land Institute. 1992. *Downtown Development Handbook*. Washington, D.C.: Urban Land Institute.

CHAPTER 13

An Evaluation of Approaches to Downtown Economic Revitalization

NORMAN WALZER and STEVEN KLINE

The past two decades have brought major shifts in retail patterns in most U.S. cities and made downtown revitalization an on-going challenge for local governments and other civic leaders. Since the end of World War II, main street has been described as the unrivaled center of retail trade and the cultural heart of small-town communities (Moe and Wilkie 1997, 142). However, as society has become increasingly mobile, small to medium size cities, in or near metropolitan areas, have also had to compete with regional shopping centers, in some instances, the same locations with which the central cities must compete. Many places, where people were once plentiful on main street (because many lived within walking distance of everything in town), experienced a relatively swift breakdown of the local economy in recent years.

Efforts to counteract the suburbanization of metropolitan areas spawned a variety of strategies for maintaining downtowns. Urban renewal programs in the 1950s, for example, heavily concentrated efforts on redeveloping central business districts (Frieden and Sagalyn 1989). Keating *et. al.* (1996) argue that even the approaches to downtown development in the 1990s (e.g., festival marketplaces, office and retail development, convention centers, sports arenas, and waterfront-related tourist attractions) are designed as urban growth machines and originated from close knit coalitions between businesses and government agencies promoting economic development. Emphasis on downtown development was so strong that, in some instances, the quality of life needs of distressed neighborhoods were neglected (Stone and Sanders 1987). Keating *et. al.* (1996) propose that trickle-down economics of downtown development in central cities did not work to the benefit of low income residents in distressed neighborhoods except those in the lowest-paid jobs (e.g., parking cars, cleaning office buildings, and working in downtown restaurants and hotels). Consequently, central cities gained a negative image because most Americans did not want to live in places they typically associated with crime, poverty, congestion, and decay (Keating *et. al.* 1996). Today we still see businesses in the downtowns of large central cities threatened by population migration to the suburbs and the subsequent movements of stores in pursuit of these expanded markets. Free parking, less congestion, and indoor shopping have made it difficult for traditional downtown businesses to retain market share. In some instances, the response has been to open a branch store in the suburbs to enter these new markets while, in other cases, the downtown establishment closed altogether when several stores opened in the suburbs.

Even places with viable economies have encountered difficulty sustaining an economically healthy downtown. Moe and Wilkie (1997) reported that the average trade area of an American small town in 1945 was about 15 miles. However, with evolutionary changes in transportation (i.e., from horse to car), the average trade area quickly broadened to more than 50 miles. More recently, the growth of regional shopping centers and discount chains have intensified competitive pressures on downtown businesses in rural areas with the result that many downtowns in relatively small communities in rural areas have seriously eroded. Many public officials and business leaders in these communities have actively responded in an effort to preserve the downtown.

This chapter examines goals and practices followed by local public officials in pursuing downtown stabilization and revitalization in U.S. cities smaller than 250,000. The presentation has five sections. First, the literature on trends and concerns facing downtowns is reviewed. Second, the overall condition of downtowns is examined, by type of city (metro versus rural, population size, and location) based on a national sample of cities. Third, local goals for these downtown areas and the strategies pursued to reach them are analyzed and compared in relative importance to those for the industrial and/or service sectors. Fourth, the relative success in reaching the stated goals is examined with special attention paid to ways in which partnership arrangements were used. Finally, specific examples of relatively small cities that have succeeded in maintaining a viable downtown, even with competition from larger shopping centers, are provided with insight into strategies implemented.

Subsequent analyses are based on three main data bases. In 1994, the International City and County Management Association (ICMA) surveyed U.S. cities to identify economic development practices. Respondents were asked to indicate whether an active public-private partnership was used in economic development efforts.

The Illinois Institute for Rural Affairs (IIRA), in 1996, surveyed the 344 cities that had reported an on-going partnership and requested additional information about goals, practices, and outcomes. The response rate was 56.3 percent (194 cities) and includes cities ranging in size from 1,221 to 1.11 million in 42 states. In addition, IIRA surveyed Illinois cities regarding the status of their downtowns and factors underlying these conditions, with 197 responding.

Issues in Central Business Districts

Urban sprawl, commonly defined as low-density, land-consuming, automobile-oriented development that moves farther and farther out from the fringes of existing metropolitan centers, is now being compared in magnitude with postwar suburbanization (Gratz and Mintz 1998). This trend became especially pervasive since the mid 1970s when large discounters and category-killers such as Kmart, Target, Wal-Mart, Home Depot and Toys R Us found independent Main Street merchants easy competitive prey. Many "mom-and-pop" establishments had reinvested relatively little of the profits in their operations and continued doing business as they had for years. A 1995 study by Iowa State University economist Kenneth Stone reported that five years after a Wal-Mart opened in Iowa, nearby communities of 5,000 or less within 25 miles of the new store often experienced a cumulative net sales reduction of 25.4 percent. Ten years after the Bentonville, AR discount chain entered the state, Stone (1995) found that half of the men's and boy's apparel stores and 37 percent of the hardware stores in Iowa had closed.

A similar study in Illinois confirmed Stones findings, and further noted that the communities hosting large discount centers expanded the local trade area, generated more traffic, and captured, on average, an additional 15.25 percent of total sales dollars in the region (Gruidl and Kline 1992). While this is relatively good news for the host community, it spells potential disaster for downtowns in communities within 20 to 30 miles of the discount chains.

Even for some host communities, the sprawl of residential development accompanying retail expansions on the outskirts of the city significantly increased costs for local home buyers and taxpayers. Gratz and Mintz (1998) cite examples of places where the cost of services far exceeded the amount of income derived from new development. Despite successful attempts to manage these conditions, "sprawl-marting" has become a household word and, according to recent literature on the subject, still continues to be fueled by a combination of public policies and private development practices that persist in many parts of the U.S. (Gratz and Mintz 1998).

In the 1980s, the competition from retail giants was exacerbated by the over-all weak U.S. economy and job declines in small rural communities. Residents commuting to large employment centers or urban areas shop in those locations as well. Instead of peeling paint, cracked sidewalks, and parking meters in an old downtown, shoppers of the 1990s prefer stores offering greater selection, competitive prices, spacious parking, and flexible shopping hours.

Despite these difficult circumstances, downtowns are still seen as a reflection of the economic well-being of many cities. Local public officials hold fast to the heritage of old buildings, county seats, and appealing public space where residents can still gather for casual conversations, holiday parades, and local festivals. This commitment to main street USA intensifies concerns about empty store fronts and buildings that quickly deteriorate without occupancy.

However, community leaders not only confront empty buildings downtown, but many now have boarded-up first-generation shopping centers or strip malls that failed to compete in the ever expanding wave of retail space during the past 10 to 20 years. Moe and Wilkie (1997, 147) reported that with nearly 5 billion square feet of retail space, the U.S. has more than 19 square feet for every

American, up from 4 square feet in 1960. Half a billion of that sits empty, the equivalent of more than 4,000 abandoned shopping centers or dead malls. If retail construction came to a halt, analysts predict that it would still take Americans decades to fill all the space that exists already.

Why then, are local public officials and other business and civic leaders still willing to add and/or renovate more space sometimes at almost any cost? Many are concerned about the loss of retail sales taxes, despite the fact that a discount store on the outskirts of town is still in the city limits. In many communities, new retail expansions on the edge of town caused anchor stores once occupying large space in the downtown to vacate, leaving empty buildings to fill. Grocers, for example, were often among the first main street merchants to leave downtown in search for large tracts along outlying highways where greater inventories could be maintained (Moe and Wilkie 1997). Large, open-format store buildings remaining in the downtown are less suitable for services or government office use and, while a building may be partitioned, it is often difficult to find compatible businesses. This situation poses a real dilemma for many small communities and, at the very least, complicates the decision-making process. City officials, concerned about the consequences of declining sales and property taxes, also worry that vacant buildings in the downtown may signal to other businesses that their city is not worthy of a strong retail environment, further triggering more economic disinvestment and outmigration.

What is clear is that successful revitalization of downtowns often requires a partnership between public officials and private businesses. These partnerships increased in importance as both groups realized that neither could solve downtown deterioration problems alone. Cities or economic development groups provide low cost loans, assistance with capital improvements, technical or business planning support, promotion, and other services to prospective business owners. Entrepreneurs tend to be more willing to invest in places offering these incentives.

It should be noted, however, that despite good intentions, dedicated leadership, and an impressive portfolio of incentives, even the most innovative and ambitious plans may not always reverse years of economic decline (or in some suburban cases unbridled growth).

Condition of Downtown

Assessing the overall condition of a downtown is difficult because of so many factors involved. The buildings may be in relatively good condition but the stores are not profitable or there may be vacancies. Detailed information on physical condition is not available on a systematic basis. It is often difficult even to find information on sales in the downtown area compared with the outskirts of the city.

A healthy downtown includes stores with goods and services desired by shoppers. That stores are occupied does not necessarily mean that goods and services are available in sufficient diversity, quality, and quantity to attract shop-pers over the long-term. Too often, a mayor or economic development group learns from the corporate office that a store will close because it did not reach a specific profit level, even though outward appearances suggest a prosperous store.

More and more, downtowns must contain an entertainment attraction. For a downtown to truly be the hub of a community, residents expect to see festivals, parades, and other events on weekends and special occasions. While these activ-ities may actually reduce sales on that specific day due to the congestion, the hope is that residents and visitors will return at a later time to make selections because of their visit to the downtown area.

The most complete assessment of conditions in the downtown is an evalua-tion by policymakers. In a 1998 mail survey of Illinois cities (Table 12), respon-dents were given a five point Likert Scale of downtown conditions, ranging from our downtown is nearly gone and only a few stores remain open (1) to the down-town is prosperous and expanding in sales (5).

Approximately one in five cities (22.8 percent) reported that the downtown is prosperous and expanding in sales. Condition rating does not vary with rural versus metro status (OMB designation).

In general, size of city is a factor and downtown condition improves with city size. The exception is that nearly half of respondents in cities smaller than 5,000 reported a prosperous and healthy downtown. This is an unexpected find-ing and could be attributed to the small number of cities in this category and, perhaps, by unique factors relating to specific location or lower expectations regarding the potential of the downtown.

Other than the experience reported in the smallest cities, the 5,000 to 9,999 category is at the overall average and only 26.7 percent of the cities with popu-lations of 25,000 or larger reported a prosperous downtown. The larger cities have significant retail centers in the past and retail developments on the outskirts of these cities may draw businesses from their main street as well as from smaller surrounding cities. The current data set makes it difficult to assess the impact of suburban development either on the downtown or surrounding communities.

The largest group of respondents (42.6 percent) rated the overall condition of downtown businesses as stable and reasonably prosperous, but definitely not expanding. Once again, rural and metro designation does not matter (43.6 per-cent and 42.4 percent). One explanation may be that cities in rural areas repre-sent small regional shopping sites and they, in turn, are less adversely affected by growth in suburban areas, especially when the local economy has stable employ-ment.

Except for the less than 5,000 population where 27.3 percent reported the stable but not expanding category, the response to this condition category declined with size from 53.5 percent (cities with 5,000 to 9,999) to 31.1 percent (25,000 and larger). One explanation could be reporting variations by respon-dents in the various size categories. When the two categories of condition are

Table 12: Condition of Downtown Retail Establishments

Describe the overall condition of retail establishments in your downtown:

	Stable and reasonably Prosperous and expanding in sales	Prosperous, but definitely not expanding	Some, but not serious declines	Major declines with several empty storefronts	Our downtown is nearly gone, only a few stores remain open
All Respondents					
Percent	22.8	42.6	21.3	9.6	3.6
Number	45	84	42	19	7
Metro Status					
Nonmetro					
Percent	23.1	43.6	12.8	17.9	2.6
Number	9	17	5	7	1
Metro					
Percent	22.8	42.4	23.4	7.6	3.8
Number	36	67	37	12	6
Population Size Categories					
Less than 5,000					
Percent	45.5	27.3	18.2	9.1	0.0
Number	5	3	2	1	0
5,000 through 9,999					
Percent	18.3	53.5	18..3	7.0	2.8
Number	13	38	13	5	2
10,000 through 24,999					
Percent	21.4	41.4	28.6	8.6	0.0
Number	15	29	20	6	0
25,000 or more					
Percent	26.7	31.1	15.6	15.6	11.1
Number	12	14	7	7	5

combined, however, the percentage of cities reporting stable or prosperous downtowns decreases with size, above 5,000, suggesting that downtowns in larger cities are more adversely affected by recent events.

Statewide, one in five cities (21.3 percent) reported a "some but not serious declines" rating with substantial differences by rural and metro status. Rural cities, on average, were less likely (12.8 percent) to report this condition than metro cities (23.4 percent). Likewise, major differences are uncovered by size of city, although the pattern is less clear. Cities in the 10,000 to 24,999 size category most often reported some declines (28.6 percent) compared with 15.6 percent in the largest cities. Respondents less than 10,000 are at or near the state average.

Thus, it would appear that the 10,000 to 24,999 group have experienced the beginnings of declines in downtown businesses. One explanation for this trend is that discount centers are moving to cities in this size group more frequently. When these stores locate on the outskirts, they compete with downtown stores that typically are locally owned, relatively small, and specialized. For these reasons, they often are not open on evenings and Sundays, when many families with two wage-earners want to shop.

While, statewide, 13.2 percent of the respondents reported major declines or only a few stores remaining downtown, this experience seems to be concentrated in the largest cities (26.7 percent). Likewise, cities in rural areas more often reported this status (20.5 percent compared with 11.4 percent). Because the question was stated in a fairly general way, reporting differences may affect interpretation of the results.

Based on the downtown condition findings, one might conclude that, at least for the cities of 25,000 and larger, there are two groups, those that are doing very well and those that are experiencing declines. Location in a rural area, in some instances, seems to place cities at a disadvantage but this is certainly not true in all instances. There is some evidence that downtowns in large cities may be more adversely affected by expansions on the outskirts. Much of the decline in rural cities may have occurred in the early to mid-1980s when rural areas, in general, underwent significant outmigration and economic stagnation.

Factors Affecting Prosperity

To better understand reasons for changes in the downtown, respondents were given a list of possible contributing factors and asked to indicate the two most important ones affecting their city. Because respondents reported more than one factor, the percentages do not always sum to 100. Likewise, the questionnaire did not ask respondents to indicate the relative importance of each factor reported.

Far and away, the most often (73.3 percent) reported factor contributing to declines is "competition from neighboring large retail centers" (see Table 13). Responses from rural cities (75.0 percent) differ only marginally from cities in metro counties (72.7 percent). While the reported differences are slight, the

Table 13: Factors Contributing to Economic Decline

If your community is declining economically, what are the two most important factors contributing to the economic decline?	Percent	Number
competition from neighboring larger retail centers	73.3	44
subsidy or tax incentives by other towns to lure businesses away	36.7	22
loss of manufacturing or other employers in area	23.3	14
closing of large retaliers in your town	20.0	12
loss of population	11.7	7
business closings because of retirements of owners	8.3	5
lack of information/expertise in finding replacements for employement declines	8.3	5

Source: IRA Municipal Survey, 1998.

explanations are probably very different. In large urban areas, shopping malls that draw populations from several hours away tend to siphon sales away from neighboring communities. On the other hand, in more remote rural areas, the important draw may be smaller shopping centers or discount stores at the out-skirts of medium-size regional centers or perhaps downtown stores in a nearby regional center.

Another important factor, according to respondents, is a decline in the over-all economic condition in the region: For example, either the loss of manufac-turing or other employers (23.3 percent) or a general loss of population (11.7 percent). Loss of employment as a contributing factor was reported much more often by cities with a stable or expanding downtown (38.9 percent) than cities with declining downtowns (15.0 percent).

Loss of a major employer was not reported substantially more often in rural than metro areas but population loss was reported more frequently (25.0 percent compared with 6.8 percent). A vast majority of rural counties in Illinois lost pop-ulation during the 1980s and a significant number (32.4 percent) have continued the trend in the 1990s. These declines mainly reflect the outmigration of resi-dents in search of better employment opportunities, often in urban areas. Loss of population equates with declining markets for goods and services available in these communities.

Analyzing cities by size offers other insights into the capacity to respond to these trends. For example, the smallest cities typically do not have a staff to promote economic development. Cities larger than 5,000 were more likely to report that subsidies or incentives by other communities lure businesses away and have contributed to the economic declines in their region. The tendency to report this factor as important increased with city size, 29.2 percent in cities between 5,000 and 9,999 compared with 46.2 percent in the largest cities.

While attracting manufacturing firms through property tax concessions is fairly common, it is becoming more common for city governments to attract commercial or retail businesses by sharing retail sales tax receipts. In some instances, private developers make infrastructure investments that benefit the public and are reimbursed by the city from sales taxes. In other cases, city governments share the additional retail sales taxes generated by a business willing to relocate or start in the city.

Loss of large retailers as a factor contributing to economic decline was reported most often in large cities, mainly because not many large retailers are in very small towns. However, among cities between 10,000 and 24,999, more than one-third (35.0 percent) and in cities larger than 25,000, almost a quarter (23.1 percent), reported large retail closures as an important factor in economic declines. Certainly, when a large retailer closes in a downtown, it adversely affects the local economy.

Responses by Public Officials

As noted previously, status of downtown businesses is closely linked with the overall economic condition of the surrounding area. Thus, one might expect cities facing economic cutbacks to more aggressively pursue intervention programs such as tax concessions to lure businesses or to encourage expansions. Respondents were asked which in a series of development tools or techniques they had used during the previous five years (1993 to 1998) and they had three options to report frequency of usage: often, infrequently, or never.

The strategies provided differ with type of business sector targeted (Table 14). Because of the large number of permutations, only the average statewide responses are shown with important differences by city location or size reported. Overall, the economic development tools and techniques were not often used in the previous five years by many cities in this sample.

The most often-used development tool is a tax increment financing (TIF) district as reported by 38.0 percent of responding cities. TIF districts are used by cities to revitalize blighted areas by freezing property tax assessments at current levels and issuing bonds to make capital improvements and then using increases in the property tax revenues resulting from improvements to retire the debt. TIF districts can include the downtown and, in some instances, may involve recapturing increased sales taxes as well as increased property taxes.

The attraction of TIFs for local officials is that improvements can be made to stimulate economic expansion without increasing the property tax rate. The

Table 14: Economic Development Tools Used by Cities, 1993–1998

Tool/Technique		All Respondents	
		Percent	Number
Tax Increment Financing	often	38.0	81
district	infrequently	28.6	61
	never	33.3	71
Business retention and	often	28.7	58
expansion programs	infrequently	40.6	82
	never	30.7	62
Property tax abatement	often	22.0	45
	infrequently	30.7	63
	never	47.3	97
Low cost loans from	often	19.5	40
city funds	infrequently	28.3	58
	never	52.2	107
Sales tax rebates to	often	14.4	30
incoming businesses	infrequently	44.0	92
	never	41.6	97
Industrial or commercial	often	14.2	29
revenue bonds	infrequently	49.5	101
	never	36.3	74
Small business	often	10.7	21
assistance programs	infrequently	34.2	67
	never	55.1	108
Free or reduced price	often	9.0	18
for land/buildings	infrequently	36.8	74
	never	54.2	109
Free or low cost city	often	8.5	17
services	infrequently	29.0	58
	never	62.5	125
Jobs Training Partnership	often	6.0	12
programs	infrequently	27.6	55
	never	66.3	132
Worker retraining	often	3.6	7
programs	infrequently	16.8	33
	never	79.6	156
Subsidized wages or	often	2.5	5
training	infrequently	12.7	25
	never	84.8	167
Subsidized office or	often	1.0	2
building rent	infrequently	9.5	19
	never	89.4	178
Clawback* provisions for	often	1.0	2
incentive	infrequently	9.2	18
	never	89.8	176

Source: IRA Municipal Survey, 1998.

increased property tax revenues can also be leveraged to cause further expansions. For instance, if a city wishes to start a housing subdivision, it can borrow, improve lots, and retire the debt with TIF revenues. Expansions of this type can support a variety of development programs including improvements to the downtown.

The second most often reported technique is business retention and expansion programs used frequently by 28.7 percent of cities reporting and used infrequently by 40.6 percent. These programs involve retail as well as industrial companies and include working with businesses to identify new markets, find alternative suppliers, and otherwise help businesses be more competitive. These programs were reported more often in nonmetro areas (44.7 percent) than in metro counties (25.0 percent) which may reflect a greater need by these communities for public intervention to promote the development process. In fact, 41.5 percent of cities in metro areas reported never using this tool.

Business retention and expansion programs are reported more often in larger than small cities. For instance, 83.0 percent of cities larger than 25,000 reported using this approach, compared with 60.9 percent of cities between 5,000 and 9,999. Some of the variations may reflect differences in interpretation of a business retention and expansion program. In some cases, this may mean simply meeting with businesses every so often to have a general discussion about overall conditions; while, in other instances, it may involve agreeing on a strategy through which the city helps a business solve problems or expand its opportunities.

Third in the list of development tools used are property tax abatements as reported by approximately one city in five (22.0 percent). Infrequent use was reported by 30.7 percent of respondents and no use by 47.3 percent. Somewhat unexpectedly, 63.2 percent of cities in nonmetro counties reported using property tax abatements often while only 12.6 percent of respondents in metro counties reported frequent usage. Given that urbanized areas are likely to have more opportunities to participate in economic development projects than rural areas, one might have expected them to be more aggressive in pursuing development efforts. However, it may also be that these cities do not have to use incentives as often to lure businesses or that current businesses have more opportunities to expand and may require less intervention by public agencies. This point is emphasized by the fact that 55.7 percent of respondents in metro counties reported never using property tax abatements.

Of special interest for the current discussions are sales tax rebates to incoming businesses, especially when used to lure retail businesses to the downtown. Statewide, 58.4 percent of respondents in Illinois reported using this development technique, either infrequently (44.0 percent) or often (14.4 percent). Some difference is found in usage between nonmetro (34.2 percent) and metro areas (47.5 percent); however, it makes sense that metro areas have higher sales taxes due to the larger volume of retail activity. Thus, they are probably more attractive to retail establishments and have more resources with which to work. Size of city does not make much difference until 25,000 or larger where 69.3 percent of the respondents reported at least some use, but 55.8 percent reported only infrequent usage.

In recent years, some local governments have paid much more attention to making sure that in-coming businesses receiving incentives meet their commitments. Cities include "clawback" provisions that require paying back some or all of the incentives if an agreed-upon number of jobs are not created or some other stipulation is not met. When asked about use of these requirements, a vast majority of cities (89.8 percent) reported that they had never used them in economic development activities. It may be that they are included in contracts or negotiations with businesses but that, because the most common development tool cited is TIF, these provisions are not visible. Alternatively, it may mean that cities in the sample have not taken this step in working with prospective businesses.

Economic Development Goals

We turn next to the types of goals that local public officials have for the downtown. While detailed information on overall economic development goals or objectives are not available for the Illinois cities, extensive data are available for U.S. cities from the 1996 national survey described earlier. To keep the focus on small to medium size cities, the analysis is limited to cities of 250,000 or less.

Specific information was collected on goals for the retail and wholesale trade sector (Table 15). Because city goals are influenced by current economic conditions, the sample cities were grouped into those that had experienced decreases in retail/wholesale trade employment between 1987 and 1992 and those with increases.

By and large, retaining and expanding existing businesses is the most often reported development strategy (77.1 percent) in both cities with decreases in retail trade and (78.7 percent) in cities with growth in this sector. The reported difference is minor, but it is somewhat surprising that cities with past increases have further growth as a first or second goal. However, this strategy could just reflect a continuation of similar efforts in the past and, therefore, the past growth may be a result, rather than a cause, of the strategy.

A related goal involves attracting new businesses and was reported by 72.7 percent of cities with past declines compared with 71.7 percent of cities with increases. Again, the difference is minor suggesting that virtually all cities in the sample see attracting new businesses or retaining current businesses as a major economic development goal.

As one might expect, past economic trends in retail and wholesale employment matter. For instance, 56.4 percent of the cities experiencing previous declines in trade employment included downtown development or redevelopment as a first or second priority in their overall efforts compared with 43.6 per-

Table 15: Economic Development Goals

Retail and Wholesale Trade Employment, 1987–1992					
	Decrease		Increase		
	Percent	Number	Percent	Number	t-test
Retain/expand existing businesses					
1st or 2nd priority	77.1	37	78.7	85	-0.032
Not a priority	0.0	0	1.9	2	
Attract new businesses					
1st or 2nd priority	72.7	32	71.7	76	0.571
Not a priority	2.3	1	0.9	1	
Industrial development[1]					
1st or 2nd priority	45.0	18	67.0	65	2.642
Not a priority	17.5	7	7.2	7	
Downtown development/redevelopment[1]					
1st or 2nd priority	56.4	22	43.6	44	-2.317
Not a priority	7.7	8	11.9	12	
Small business development					
1st or 2nd priority	38.7	12	35.3	30	0.355
Not a priority	32.3	10	15.3	13	
Office development					
1st or 2nd priority	16.1	5	18.8	16	1.515
Not a priority	58.1	18	35.3	30	
Service sector growth					
1st or 2nd priority	12.9	4	12.6	11	0.668
Not a priority	54.8	17	41.4	36	
Neighborhood commercial development					
1st or 2nd priority	18.2	6	10.6	9	-0.048
Not a priority	51.5	17	49.4	42	
Minority business growth					
1st or 2nd priority	9.4	3	11.5	10	-0.313
Not a priority	46.9	15	51.74	5	

[1] A significant difference was discovered between municipalities with increased and decreased trade employment.

Source: IRA Survey of incentives and Partnerships, 1996.

Table 16: Incentives Provided to Retail/Wholesale Trade Businesses

Cities that provide incentive:	Decrease Percent	Decrease Number	Increase Percent	Increase Number	Chi-Squared	Significance	All Respondents Percent	All Respondents Number
Infrastructure improvements	51.1	23	64.2	61	2.183	0.140	60.0	90
Direct loans to private businesses	37.8	17	34.7	33	0.123	0.726	36.0	54
In-kind services	46.7	21	25.3	24	6.414	0.011	31.3	47
Tax abatement	31.1	14	18.9	18	2.562	0.109	24.0	36
Grants	24.4	11	16.8	16	1.134	0.287	20.0	30
Cash contributions to projects	22.2	10	13.7	13	1.621	0.203	15.3	23
Employee training/retraining programs	17.8	8	13.7	13	0.401	0.526	14.7	22
Loan subsidies	20.0	9	10.5	10	2.336	0.126	14.0	21
Issuance of bonds for private development	13.3	6	14.7	14	0.049	0.825	14.0	21
Tax credits	13.3	6	12.6	12	0.013	0.908	12.7	19
Loan guarantees	17.8	8	8.4	8	2.641	0.104	12.0	18
Training support	17.8	8	6.3	6	NA[1]	NA[1]	11.3	17
Subsidized buildings	13.3	6	10.5	10	0.238	0.626	10.7	16
Free land	11.1	5	9.5	9	NA[1]	NA[1]	10.0	15
Shared equity in projects	11.1	5	7.4	7	NA[1]	NA[1]	8.7	13
Employee screening	15.6	7	5.3	5	NA[1]	NA[1]	8.7	13
Sale-lease back	11.1	5	3.2	3	NA[1]	NA[1]	5.3	8
Donation of unused real property	6.7	3	3.2	3	NA[1]	NA[1]	4.0	6
Deferred tax payments	4.4	2	3.2	3	NA[1]	NA[1]	3.3	5
Centralized management services	4.4	2	2.1	2	NA[1]	NA[1]	3.3	5

Trade Employment, 1987–1992

1. Some cells have counts less than 5, which may distort the statistics.

Source: IRA Survey of Incentives and Partnerships, 1996.

cent of cities experiencing increases. Downtown expansion is the third most often reported strategy for cities with past declines so it clearly is considered an important option. Similarly, 11.9 percent of cities with past increases in trade employment rated downtown development as not a priority suggesting that there is little pressure to revitalize the downtown. On the other hand, 7.7 percent of the cities with decreases in the past rated downtown development as not a priority.

Since offices are an integral part, and growing, activity in many downtowns, we also examined the importance of expansions in office activities as a goal in cities with past trade increases or decreases. Overall, relatively little difference exists between the two city groups. In fact, those cities with past declines in trade employment were slightly less likely (16.1 percent) to have office development as a 1st or 2nd goal than cities with increases (18.8 percent). On the other hand, the two types of cities differ widely with respect to reporting office development as not a priority and cities experiencing decreases (58.1 percent) were much more likely than cities with increases (35.3 percent) to disregard office development as a strategy.

Explaining why cities with previous declines in trade employment do not actively pursue office development is difficult with current data. One possibility may be that cities with employment declines do not have opportunities for expansions in office development simply because economic conditions do not support these efforts. An alternative explanation could be a perennial hope that stores can be attracted back to the downtown and there is an aversion to having offices occupy the store fronts.

The causation also could run the other way in that cities without an aggressive downtown development strategy may have missed opportunities in the past to stimulate this sector and, consequently, have experienced declines. Because the survey was undertaken in 1996 and the trends are from 1987 to 1992, this hypothesis cannot be tested.

City officials were asked about goals regarding service sector growth since services also are located in the downtowns of many cities. Virtually no differences were reported in goals for service sector growth (12.9 percent and 12.6 percent) between cities with trade declines compared with those with increases. This finding suggests that cities in this sample do not see growth in the service sector as a strong economic development goal. In fact, 54.8 percent of cities with decreases in trade employment and 41.4 percent with increases reported that service sector growth is not a priority.

The service sector, especially in rural areas, often does not pay well, although it may be comparable with retail. Because of past land uses and attitudes, local development officials may prefer to keep the downtown as a retail sector. In these instances, they may be reluctant to actively pursue service businesses when they are small and do not represent high-paying employment. Another possibility is that service businesses tend to follow populations and local development agencies simply do not pursue them as a general development strategy.

Incentives Provided

Respondents were asked next about specific incentives provided to retail/whole-sale businesses with the cities again grouped by previous changes in employment (Table 16). Far and away, the most often reported incentive (60.0 percent of respondents) was infrastructure improvements. City groups differed in these responses with those having increases (64.2 percent) somewhat more likely to report these incentives than cities with trade employment declines (51.1 percent). However, this difference is not statistically significant. Again, one cannot be sure that the incentives reported in 1996 are not a continuation of earlier trends that, in turn, led to growth in trade employment.

Those cities reporting declines, however, much more often reported in-kind services (46.7 percent) compared to cities with growing trade employment (25.3 percent). This difference is statistically significant at the one percent level. Detailed information was not provided on specific services provided but one might expect water/sewer, parking, streets, and lighting projects to be included.

Also important are direct loans to businesses but only minor differences are reported by type of city in this incentive category. One explanation may be that businesses obtain loans from development agencies rather than city govern-ments. Revolving Loan Funds, for example, are sometimes managed by local economic development agencies.

Of special interest are tax abatements for retail and wholesale trade busi-nesses. Based on this survey, approximately one city in four (24.0 percent) pro-vides these incentives for retail and wholesale businesses. Also interesting, but consistent with expectations, is that fewer cities (18.9 percent) provide this incentive if they have had previous increases in trade employment, compared with 31.1 percent in cities that have had declines. These differences suggest that some cities actively try to attract retail/wholesale businesses, although the data are not specific enough to determine whether these businesses are being lured to the downtown area.

Thus, differences are found in approaches taken by cities to pursue eco-nomic development goals for retail and wholesale trade, depending on past employment trends. Infrastructure improvements are used most often, especially in cities with previous growth. Some of these improvements may have been required to accommodate previous growth. Tax abatements, a mainstay of indus-trial development, are not as common in attracting retail and wholesale trade but are used nevertheless, especially in cities with previous decreases in employ-ment.

Successes in Development Programs

City respondents were asked whether development programs had generally exceeded, met, or fell short of expectations with cities classified by past changes in trade employment (see Table 17). Overall, downtown development programs

Table 17: Expectations of Economic Development Programs

| | Trade Employment, 1987–1992 | | | | | | | | | |
| | Decrease | | Increase | | | | All Respondents | |
	Mean	Number	Mean	Number	t-value	Significance	Mean	Number
Retain Existing Business	2.1	48	2.2	108	-0.366	0.715	2.1	173
Attract New Business	1.9	47	2.1	107	-1.296	0.197	2.0	170
Industrial Development	2.1	46	2.0	99	0.741	0.460	2.0	159
Service Sector Growth	2.0	38	2.0	85	0.618	0.538	1.9	137
Small Business Development	2.1	43	1.8	100	2.657	0.009	1.9	160
Downtown Redevelopment	1.7	46	1.9	99	-1.561	0.121	1.8	162
Office Employment Growth	1.8	40	1.8	85	0.559	0.557	1.8	139
Neighborhood Commercial Development	1.7	36	1.8	78	-0.792	0.430	1.7	127

Since 1989, have your economic development programs generally exceeded, met, or fell short of expectations?
(Code: 3 = exceeded expectations, 2 = met expectations, and 1 = fell short of expectations)

Source: IRA Survey of Incentives and Partnerships, 1996.

averaged 1.8 on the 3.0 scale, where 3.0 is "exceeded" and 1.0 is "fell short". Strategies to retain existing businesses, attract new businesses, and industrial development all ranked as the most successful strategies. Also service sector growth and small business development strategies ranked higher than downtown redevelopment. No significant difference is found between whether a city had previous increases or declines in wholesale/retail trade employment and the success of the downtown development strategies. In fact, the only statistically significant difference between the two city groups is in small business development strategies where cities with previous decreases in wholesale/retail trade employment reported more success with strategies to expand small businesses.

The relative success of downtown redevelopment tied with office employment growth (1.8). These two strategies may be related because, in some cities, retail stores in the downtown are being replaced by offices, although previous findings suggest that office activities in the downtown may not be the preferred approach. However, offices may be better than vacant store fronts.

Reasons for the relatively low success of downtown redevelopment strategies are not completely clear due to the multitude of factors involved, both within the city and the surrounding area. Retail sales in a downtown are determined by overall economic conditions because many customers reside outside the city limits.

Differences in perceived success of the downtown redevelopment strategies may also have resulted because of differences among local officials in what is seen as success. Small communities, for instance, may accept the fact that retail will no longer be a major role in the future of their city. The downtowns in larger cities have had to deal with shopping malls and expansions on the outskirts of the city for many years. In some cases, the nature of the downtowns have changed to more services and these activities may have been accepted by local officials. Thus, success of the strategies may not mean the same results to all respondents.

The goals, strategies, and aggressiveness with which the strategies are pursued vary with cities. Local enthusiasm in implementing the downtown redevelopment strategy(ies) may, in fact, be the most important factor in determining success. While most local officials, conceptually at least, would probably prefer that the downtown regain its vitality, they may also realize that the downtown no longer meets the space needs for large stores and the volume of retail business activities needed in the community.

Overall, the downtown redevelopment strategies do not seem to have met expectations for success as much as other development approaches. Nevertheless, many communities have been able to revitalize the downtown through aggressive marketing and other approaches. In the next section, we examine several successful approaches built on public-private partnerships.

Successful Approaches to Downtown Revitalization

One community's answer to filling downtown space and preventing undesirable sprawl was to invite Wal-Mart to locate near the middle of downtown. In early 1991, downtown Carroll, Iowa (population 9,579) retailers asked local officials to partner with them to devise a strategy for successfully locating Wal-Mart in an area adjacent to the central business district, instead of a remote site being considered by the large discount merchandiser. The effort was successful and has since helped make Carroll a regional retail, commercial, and industrial center in west central Iowa. Downtown Carroll boasts a thriving economy and makes the community's novel approach worth a closer look.

Although the majority of the current retail space in Carroll was built or renovated in the early 1990s, the community's innovative efforts to retain a thriving downtown began in the 1960s when local officials, business owners, developers, and residents cooperated to create a plan for converting the existing building stock into a downtown shopping mall.

Following a fire that destroyed several businesses in the late 1960s, Carroll officials took advantage of an urban renewal program to develop West Gate Mall by aggressively relocating approximately 90 businesses and renovating a four-square block section of downtown. The creation of CitiPlaza, complete with canopy-covered sidewalks and several blocks of street front stores, was accomplished by initially retaining the outward appearance of two blocks of downtown containing a majority of the community's retail stores. At the same time, the interiors of the buildings were connected via an enclosed service alley so that shoppers could pass from one business to another through a central corridor.

The initial phase of the project made it possible to join several buildings with JC Penney, the downtown's existing anchor store. In the 1980s, a second portion of the downtown was incorporated into the plan adding six more business sites in the process. By 1991, and despite the closing of the community's longtime, 20,000 sq. ft. Sernett Department Store, new and relocated businesses filled Carroll's West Gate and Old Alley malls. Downtown Carroll now offers a variety of unique gifts, crafts, men's and women's apparel, specialty boutiques, and several other popular chains.

When Wal-Mart announced its intention to locate a store just outside of Carroll in 1992, the city created a tax increment financing district (TIF) to help finance the development of property immediately adjacent to the CitiPlaza mall area. The city agreed to share the costs of water main and storm drainage improvements and obtained a grant from the Iowa Department of Transportation to finance traffic control improvements. With TIF, the city used funds acquired from the captured assessed value of the downtown area to finance the infrastructure improvements. What is now known as Carroll's 30-acre CitiCentre, is the site where local leaders encouraged Wal-Mart to build a 72,000 sq. ft. store. With only a small green space area separating CitiPlaza from Wal-Mart's mammoth size parking lot (half of which Carroll persuaded Wal-Mart to pay), the new

CitiCentre development is contiguous with the original downtown.

Soon after Wal-Mart's announcement to build, an existing Kmart relocated from several blocks away to the new downtown area and built a 92,000 sq. ft. store just west of Wal-Mart where the two stores still share a service road. With the coming of the discount chains, also came a new 44,000 sq. ft. Hy-Vee Grocery Store, Burger King, Payless Shoes, U-Save Rentals, GNC, and several small businesses in the CitiCentre.

In 1992, approximately 4,000 people participated in what was called the world's longest ribbon-cutting ceremony when an 8-inch ribbon was stretched around downtown's entire $10 million CitiPlaza and CitiCentre complex. According to chamber of commerce officials there are currently no vacant commercial properties in downtown Carroll.

As of 1999, Carroll residents are still very enthusiastic about the community's accomplishments. Although the relatively swift increase in retail space contributed to an increasing shortage of housing in the early 1990s, four housing projects and two apartment complexes are in varying stages of completion as of the time of writing. Given an estimated trade radius of approximately 50 miles, the community's location, and access to two intersecting highways, long commutes are not uncommon. Building is underway as Carroll officials recorded $24 million dollars in building permits in 1997 alone. Interestingly, residents pay only $2.82 in property tax per $100 of assessed valuation. The population growth has been manageable and the value of new development has outpaced the costs of providing high quality public services.

It is likely that Carroll's retail expansion contributed, along with the national economic expansion, to an increasing labor shortage in the area. By 1997, Carroll's 3.2 percent unemployment rate left relatively few people available for commercial and/or industrial growth. However, recent attempts to expand several third-generation employers have successfully begun to raise wages and attract people into the community. Local leaders in neighboring communities have also joined forces with Carroll to collaboratively promote a four-lane expansion of Highway 30 and enhance the regional economy.

Knox (1991) reports that, rather than using the urban renewal funds to demolish old buildings and start over, Carroll's efforts represent a significant financial, economic and political commitment to building a strong downtown economy while retaining a small-town, socially acceptable living environment. That philosophy appears to continue today and guides the city's goals for downtown and the rest of the community as well.

Main Street's 4-Point Approach

The National Trust for Historic Preservation (NTHP) is celebrating its 50th Anniversary in 1999 as the oldest national not-for-profit preservation organization in the U.S. In 1977, the Chicago Office of the NTHP initiated a pilot program to help America's Main Streets compete against forces eroding historic downtowns (Moe and Wilke 1997). Three communities of various sizes were selected for the pilot project: Galesburg, Illinois; Hot Springs, South Dakota; and Madison, Indiana. The philosophy behind this project is to work with each community to customize a plan that addresses unique needs and concerns relating to the preservation of historic buildings. The Chicago staff designed an approach to restructure the economies of the commercial districts, adapt old buildings for new uses, provide training to local merchants, and offer technical assistance for promoting, marketing, and revitalizing consumer interest in the downtowns.

Galesburg, IL (population 33,530) developed a well-known Seminary Street Historic District as one of the original "Main Street" pilot projects. Named after the original Knox Female Seminary (a women's educational facility constructed by the Knox Manual Labor College, circa 1841), Seminary Street evolved from a single retail shop in 1968 to more than 20 businesses that now include nationally recognized restaurants, a bakery, winery, pub, antique mall, and several other distinctive specialty shops. The Galesburg Railroad Museum is located on the site of the former Seminary school. Although the Seminary Street Historic District includes only two blocks, it has become a popular tourist attraction in western Illinois. Galesburg was selected in 1978 by the Chicago NTHP office because it was experiencing one of the most serious forces that the NTHP believed was eroding historic downtowns, a new shopping mall on the edge of town.

With the opening of a regional shopping center in the mid-1970s, downtown Galesburg was left with several vacant buildings that once housed a 100 year old O.T. Johnson Department Store, Carson Pirie Scott & Company, Sears & Roebuck, JC Penney, and several other smaller retailers. In 1977, and prior to the NTHP pilot project, owners of the one remaining retail shop on Seminary Street formed a partnership with a group of local investors, acquired the backing of a community bank, and purchased a majority of the vacant properties on Seminary. Their early revitalization plan called for promoting the area's heritage as a railroad town and bringing back specialty, niche-market businesses that could co-exist in Galesburg's competitive retail environment.

The NTHP project began the following year and provided the group with guidance for organizing an historic district and further developing an economic development game plan. By 1981, Seminary Street received national attention when the *Wall Street Journal* cited the Packinghouse Dining Company in a feature on downtown revitalization. By 1987, more than half of the buildings on Seminary Street had been restored (Seminary Street Web Site 1999).

In 1980, the National Trust for Historic Preservation formally created the National Main Street Center. The program has since grown into a national network of more than 1,400 communities. Today, the National Main Street Center reports that, on average, for every new dollar a participating community spends to support an organized Main Street program, $35.43 is reinvested in the local economy (Main Street Web Site 1999). Nationwide, there have been more than 60,000 building renovations and nearly $11 billion of public and private reinvestment in Main Street communities since the program began 19 years ago.

Following the four-point Main Street approach (i.e., design, organization, promotion, and restructuring), communities such as Burlington, Iowa; Lanesboro, Minnesota; Holland, Michigan; Lafayette, Indiana; San Luis Obispo, California; New Cordell, Oklahoma; and hundreds of other communities of various sizes have implemented local efforts. They have adopted the approach that historic buildings, existing infrastructure, and existing local businesses are resources from which thriving downtowns can be born again. Lanesboro, Lafayette, and Cordell, all Great American Main Street Award winners featured below, have recently been recognized for exceptional accomplishments in revitalizing historic and traditional downtowns and neighborhood commercial districts.

Lanesboro, MN (population 858) rallied 250 volunteers to create a plan with local officials and other civic leaders focusing on natural resources, the arts, and historic preservation to revive main street following the unexpected demolition of an 1870 vintage depot that was once part of the Milwaukee Railroad. The group listed the entire downtown district on the National Register of Historic Places in 1985 and constructed the Root River State Bike & Recreation Trail on the former Milwaukee rail bed. Today, more than 40 miles of paved trail invites visitors to Lanesboro annually. The depot has since been reconstructed through volunteer efforts and serves as Lanesboro's Visitor Center, Minnesota Department of Natural Resources Trail Office, a community meeting center, and a public restroom.

Lanesboro gained recognition as one of The 100 Best Small Art Towns in America (Villani 1998) due to the successful efforts of the Lanesboro Art Council to give the downtown a new image as a serious supporter of the arts. The Cornucopia Art Center sponsors exhibits of national and international art along with a sales gallery for regional artists. In addition, the Art Council purchased and restored a movie theater that is now called the Commonwealth Theater Company.

While maintaining the highest artistic standards, the Commonwealth Theater, in its 11th season, is a not-for-profit collective of artists providing quality, live professional stage productions (classic and contemporary) for people of all ages. What has this meant to Lanesboro's economy? Many businesses essential to the needs of local residents as well as those important to the thousands of Lanesboro visitors each year have returned to the community. Main Street reports a 200 percent increase in number of jobs downtown and more than 20 small lodging establishments have opened to provide 102 overnight accommodations (Main Street Web site 1999).

Lafayette, IN (population 46,000), was founded in 1825 because of a strategic location on the Wabash River. For 50 years afterward, virtually all residential, commercial, and industrial development were tied to the river. By 1843, the ill-fated Wabash and Erie Canal project proved troublesome for the State of Indiana, but not before the 250 mile stretch between Toledo and Lafayette introduced economic expansion to Lafayette (City of Lafayette Web Site 1999). Dug primarily by immigrant labor, the 30 foot wide, six foot deep canal opened new grain markets for farmers throughout the Lafayette region.

By the time of the railroads in the 1850s, Lafayette's population had grown from 2,000 in 1840 to 13,506 in 1870. With rail, came tremendous economic expansion including manufacturing, wholesale trade, and meat packing. Technology (e.g., electricity, telephones, radio, and gas engines), education (i.e., Purdue University), and urban development (e.g., street cars and mass transit) set the course for Lafayette between 1873 and 1920. Since 1945, suburban expansion caused growth to come rather haphazardly. Suburbanization so far beyond the city border resulted in no clearly defined separation between city and the rural landscape (City of Lafayette Web Site 1999). By 1960, an Area Plan Commission was formed to restore orderly growth of Lafayette and the county. In 1966, the Redevelopment Commission was formed to address issues confronting the future of the downtown area.

To restore the vitality and productive uses of the central business district, the emphasis in recent years has been to keep the downtown attractive and as user-friendly as possible. Early commitments by the Area Plan Commission and the Redevelopment Commission to manage growth and ease the stresses downtown carried through to the Lafayette Main Street Program. The city has retained approximately 175 of its original stock of pre-1920 buildings by encouraging private investment in several historic downtown buildings.

A totally restored, one square block (including the 1884 Tippecanoe County Courthouse) in the downtown has had more than 90 building renovations in recent years. Fifty of these projects were funded by private investment and 43 were completed through a façade rehabilitation program. The façade program will pay 45 percent of actual exterior rehabilitation costs, up to a maximum of $9,000 per storefront bay (City of Lafayette Web Site 1999).

As part of an extensive $180 million downtown improvement program, the city relocated several railroad lines away from the downtown to a controlled access corridor along the Wabash River. The purpose for relocating the rail lines was to remove more than 40 at-grade rail tracks and create a large public plaza featuring a restored train depot. The depot serves as a community center and a transportation hub for Amtrak and local commuter buses. With Purdue University (enrollment 36,000) across the river in West Lafayette, the downtown transportation linkages are major attractions. "Today, Lafayette is the regional center for industry, commerce, retail, agriculture, finance, education, religion, recreation, "Big Ten" sports, and health care" (Main Street Web Site 1999).

New Cordell, OK (population 2,903). Crisis often provides a terrific motivation for change. During the mid-1980s, New Cordell, OK, as with so many rural midwestern towns, was in an economic tailspin. New Cordell was founded in 1892 with the opening of lands made available from the Cheyenne-Arapaho land rush. Of Oklahoma's 77 counties, the county ranks 6th in total receipts of agricultural output including wheat, cotton, alfalfa, peanuts and livestock (City of New Cordell Chamber of Commerce Web Site 1999).

During the 1980s, when the national economy experienced double-digit interest and inflation rates, the agricultural and petroleum industries underwent severe economic reversals. These events precipitated the closing of three locally-owned banks and a savings and loan, a devastating blow to any small community. To revive local commerce and inspire confidence in local residents, New Cordell officials used the main street approach to organize volunteers for an aggressive community renewal program including a $1.25 million downtown streetscape project funded through the Intermodal SurfaceTransportation Efficiency Act (ISTEA). More than 14 linear blocks of New Cordell's main street received new water lines, period street lights, and over 5,000 feet of new sidewalks. According to Main Street reports (National Main Street Web Site 1999), New Cordell created a $1.3 million adaptive-use housing project that converted a hospital and dry goods store into moderately priced housing for the elderly. The project includes a beauty shop and a hospital museum within the housing complex.

The city also converted an old tire shop and gas station into a state-of-the-art police complex. Valued at $275,000 (the city spent $125,000 for improvements), this 6,500 sq. ft. facility offers a large community room overlooking the courthouse square and provides space for public meetings and events on an ongoing basis. Other city activities include a $175,000 public improvement project for New Cordell's Centennial Park on the Square. A Main Street Brick Sales Committee raised an additional $85,000 in 18 months for park improvements.

The National Main Street Center credits much of New Cordell's success to the public-private partnerships evolving since the mid-1980s for aesthetic improvements in the downtown (National Main Street Web Site 1999). Sales tax revenues have increased at an average annual rate of $62,000. From the total $4.6 million of public-private sector investment to date, 87 storefronts have been restored or rehabilitated. More than 80 new jobs have been created through business start-ups or through expansion of downtown enterprises.

New Mindset for Downtowns

Gratz and Mintz (1998) suggest that although there are numerous perceptions of what is increasingly referred to as the "New Urbanist" movement, the fundamentals generally follow the pre-automobile age principles that shaped the most enduring communities in the U.S. Contemporary downtown planners and visionaries are translating old common sense principles into new development (or redevelopment) strategies. The principles include: density, pedestrian orientation and disdain for the automobile, encouragement of transit, mixed land uses, and the dedication of public open space. According to Johnson (1999), "The model is a relatively urban one by American standards, allowing closer contact between people and a greater commitment to the community as a whole" (Johnson Web Site).

The current literature on downtown/Main Street revitalization often cites the importance of pedestrian movement and comfort, rather than vehicular mobility even in small rural areas where "urban planning" is less frequently associated with community and economic development. This is also what leaders in the successful cities examined in this chapter have concluded. Gratz and Mintz (1998, 329) sum it up by suggesting that "to make a development a place, people have to make it theirs." They suggest that well-groomed, perfectly coifed suburban communities and shopping districts are often developer-built and laced with overly constrictive rules that can stifle individual expression.

To build local economies and continue the tradition of free competition, Gratz and Mintz (1998) recommend a different planning mindset. Local governments must resist the temptation to create expensive infrastructure on the edges of towns for developers who offer projects with short-term appeal, but still require publicly-financed infrastructure. Revitalizing downtowns and preserving publicly developed infrastructure before it needs expensive reinvestment is a public process that requires the participation of city planners, community advocates, private developers, innovative architects, historic preservationists, transportation planners, environmentalists and local public officials who recognize the social value and fiscal wisdom of husbanding existing places, infrastructure, and resources.

As shown in the Carroll, IA case, respect for existing buildings does not mean a city is forbidden to replace or modify some structures. Carroll leaders realized that a row of main street buildings should not lose out to a single-story super store. Clearly, there are no cookie-cutter, one-solution-fits-all answers to downtown revitalization programs, but most will agree that given sufficient attention and commitment, many downtowns are filled with buildings of all sizes, styles, and age that can be adapted for new uses again and again. Increased coordination of infrastructure development and enhancements in downtowns are often the result of open-minded, productive partnerships between public and private agencies genuinely interested in making long-term investments rather than improving short-term bottom lines.

References

City of Carroll Chamber of Commerce (1999, June 30). Carroll Central Business District [WWW document]. URL http://www.carrolliowa.com/carolbzc.htm

City of Lafayette, Indiana (1999, July 2). *History of Lafayette* [WWW document]. URL http://www.city.lafayette.in.us/features/hist_frames.htm

City of New Cordell, Oklahoma (1999, July 2). [WWW document]. URL http://www.cordell-ok.net/

Frieden, Bernard J., and Lynne Sagalyn. 1989. *Downtown, Inc.: How America Rebuilds Cities.* Cambridge, MA: MIT Press, 1989.

Gratz, Roberta Brandes with Norman Mintz. 1998. *Cities Back from the Edge: New Life for Downtown.* New York, NY: John Wiley & Sons, Inc., 1998.

Gruidl, John, and Steven Kline. *The Impact of Large Discount Stores on Retail Sales in Illinois Communities.* Macomb, IL: Illinois Institute for Rural Affairs 3: 2 (Winter 1992).

Johnson, Don. (1999, July 6). *Testing the New Urbanism* [WWW document]. URL http://solar.rtd.utk.edu/planner/fall95/djohnson.html

Keating, Dennis W., Norman Krumholz, and Philip Star, *et. al.* 1996. *Revitalizing Urban Neighborhoods.* Lawrence, KS: University Press of Kansas.

Knox, Jerry. 1991. Dealing with a Volume Chain Store: Carroll, Iowa, Guides Development and Protects its Downtown. *Small Town.* (September-October): 19-23.

Moe, Richard and Carter Wilkie. 1997. *Changing Places: Rebuilding Community in the Age of Sprawl.* New York, NY: Henry Holt and Company.

National Main Street Center: Economic Statistics (1999, July 2) *1998 National Reinvestment Statistics* [WWW document]. URL http://www.mainst.org/about/numbers.htm

National Main Street Center: Award Winning Districts (1999, July 2) *Cordell*, OK [WWW document]. URL http://www.nthp.org/main/awards/mainstreet/cordell.htm

National Main Street Center: Award Winning Districts (1999, July 2) *Lafayette*, IN [WWW document]. URL http://www.nthp.org/main/awards/mainstreet/lafayette.htm

National Main Street Center: Award Winning Districts (1999, July 2) *Lanesboro*, MN [WWW document]. URL http://www.mainst.org/conferences/lanseboro.htm

Seminary Street Historic Commercial District (1999, July 2). *History of Seminary Street Commercial Development, researched by Martin Litvin* [WWW document]. URL http://www.seminarystreet.com/history.htm

Stone, Clarence, and Heywood Sanders, eds. 1987. *The Politics of Urban Development.* Lawrence, KS: University Press of Kansas, 1987.

Stone, Kenneth E. 1995. *Competing with Retail Giants: How to Survive in the New Retail Landscape.* New York, NY: John Wiley & Sons.

Villani, John. 1998. *100 Best Small Art Towns in America: Discover Creative Communities, Fresh Air, and Affordable Living.* Santa Fe, NM: John Muir Publications.

CHAPTER 14

Does Size Matter? Successful Economic Development Strategies of Small Cities[1]

AKHLAQUE HAQUE

The engine of economic growth of cities has largely been driven by business retention and expansion efforts, generally undertaken by cities' economic development offices and their Chambers of Commerce. The majority of new jobs in cities within metropolitan areas are created by established businesses and a very small percent of jobs lost can be attributed to moving or downsizing of existing businesses (Morse 1990; Vaughan 1980). Successful retention strategies require innovative programs, including programs for downtown revitalization. The key to successful economic development in small cities has been a partnership with various local agencies, including local educational institutions, voluntary agencies, and private businesses. In addition, creative ways of using federal funds have proven to be valuable weapons for attracting businesses and revitalization of the downtown. This chapter looks at economic development efforts and their impacts on downtown revitalization for small cities in the deep South.

The purpose of this chapter is in part to discuss the theories of local economic development and show how these theories can be applied to the revitalization of small city downtowns. Case studies of two, stand-alone, small sized cities in Alabama will be used to provide examples of recent successful development strategies—the City of Auburn and the City of Dothan, AL. Both cities have undertaken innovative economic development strategies and created a market niche for revitalizing the economies of the cities in general and their downtowns in particular. The case studies show that the survival and revival of small city downtowns can succeed when there is a partnership between public and private sectors and the utilization of their local educational institutions. The study is divided into three broad sections. The first section describes general economic development strategies with an emphasis on smaller sized cities. The second two sections discuss economic development success stories of two-small cities in Alabama followed by implications of the study.

Strategies of Economic Development

For analytical simplicity strategies of economic development can be broadly divided into two schools of thought. The first focuses on locational advantages of cities, primarily based on competitive advantage in a specific area. According to the first school of thought pioneered by Chinitz (1960a 1960b) and later supported by other studies (Hoover 1971; Mills 1972; Puryear 1975), specialization of activities or role of a few dominant industries in a city gives them a competitive advantage over other cities in economic development. From a traditional international trade standpoint, these authors emphasize the comparative advantage that gives rise to urban areas and fosters specialization among them. Comparative advantage is attained through the creation of localization economies (or agglomeration economies) where businesses lower their transaction cost by localizing themselves into one area. Localization economies occur when increases in the output of an entire group of firms at a particular place result in lower costs for firms in that industry at that location. Based on this rationale, economic development officials develop strategies designed to create a cluster of closely related industries in order to attract further growth from firms seeking the benefit from localization economies (Sternberg 1991).

In contrast to localization, the second school of thought argues that due to cyclical economic instability of local economies, diversification of industrial activities is a necessary condition for economic development; Clement and Sturgis 1971; Crowley, 1973; Paraskevopoulos 1975). The economic downturn in the industrial belt during the late 1960s and early 1970s is attributed to cities' economic dependency on a few specialized industries. The economic rationale behind diversification is that specialization attracts new population and businesses, however, once a threshold level is reached, it diversifies to meet the demand of a larger population size. This type of agglomeration economies, termed urbanization economies, are based on cost savings that accrue to a wide variety of firms when the volume of activity in an entire urban area increases. The firms that share in urbanization economies may be unrelated and may result from economies of scale in public infrastructure (roads, sewers, fire protection, and health facilities etc). Urbanization economies may also result from a more extensive division of labor made possible by greater size and activity.

The above strategies can be summarized by the types of approaches undertaken for economic development purposes. The approach to economic development could be either demand driven or supply driven. Demand driven approach is used for gaining competitive advantage in a specific activity and thereby bringing "new money" into the local economy. Such demand-side approach (also termed export driven) has the logical appeal of devoting resources to few areas for the purpose of specializing in that activity and gaining the competitive advantage. On the other hand, the supply-side approach could be undertaken to capitalize on existing resources (entrepreneurship, productivity, increase in capital and labor). Economists recognize that both supply and demand are necessary to induce production. There is however, disagreement regarding which approach should be used. When supply is very responsive to increases in demand, then the demand-side approach is the best option to follow. Alternatively, if demand for the region's output is responsive to changes in local supply, then an increase in supply will quickly create a market for what was produced. In this case, supply-side theories will have good predictive power.

Challenges for Small Cities

Small cities tend to be less diverse in the range of economic activities they perform and this tends to slow the pace of their economic growth (National League of Cities 1991). Many firms require a wide range of business services that are more likely to be available in larger cities, which influences their location decisions. To overcome the disadvantage of their smaller size, the smaller and mid-size cities often focus on development efforts in two areas. First, smaller cities focus on their urbanization economies by attracting as wide a range of business service activities as possible to maximize their desirability as a business location. Second, they attract industries with a relatively narrow range of business service needs. Successful implementation of these approaches require strategic planning that (i) appropriately identifies assets of the city; (ii) encourages business start-up through innovative financing plans; and (iii) include local leadership. While implementation poses significant challenges, local leadership and community involvement can overcome some of the major obstacles.

Successful Leadership Strategies

Although small cities and towns typically possess a significant amount of determination, energy and spirit, studies suggest that small cities lack proper understanding of their strengths and how to undertake economic development planning (National League of Cities 1991). Successful leadership strategies are two pronged—business retention and expansion, and downtown improvement. This plan involves a variety of factors starting with local leaders who inventory their local business and labor sector and conduct an overall assessment of the community's strengths and weaknesses. The assessment of local inventories is followed by a comprehensive business retention and expansion plan.

Successful retention and expansion strategies build on a city's known economic strengths and minimize its weaknesses. By targeting resources, successful business retention and expansion strategies help revitalize business and employment growth in targeted areas that already have established linkages. For long term economic stability and economic viability, small cities must investigate how existing firms can be given financial, managerial, and technical assistance for economic growth. Existing firms have already made an investment by locating in the community. They have invested in a trained workforce and the community has made an investment in the firm. For small city businesses, often the most immediate assistance that is required is financial. One creative way of handling the problem is through the establishment of revolving funds for low-interest loans to industrial firms. These funds often leverage private financing for firm expansion and retention. Another retention and expansion program used in small cities is the creation of technology parks to provide technical assistance and empower businesses through introduction of new and emerging technologies. Older manufacturers and start-up firms are the most likely beneficiaries of this assistance. Local technology programs must often be funded at least partially by a local Chamber of Commerce, the state, or federal government.

The second significant aspect of leadership in a small city must address the downtown revitalization issue. Downtown is the heart of small cities. Downtown reflects the character and image of the city and provides the first impression of its overall quality of life. The Main Street approach is the most comprehensive and widely used downtown revitalization strategy for economic development. According to Smith *et. al.* (1991), Main Street's success lies in committing and integrating four key elements in revitalization efforts: (i) design (improving the downtown's image by enhancing it's physical appearance); (ii) organization (building local community consensus and cooperation); (iii) promotion (marketing downtown's uniqueness) and (iv) economic restructuring (strengthening the existing economic base and diversifying it). Smith (1991, 1) notes that, "A healthy, viable downtown is crucial to the heritage, economic health and civic pride of the entire community and are symbols of community caring and high quality of life."

Finally, human skill is probably the most important determining factor for the success of economic revitalization in a small city. Economic development requires the participation of multiple interest groups through collaborative strategies. Community leaders seeking to manage economic development must learn how to facilitate cooperative and collaborative efforts among the public, private, and nonprofit sectors as well as among the local, regional, state and federal levels of government. The leaders as facilitators must manage a process where diverse groups and individuals can come together to discuss and disagree with openness, and find common ground for consensus. In order to facilitate the development of a common vision and sense of direction, community leaders must develop and refine their skills in collaboration, networking, bargaining, and negotiation. To ensure success of economic revitalization in the small city, leadership and community participation is critical. We now turn to the discussion of the two case study cities below.

Auburn, AL

With a population of 40,400 in 1999, the City of Auburn is a vital college town in Southeast Alabama. The nearest larger cities are Montgomery, AL, 60 miles to the west; Columbus, GA, 30 miles to the east; and Birmingham and Atlanta both approximately 100 miles to the north. With 14 schools and colleges, more than 21,775 students and approximately 1,200 faculty members, the University of Auburn is the heart of economic vitality in this city. In recent years, the city's proactive economic development initiatives and innovative public-private partnership programs have made it one of the most successful small city economic development stories. Since a comprehensive revitalization plan was implemented in the late 1980s, population for the city increased from 33,830 in 1990 to 40,966 in 1999 (21.1 percent increase) and median family household income rose from $36,348 in 1989 to $46,237 in 1999, a 27.2 percent increase (see Table 17). Improvement in the quality of life is also reflected in a decline in the lowest income group population. The percentage of people with an income below $10,000 decreased from 15.4 percent in 1989 to 11.4 percent in 1999. At the same time, the percentage of people in the highest income group ($100,000 or higher) also increased from 6.5 percent in 1989 to 15.4 percent in 1999.

Several factors can be attributed to the success of the city's initiatives. The turning point was in 1984 when the city created its own economic development department and initiated a proactive and comprehensive program aimed at increasing non-university employment opportunities. In 1983, voters approved changing the system of government to a council-manager system, and this went into effect in 1986. The city's professionalism increased and produced tangible results. During the past ten years the city periodically conducted annual citizens' surveys. Throughout this period, an average of 86 percent of the city's households have consistently rated the level of public services they receive as either excellent or good (Citizens Survey 1995). The strategies undertaken by the Economic Development Office, primarily through the Directors initiative, made the difference.

**Table 18: Income Data for the City of Auburn
and the City of Dothan, AL, 1980–1999**

City	Population			Median HouseholdIncome	
	1980	1990	1999	1989	1999
Auburn	30,188	33,830	40,400	36,348	46,237
Dothan	49,507	53,589	56,500	32,342	42,357

City	Per Capita Income		Income Below $10K (percent Hhs)		Income Above $100K (percent Hhs)	
	1989	1999	1990	1999	1990	1999
Auburn	10,532	14,825	15.4	11.4	6.5	15.6
Dothan	13,101	19,082	12.6	8.1	3.6	9.6

Source: 1990 U.S. Census and 1999 U.S. Census Population Estimates. Income data was obtained from Claritas Data Inc.

URBAN DEVELOPMENT ACTION GRANT (UDAG)

The Urban Development Action Grant (UDAG) was initiated in the 1970s. For the first time, a grant program required extensive negotiation between public and private participants. For public participants, it also required a great deal of understanding of how investments were made and what resources were necessary for projects to occur. Localities seeking UDAG grants had to learn how to negotiate with private developers and investors, understand investment decisions and investors priorities. As a result of these experiences, several elements of successful public-private negotiation efforts were identified. The City of Auburn had the advantage of having a progressive and visionary City Manager who hired an economic development practitioner who understood the importance of public-private partnerships and had experience with the UDAG program. Between 1984-89, the economic development director was successful in bringing $10 million into the community through the UDAG program (Watson 1996).

The first UDAG initiative provided mortgages to purchase 114 new homes for low- and moderate income citizens in the city. The program allowed citizens to receive a second mortgage equivalent to 25 percent of the cost of the new home. If the buyer sold the house before the first mortgage was paid off, then the second mortgage came due. This allowed the city to recover mortgage for people who did not have a long-term commitment to live in the city. By 1993, the city had already recovered over $400,000 of the $1.4 million UDAG funds used as second mortgages.

The second UDAG project was devoted to downtown redevelopment. A five story mixed-use facility building (office/retail/apartment building) of 90,000 square feet was constructed on a large vacant lot that was owned by two local developers. With UDAG incentives, the local developers invested nearly $4 million and created sixty-one new jobs in the downtown area. For the city it provided an additional $33,000 in taxes. The city also constructed parking decks for the building; for shoppers, businesses, a bank that occupied one-half of the commercial space and for tenants who lived in the building. After several years the first floor of the building was leased to new businesses from outside the city.

The city did not have a conference center to facilitate large conventions or conferences. Through the UDAG program, Auburn continued its success—a hotel and conference center was constructed across from the university campus. The 250 room and 3,000 square foot conference facility soon became the perfect place for university sponsored conferences. About $858,000 was secured from the UDAG project and tax free financing for the project was arranged through the city's Industrial Development Board (IDB), established in the 1970s. The university leased and managed the conference center while the developer of the hotel hired a management firm to run the day-to-day operations. As per the terms of the agreement, the full amount secured through UDAG was paid back in five years. The project not only improved the city's image as a vibrant community catering to the needs of large businesses, but also paved the way for building a capacity for the future growth of the city. The facility provided 175 new jobs to low and moderate income groups and generated in excess of $150,000 in new taxes for the city.

The city also utilized its internal resources to recruit businesses and improve the downtown image. Auburn's first theater, located in the heart of downtown, was abandoned for many years. The city's economic development director again took the opportunity to utilize this building by converting it to a mixed-use facility. Because of the historical significance of the building, the potential developers were asked to keep its old architectural beauty including the gazebo. Another UDAG loan of $88,000 helped the developer undertake this project of preserving a historic building and making it a viable part of the downtown. After the completion of the project, twenty new jobs were created with $5,000 of additional taxes for the city.

In 1987, the state of Alabama selected Auburn as one of the sites for the incubator program and awarded $369,000 in CDBG funds to the city. A 12,000 square foot building was completed in 1988 opening the state of the art Auburn Center for Developing Industries. By 1989 the incubator was at its full capacity and had to be expanded in 1992 with two new buildings. The new buildings were immediately occupied by start-up industries, almost all occupied by industries that were a product of research at Auburn University. From an economic development stand point this is a typical example of how local resources can be leveraged to generate additional funds for the City.

CREATIVE FINANCING

Although the UDAG program terminated in 1989, the cities' visionary leadership continued the investment strategy based on the UDAG model. By creating a revolving load fund (RLF) from the developers payback of the loans, the city was able to have a $10 million revolving fund at its disposal. This significant backup cash gave the city the ability to attract quality jobs and quality investors. In a few years, a $785,000 loan was approved from the RLF funds for nine projects as well as guarantees to banks for two small industrial projects. As noted by Watson (1996, 59), "the private sector investment for these eleven projects exceeded $11.2 million and resulted in the creation of approximately 315 new jobs." It is important to note here that all loans are secured so that the city does not lose its RLF funds. Furthermore, if borrowers did not have sizable personal worth, the city required letters of credit from banks to secure the loans.

AUBURN'S KEY TO SUCCESS

The presence of an educated work force with a stable economic base provided Auburn the opportunity to capitalize on revitalizing this small city. However, without entrepreneurial leadership such turnaround would not have been possible. Clearly, the strong support from the city's elected officials and the competency of the staff, particularly the entrepreneurial leadership of the Economic Development Director, was critical. The city developed partnerships with other organizations and groups. Of special importance was the role played by the university in developing the incubator and the hotel conference center. Local businesses invested in rehabilitating the older theater and supported other initiatives undertaken by the economic development office. Tax incentives have commonly been the primary vehicle for economic development. However, Auburn's experience has been quiet the contrary. Its incentives have been based on priorities of the community—building a cluster of closely related businesses that match the community's long term goals.

Dothan, Alabama—The Mural City

A 1930s Chamber of Commerce promotional postcard reads,

> We extend you a cordial welcome and invite you to visit and closely observe us and our environments. We are not much on 'blowing our own horn,' but first chance you get, take a stroll through the business section and note the marks of progress made since it was a mere crossroads village. A ride over the beautifully shaded streets will give you an idea of this fast growing city. We hope your visit to us will be mutually profitable in every way. (Annamarie Saliba Martin *et. al.* 1998, 6)

Today, Dothan, Alabama has a population of 56,500 and serves as the regional center in medical services, finance, retail trade, agri-business, and light manufacturing. The city is approximately equidistant (200 miles) from Atlanta, GA, Birmingham, AL, Jacksonville, FL and Mobile, AL. Also known as the "Peanut capital of the world,"[2] the city is in the southeast corner of Alabama. The local area is tied closely to southwest Georgia and the eastern end of the Florida Panhandle. The city's Chamber of Commerce is in the third year of a comprehensive 5-year economic development initiative. Called "Dothan by Design," this public-private partnership is designed to ensure the continued prosperity and economic growth of the city and downtown.

Due to Dothan's strategic location, it historically attracted consumers from nearby towns without clothiers, movie theaters, and hospitals. U.S. Highways 52, 84, 231, and 431 made it the "Hub of the Wiregrass", drawing in cars and buses from nine Alabama counties and another dozen in southwest Georgia and northwest Florida. Serving a 50-mile trade area, Dothan professionals provide one-stop shopping for merchandise, medicine, news, and entertainment. In 1997 reports counted 1,235 trade businesses employing 14,508 in the county (Houston county) and serving 515,000 within a 50 mile-radius (Martin 1998). Table 17 showed the recent income and population figures for the city. Median household income rose from $32,342 in 1989 to $42,357 in 1999 (31 percent increase).

Increasing distress conditions in the city sparked city officials to focus on economic development programs targeted to improving the quality of life of the population and improving the image of the city. During the last decade the city has been taking proactive steps to improve the quality and image of the downtown area. Today, the city offers a better quality of life as evidenced by a decrease in the percentage of households earning below $10,000 from 12.6 percent in 1989 to 8.1 percent in 1999. At the same time, the percentage of the population earning above $100,000 increased from 3.1 percent to 9.6 percent during the same time period.

During 1987 a powerful citizens group, later to become a non-profit organization, in the city raised funds for cultural consciousness and a better image of the city's downtown. The funds raised were used to create the Landmark Park—home of the state's agricultural museum, the Wiregrass Museum of Art, and the Wiregrass festival of Murals—an outdoor art project designed to attract tourists and engender downtown revitalization. Later, a new mayor in the early 1990s proposed a sales tax increase. Despite great opposition, the commission passed the tax and the city collected enough revenue to address infrastructure needs through a funded five-year capital improvement plan. Various support agencies coordinated programs in a Family Service Center, which in its first two years, assisted and educated more than 2,000 low-income families. Private businesses as well as county and city governments pledged dollars and support for a cooperative industrial expansion program administered by the Chamber of Commerce. In 1996, two hundred health service businesses employed more than 6,000 Dothan residents, and in a flourishing tourism industry, 171 eating and drinking establishments joined 27 lodging businesses and 54 amusement spots.

THE DOWNTOWN GROUP (DTG)

Dothan's Downtown Group (DTG) and the city manager's office in Dothan developed a plan to breathe new life into the downtown's historic core using funds raised directly from the Dothan community and from the U.S. Department of Housing and Urban Development for public improvements to streets, sidewalks, lighting, and signal improvement. The Downtown Group, Inc. was formed in 1989 as a non-profit 501 3(c) organization. The annual operating budget which includes the streetscape account (murals, landscaping, banners, bricks, fund raisers etc.), is approximately $120,000. The City of Dothan, the Houston County Commission, individuals, and private business fund the organization. Funds are leveraged with regular county and city budgets to undertake public works projects. To date, since the Downtown Group was formed, over $35 million have been invested in the core area of downtown Dothan and over 80 buildings have been revitalized or constructed. In the Downtown Core area, over 250 jobs have been created in 1999 alone. The group has gained tremendous community support since its inception. The DTG's image building campaign and public education about the importance of downtown revitalization via local radio stations and television has attracted investors and visitors from outside the local area. The organization is headed by an executive director who is paid by the organization and a board of 25 members who work closely with the city and county officials. Funds raised through grants, brick sales, and community support, are utilized to improve the aesthetic beauty of the downtown, make it more attractive for visitors, and give the community a sense of identity. In 1997–98 the group spent $10,000 on thoroglaze coating for preservation of older murals. The group has taken the lead role in long-term mural preservation and has identified a total of 15 murals in 5 years to be preserved.

Recasting downtown as a professional and cultural center, city governments, corporations, and individuals united to restore the Municipal Light and Water Plant and Opera House. From 1993 to 1995, American and Canadian muralists memorialized history through art, as the Wiregrass Festival of Murals recounted the region's defining events on the painted exteriors of buildings. Dothan presently has seven murals in its downtown district with eight more being planned. Because of its importance to the Wiregrass area, the peanut is the subject of the premiere mural by Canadian artists Susan Tooke and Bruce Rickett. The 30-foot tall, 150-foot wide mural features the late Tuskegee Institute botanist Dr. George Washington Carver, who developed more than 300 uses of peanut, alongside a modern day peanut farmer. Other historical vignettes include Elizabeth Stewart's kidnapping on the Chattahoocoche River; George Washington Carver's address at the Wiregrass Stadium; and Chief Eufaula's farewell speech. Today's renovated brick sidewalks and street crossings, nostalgic street-lights, restaurants, antique shops, and dinner theaters give a new life to the downtown and the city. Based on *Money Magazine* surveys, Dothan was titled the "Most Livable City in Alabama" from 1994 to 1996.

Further improvement in downtown is expected with a lucrative incentive package for downtown businesses introduced by the city in collaboration with support from DTG and the local chamber of commerce. The incentive package is a capital investment of more than $150,000 from the city, that includes a fifty percent reduction of landfill fees, complete waiver of construction permit fees and a significant reduction of the business license fees for the first two years (first year 75 percent; second year 50 percent) of business operation. The purpose of the incentive package is to encourage businesses to improve the façade/exterior of the businesses as well as to help improve the downtown aesthetics.

The city's five-year capital improvement plan is upgraded annually to support an infrastructure necessary for growth with ongoing attention to roads, water, sewerage treatment, public safety, cultural programs and facilities, and leisure services. The City of Dothan works closely with *Dothan by Design*, the economic development arm of the Dothan Area Chamber of Commerce, to recruit new business and industry that help to bring in new money to revitalize the city. With revitalized infrastructure in place, joint private ventures continue to upgrade old buildings with new restaurants and commercial outlets that capitalize on Dothan's refreshed historic district.

Implications of the Study

Community support, private-public partnership and innovative investment strategies are the keys to economic revival and downtown revitalization for small cities. Economic development strategies are bound to differ due to history, strategic location, and community commitment. The City of Auburn, being in the middle of a large world-class university has been able to create its niche by utilizing the available human capital and finding creative ways of attracting businesses. Its strong and stable economic base, due mainly to the university's presence, allows continued demand for goods and services. The local officials found creative ways to capitalize on their local resources. The city had the option of providing incentives to any business that would help to revitalize and expand its tax base. However, it did not arbitrarily choose businesses. Incentives were provided only if the investment improved resources already available that had the possibility of a long-term success. The idea was to create a cluster of industries that matched the need of a college town—research, innovation, and a vibrant downtown. Community strategies that focus on a cluster of related activities or a particular development path for which the community already has an economic advantage often contribute to positive-sum outcomes (Blair and Kumar 1997). Targeting industries that do not have cost advantages in the region can have a negative result because if the incentives attract such a firm, it will be an inefficient location and such a firm is very likely to move out once the incentives end. This is particularly important for smaller cities since a large portion of their investment is based on a hope that the industries that are lured will become the prime engine of growth for the city. In that regard, economic development can only become a zero sum game. Therefore, if incentives are used they must be carefully targeted to specific industries.

As a result of fundamental changes in society and the economy, universities today face a broader and more complex set of demands than they did a few decades ago. In addition to traditional teaching and research functions, universities today are expected to provide leadership and infrastructure, to stimulate the economy through technology transfer and expenditures, and to create a milieu that is favorable for economic and societal development. Knowledge of infrastructure stimulates economic development by effectively lowering the costs faced by individual businesses for some critical inputs needed for successful innovation. Indeed, economic development is positively influenced by a region's knowledge-based infrastructure, including the prominence of one or more research universities, and its capacity for generating innovative businesses and sustained economic development. Clearly, Auburn has used the localization strategy by clustering closely related industries to attract further growth from firms seeking the benefit from localization economies.

Numerous studies have shown that keeping industries that are already located in a community is easier than bringing in new ones. Evidence also suggests that the majority of new jobs are created from existing businesses and, thus, the closing of a company in a small community can be devastating (Luke 1988). For small cities it may be more beneficial in helping existing businesses than in chasing down new leads. Unlike Auburn, the city of Dothan did not have the option of attracting businesses for building a particular type of industrial cluster. Due to its strategic location as a thoroughfare, for decades it has been serving as a hub and symbol of diversity, meeting demands of a tri-state population group. The community realized that its pride is in the downtown. So, with exemplary community participation, the city invested a large amount of money and energy to revitalize the downtown and capitalized on the history of the city, building murals and preserving history on walls, unlike other small cities in the United States. For older, small cities, there is much to learn from Dothan's experience. The Main Street redevelopment components of downtown image building, community commitment and participation, promotion of downtown, and economic restructuring, have been fully realized by Dothan. As noted by Smith and his colleagues;

> The key to success of the Main Street approach is its comprehensive nature. By carefully integrating all four areas into a practical downtown management strategy, the Main Street approach produces fundamental changes in the downtown economic base, making it economically feasible to put historic commercial buildings to productive use again (Smith *et. al.* 1991, 3).

Given the two examples of small city revitalization efforts, we can argue that successful economic development strategies may not have to do with being larger or smaller in population (size). Rather it may have more to do with how successfully communities capitalize on their uniqueness. Indeed, unlike larger cities, smaller cities that are more homogeneous have the advantage of making this happen more easily, they just have to look at the problem with visionary spectacles.

Reference

Blair, J., and Rishi Kumar. 1997. "Is the Local Development a Zero-Sum Game?" In The Dilemmas of Urban Economic Development. edited by Richard Bingham and Robert Mier (1-20). Thousand Oaks, CA: Sage.

Chinitz, B. 1960b. "Contrast in Agglomeration: New York and Pittsburgh," *American Economic Review Papers and Proceedings*: 279-289.

Chinitz, B., and R. Vernon. 1960a. "Changing Forces in Industrial Location." *Harvard Business Review*: 38:126-136.

City of Auburn. (1995). *Citizens Survey. Reports of the Annual Surveys for 1986 through 1995*. Auburn: City of Auburn.

Clemente, F., and R. B. Sturgis. 1971. "Population Size and Industrial Diversification." *Urban Studies* 8: 65-68.

Crowley, R. 1973. "Reflections and Further Evidence on Population Size and Industrial Diversification." *Urban Studies* 10:91-94.

Eichner, A. 1970. *Development Agencies and Employment Expansion*. Detroit: Wayne State University Press.

Haque, Akhlaque. 1997. *Regional Development Issues and Opportunities: An interpretation of Demographic, Economic, and Transportation Related Data for Jefferson and Shelby Counties, Alabama 1980-90*. Birmingham: Center for Urban Affairs, University of Alabama at Birmingham.

Hoover, E. 1971. *An Introduction to Regional Economics*. New York: A. Alfred Knopf.

Luke, Jeffrey, Curtis Ventirss, B. J. Reed, Christine M. Reed. 1988. *Managing Economic Development*. San Francisco: Jossey-Bass.

Martin, Annamarie S. 1998. *A Place of Our Own: The Stories of Dothan Houston County*. Montgomery: Ronald P. Beers and James Turner.

Mills, E. 1972. *Studies in the Structure of Urban Economy*, Baltimore: John Hopkins Press.

Morse, G. 1990. "Moving from R @ E's to Jobs." In *The Expansion and Retention of Existing Businesses*. Ames: Iowa State University Press.

National League of Cities. 1991. *Small City Economic Development: Road to Success*. Washington, D.C: National League of Cities.

Paraskevopoulos, C. 1975. "Population Size and the Extent of Industrial Diversification: An Alternative View." *Urban Studies* 12:105-107.

Puryear, D. 1975. "A Programming Model of Central Place Theory," *Journal of Regional Science* 15:307-316.

Smith, K. 1991. *Revitalizing Downtown*. Washington D.C.: National Trust for Historic Preservation.

Sternberg, Ernest. 1991. "The Sectoral Cluster in Economic Development Policy: Lessons from Rochester and Buffalo, New York." *Economic Development Quarterly* 5 (4): 342-56.

Vaughan, R. J., (1980). *Local Business and Employment Retention Strategies*. Washington, D.C.: Public Technology.

Watson, D. 1996. "Joining Battle: Two Competitive Cities," In *Workable Government: Auburn Provides Solutions for Community Challenges*, Auburn: City of Auburn: 53-74. .

END NOTES

1. Many persons contributed their time and efforts to make this chapter a reality. My thanks to Douglas Watson, City Manager for the City of Auburn for his assistance and time. Also, thanks to Matt Parker, President of the City of Dothan Chamber of Commerce for his insightful suggestions and for providing me with data on the city. I also wish to thank Janice Hitchcock, the MPA Program Coordinator at the University of Alabama Center for Urban Affairs for her help in getting in touch with the right persons and for her editorial review and suggestions.
2. The peanuts now harvested within 75 miles of Dothan equal one-fourth of the entire U.S. peanut crop. With this acclaim, Dothan-Houston County prides itself in being the Peanut Capital of the World!

Part Five

Conclusion

CHAPTER 15

Keeping Faith

What We Know About Downtown Revitalization in Small Urban Centers

MICHAEL A. BURAYIDI

The shared experiences of downtown revitalization in small cities around the country give evidence that downtown is still considered a vital part of the health of cities. Rarely does a community give up on its downtown. This is, in part, because downtowns still occupy a special place in the psyche of many Americans. These are places where colorful festivals are held and where civic activities bring the community together. Communities across the country are working hard to ensure that downtowns remain viable centers of community life. Even so, competing with the suburban malls for business and economic activity has been a daunting task for downtown promoters. But as the contributors in this volume have made clear, many communities have succeeded in bringing life back to dying downtowns. So what lessons can other small cities learn from these stories in the process of revitalizing their downtowns? The following is a summary of the key issues to downtown revitalization from the discussion of city experiences in this book.

Work Within the Political Culture

Local governments, organizations and groups, which seek to revitalize their downtowns must first understand the political culture within which they work. Planning and economic development do not take place in a vacuum. Thus, understanding the local political culture is important to revitalizing downtown. Redevelopment is generally not a favored economic development strategy for politicians working within the political life cycle. The outcomes of community redevelopment may not be visible for a long time and politicians prefer programs that show quick returns and that are visible to the electorate. Because of these constraints, bringing downtown revitalization to the forefront of the political debate is often difficult. A pro-growth local regime may simply want to promote economic development regardless of where such new growth takes place. As Garr discussed in chapter nine, in the case of Santa Cruz's "progressive regime", building a community-wide consensus and involving the key stakeholders, especially members of the Santa Cruz Action Network (SCAN) was key to getting downtown revitalization off the ground after the Loma Prieta earthquake, even if this meant project delays.

There is also a need for grassroots mobilization of support for downtown revitalization. In some cases, this may require educating the public about the importance of downtown to the community in order to win a broad based support for downtown programs. Widespread community support also encourages donors to contribute to programs. The lack of community support for downtown revitalization in Newport, OR, as Klebba *et. al.* discussed in chapter five, stifled the process and led to frustrations. In some instances, internal squabbles within a community could make revitalization efforts a nightmare. Such has been the case in Lincoln City, OR, where consolidation of five previously distinct communities has created serious disagreements that no single vision could be reached for the communities' downtowns. It is, therefore, necessary to understand the local political system so as to be able to effectively work within it to promote downtown programs.

Place Emphasis on Local Funding of Downtown Programs

Communities ranging from Colfax, WA, and Auburn, AL, to Santa Cruz, CA, have benefitted from state and federal funding to revitalize their downtowns. As Haque discussed in chapter fourteen, Auburn, AL received $1.4 million through the Urban Development Action Grant (UDAG) program to help promote low and moderate income housing in the community. Sheboygan, WI, used funding from the State Highway Program and from the Federal Waterways Program to help revitalize the city's downtown. Thus, the importance of such funding should not be down-played.

Unless a community feels ownership for its downtown programs, however, revitalization will be a failure. The seed money of $1 million for the downtown revitalization of Sheboygan, for example, came from local businesses and residents. So while local financiers may not have the capacity to provide all of the funding needed for downtown revitalization, their contributions signify a commitment to the process. Since they live in the community, they have a stake in seeing to it that projects succeed and can also monitor the process and initiate changes to programs where needed. The historic district in Billings, MT, was redeveloped largely through local initiatives and by relying entirely on local funding from businesses located in the district. This was much more successful than efforts at revitalizing downtown Billings that did not elicit similar commitment from property owners in the downtown.

Create an Image and Sense of Place for Downtown

Physical renewal must go hand in hand with economic renewal of the downtown. Downtown revitalization must build on and recreate the historic image of the city. Sen and Bell in chapter eight discussed how the design of the physical space in the downtown can affect a city's vitality. Thus, York, Reading and Easton, PA, as well as Wilmington, DE, and New Bedford, MA are now recreating their historical image through urban design and by reclaiming "lost spaces and cracks" through better street layout, and pedestrian friendly design of their downtowns.

The design of the built space may either impede or enhance the use of a city's waterfront. As Kotval and Mullin have observed in chapter ten, while Baltimore's Inner Harbor and New York's South Street Seaport have enabled pedestrians to enjoy the use of the cities' waterfronts, in smaller cities such as Point Judith, RI, and Stonington, CT, the built environment has impeded the enjoyment of the waterfront.

One of the instruments for ensuring that downtowns are both aesthetically pleasing and retain a distinct historic image is the use of design guidelines. Design guidelines stipulate what physical changes are acceptable in the downtown and, thereby, enable a community to control alterations to downtown buildings and how new structures are built. Community residents, through workshops and charettes, can play an active role in determining what features of the downtown need to be preserved. This was the case in Colville, WA where McClure and Hurand (see chapter seven) helped community residents to identify and define design recommendations for the city's downtown to guide the building of streets and sidewalks, street signs, and buildings.

Monitor Programs and Progress

Most cities that have engaged in downtown revitalization have a vision of what they want for the downtown. Walzer and Kline in chapter thirteen identified the top two objectives of economic development for Illinois cities as that of retaining and helping existing businesses to expand and to attract new businesses. Simmons in chapter eleven also discussed the goal of Fox City communities to restore their waterfronts and brownfields. What is lacking for these cities is a tracking device for monitoring changes in the downtown. My examination of downtown revitalization in the Fox cities of Wisconsin led me to conclude that these cities have not established a means for monitoring the outcomes of their downtown redevelopment programs.

Evaluating the effects of downtown redevelopment programs seems to be an issue that is not given attention by cities. In order to demonstrate to the public and financial contributors of downtown programs that such programs work, it is important that cities establish indicators for monitoring changes in the downtown districts. This also enables cities to gauge the effectiveness of their downtown redevelopment initiatives. Some of the indicators for which cities need to keep data are provided in chapter four.

Downtown Revitalization Should be a Community Effort

One of the challenges to downtown revitalization especially in small cities is the preponderance of absentee landlords of downtown property and the dearth of personnel resources. Since most retailers in downtown districts do not own these properties, they do not have a vested interest in the physical outlook of the property beyond the economic benefits that such changes may bring to their businesses. Hence, involving both tenants of downtown property and property owners is crucial to downtown renewal. A bigger downtown crowd is economically beneficial to businesses, and physical improvements to the downtown help improve downtown property values. Having said this, revitalizing downtown is not a job that should be relegated to experts or to businesses and property owners in the downtown. Downtown is so important to the image of a community that its renewal should be a community-wide endeavor. While outside expertise should be used wherever possible (engineers, planners, architects, etc.), experts should only provide guidance and work alongside the community, not replace the experiential knowledge of community residents. In the case studies discussed in this volume, downtown revitalization succeeded only when the entire community has been involved right from the start. Initial efforts at revitalizing downtown Billings failed because the city relied on outside experts who did not consult the community in the preparation of the downtown redevelopment plan. This has paralyzed subsequent efforts at downtown revitalization. An apathetic community in Newport, OR has stalled efforts at downtown redevelopment while an engaged community in Brandon, Canada (see Horne's discussion in chapter six) and in Seaside, OR (chapter five), Los Gatos, and Capitola, CA (see chapter nine) have catalyzed downtown revitalization in these communities.

There Must be a Long-term Vision for the Downtown

Contributors in this volume have noted the need for cities to engage in incremental redevelopment of the downtown. Such small steps build confidence and morale because they show accomplishments. However, a city can lose its vision if such incremental projects are not placed within the scope of an overarching long-term goal for the downtown. Hence, downtown revitalization must be both incremental as well as comprehensive. Simmons in chapter eleven and Klebba, and others, in chapter five have suggested that downtown redevelopment should proceed within a framework of sustainable development. This ensures that cities not only pursue the regeneration of their downtowns but that such redevelopment is both environmentally friendly and that it leads to genuine progress, not simply quantitative changes in the conventional measures of economic development.

Finally, Don't Live in Isolation

Downtown revitalization initiatives are taking place in hundreds of smaller communities around the country. While programs that work well in other communities may not necessarily work in others, networking will enable communities to learn from each other and avoid the, sometimes, painful experiences that have characterized many a downtown redevelopment approach. There is no need to reinvent the wheel!!

In conclusion, it is important to stress that downtown revitalization can work. The discussions in this book make this all too clear. Cities can be brought "back from the edge," and small cities can revitalize their downtowns through a sustained effort, galvanizing community resources and tapping those of higher levels of government and the private sector. The road to downtown recovery will not be smooth and communities should not be despaired by short-term failures that are bound to occur. The longest journey begins with one step!

Contributors

Matthew J. Bell is an architect and an Associate Professor at the University of Maryland School of Architecture. His published work can be found in journals such as *Cornell Journal of Architecture* and *The New City*. He has participated as a designer for numerous projects and was also the vice president of the Neighborhood Design Center of Baltimore and Prince George's County in Maryland.

Michael A. Burayidi is Associate Professor of Urban Planning and Coordinator of the Urban and Regional Studies program at the University of Wisconsin, Oshkosh. His professional interests are in the area of comparative economic development, downtown revitalization, sustainable development, and urban land management. Burayidi has published several articles in his area of expertise in such journals as the *Journal of Planning Education and Research, Journal of Agriculture and Human Values,* and the *Journal of Economic Issues,* among others. In additon he is author/editor of the following books: *Urban Planning in a Multicultural Society* (Praeger, 2000); *Multiculturalism in a Cross National Perspective* (University Press of America, 1997), *Race and Ethnic Relations in the First Person* (with Alfred T. Kisubi, Praeger 1998).

Bryan T. Downes is a Professor in the Department of Planning, Public Policy and Management at the University of Oregon. He has longstanding research and teaching interests in leadership and management of public sector change efforts; local government capacity building; strategies for achieving organizational excellence in the nonprofit sector; and the development of sustainable communities.

Daniel J. Garr is a member of the American Planning Association and Professor of Urban Planning at San Jose State University. Professor Garr specializes in urban history, housing and neighborhood studies, and planning in developing countries.

Mindee D. Garrett is a second year graduate student in the Public Policy and Management Master's Degree Program at the University of Oregon in Department of Planning, Public Policy and Management. Her thesis focuses on downtown revitalization in Oregon's coastal communities. She has recently worked with the Southern Willamette Private Industry Council as grant writer, implementing a one stop career network, and creating a marketing plan.

Akhlaque Haque is an Assistant Professor of Government and Public Service and senior research associate at the Center for Urban Affairs at the University of Alabama at Birmingham (UAB). Haque's research interests are in the areas of economic development and policy analysis, public administration, and geographic information systems. His published works have appeared in several refereed journals including *Journal of Rural Health, Administration and Society, Journal of Urban Technology, Annals of Epidimeology,* and the *Journal of History and Management.*

Mark D. Hardt is Associate Professor of Sociology and Director of General Education Assessment at Montana State University-Billings. His research interests include urban development and the ecological analysis of communities.

William R. Horne is a member of the Geography Program, University of Northern British Columbia in Prince George, BC, Canada. His interests are in social and economic development in small cities and he has worked as a consultant and planner in Ontario and Manitoba.

Fred A. Hurand, FAICP, is Professor of Urban and Regional Planning at Eastern Washington University. He holds degrees in architecture (Ohio State University), urban planning (University of Washington), and man-environment relations (Ph.D., Pennsylvania State University). A Fellow of the American Institute of Certified Planners, he teaches and provides community service consultation to communities throughout Eastern Washington. He is the author of more than ten community and downtown plans and development ordinances, several flood damage mitigation plans, and "Preparing Your Comprehensive Plan Foundation: A Land Use Inventory Guide," a manual used in the State of Washington's Growth Management Program. He has served on the Spokane City/County Landmarks Commission, King County Design Commission and the City of Spokane Design Review Committee. His current research interest is in the urban morphology of small towns and central business districts.

Jennifer R. Klebba is a second year graduate student in the Public Policy and Management Master's Degree Program at the University of Oregon in Department of Planning, Public Policy and Management. Her main interests are in environmental policy and citizen participation in public processes at the local community level. Her thesis focuses on mediating institutions and their role in the revitalization of civic participation in local communities in the U.S.

Zenia Kotval is an Assistant Professor of Urban Planning at Michigan State University. She was the former project director for the Center for Economic Development at the University of Massachusetts. Her training and experience combine project administration, data collection and analysis, coordination with clients and evaluation of fiscal impacts of planning and development issues. Dr. Kotval's expertise is in economic impact computer models, quantitative methods and economic base analysis. Over the past six years, Dr. Kotval has conducted research projects in over twenty communities and has been responsible for data interpretation and economic base analysis on a number of projects in Massachusetts, Connecticut, Rhode Island, New York, and Pennsylvania. Dr. Kotval also worked with the Lexington Planning Department as a planning analyst prior to receiving her Ph.D. in planning.

Kirk McClure is an Associate Professor with the Graduate Program in Urban Planning at the University of Kansas. His teaching and research work are in the fields of housing and community development. Before moving to his current faculty position, McClure worked with the Boston Redevelopment Authority dealing with modeling the dynamics of real estate markets.

Wendy McClure, AIA, is a professor of Architecture at the University of Idaho. As an architect in New Orleans she was the 1987 recipient of a New Orleans Historic District Landmarks Commission Design Award for "outstanding achievemnt in preservation." Since joining the faculty at the University of Idaho in 1987, she has received several other preservation awards including the Idaho Preservation Council's "distinguished preservationist award for superlative achievement in preserving the Idaho's heritage." McClure created a community design program that targets the revitalization planning and design needs of Northwest communities through collaborative teaching, research, and outreach projects. She is the editor and a contributing author of a book entitled *The Rural Town: Designing for Growth and Sustainability*, has published articles in the APT (Association for Preservation Technology Journal), and is currently preparing a manuscript about the evolution of town development in the Pacific Northwest.

John R. Mullin is a Professor of Urban Planning and former Head of the Department of Landscape Architecture and Regional Planning at the University of Massachusetts. He is also the Director of the Center for Economic Development at the University of Massachusetts. He has an active and extensive research and planning consultation practice which has included studies and recommendations for economic impact assessment, industrial development, historic preservation, urban revitalization, industrial plant siting, zoning and subdivision regulations, building code revisions, and waterfront redevelopment. Dr. Mullin has written or edited over fifty book chapters, book reviews, technical reports, journal articles, and conference proceedings. He has presented papers at numerous national conferences dealing with planning and public policy. He is a Colonel in the Army National Guard.

Autumn Lyn Radle is a second year graduate student in the Public Policy and Management Master's Degree Program at the University of Oregon in Department of Planning, Public Policy and Management. Her main interests are in environmental policy and resource management, and land use planning. She is currently on-leave from the graduate program working on a long term land use plan for the City of San Diego, CA.

Kent Robertson is Professor of Community Studies at Saint Cloud State University (Minnesota). He has published over 20 journal/magazine articles on downtown development, spoken widely on this topic, and assisted numerous small cities with their downtown revitalization efforts.

Siddhartha Sen is an Associate Professor and Program Coordinator of the Graduate Program in City and Regional Planning at Morgan State University in Baltimore. He has assisted numerous cities and communities in their design endevours. His current research focuses on urban design, international planning, and race, gender, and ethnicity in planning.

James R. Simmons is Chair of the Political Science Department. He also directs the department's undergraduate Public Administration and Government Internship programs. He received his doctorate in Political Science from Indiana University-Bloomington. Jim teaches and does research in Public Policy, Public Administration, American Politics, and Environmental Studies. He has published work extensively in journals ranging from the *New Political Science* and the *Policy Studies Journal* to *Extrapolation and Environmental Impact Assessment Review*. He is the co-author (with Benjamin I. Page) of *What Government Can Do* (University of Chicago, forthcoming).

Norman Walzer has a Ph.D. in economics from the University of Illinois (Urbana) and directs the Illinois Institute for Rural Affairs at Western Illinois University. He has published in the areas of local public finance, urban/regional analysis, and local economic development with articles in Land Economics, Review of Economics and Statistics, National Tax Journal, Public Finance/Finances Publiques, and Journal of the Community Development Society among others. He also has written or edited 13 books on a variety of local public policy issues.

Index